BOOKS BY JULES WITCOVER

85 Days
  The Last Campaign of Robert Kennedy

The Resurrection of Richard Nixon

White Knight
  The Rise of Spiro Agnew

WHITE KNIGHT

WHITE KNIGHT

The Rise of
Spiro Agnew

JULES WITCOVER

RANDOM HOUSE NEW YORK

Copyright © 1972 by Jules Witcover
All rights reserved under International and
Pan-American Copyright Conventions. Published
in the United States by Random House, Inc.,
New York, and simultaneously in Canada
by Random House of Canada Limited, Toronto.
Library of Congress Cataloging in Publication Data

Witcover, Jules.
White knight; the rise of Spiro Agnew.

1.   Agnew, Spiro T., 1918–   I.   Title.
E840.8.A34W5   973.924'0924   [B]   76–37425
ISBN 0–394–47216–0
Manufactured in the United States of America
by American Book-Stratford Press
2 4 6 8 9 7 5 3
First Edition

To Marian

"It's time to take my gloves off. No more of this Mr. Nice Guy. Starting tomorrow I will try to switch off my low-key approach and start calling a spade a spade. Maybe then I can attract some attention."

—*Vice-President Spiro T. Agnew, addressing the Navy League dinner at the Waldorf-Astoria Hotel, New York, on October 27, 1970*

ACKNOWLEDGMENTS

In the early stages of research for this book, I had a long interview with one of Vice-President Agnew's old political associates in Maryland. Near its close, he told me he had agreed to talk to me only after having obtained the acquiescence of the Vice-President's aides. One of them remarked to him, "He'll speak to our enemies; he might as well speak to our friends." That is what I have tried to do in a year of researching and writing this book. Many of the 120 persons interviewed frankly characterized themselves either as friends or enemies of Mr. Agnew; others did not, but all generously gave their recollections of the man in both his public and private moments. To friends, foes and the noncommittal alike goes my appreciation; the conclusions expressed in this book are my own, but what I have been told by all of these personally knowledgeable sources has been an invaluable guide.

I am indebted first of all to Vice-President Agnew for granting me a lengthy interview and for permitting his aides to talk to me. Next, I am grateful to Governors Nelson A. Rockefeller of New York, Marvin Mandel of Maryland and Tom McCall of Oregon, and to a host of Mr. Agnew's old associates in Baltimore, in the Army, and in Towson, Annapolis and Washington—especially the following: Al Abrahams, Charles Bresler, Frank DeFilippo, Edgar Feingold, Victor Gold, Robert Goodman, J. Walter Jones, Sam Kimmel, Colonel Robert J. Lally, Ormsby and Scott Moore, W. Roy Pollard (Mr. Agnew's half-brother) and Herb Thompson. Several members of the White House staff were also very helpful.

Colleagues in the national press corps, too, gave me invaluable assistance, especially Walter Mears of the Associated Press, James Naughton of the *New York Times*, Gene Oishi of the Baltimore *Sun*, Lucy Salinger of CBS News, and Robert Shogan of *Newsweek*, as well as the library staffs of the Baltimore *Sun*, the Washington *Post* and the Washington bureau of the Los Angeles *Times*. Observations by the Vice-President, by his predecessor, Senator Hubert H. Humphrey of Minnesota, and by former presidential adviser and Secretary of Defense Clark Clifford were particularly helpful in connection with the final chapter, on the role of the Vice-Presidency.

Finally I want to thank my agent, Robert Lescher, for constructive advice and guidance, and above all my wife, Marian, whose encouragement, editorial counsel and assistance in refining the manuscript were vital. My children, Paul, Amy and Julie, also contributed by sacrificing many weekend outings through a long year.

J. W.

Washington, D.C.
January 5, 1972

CONTENTS

ACKNOWLEDGMENTS   *xi*

1 ◊ THE SERENDIPITY EFFECT   *3*

2 ◊ ROOTS OF A MIDDLE AMERICAN   *30*

3 ◊ THE BOTTOM RUNG   *54*

4 ◊ THE RIGHTS OF MAN   *74*

5 ◊ SKIN-DEEP LIBERAL   *101*

6 ◊ MOVING UP   *116*

7 ◊ THE HOLY LIBERAL CRUSADE   *137*

8 ◊ ANNAPOLIS   *150*

9 ◊ THE COURTSHIP OF NELSON ROCKEFELLER   *180*

10 ◊ THE SWITCH TO RICHARD NIXON   *200*

11 ◊ SPIRO WHO?   *216*

12 ◊ THE ROAD TO RIDICULE   *234*

13 ◊ THE "FAT JAP" FLAP   *252*

14 ◊ MUDDLING THROUGH   *264*

15 ◊ PITCHER OF WARM SPIT   *283*

16 ◊ THE BIRTH OF AGNEWISM   *298*

17 ◊ STRONG RIGHT ARM   *322*

18 ◊ WAR ON RADICLIBS   *350*

19 ◊ GOOD-BYE CHARLIE   *372*

20 ◊ DON'T BLAME ME   *396*

21 ◊ WHAT PRICE AGNEW?   *429*

INDEX   *455*

WHITE
KNIGHT

1

◇•◇•◇•◇•◇•◇

THE SERENDIPITY EFFECT

O N the early afternoon of March 21, 1968, the world of Spiro
Theodore Agnew was one of confident anticipation. As the
freshman governor of Maryland sat in the reception room of his
Annapolis office conducting a routine press conference, a scene of
great political importance was about to unfold in New York City
that would prove to all the wiseacres that Ted Agnew had been no
fool.

Momentarily, in a crowded, festive ballroom of the New York
Hilton, Governor Nelson A. Rockefeller was going to announce
his plans concerning the 1968 Republican presidential nomination. The *New York Times* had already reported that he would
run, and the *New York Times* was gospel. For most of the sixteen
months since his election as governor, Agnew had been working
to bring Rockefeller into the race, undeterred by the New Yorker's
repeated disavowals of interest and his public and financial commitments to the White House aspirations of Governor George W.
Romney of Michigan. All through 1967, as Romney engaged in a
drawn-out chautauqua of political self-immolation fired by his
unhappy penchant for obfuscation, Agnew had persevered as a
one-man "draft Rockefeller" committee. Among his fellow governors he had lobbied resolutely at every private and public opportunity. Circumstances would eventually conspire, he had told
them, to bring Rockefeller into the race in spite of his disclaimers.

But they had just smiled tolerantly. Then, just three weeks earlier, Romney had suddenly quit cold, confronted with the dismal reality of public opinion polls indicating he was about to be inundated by Richard M. Nixon in the first 1968 primary, in New Hampshire. All at once, the path was clear for Rockefeller to transform Ted Agnew from windmill-tilter to prophet.

A transformation in the political fate of Ted Agnew was indeed about to take place, in which Rockefeller's decision, and the manner in which he conveyed it to Agnew, would be only the first of three key circumstances. From this moment through the next twenty-one days, events were to unfold that would affect much more than Agnew's public image as a political prognosticator. Many would contend that the man himself had changed radically overnight as a result of them. But Agnew would insist through it all that he really had not changed—that those around him, and the circumstances affecting their political thought, had undergone the transformation. What was politically important, however, was the public perception of the man, and that perception would shift drastically between March 21 and April 11, 1968.

Propelled into national Republican affairs by a series of political flukes in the previous decade, Agnew had been elected governor of Maryland in November 1966 as a sane alternative to an ultraconservative segregationist, Democrat George P. Mahoney, who campaigned on the transparent slogan "A Man's Home Is His Castle—Protect It." More out of fear of Mahoney than love of Agnew, moderates and liberals of both parties had flocked to the side of the Republican alternative, and Agnew, in the act of embracing these converts, had recited the campaign liturgy of liberalism. It seemed only natural afterward, then, that he would gravitate toward Nelson Rockefeller. Indeed, Agnew had become the New Yorker's John the Baptist, and now he expectantly awaited Rockefeller's presidential coming. Out of that expectation, however, and two unforeseen developments insinuating themselves into Agnew's political and emotional consciousness in the days immediately to follow, was to come what appeared to be a different Spiro Agnew—and the synthesis of a new and vastly divisive phenomenon in American political life.

Because Agnew was above all else a supremely proud man, the condescending attitude of others—and particularly of the press—toward his seeming fantasies of a Rockefeller candidacy had hurt. And so, now that his moment of public vindication was apparently at hand, he wanted the world to know and share it. As the time for Rockefeller's press conference approached, Agnew concluded his own session with the Maryland reporters, and an aide brought in a portable television set, which was switched to the channel about to transmit the announcement from New York for which he had waited so long. Agnew sat several feet from the set and watched intently, the barest trace of a smile on his usually expressionless face. The dozen or so reporters present, invited to share the delicious moment, stood in an arc behind him, and a television cameraman across the way alertly panned the scene. It would be interesting to see how Agnew reacted, this cool and unflappable man, when after more than a year of tenacious pursuit, his reluctant quarry was finally bagged.

"Governor," a reporter had asked only a moment earlier, "has Governor Rockefeller indicated to you what he plans to say at his press conference today?" And Agnew had replied, "No, he hasn't, and I'm just as glad, to tell you the truth. I haven't really placed any heavy pressure on him to let me know what his decision is because, at the moment, it's more comfortable to be in the dark." Now, as they all awaited Rockefeller's appearance, he repeated, "I'm just as much in the dark as all of you." But the way he said it suggested otherwise.

On the black-and-white screen, the Rockefeller that Agnew and his guests saw should have been nominated later for an Emmy award. As his hangers-on whistled and applauded, the three-time New York governor strode cheerfully down the aisle between the seated reporters, his famous lopsided grin at its widest. He mounted a platform, stood behind a battery of microphones, waved his hand for indulgence and launched into his speech in the best upbeat style of the hopeful candidate embarking on his campaign. Having thus set them up, he let the nation—and Spiro T. Agnew—have it right in the political solar plexus. But his manner was so matter-of-fact that it was more like administering an anesthetic than a haymaker when he said: "I have decided to reiterate unequivocally that I am not a candidate campaigning directly or indirectly for the Presidency of the United States."

The words did, indeed, seem to anesthetize Agnew as he watched there in his Annapolis office, his expected vindication turned to the rankest public humiliation—and in the presence no less of that group of certified know-it-alls, the press. He just sat there, frozen. Some of the reporters present said later they thought they saw his jaw open slightly for a second; others recalled that a kind of barely perceptible, sick grin came over his face for an instant. But the television tape that was recording the scene captured only the image of a stolid man, staring with no expression at all at the screen in front of him.

Rockefeller went on at great length explaining why, led to the water's edge by Agnew and others, he now was refusing to drink. But these words summed it up: "Quite frankly, I find it clear at this time that a considerable majority of the party's leaders wants the candidacy of former Vice-President Richard Nixon, and it appears equally clear that they are keenly concerned and anxious to avoid any such divisive challenge within the party as marked the 1964 campaign [between Senator Barry Goldwater and himself]. It would therefore be illogical and unreasonable for me to try and arouse their support by pursuing the very course of action that they least want and most deplore."

The decision not to run was shocker enough for one afternoon; on top of it, this apparent invitation to the party to nominate Rockefeller's long-time archfoe, Nixon, was too much for the assembled faithful in the hotel ballroom. Dumbstruck at first, some of those standing along the walls loudly moaned their disappointment and displeasure. Meanwhile, down in Annapolis, Agnew just sat there and stared.

Rockefeller went on: "At precisely this time the Democratic party, while in control of both the executive and legislative branches, threatens to be torn asunder. How should a responsible Republican act in a period of such crisis? I cannot believe that the Republican retort to the Democratic scene should be, 'Any din that you can raise, we can raise higher.' " Translation: His candidacy against Nixon would be not only fruitless but also irresponsible.

Still, said Rockefeller, if the party ultimately wanted him he would be available. "I have said that I stood ready to answer any true and meaningful call from the Republican party to serve it and the nation. I still so stand. I would be derelict or uncandid were I to say otherwise. I expect no such call and I shall do nothing in the future by word or deed to encourage such a call." That last was a direct message to the Agnews who had pursued him through 1967, and to underline it he added words that soon were to take on the hollowest of rings: "We live in an age when the word of a political leader seems to invite instant and general suspicion. I ask to be spared any measure of such distrust. I mean I shall abide by precisely what I say."

Rockefeller closed the press conference by reporting that he had already sent wires to existing "Rockefeller for President" groups expressing "my deep appreciation to them for their faith and their effort and their work," but asking them "to desist." Agnew obviously hadn't received his. "This comes as a complete surprise to me," he said to the reporters in the room, who by now had no doubt of it. "I must confess I am tremendously surprised. I also frankly add that I am greatly disappointed." There could be no doubt of that either, especially when the crestfallen Agnew added that in his view Rockefeller still was "clearly the best possible candidate." According to one Agnew insider, the governor had prepared elaborate remarks outlining how he intended to help Rockefeller get the nomination. But now they were useless.

During Agnew's press conference, several aides said later, a phone call had come in to the Annapolis office for him from Rockefeller in New York. According to the aides, the secretary who took it, Alice Fringer, supposedly reported that the governor was in a press conference, and the caller left no message. Mrs. Fringer, however, said later that while there were two phone calls from Rockefeller's office that morning and early afternoon, neither was from the New York governor personally. The first, she said, came at about eleven o'clock to inform Agnew that Rockefeller would be calling him between noon and one o'clock. "I told him [Agnew] right away, if you're at Government House I'll switch it over there," Mrs. Fringer said. "I warned him to expect it. He came back from lunch around one o'clock and asked me if there had been a call, and I told him there hadn't. Then, around one-thirty, there was another call from Rockefeller's office saying the governor [Rockefeller] was sorry he couldn't talk to him but he had too much to do." While Agnew was watching Rockefeller on television, a call did come for him. It was another surprised and disappointed gubernatorial suitor, the salty Tom McCall, who had been watching in Oregon. To a fuming Agnew he said, "I'll bet your wattles are as red as an old turkey gobbler's!"

Much later, reviewing the whole incident in his New York

office in an interview, Rockefeller denied ever having attempted to call Agnew. Of this most-discussed political omission of a stormy year in which things said, done, unsaid and undone kept the presidential picture spinning wildly, he gave this explanation:

"There had been a speculation in the *New York Times* two days before. Nobody from the *Times* checked. This was a planted story. It had absolutely no substance. It was a complete misrepresentation based on nothing. I was very concerned about it because I was coming to the conclusion I was not going to go. When I came out two days later and said I wouldn't, it made it look like I was flip-flopping. A lot of this stuff about vacillation was due to that story, which had no foundation, which was planted. There were a number of people who were working very hard, and in view of this story, I didn't want another leaked story. I wanted to put my own story out. So I did not say to Spiro or to any of the other governors what I was going to do.

"We discussed whether I should call them. I had seen him [Agnew] in Washington a matter of days before this, gone to a big meeting, a national conference of Greek leaders—the Ahepa society. And at that time I said to him, 'Ted, don't take for granted that I'm going to go into this thing because I've not come to a conclusion, and anyone who would assume that I was going to go is doing it without any foundation.' I was trying to slow him down because I figured the way he was talking, that he was pretty well convinced that he had persuaded me to go. I was very dubious about this. I didn't want to go, which is what I had been saying all along, but I was still giving it consideration. I did not want to say or give any intimation.

"Where the real problem came with Ted was that I didn't call him before. He had assumed I was going to go. He had a big group of newspaper people immediately in his office to listen to my acceptance. And of course when I said that I was not going to, this was a very great shock to him, and I think he felt in a sense sort of a betrayal of his support. I think it was an embarrassment because the people were there, and he told them that I was going . . . We didn't want the thing to get out because I wanted to give my own reasons clearly and not have another garbled story after the *Times* story . . . I didn't contact anybody. A lot of other people felt badly about it, but he felt the worst."

Rockefeller acknowledged in retrospect that he should have

made the call "in the point of view of courtesy and friendship." But if he was wrong about that decision, he was absolutely right about Agnew's reaction to it—the governor of Maryland was mortified. If ever there was a politician who climbed out on a public limb and had it sawed off behind him, that politician was Spiro Agnew. It might not have been so bad had he not confidently invited the local press to share his moment of glory. But there he was, not only naked in his humiliation, but naked on television. And it might have been more bearable had he been only an informal Rockefeller admirer; there were many of those within the liberal-moderate wing of the Republican party. What made it so humiliating was that Agnew was the national chairman of the new "Rockefeller for President" citizens' committee, established only three weeks before as a holding action while the New York governor weighed his decision about running. Also, Agnew had recruited all his most prominent Maryland backers into open support of Rockefeller; thus they both shared and compounded his vexation and embarrassment in the state's political community.

Agnew probably would have felt even more humiliated had he known that he was not Nelson Rockefeller's first choice for the role of national citizens'-committee chairman, nor even his second. Former Governor William W. Scranton had been asked first and had agreed to serve. George Hinman, Rockefeller's chief political adviser, summoned a veteran Washington political organizer, Al Abrahams, to New York to discuss the matter with him and Scranton, but Scranton backed out. Now who would front the effort? "Nelson thinks we should get J. Irwin Miller," Hinman told Abrahams. Miller was the relatively obscure president of the Cummins Engine Company in Columbus, Indiana, who in October 1967 suddenly had been introduced to the world on the cover of *Esquire* magazine as its choice for the next President of the United States. The article had immediately caused a stir in Columbus, Indiana—and nowhere else. Abrahams didn't think much of Miller as the "draft Rockefeller" front man. There was no time to bring in a political novice.

"Who then?" Hinman asked Abrahams.

"Who else but Spiro T. Agnew?" was the reply.

Agnew's main attraction, it turned out, was not his political acumen, nor his dedication, nor his long fealty to Rockefeller, but the fact that he was available. He had never been on the cover of

Esquire, but he was, after all, a governor. Agnew apparently didn't know he was the third man considered; even so, he had every reason to expect that he would be personally informed by Rockefeller of his negative decision at least a minute or two before the rest of the country.

Later, after Rockefeller's electrifying telecast when the reporters had left, Mrs. Fringer asked her boss in his inner office, "Were you as surprised as I was?" He replied, "Alice, I have never been more surprised." It was a hard and unexpected blow—and a low one, in Agnew's view. As everyone around him knew, Ted Agnew was a man who put great stock in personal loyalty; accordingly, Rockefeller's failure to advise him personally in advance hurt deeply. A phone call from Rockefeller later that afternoon did not ease the blow. And because, as everyone also knew, Ted Agnew was a man of great personal pride, the very public nature of the indignity compounded the hurt.

As events were to demonstrate in the next three weeks, however, this was only the first of three very public affronts to Agnew's pride. The second already was beginning to take form less than twenty miles west of Annapolis, at Bowie State College, an overwhelmingly black state-supported school out of sight and mind of most Marylanders, including their governor. The college was far removed, as well, from the political battleground of 1968 which was now in disarray from the shocks administered by the two reluctant dragons of the Republican party, first George Romney and then Nelson Rockefeller. But Bowie State soon was to be thrust unwittingly into The Making of a Vice-President that now, unrecognized by even the most astute of politicians and Agnew himself, was unfolding.

A few weeks before Rockefeller shook Spiro Agnew's political world, a black young man named Roland Smith, president of the student body at Bowie State College, had written a letter to the governor of Maryland. In it he expressed his colleagues' growing impatience with the deplorably dilapidated state of the dormitories and classroom buildings, and pleaded with Agnew to take some action. An aide to the governor replied that the college's operating budget was the highest it had ever been, nearly twice the previous budget, which was true. But much of that increase was required to handle a burgeoning student body, severely taxing the already inadequate sixteen red-brick buildings. The problem was in the capital budget, which left no room for the need to rehabilitate facilities about which Smith and his fellow students, about 70 percent of them black, were exercised.

On March 15, in that period when Ted Agnew was busy fronting for the new "draft Rockefeller" committee and looking hopefully ahead to the New Yorker's candidacy, about forty students met at the Bowie State student union to air their gripes and consider action. Moderation had long been the byword on this rather quiet campus, spread over 187 attractive acres of hilly countryside just north of the famed Bowie race track. Two years earlier, students had staged a boycott that produced repairs to their dormitories and an announcement that the school's president of twenty-five years, William E. Henry, would retire. His successor, a former State Department official and educator named Dr. Samuel L. Myers, improved the campus climate greatly; through the previous fall he had held weekly dinner meetings with students to keep attuned to their moods and problems. In general he was regarded as a decent man who tried his best, but good intentions were not enough; Bowie State was falling apart around him, both physically and spiritually.

For the next twelve days, dissatisfaction and tension built on the campus. Then there occurred an essentially minor incident that sparked the smoldering mood into open rebellion. A twenty-nine-year-old history professor named Virginius B. Thornton III, a favorite of the students, was refused tenure, and under college policy no reason was made public. On Wednesday, March 27, tall, mild-mannered Roland Smith led more than two hundred of Bowie State's students in a peaceable, effective boycott of classes. Starting with sit-ins at campus libraries, the protest soon spread to the halls and corridors of the main buildings. Almost at once it brought normal school activities to a halt; class attendance dropped about 90 percent, and from Howard University in nearby Washington, scene of a recent five-day strike, about ninety young people came to lend moral support. And with that boycott, the Bowie State students helped lift Agnew's now uncertain political star out of the confusion into which Rockefeller's statement had plunged it the week before, and onto a new and fateful path.

The students wanted their governor to come to Bowie State and see conditions for himself, but Ted Agnew was a man who did not believe in softness, in permissiveness, and above all in knuckling under to threats and pressure. Under the circumstances, a personal visit to the campus by the governor of the state was out of the question. He did, however, send a representative—a fast-talking real estate developer named Charles Bresler who had run unsuccessfully for state comptroller on the Agnew ticket in 1966. To convey the campus mood and the Agnew administration's response, the visit is best described by Bresler himself: "Word got out that there was somebody from the governor's office there. I came out, and all of a sudden there was a tremendous crowd. There were epithets thrown—'Tell that no-good SOB to come up here; if he don't, we'll burn the place down'—and all the rest. . . . [They shouted] 'Tell Agnew to come down here or we'll burn the goddamned place down,' things of that nature. So I stated very quickly, I said, 'Look, you want to prove you can out-holler me? You win.' I said, 'You want to talk? Here I am.' I said, 'You want to burn the place down?' I took my cigarette lighter out and I went like that [lighting it]. I said, 'Here' [extending it]. I said, 'I want to tell you something. It costs us eleven hundred dollars a year in capital and otherwise for every student here. The place is fully insured, it's going to take three years to build it back up. You think it's going to solve any problems? You're doing the state of Maryland the biggest favor in the world. Burn it down, save the state six hundred times a thousand dollars, you save them six hundred thousand dollars immediately a year every year for three years, two million dollars, and you don't have any education. Now, what does that prove? Now, if you want to talk, I'll tell you what I can say.' We reported what went on and we calmed it down a little bit. There were a lot of outsiders who were very evident and who were only intent on making trouble. A number of the students did come over afterwards and say they were frightened. They couldn't be against the people who were there. The militant or the organizer has a very good thing going for him in this—'Either you're with me or against me.' So now you get a kid who's out there, all he's there to do is get an education. He couldn't care less about joining into these things. He might be walking across campus and all of a sudden he's part of a crowd and pushed in. Well, he's not going to stand up and say, 'Hey, I'm for the governor and I think what these kids are doing is wrong.' He either keeps his mouth shut or goes off."

Dr. Myers has a different assessment of the scene. "It was a fiasco," he said in an interview when Agnew was Vice-President. "That man Bresler rubbed the students the wrong way. He was brusque, it was offensive to the students, and this caused the situation to be much worse. I can assure you that from the students' viewpoint the man was not the one to come here. It was condescending, it was insensitive to the bad situation that physically existed here. He certainly wasn't an ambassador of good will, and it helped to exacerbate the entire situation. In [Agnew] not talking to the students, and in sending a person who was not very tactful, the reaction of the students was that much worse."

A complete campus takeover followed in a few days. Pressures mounted on Agnew to go to Bowie, but his resolve not to do so only stiffened. Police were moved onto the campus and a tentative, tenuous settlement was finally reached. For the next few days, peace hung by a narrow thread as students waited with increasing pessimism for some evidence that their grievances would be assuaged.

On Thursday morning, April 4, a report spread across the campus that as a result of a student protest over teachers' salaries at predominantly white Towson State College, Agnew had gone there, or was going. The story was not true, but the rumor plus the lack of tangible response from Annapolis was enough to snap the inertia of the preceding days.

According to Dr. J. A. Wiseman, chairman of the department of education at Bowie, who was in close touch with the student leaders, "they had a promise from the governor's office that something would be done that day, and they were to wait for a telephone call from the governor's office . . . as to whether he would receive a delegation to put their grievances before him. Somehow that morning, there was word from some source that the governor was not going to see them." Roland Smith and other student leaders then telephoned Agnew's office and were told he would be in all day. That was all they needed to hear. Students poured out of their classrooms; hurried leadership meetings were held; a caravan of two chartered buses, supplied by the NAACP, and more than twenty private cars formed and at about one o'clock departed for Annapolis. "The faculty deplores what our students are now doing," Dr. Myers told newsmen as the protesters drove off, but nothing he could say would stop them.

The group, which totaled more than two hundred, gathered on the capitol grounds and marched directly to the State House, expecting to find Agnew in his second-floor office. He knew from state police reports that the students were coming, so he had decided to stay in the governor's mansion across the street. "It looked like they were expecting us," Smith said afterward. "They had state police at every door. We were all dressed in coat and tie and some of us had books. We tried to put on the appearance of adults trying to do something through legal channels, seeking a redress of grievances. We tried to go in but the state troopers blocked our way. An aide to Agnew came down and said, 'The governor is not in.' So we said we'd stay and wait. We just sat down on the marble floor and read or stood around and talked. In about two hours, the aide came down again and said the governor would not see us, and if we didn't leave by closing time, at five o'clock, we would all be arrested."

Shortly before that hour, Dr. Wiseman and other faculty members arrived and tried to persuade the students to leave, but they refused. They picked up their books and gathered in an orderly fashion at one end of the first-floor corridor to await arrest. At the direction of Kenneth Brown, an NAACP leader, they bowed their heads and softly hummed "The Lord's Prayer." All this time Agnew remained in the mansion across the street, digging in his heels and taking reports from his lieutenants on the scene. "He maintained the utmost calm," according to an aide who was there, and never considered yielding to them.

Finally Agnew ordered Charles Davis, the building superintendent, and Colonel Robert J. Lally, superintendent of the state police, to get it over with. Lally explained the trespass law and penalties to the students, and Davis then declared the building closed for the day. "We're not leaving," Kenneth Brown told Lally. "You arrange some kind of peaceful eviction so we won't have any hanky-panky." Together, Lally, Brown and Smith worked out the details, and "it was all quite orderly," Lally recalled. "We had buses outside, and they simply lined up two by two and passed by a state trooper's desk almost in assembly-line fashion." Smith was the first one taken into custody, then Brown. They led the procession down to a basement exit and then out into waiting buses, which took them in shuttle runs to the nearby Anne Arundel detention center. In all, 227 Bowie State students, plus Brown, were arrested and taken to the center that night for arraignment.

At the same time Agnew, "with great reluctance," summarily ordered Bowie State College closed "for a very short period of time." The issue was, he said, "whether or not to excuse and thereby condone a deliberate flouting of the law." As the lobby of the State House was being cleared, Lally set off in a police car for Bowie State, armed with the governor's order to close down the campus. On the way, over the car radio, he heard a news bulletin that turned the already tense night into a nightmare of potential violence. Dr. Martin Luther King, Jr., standing on the balcony of a motel room in Memphis, had been gunned down in cold blood from across an alleyway. Lally pressed on. "We were concerned now that it might arouse their emotions that much more," he recalled.

At the detention center the students were being bedded down on mattresses on the floors of dormitory-style cells when, sometime after eight o'clock, the word of Dr. King's murder came. Exhausted from lack of sleep for several days, many were already asleep, but the others heard the news of the assassination with utter shock. "A number of them cried; the girls did especially," said Dr. Wiseman, who had been called there to arrange bond. "The word came to the desk where I was filling out the bonds. Somebody went down to the detention rooms and told them. A moan rose and swelled from the whole group." But still there was no violence.

As the students were being brought in, it had become clear that the detention center could not hold them. The county executive, Joseph W. Alton, called Agnew and told him about it, and recommended that they be freed in Dr. Wiseman's custody. Agnew agreed.

At Bowie State, according to Dr. Myers, Dr. King's death "caused a shock to go through the entire campus. Because of this, and the rainy, dreary, dismal atmosphere of that night, the governor said the campus had to be evacuated immediately, and persons would not even be permitted to stay overnight. Some people looked at this as being a very cruel decision because this late at night it was difficult to get transportation. It therefore was modified somewhat so that students who could not get transportation were permitted to stay in one of the residence halls. Many of the people in the community opened up their homes." To some, the decision to put the students out in the rain seemed especially harsh. In retrospect Dr. Myers said, though it was unwise of Agnew not to see the students and unwise to order them arrested at Annapolis, "given the fact that this nation was shocked by the death of Martin Luther King, and particularly the black community, I think it was a very wise decision to disperse the students and close the campus for that night."

But the Bowie State students saw it otherwise. Roland Smith, who went directly back to the campus after having been released on Dr. Wiseman's bond, described the scene later: "The school was closed tight by the time I got back. It was raining, and there were state troopers all over. They told us the campus was closed and all we could do was get our clothes and get out. They came and banged on our doors with their night sticks." Of Agnew's conduct through it all, Smith said, "It started with the fact he wasn't going to knuckle under to our demands. And because of—in his eyes—our belligerence, he was going to go through this for spite, because we were putting him on the spot."

Smith's view doubtless was colored by his personal experience and the heat of the inflammatory situation. But it would not be very long before other Maryland blacks, in still another direct confrontation with their governor, would be saying that they too, having put him on the spot, had felt the wrath of Spiro Agnew. Already the last of the three episodes that were to have such critical impact on his political future was unfolding, and again the black community would be at the vortex.

On April 11, one week after the Bowie State arrests, Agnew sat tight-lipped and determined before a group of about one hundred black leaders in the legislative council chamber of the State Office Building in Baltimore. Outside, great sections of the city were in ashes. Colonel Lally's fears that the assassination of Martin Luther King would exacerbate the Bowie State crisis did not materialize, but as the last of the college's docile student demonstrators were moving off the closed-down campus, a combustion had occurred north in Baltimore city that dwarfed all Governor Agnew's earlier problems. The rioting had begun sporadically on Friday night, April 5, in an overwhelmingly black section of the city's east side, with scattered acts of vandalism and looting and the starting of fires. Black moderate leaders took to the streets to cool matters, but to little avail. Before it was over, there were six deaths, seven hundred persons were injured and five thousand arrested.

Dr. King was buried in Atlanta on April 9, and now, two days later, the black leaders were assembled, having been invited sometime earlier. Agnew's aides say the invitations had gone out well before the Baltimore riot; some black leaders say they received them only afterward. On April 3, the day before Dr. King was shot, Baltimore had had a notorious visitor. Stokely Carmichael, former leader of the Student Nonviolent Coordinating Committee and now one of the more inflammatory evangelists of black power, set up shop in a Pennsylvania Avenue café, in a tough black neighborhood, where he met with various black leaders. An undercover man was in the next booth, and he reported to Colonel Lally that Carmichael had said at one point, "The only way to deal with a white man is across the barrel of a gun." Carmichael had also been heard to say, according to Lally, that riots were part of the war against the white power structure. A full intelligence report on the incident had been submitted by Lally to Agnew. "This perturbed him no end," Lally says, "and this was the thing that instigated the meeting. The black leaders with whom he was trying to work literally ignored his efforts to bring about peace in the community. He couldn't understand their dealing with extremists." Whether listening to Carmichael was "dealing" with him was, of course, the crucial point. There was no evidence that the moderate blacks ever acted on anything Carmichael had said, but as a number of them pointed out later, they all had a realistic problem of maintaining their credibility in the black ghetto; to do that, one could not simply turn off Stokely Carmichael, a grass-roots voice of immense prestige, or others like him.

An hour or so before the April 11 meeting, at about one o'clock in the afternoon, Agnew met in his office on the fifteenth floor of the State Office Building with the law-enforcement leaders— Colonel Lally, City Police Commissioner Donald D. Pomerleau and Maryland National Guard General George M. Gelston among them, some in riot uniform. The governor briefed them on what he was going to say, and asked them to attend the meeting so that (according to Lally) they would be available to participate in whatever discussion ensued. "He anticipated some sort of reaction from the black leaders," Lally recalls, "but he never exactly expressed what he expected. He mentioned at one point that he was probably committing political suicide because of what he was going to tell them, but he felt it was necessary to bring about peace in the community."

Others who saw or got wind of the remarks the governor intended to deliver did not agree with him that "peace in the community" would be its product. One of them was Mayor Thomas D'Alesandro, a Democrat but an old friend and colleague in the law and in local government affairs, who saw a press copy of the speech about an hour before scheduled delivery. Deeply involved himself in the tragic events of the previous days, D'Alesandro telephoned Agnew and urged him not to make the speech. One of Agnew's closest aides, E. Scott Moore, said later he had been told that the governor had received a threat against his life the day before. "I think that had an impact," he said. "The times were rough. But as a lawyer who would not want to be chewed out by a judge in open court, you would have thought he would have been more sensitive to how the black leaders would feel."

Meanwhile, downstairs, the black leaders were suspicious. A state patrolman was stationed outside the legislative council door, screening each arrival before permitting entry. "I knew it was going to be a fiasco when I went over there," said State Senator Clarence Mitchell, a member of one of the city's most prominent black families and one of the black community's most moderate voices. "My instincts told me it would be, but I went." This apprehension mounted when the invited guests, once inside the small rectangular room, saw that three television cameras and crews were ready to record the scene. "We were terribly surprised, because we thought it was going to be a private meeting," the Reverend Marion C. Bascom, a Republican, said later. The choice of the meeting place did not allay suspicions, either. The legislative council chamber resembles a jury room without a jury box, or perhaps more accurately the site of a court-martial. On the platform at the front of the room was a long table with five empty chairs behind it. On the floor itself were the press tables, and from about the center of the room to the rear, the spectators' section—about ten or twelve rows of attached theater seats.

There were some early signs of what was coming. When most of the black leaders had arrived, Agnew dispatched Charles Bresler to set the stage for his appearance. Bresler entered the chamber and began to deliver a very patronizing sermon about the governor's and his own humble beginnings: how their parents had come to the United States with nothing, and how they had picked themselves up by their bootstraps. He was proud, said Bresler, as the son of Jewish immigrants, to be serving in state government with the son of a Greek immigrant and with descendants of African "immigrants" such as those present at this meeting. Before he finished, Bresler had mouthed most of the other rags-to-riches clichés of the white immigrant that had ever been uttered in a Grade B movie. Christopher Gaul, then a reporter for the Baltimore *Sun*, remembers Bresler's "audience warm-up" as "the most offensive thing I had ever heard north of Mississippi." Ormsby S. "Dutch" Moore (Scott's brother), who was running Agnew's Baltimore office, said later that Bresler had in fact been "the prime mover" behind the meeting. "Maybe Charlie did more to make Ted Vice-President than anyone, but he didn't know it." Perhaps Bresler's description of what happened next is the most interesting, coming as it does from an Agnew aide of unquestioned loyalty:

"In the midst of my speech, in they came. The door flung open, and by law, in front of the governor and behind the governor came state troopers. And of course the troopers' detail is always the biggest and the most state-trooper-looking detail. You know what they look like—like an honor guard. Bang!—the door opens up and in comes, in the midst of my remarks, this entourage. . . . There was General Gelston in his paratrooper jumpsuit; you know, fatigues with his paratrooper boots, and he had a habit of carrying under his arm a crop, a riding crop. With his shaved —you know, crew-cut—head, typical military man all the way down the line. There was Bob Lally, head of state police; there was Pomerleau, who was commissioner of the Baltimore police and there was Gil Ware [Agnew's human relations aide, a black man]. Well, Gil of course followed up the crowd and of course each of these had two military aides with him; the general had his aides, and the police commissioner had his, and I'm sure Bob

Lally had a couple of state troopers running with him, and this whole group comes—bang!—right through the door, walk right up and they go for the seats.

"Well, there I'm standing up there like this, and there's not enough chairs. . . . I stopped. . . . What do you do at that point? [I said] 'Ladies and gentlemen, the governor of Maryland.' He walks in, Gelston puts his crop down there, I look for—there's no place for Gil to sit down. So Gil has to stand at the end. Now you look at this line-up . . . you talk about a foreboding, all-white military line-up. It looked like the Gestapo was ready to interrogate you, you know. And there I'm stuck in the middle next to the governor. . . . I mean, really, if I ever set up something that was badly [organized], that was it, but of course you know those things happen. . . . Supposed to be at that table, alongside of the governor, was the head of OEO, a black; two blacks from the education system; somebody from the human rights commission; Gil Ware. Because this was not to be whites, other than the governor, speaking to this group. . . . They had come in and they were all stuck against the wall. . . . Now, Lally and all the rest weren't supposed to be there. They were upstairs; they had just reported to the governor on conditions and everything. Well, he said, 'I've got to go downstairs'; they came along with him. You know, it was just one of those goofs that happen in time and situation [that] I guess you'd say maybe helps make Vice-Presidents —or Presidents. Who knows?"

The impact of this scene on the black leaders, with the streets of Baltimore still smoldering and patrolled by federal troops, was devastating. Reverend Bascom said later of his immediate impression, "Agnew had the establishment there to give license and credentials to what he was saying. It looked like the supreme court of Maryland. Awesome authority facing black people; it was a power bloc across the front." The moderate black leaders' negative reaction was compounded when they saw Gelston at the head table place his riding crop before him, in the best tradition of the stereotype authoritarian. It was obviously a small thing, but in the ominous and distrustful atmosphere already created, an unfortunate gesture.

Finally Agnew began to read his statement, seldom looking up, seldom raising his voice, plodding on with the determination of a man steeled to accomplish a task he has assigned himself:

"Ladies and gentlemen: Hard on the heels of tragedy come the assignment of blame and the excuses. I did not invite you here for either purpose. I did not ask you here to recount previous deprivations, nor to hear me enumerate prior attempts to correct them. I did not request your presence to bid for peace with the public dollar."

It was, in all probability, the bluntest, most insulting opening remark ever delivered by the governor of a state to a gathering of responsible, moderate civic leaders anywhere. Don't try to divert me with bleeding hearts, he was telling them, and don't think I'm going to try to buy you off with new programs. And then, lest anybody miss the significance of his call to the men who prided themselves as moderates in the black community, he spelled it out for them:

"Look around you and you may notice that everyone here is a leader—and that each leader present has *worked* his way to the top. If you'll observe, the ready-mix, instantaneous type of leader is not present. The circuit-riding, Hanoi-visiting type of leader is missing from this assembly. The caterwauling, riot-inciting, burn-America-down type of leader is conspicuous by his absence. That is no accident, ladies and gentlemen, it is just good planning. And in the vernacular of today—'That's what it's all about, baby!' "

Even before the Baltimore riots, Agnew's righteous indignation had been building toward the black community. In February, a split had developed between the city's black moderates and militants. Robert B. Moore, head of the Baltimore office of SNCC, called Mayor D'Alesandro's campaign against street crime "a war on the black community," and the police "the enemy of the black community"—remarks that Clarence Mitchell on the floor of the State Senate had denounced as "bigotry." Although Mitchell's observation was hailed by white leaders, it had deepened the breach within the black community and finally led to a "black unity" meeting in March, bringing together leaders covering the spectrum from orthodox politicians, including Mitchell, to the most outspoken advocates of black power, including Moore.

In that accommodation, the governor sought now to find the tinder that had sustained the riots. "Some weeks ago," he lectured the moderates, "a reckless stranger to this city [apparently Robert Moore], carrying the credentials of a well-known civil rights organization, characterized the Baltimore police as 'enemies of the black man.' Some of you here, to your eternal credit, quickly condemned this demagogic proclamation. You condemned it because you recognized immediately that it was an attempt to undermine lawful authority—the authority under which you were elected and under which you hold your leadership position. You spoke out against it because you knew it was false and was uttered to attract attention and inflame.

"When you, who courageously slapped hard at irresponsibility, acted, you did more for civil rights than you realize. But when white leaders openly complimented you for your objective, courageous action, you immediately encountered a storm of censure from parts of the Negro community. This criticism was born of a perverted concept of race loyalty and inflamed by the type of leader who I earlier mentioned is not here today."

And then came the most brutal phrase. "*And you ran,*" said Agnew of their participation in the black unity meeting. "You met in secret with that demagogue and others like him—and you agreed, according to published reports that have not been denied, that you would not openly criticize any black spokesman, regardless of his remarks. You were beguiled by the rationalizations of unity; you were intimidated by veiled threats; you were stung by insinuations that you were Mr. Charlie's boy, by epithets like 'Uncle Tom.' God knows I cannot fault you who spoke out for breaking and running in the face of what appeared to be overwhelming opinion in the Negro community. But actually it was only the opinion of a few, distorted and magnified by the *silence* of most of you here today."

That did it. Parren Mitchell (now a congressman), who had learned of the contents of the speech earlier, got up, announced that a black caucus would be held in the corridor, and walked out. First one, then another, then about a dozen black leaders followed him. "If you want to talk to us like ladies and gentlemen, Mr. Governor," one of them shouted on his way out, "we'll stay and listen." But Agnew, after a moment of confusion, droned on, seemingly impervious to the commotion. Reverend Bascom, one of his first black supporters for governor in 1966, was one of the first to leave. Outside, visibly shaken, he said of Agnew, "He is as sick as any bigot in America. He is as sick as anything I have seen in America." And later, reflecting on the speech, he gave this appraisal: "It demonstrated that Agnew has a messiah complex, and anything he says is said sort of *ex cathedra*. He doesn't argue; he testifies to what has happened and what is happening. He was speaking for the great benefit of the press. He did not come to ameliorate the situation. The blacks came to hear what he had to say, but what he said was not ameliorative, but punitive and condescending. This is where the thing hit the fan."

Those who remained in the room then heard Agnew attribute the Baltimore riots to nothing short of conspiracy by Stokely Carmichael and others. "You know who the fires burned out just as you know who lit the fires," he said, not looking up from his text. "They were not lit in honor of your great fallen leader. Nor were they lit from an overwhelming sense of frustration and despair. Those fires were kindled at the suggestion and with the instruction of the advocates of violence. It was no accident that one such advocate appeared at eight separate fires before the fire chief could get there." This remark apparently was a reference to Walter H. Lively, director of the Baltimore Urban Coalition and a local group called U-JOIN (Union for Jobs or Income Now), who had been accused by police of having been at the scene of several fires during the riots.

Finally, it was Carmichael's turn. "The looting and rioting which has engulfed our city during the past several days," the governor intoned, "did not occur by chance. It is no mere coincidence that a national disciple of violence, Mr. Stokely Carmichael, was observed meeting with local black-power advocates and known criminals in Baltimore on April 3, 1968—three days before the Baltimore riots began. It is deplorable and a sign of sickness in our society that the lunatic fringes of the black and white communities speak with wide publicity while we, the moderates, remain continuously mute. I cannot believe that the only alternative to white racism is black racism."

Now Spiro Agnew was at the peak of his sermon, undeterred by the fact that his audience was shrinking by the minute. He was going to talk some sense into their heads, if only one of them remained. "Somewhere the objectives of the civil rights movement have been obscured in a surge of emotional oversimplification," he lectured. "Somewhere the goal of equal opportunity has been replaced by the goal of instantaneous economic equality. This country does not guarantee that every man will be successful, but only that he will have an equal opportunity to achieve success. I readily admit that this equal opportunity has not always been present for Negroes—that it is still not totally present for Negroes. But I say that we have come a long way. And I say that the road we have trodden is built with the sweat of the Roy Wilkinses and the Whitney Youngs—with the spiritual leadership of Dr. Martin Luther King—and not with violence. Tell me one constructive achievement that has flowed from the madness of the twin priests of violence, Stokely Carmichael and Rap Brown. They do not build—they demolish. They are agents of destruction and they will surely destroy us if we do not repudiate them and their philosophies—along with the white racists such as Joseph Carroll and Connie Lynch—the American Nazi party, the John Birchers, and their fellow travelers."

Agnew went on in the same vein, quoting harangues attributed to Carmichael and Brown, and asking, "What possible hope is there for peace in our community if these apostles of anarchy are allowed to spew hatred unchallenged? If we are to learn from bitter experience, if we are to progress in the battle for equal opportunity, we must plan together and execute those plans together. To do this we must be able to communicate. We cannot communicate and progress if the lunatic fringers are included in the problem-solving team. I publicly repudiate, condemn and reject all white racists. I call upon you to publicly repudiate, condemn and reject all black racists. This, so far, you have not been willing to do."

Unless Brown and Carmichael were repudiated by the black moderates, the governor warned, most of Maryland's blacks "will be unjustly victimized by a hardening of attitudes in the responsible, decent white community." His greatest fear, said the man who later would preach "polarization along authentic lines" as a prescription for national catharsis, "is this polarization of attitudes as an aftermath of violence. . . . Together we must work first to prevent polarization and second to reduce tension." And this speech, obviously, was to be the first step in that effort. Only about thirty of the original hundred black leaders were still in the room to hear the governor conclude his sermon with a conciliatory call on them to "rebuild our city and to rebuild the image of Baltimore," and those who remained were distinctly not in a conciliatory mood.

One of the first blacks to stand and speak was Mrs. Juanita Jackson Mitchell, matriarch of a prominent Baltimore family, an official of the National Association for the Advancement of Colored People and a civil rights pioneer in the city—a symbol of old-line, responsible, moderate black leadership. Mrs. Mitchell said she deplored both black and white racism and violence, but added that the history of the United States indicated "it is only when there is violence or the threat of violence that the body politic moves." Agnew snapped back, "It's going to stop being the history of this country or we're all going to be dead, every one of us."

Then, his voice rising, Agnew went on the attack. "Do you repudiate black racists?" he shouted at the old woman. "Are you willing, as I am willing, to repudiate the white racists, are you willing to repudiate the Carmichaels and the Browns?"

"We have already done so!" she shouted back. "Didn't you read our—"

But Agnew was in no mood to listen. "Answer me! Answer me!" he broke in, bullying her. "Do you repudiate Rap Brown and Stokely Carmichael? Do you? Do you?"

"We don't repudiate them as human beings," Mrs. Mitchell replied. "We repudiate—"

But he wouldn't let her finish. "That's what I was afraid of," he said insinuatingly.

"Wait a minute—" Mrs. Mitchell said, but Agnew had heard all of the answer he cared to. Mrs. Mitchell, reduced to tears, tried to go on. "This city, this government, have made them what they are," she said, "have made our children burners and looters."

Her son Clarence came to his mother's aid. "I condemn Rap Brown. I condemn Stokely Carmichael. I condemn George Wallace. I condemn Ross Barnett. I condemn all of the racists in this country. But I'm not going to pick out Negro racists . . . and Negro racists only."

"I didn't ask you to," the governor said.

"Let's condemn the entire broad spectrum of this—"

Agnew interrupted Mitchell. "That's exactly what this is all about. If we can get that done, then we can start without those people to solve some problems."

A former director of Baltimore's human relations commission, Samuel T. Daniels, told the governor his statement was "offensive to me and it is insulting. . . . Those who have advised you," he said, "have ill advised you." And one of the few whites invited, Miss Mae Gitling, a director of the Joseph House, a community center in west Baltimore, told him, "You're listening, but you're not hearing. This is not the time to repudiate people, but causes." The black militants, she said, were "speaking the truth but not the way to the truth. They're speaking the mind of the common people and you'd better hear it."

But Agnew had come to tell, not be told. For more than an hour it went on like that, with several black leaders engaging him in a stormy exchange while the walkouts convened a black caucus at the Reverend Bascom's church up the street. "We are shocked at the gall of the governor," their eventual statement said, "suggesting that only he can define the nature of the leadership of the black community. Agnew's actions are more in keeping with the slave system of a bygone era. At a time when the chief executive should be calling for unity, he deliberately sought to divide us."

If that was Agnew's intent, he certainly failed dismally. As a result of his insulting sermon, the black community undoubtedly emerged more unified than before. Although he professed to be satisfied after the stormy session that a candid and constructive exchange of views had taken place, he acknowledged to reporters back in his fifteenth-floor office that he had not expected "the depth of reaction" that occurred. He said no apology was in order for views that "clearly needed to be stated." He pulled out the intelligence report Colonel Lally had supplied him and quoted parts of it to the newsmen. In addition to the one that had Carmichael saying that "the only way to deal with a white man is across the barrel of a gun," another had him observing that "Bobby Kennedy is the last hope of this country."

"What's so inflammatory about that?" one of the reporters asked Agnew. The governor just shrugged. When the newsman asked to see the report, he declined. He had done what in his view needed doing, and he would accept the consequences.

The April 11 confrontation with the black leaders climaxed a remarkably rapid transformation in the public image of Spiro Agnew. The governor himself insisted it was only that—a change in his image, in how he was perceived by others; he was, he said, the same man he had been. "I've stood still," he told Gene Oishi of the Baltimore *Sun* shortly afterward, "while the rest of the country, led by the press, has rushed headlong to the left."

But others were not so sure. Almost immediately after the Rockefeller withdrawal, political agents of Richard Nixon had been in touch with Agnew, eager to field him on the first short bounce. Robert Ellsworth, then one of Nixon's chief campaign directors, went down to Baltimore from New York. He found the Maryland governor personally embittered by the way in which Rockefeller had cast him aside, and supremely interested in Nixon. A meeting was arranged between Nixon and Agnew, who had talked to each other at length only once before, about two months earlier at a New York reception given by Maryland State Senator Louise Gore, niece of Democratic Senator Albert Gore of Tennessee. On March 29 Agnew called on Nixon in New York for a two-hour talk that left a strongly favorable impression on both men.

Nixon was and always had been, of course, a law-and-order man. While Agnew was having his troubles, Nixon had breezed through the New Hampshire and Wisconsin Republican primaries warning darkly that "some of our courts have gone too far in weakening the peace forces as against the criminal forces, and we must restore the balance." And with the outbreak of street crime and violence that spring, a tough line in this area certainly would be an integral part of the Nixon presidential candidacy. A governor from a border state like Maryland who could demonstrate that he too was tough on crime and violence would have something going for him when the time came for Nixon to pick a running mate. The fact that he had been for Rockefeller didn't hurt either, nor did the fact that he had managed to support him without ever being critical of Nixon. (In an interview with Agnew in his Baltimore office in late February, while Romney was still in the Republican race, Agnew was asked whether his work in Rockefeller's behalf constituted a stop-Nixon effort. "Absolutely not," he said. "If Rockefeller doesn't make it, Nixon may very well be my second choice. I don't have a thing against him. I like him.")

Whatever Agnew's intent, his conduct in the three weeks between the Rockefeller pull-out and the black-leaders confrontation proved to be critical in his political life. One of Nixon's most conservative aides, Patrick J. Buchanan, later a White House speech writer, was himself very impressed with how Agnew had handled the Bowie State and Baltimore racial crises, and he made certain that his boss saw clippings of what the governor had said and done.

In light of subsequent events, many of those who observed Agnew at close range in that twenty-one-day period are convinced that his transformation of image was more than coincidental. Clarence Mitchell later remarked concerning his performance at the April 11 meeting, "I was shocked primarily because it had not been his pattern as governor. He had been open, listening to our problems. I have a tendency now to believe it was politically inspired. It was calculated to create a conservative image for political purposes. After Rockefeller insulted him, I believe Agnew decided he had to cast his lot with the conservatives. I believe he will do whatever the person over him suggests that he do." Marshall W. Jones, a Republican Baltimore committeeman who walked out on the governor on April 11, agreed. "You take a poll one day," he said, "and you say, 'I'm going to move to bigger and better things.' You go with the breeze."

But others who have known Agnew a long time, including some Democrats, do not believe the Baltimore meeting was a product of political expedience. "The embarrassment caused by Rockefeller's announcement had a real telling effect on Ted," Mayor D'Alesandro observed. "It was like being shot in the back, and he didn't have the political sophistication and the background to realize that Rockefeller's decision could be 'No.' But I don't believe he thought that by giving that speech to the black leaders he was setting himself up as Mr. Conservative or attracting that element of the voting constituency. I believe he believes in what he's saying. There's nothing phony about the man."

Another long-time Agnew friend in Maryland, Republican state legislator Jervis Finney, looking back at the twenty-one-day period later, when Agnew had become Vice-President, said Rockefeller's conduct did jolt and disappoint Agnew because "he has an unusually high belief in loyalty. He's unusually loyal himself and he senses the presence of disloyalty early. But if he ever had a conscious thought about the vice-presidential nomination, I doubt it. He wasn't angling for that. People now have a preconceived notion of Agnew and try to fit all past events into it. Agnew is an able man. The big thing that people don't realize is that he is a very able man, an able administrator, he has a good mind, he gets things done; he has a good intellect and unbelievable political instincts when he needs them. Some say one of the times those instincts were working was when he gave that speech. Maybe it was, but there never was a conscious connection. It probably helped him politically, but that was a result—a matter of luck. It was sort of a serendipity effect."

"Serendipity"—an Agnew kind of word that sends the average listener to the dictionary for elucidation. *Webster's Third New International* defines it as "an assumed gift for finding valuable or agreeable things not sought for," and it might well describe the man's sudden emergence in 1969 as the Vice-President of the United States. But luck as an explanation for the rise of Spiro Agnew is too easy, too convenient. The elements in his character and motivation that mark him as one of the most controversial figures on the American political scene today had their roots in the people, circumstances and places that came before; to understand why he was so deeply affected by the Rockefeller withdrawal, by the Bowie State sit-in, by the Baltimore riot and black confrontation, it is necessary to look back at who Spiro Agnew was, and where he was, before he became a household word.

2

ROOTS OF A MIDDLE AMERICAN

To start tracing the roots of Spiro Agnew, one need go only a very short distance from Baltimore's State Office Building where in April 1968 he confronted the city's black moderates with their "sins." About two long blocks down Howard Street, on the corner where it intersects Madison Street, there stands an old three-story red brick building whose first floor is occupied by the Mary Johnson Florist Shop. Over the shop are five apartments, one of which, at the second-floor rear, in November 1918 housed the small family of Theodore Spiro Agnew, a Greek immigrant originally known as Anagnostopoulos.

It was to this apartment that the senior Agnew, an erect and stern man who operated a small restaurant farther down Howard Street, brought his infant first-born, named Spiro Theodore in the Greek tradition of reversing the father's name. The apartment of three rooms, kitchen and bath made for cramped quarters for Agnew, his wife Margaret, whom he had married only about a year earlier; eleven-year-old Roy, Margaret's son by a previous marriage; her sister "Teddy" and the new baby. But it was comfortable, it was near the restaurant and it was in a good, respectable section of old Baltimore.

That was fifty-three years ago. Today, in the short walk from the State Office Building to 226 Madison Street, one travels several light-years from the respectability of the old Baltimore that the senior Agnew knew. A knock on the door of the old Agnew apartment produces twenty-one-year-old, mini-skirted Kim Davenport, a Maryland Institute of Art student with long straight red hair and strands of hippie beads around her neck. Over her head, fastened to the ceiling of the hallway behind her, is a huge papier-mâché-and-chicken-wire pterodactyl, green and brown and grotesque, salvaged from a recent school dance. It sets the mood of elaborate put-on that dominates the motif of Kim's pad.

Throughout, the appointments constitute a Now Generation thumb to the nose to all that Spiro Agnew and his Middle America stand for. In the kitchen, a large Jerry Rubin poster bearing his Do It! motto looks down from above the small gas stove; a Woodstock poster graces another wall; an END THE WAR placard is on a third, along with a metal plate that reads: PLEASE GIVE THE GRASS A CHANCE. The bathroom sports a poster showing a nude man sitting on a toilet bowl, under the words PHI BETA KRAPPA. And in the bedroom, on one wall next to the bed that instant history now proclaims once bore young Spiro, is an American flag displayed upside down, with the blue field toward the floor.

It's nothing personal, Kim, a placid, thin girl, insists. "The flag hung upside down is a sign the country is in distress," she says matter-of-factly. "Well, it sure is."

Kim also owns a vest she made of another American flag, and in her living room, over two mattresses on the floor arranged at right angles in the best Middle America interior decoration, is a huge Stars and Stripes hung as a canopy. Old Baltimore helps furnish the New; Kim bought the massive flag, large enough to have flown over a fort or from a ship, in an antique shop for $2.

Publication of a picture of Kim in her flag-vest, sitting on her Agnew-bed with the flag-in-distress behind her, brought her a flood of hate mail when she first moved in. Most of it was love-it-or-leave-it stuff, much of it from the Midwest, though some writers optimistically sent along a copy of a pamphlet called "How to Respect and Display Our Flag." One correspondent, a fourteen-year-old boy from Wisconsin, defended her; now they are pen pals.

Kim lives the student's life of the 1970's unimpressed though faintly amused by the fact that for $75-a-month rent, she sleeps in what is said to be the old bed of the Vice-President of the United States. "When I heard who had lived here, I just hoped no radicals would bomb the house," she says, laughing. She has no particular feeling about Agnew. "The man, I don't hate the man at all," she says. "But his ideology is intolerable in this country in this time."

Downstairs in the florist shop, however, both Agnew the man and his ideology are revered by the owner, Mrs. Isabel DeMuth, direct descendant of Mary Johnson, and the three little old ladies who assist her. There, it is Kim Davenport who is intolerable. "That's all we have around us now," Mrs. DeMuth says, obviously scandalized. "This was the central part of the city, where all the society people lived, the best section of Baltimore. Mr. Agnew would feel very proud if he could go in there today, wouldn't he? If he went up there, he'd think it was terrible, just terrible. And the whole neighborhood—students, art students. They're so noisy. They holler out the window at people. And they're mixed, white and black. The girls all go out with the colored—it doesn't mean anything any more. Just changing times, that's all. If Mr. Agnew was President, he could change things. He did all right with the riots. What he said was just the truth at the time, that's what they had against him, but he won out. He had the National Guard right on this corner. This is where they were coming— downtown." Mrs. Anna Counabaugh, a clerk in the shop for more than twenty years, puts in, "Agnew is tops with us. He's our boy. He's the only one ain't afraid of them. I'd like to see him for President. He speaks his mind. He tells the truth. We need somebody like that."

Mrs. DeMuth looks back with nostalgia and even longing at the old aristocratic days at the corner of Howard and Madison. She recalls the senior Agnew as "a nice-looking man. You could tell his nationality, you know, but yet he carried himself very straight, like royalty. Whether they were or not, I don't know. She was a very good-looking woman, and Spiro was a good-looking child. I think the father did very well; not well-to-do, but comfortable. And what I remember most is the brother, going up and down here, so quiet and well-behaved. The children were always that way, and well-dressed."

The half-brother, W. Roy Pollard, an employee at the Monumental Life Insurance Company in downtown Baltimore for forty-four years, shares Mrs. DeMuth's recollection about Spiro and his father. "Spiro was always neat," he says. "He was never a noisy individual, a bit on the studious side, and he loved to read." They were traits he obviously got from Agnew senior, whom Pollard recalls as "a disciplinarian. He was born in Greece and the Greeks do have a sterner upbringing. For example, Greece right now is run by a junta. There is a regulation over there that everybody is off the streets by nine o'clock; anybody on the street after nine, there are no questions asked, is going to be shot. As a consequence, they don't have any crime rate over there."

The senior Agnew, college-educated in Greece, "was a student," Pollard says. "He would never pick up the average book. He'd read all the philosophers; I remember a book on Socrates, on Plato and a couple of others. If he was not reading something to improve his mind, he wouldn't read. And he imbued it to a point where, occasionally if I pick up a book, just the average novel, I feel a little bit guilty that I'm not learning an awful lot from it. The only thing I might learn from it is the usage of words."

Perhaps from this background, he recalls, both he and his half-brother Spiro always have been "students of words . . . I don't go for the big words that Spiro uses. I wonder where in heck he gets all the words he tosses into his speeches. I think he's deliberately digging them up or having research on it, I don't know. I think he's doing this now simply for effect. About a year ago I said to him, 'Spiro, all of these big words you're using. You have a wonderful command of them. I think they're fine for a certain kind of people. But actually, what you're trying to do is to reach Mr. Middle-Class Man and average people. Why don't you use words that can be understood by everyone?' Well, he disagreed with me. He said, 'I'm doing this intentionally. I think I'm doing the right thing.' "

If the size and obscurity of his half-brother's vocabulary surprise Roy Pollard, the concomitant directness and candor do not. "I'm afraid that in that respect," Pollard says, "he may have inherited a little from me because I'm addicted to say what I think. Actually, when he was a little shaver I used to baby-sit with him in the afternoons. I would get his little express wagon, pile him in and we used to go tearing up and down the pavements, and I used to keep him on many a Saturday. I don't mean to say at all that I'm responsible for his candor; all I'm saying is I too have that characteristic, and it does not only date from the time Spiro has been in politics. I'm known all over as a person who really speaks his own opinion, even though sometimes it comes out to my disadvantage."

Agnew himself remembers his father as a serious man, already forty years old when his son was born. "In my early years," the Vice-President recalled in 1971 in an interview, "remembrance of my father was that he was never what you might call a participant in any childish activities. I think his age made that very difficult for him and he was a father symbol, not a comrade in any sense. He was a disciplinarian to the extent that his manner may have seemed stern to a young child, although he was quite soft inside and quite gentle. But I didn't really get to know him until the latter years of my teens, because of this age discrepancy. During the formative years he was an authoritarian symbol to me, although my mother was quite influential and quite persuasive on him. He never struck me other than a couple of blows on the rear end, I guess, if from time to time I did something that justified it. But there was never any physical punishment that I remember where I was really severely chastised. But I still had a healthy respect for him."

In an earlier interview, with James Naughton of the *New York Times,* Agnew said his admiration for his father really mounted when "he got wiped out in the depression. And I saw he just shrugged it off and went back to work with his hands without complaints, and kept the food coming in, and the coal coming to keep the house warm. I'd watch him come in, just dead tired, and having lived a rather affluent life up to that point and now hauling sacks of potatoes around. He'd come home so tired, went in the living room with a newspaper on his lap, pull out a sack of Old Durham and roll his next day's cigarettes, and then after dinner right to bed because he had to get up about three.

"With all that, a very aware person politically. This sort of helped my interest in politics, that he always knew what his congressman was doing and he had strong opinions about political figures and political issues; and after he'd finished his rounds from the produce market to the restaurants he served, he'd sit in there with a cup of coffee, and I'd be with him sometimes, and talk politics—not football—that was the big thing to talk about in those days."

According to the Vice-President, his mother also was a strong person. Born Margaret Akers in Bristol, Virginia, she was orphaned when quite young and was raised by an older brother in Roanoke. At one time she worked as a secretary in Washington, in the very building—then housing the State and War Departments —where the Vice-President now has his office. Her first husband was a veterinarian from Massachusetts, Dr. William R. Pollard. The Pollards lived in Baltimore and were friends of Agnew's father; they used to go to his restaurant and, the Vice-President recalls, "They became good personal friends, the three of them, and other people in the group. After Dr. Pollard died, my mother and father started to go together and they were eventually married in Baltimore."

Agnew remembers his mother as "a very strong-willed, very persuasive woman who sort of wrapped my father around her finger; I guess most wives do that, anyhow. I could sometimes get a reprieve from a paternal judgment by a maternal appeal." Roy Pollard recalls, though, that in general she backed her husband in his strict handling of the boy. She told her sons of her own family's roots in old Virginia, and of the graciousness of that life. But she did not attempt to soften the disciplinarian manner of her husband toward the boys. "The father was the particularly dominant influence on Spiro Agnew's life," Pollard says.

In those early days, however, young Spiro was not one whose words or actions singled him out from the crowd. According to Pollard, "Spiro was an average kid. There was nothing in his youth that would indicate he would rise to the political heights that he has." Although he belonged to the Sons of Pericles, the junior arm of Ahepa (American Hellenic Educational Progressive Association), the Greek fraternal order in which his father was a national leader, Spiro was in other ways "a typical American boy," his half-brother says. While under the strict Greek home discipline and imbued with the immigrant family's industriousness and determination to get ahead, like many second-generation Americans he nevertheless responded to the equally strong influence of the larger environment and his own generation. His friends were classmates and neighborhood boys at P.S. 69 and at Garrison Junior High School in the Forest Park section of the city, an area of larger upper-middle-class homes to which the family moved when Spiro was in his subteens. The senior Agnew was doing better now, with a larger downtown restaurant, called the

Piccadilly, but his young son still was expected to work after school. A sixth-grade Garrison classmate, "Bud" Hammerman, now in the mortgage and banking business in Baltimore County, and Agnew had part-time jobs delivering groceries from supermarkets in their wagons, at ten or fifteen cents a trip, and distributing circulars for a hardware store.

At Forest Park High School, then regarded as the city's best, young Spiro was by all accounts a run-of-the-mill student, quiet and studious but not bookish, a boy who was on the fringes of the school's mainstream, friendly and pleasant and not stand-offish, just not much of an activist either. "He was homogenized in the whole group," says classmate Eugene Feinblatt, now an urbanologist in Baltimore. Part of the reason, obviously, was that Spiro worked after school. His only entrée into the school's social life was his piano playing. He accompanied one of his buddies, Jim Ringgold, a tenor and later a star blocking back at Wake Forest, in school assemblies. Although Agnew plays by ear, Pollard says he did have some lessons in his early days.

Young Spiro participated in intramural sports, but did not have the build for football. The school's coach, C. M. "Andy" Anderson, now retired, remembers him as "a very thin, tall boy, very well-mannered, very cooperative and willing, but he happened to come along at a time we had some pretty good athletes. I had one of my better football teams. He couldn't have made my team. We would have killed him." Agnew did participate in what was called the "Jolly Junior Jubilee," an annual fund-raising demonstration of gymnastics and general calesthenics using Indian clubs, dumbbells and wands. Outside of school, he developed an interest in tennis and with neighborhood friend Emmett Queen, now a prominent Baltimore doctor, and other boys built their own clay court on a vacant lot. He also played pool in the recreation room of a neighborhood church. While still teenagers, he and Queen joined a few other boys on a ten-day sightseeing trip to New England and Canada, a rather adventurous excursion in those days.

Young Agnew was not much of a ladies' man. A classmate, Leslie Edwards, says he doubts that Agnew ever had a date in high school. A neighbor, Elaine Sturgis, now Mrs. Dempsey Williford, says she went to the movies with him once or twice "but it was no big deal. He was just the boy next door." In the class yearbook for 1937, when he was graduated, the line under Agnew's picture says: "An ounce of wit is worth a pound of sorrow." Classmates still scratch their heads over what that might mean. That's all the yearbook says, and Edwards observes, "That yearbook tells the story. You look through it and there's not much about him in it. He just wasn't very popular, or very active."

Agnew's academic performance in high school is a matter of official secrecy in the Baltimore Department of Education. Classmates recall that he was an average student, which was good enough in a highly rated school like Forest Park in the late 1930's to virtually assure college admission. Immediately upon graduation in February 1937, Agnew was accepted at Johns Hopkins, where he labored as a chemistry major until 1939, with unsatisfactory results. The first year he went to school from February through the summer and passed, but the intensity of the effort took its toll on him.

"It was a dumb thing to do," he acknowledged in an interview as Vice-President. "When I finished that summer I was so exhausted I wasn't ready to go back in September and take on the sophomore year. I didn't have any failures at all the first year, my grades were all good, and I absolved some courses—freshman English, for example—by examination, which helped take some pressure off me. But by the time the October term began, I thought, 'Oh, I've got to go back there again?' Laboratory work takes a lot of time, and in the summertime you get in these chemistry labs, three-hour sessions every afternoon, and I was pretty tired."

He was interested in chemistry, though, and he persevered. "In '38, I started the normal semester in September, but there was a multiplicity of reasons that caused a lack of concentration on my part. One of them was the financial problem that the Depression had brought. My father still wasn't doing well; he was making sacrifices to keep me in school. . . . On top of that the war thing was generating. . . . the draft hadn't begun, but there was debate about it and talk about our involvement, and a lot of distraction for me. Consequently, I lost some interest and I didn't concentrate as well as I might have. I fell off scholastically, to the extent my father was pretty sore about it. There was some question about whether he was going to continue me in school. He thought maybe if I wasn't any more interested, then I should get out.

"That continued through '38 and into '39. I began taking some of the more advanced chemistry courses and particularly a lot of laboratory work, which I disliked intensely. I decided that perhaps chemistry really wasn't what I was interested in. But I really can't blame it all on chemistry. It was a culmination of dislocations and pressures and what-not and I just wasn't dedicated, I didn't have a direction at that time. So I finally decided that the thing to do was to withdraw. I'd failed a few courses; they weren't fatal, I could have repeated them, but I just didn't feel it was the way to continue, and the tuition problem became acute. So I withdrew from the school with the right to enroll again, and in fact did enroll again in later years, in the fifties, and took accounting courses there. There's some talk that I was dropped, but that's not true. I withdrew voluntarily without any pressure on the part of the school. I took a job at that time and entered law school at night. I felt better about it; I was financing my own education at that time."

Young Agnew took a daytime job as a clerk at the Maryland Casualty Company in Baltimore, was assigned to the sprinkler-leakage and water-damage department and by 1942 had become an assistant underwriter. His job was to take inspectors' reports of new water-damage insurance coverage, or old policies being renewed, and determine the premium rates to be charged. It was strictly paper work; day after day Agnew would sit at his desk grinding away in his calm, low-key way. Fellow employees like Louis Muths, another assistant underwriter, lunched with him regularly and recall that he was friendly and cordial, with a dry sense of humor, and "immaculate" in his dress—a description that without exception is applied to Agnew by those who have worked with him throughout his career.

It was at Maryland Casualty that he met his future wife, Elinor Judefind, called Judy. She worked at the general-records counter and increasingly he would go down there to get copies of reports. Like him, she is remembered as "immaculate," and fellow employees thought they were an ideal couple.

After working hours Agnew attended law school with another Maryland Casualty employee, Gould Gibbons, now a Baltimore lawyer. Gibbons says Agnew in those days was "a pretty bright guy, always very articulate and a good sport who liked a good time." The two of them would go down to the legal department of

Maryland Casualty and use the library there to prepare for their law classes, frequently working into the small hours of the morning. Neither of them was particularly conscientious, Gibbons admits; the practice was par for the course in law school. What impressed Gibbons most was Agnew's level-headedness and self-confidence. "I considered him a sort of father-confessor I would go to with my own troubles."

Gibbons says he recalls Agnew's scholastic performance as undistinguished at the law school, and the school declines to reveal his records. Gibbons points out that to be undistinguished there was not unusual; classes were large and there was little campus life and hence little opportunity for anyone to stand out. The dean emeritus of the school, John H. Hussey of Baltimore, was impressed with Agnew, however, and later encouraged him to return to the school to teach, turning over to him one of his own courses in torts. This display of confidence hardly suggests that Agnew got through law school only by the skin of his teeth. The University of Baltimore Law School, of course, was not Johns Hopkins. It lacked national accreditation and for some years was in danger of losing accreditation by the Maryland Bar Association. But Agnew himself notes that he passed the bar examination six months before completing law school.

While Agnew was thus engaged in his erratic progression toward a career, World War II intruded. In September 1941, three months before the Japanese attack on Pearl Harbor, he was drafted into the Army. He took his training at Camp Croft, South Carolina, and then was transferred to officer candidate school at Fort Knox, Kentucky, from which he was commissioned a second lieutenant on May 24, 1942. Three days later he and Judy were married. They lived in a series of nondescript off-base apartments near Fort Knox and later Fort Campbell, Kentucky, working for a time in Special Services, organizing athletic teams, until he was sent overseas to join the 10th Armored Division, in March 1944. The Agnews by then had their first child, Pamela.

Agnew was stationed in Birmingham, England, as a casual officer until the fall of 1944, when he joined the 54th Armored Infantry Battalion in France as a replacement officer. For a few weeks he was a rifle platoon leader, then became a service company commander in charge of about 120 men. The battalion was a fast-moving combination of a headquarters company, three rifleman companies transported by half-tracks and trucks, Agnew's service (supply and maintenance) company, plus medical and other detachments. There were about nine hundred men under the command of Lieutenant Colonel James O'Hara, now retired and living in Washington, D.C. The division was moved into Metz, in the northeastern tip of France, shortly after the town had been seized by the Third Army in General George S. Patton's swift thrust toward Germany. Patton's drive was stalled there for lack of gas, and Metz and Thionville became a staging and regrouping area.

In December, O'Hara's battalion was detached and made part of a special task force, 10th Armored Combat Command "B," attached to the 101st Airborne Division under Brigadier General Anthony McAuliffe. In the weeks just before Christmas, Agnew took part in the push northward through the Ardennes Forest that culminated in the Battle of the Bulge and the isolation of McAuliffe's division, the O'Hara task force included, at Bastogne. Combat Command "B" was pinned down there, and according to John Bevilaqua, Agnew's first sergeant, the company spent thirty-nine days "in the hole of the doughnut." According to O'Hara, Agnew was under heavy fire in what was always a dangerous support role, moving constantly at the battalion's rear, bringing up tank recovery units, men, rations, ammunition, fuel and other supplies. Bevilaqua, now of Chattanooga, recalls of Lieutenant Agnew: "He was tough. He wanted it a certain way, and that was it. He was straight from the shoulder. We had some head-to-head discussions about the enlisted men, but we got along pretty well."

After the siege of Bastogne was lifted, Agnew's battalion moved east, fighting through the Siegfried Line in the bloody Saar-Moselle triangle. The unit crossed the Saar at the town of Ayl at dusk in small boats under cover of a smoke screen, and moved toward the town of Zerf, where O'Hara was wounded and knocked out of the war. Then, according to Bevilaqua, the battalion moved northward, took part in the capture of Trier, swung southeast again across Germany, through Mannheim and Heidelberg and southeast to Krailsheim, where another rugged battle took place. All through this swift push against the crumbling Nazi armies, Agnew's service company moved constantly over the countryside in close-up support of the 54th Armored Infantry Battalion, gathering the supplies and making the equipment repairs needed to keep the unit's drive going.

Though he was a service officer, the going was often rugged. "A service company is a combat operation, it's not a service-and-supply situation, in the sense of a regimental supply outfit," Agnew recalled later. "With our division, many times we were running the gamut between what we thought was occupied ground and what wasn't. I remember one time down at Krailsheim, we followed the spearhead down. We were about sixty miles behind the enemy lines; the other units went through in complete surprise without any resistance, but by the time we tried to get through, we had to fight our way through. We couldn't get back, so we stayed with the division and fought our way out with the division."

After Krailsheim, the battalion swung south and took part in the squeeze of the retreating Germans, winding up the war at Garmisch-Partenkirchen in Bavaria, a great resort area. Agnew returned home with a Bronze Star and the Combat Infantryman's Badge. (Agnew has told aides that he met General Patton briefly during a fire fight in Germany and has read books about him. But his aides say Agnew is neither a Patton nor a World War II buff.)

When he came back, according to friends who saw him then, he did not dwell much on his military career, nor has he said much about it in building a political life, which is somewhat unusual for the American politician on the rise. His half-brother Roy says, "Actually, we didn't know an awful lot about his actual experience. . . . Because my mother was a very excitable person, all this was kept completely from her; to her, his Army career was completely without incident. Well, judging from the different stories he tells here and there, it wasn't without incident. He was driving along in a jeep and the mortars or larger shells began zeroing in, and he jumped over into the ditch and almost immediately after jumping, a damn shell hit the jeep. But, again, all these actual experiences, they were kind of soft-pedaled around his mother. And after she died, in the sixties, the war had been over so very long that he just no longer talked about the war. It wasn't an effort on his part to withhold."

Lou Muths, who corresponded with Agnew during the war and was a bowling companion afterward, agrees that "he didn't like to talk about it. He was very reluctant to talk about the Army whatsoever." But in V-mail Muths received, he recalls, "he used to tell me that he was writing by candlelight and you could hear the German 88's go over. He said they made a different noise than the ordinary artillery shell." Once Agnew sent Muths a Mauser as a souvenir, and later, his old Maryland Casualty buddy remembers going out to the Judefinds' home, where the returned veteran and his wife lived for a while, and watching Agnew stretch a map on the living room floor. He traced his wartime travels across Europe, and displayed a boxful of combat souvenirs—"German medals, German shoulder patches, belt buckles, stuff like that."

By coincidence, a man soon to become Agnew's law partner, Sam Kimmel, was the commander of an LST in the Mediterranean at the time Agnew's unit was preparing to move out of France toward Bastogne. His job was to ferry tanks surreptitiously out of Leghorn, Italy, to Marseilles for shipment north to Patton's armored units. After the war, the two lawyers swapped war tales. "He tells the story," according to Kimmel, "where at times things were right tough, at times things were pretty good. In fact, one time they ran their tank right into a wine cellar in one of the old French villas there, and he managed to find a good supply of old wine and they had a pretty good time for a few days. But they weren't moving much, anyway. This was the time they were sort of stalled there. It was hard to break through." Since then, Kimmel says, Agnew has had an annual reunion with about ten or twelve buddies who come from all over the country to have a few drinks and dinner with him.

Of his military experience, Agnew told Naughton: "It was my first view of the outside world, really. When I say that, outside the confines of an immediate neighborhood and a college community. I had done very little travel before I went into the service . . . the first thing I remember was going into basic training, which was before [participating in] World War II, down in South Carolina. We had regular army NCO's who, to a sheltered lad, were pretty rough customers. But very fair, and very adept at what they were teaching. I was assigned to a .30-caliber machine-gun company and they used to get us out in that mud down there and run us around the tripod and weapon for hours on end. The usual disciplines of making a bed and keeping a place clean and being responsible for yourself I found difficult, because I hadn't had many of those disciplines. But I began to see the benefit of them and the pride that goes with conforming to that style. When you successfully complete it, you feel like you've done something.

"I remember my experiences there and also at [Fort] Knox when I went to officer candidate school—a tremendous esprit de corps among these ninety-day wonders at that time . . ."

Of his twenty months overseas, almost half in combat, Agnew recalled, "That was all very beneficial, the idea about being on your own and away, with responsibilities. When I came back I knew what I wanted to do. I knew first of all I wanted to go back to law school, not just to be going to law school, but to finish as quickly as I could with the best grades I could and become a successful practicing attorney. In other words, I had a purpose, a much more identified purpose and I was so glad to get back to a peaceful existence and so grateful for the idea that I could get up in the morning and go to a nice comfortable job instead of wondering whether you're going to get back or not. . . . I found scholastically I had improved immeasurably because my power of concentration was so much higher. Before the Army I had been just sort of drifting along, doing as little as I could to get through, more interested in the social side of life than anything else."

On Agnew's return from the war, he was offered his old job at Maryland Casualty but decided he should strike out on his own. He resumed at the University of Baltimore night law school under the GI Bill of Rights, and through a friend of his father's, Michael Paul Smith, was taken on as a law clerk-trainee in his firm, Smith and Barrett (with the government paying part of his salary— about $50 a week). The other partner was Lester Barrett, an older man who knew his way around Baltimore Republican politics. Just before the war, young Agnew had registered as a Democrat, his father's party affiliation, but politics was not a matter of particular interest to him then. Baltimore records indicate that after having voted in the 1940 election he didn't go to the polls in the city again, and his registration was canceled in 1945 for not having voted within the required five years. But as Barrett's protégé, his interest began to grow.

On graduation from law school in 1947, according to Sam Kimmel, Agnew thought he was entitled to a raise at Smith and Barrett and said so. Six months before graduation he had taken and passed the Maryland bar examination. But Smith had moved out to the firm's Baltimore County office in Towson and wanted to close down in Baltimore city, and Agnew's request was rejected. He opened his own law firm, but it was not a success.

At about this same time, Agnew went to Lester Barrett, also practicing in Towson, for some advice about getting into politics. Barrett, who later became chief circuit court judge in the county, made it short and simple: become a Republican. "If you're going to run for public office," Barrett recalls telling Agnew then, "it's difficult to be a candidate in the Democratic party because of the overwhelming Democratic registration." The figures—a four-to-one Democratic edge—provided persuasive backing for Barrett's argument, and Agnew, who had bought a small house in 1947 in the town of Lutherville just north of Towson, registered in the county as a Republican. "It was not a matter of ideology," Judge Barrett says, but of practical politics. (Agnew has denied that the greater personal prospects in the Republican party motivated his party change. More important to him, he has told interviewers, was the persuasiveness of Barrett's thinking.)

On the job front, meanwhile, Agnew's old friend at Maryland Casualty and law school classmate, Gould Gibbons, was working at the Lumbermens Mutual Casualty Company of the Kemper Insurance group. In late 1948, Gibbons helped Agnew get a job there as an investigator and casualty claims adjuster. Eugene Fulton, his now-retired superior, describes Agnew's duties this way: "It entailed going out into the field and making actual investigation of accidents under automobile or general liability coverages. In his case, he was able not only to make investigations but was equipped by legal training to make an assessment as to legal liability, claim evaluations and settlements. If necessary he participated in the defense work, within reasonable limits, in what we call lightweight cases, in contrast with the heavy cases, for which his experience was not sufficient at that point in his career." For this work, Agnew was paid about $3,600 a year, Fulton says, and he stayed on only a little more than a year, when he again went into law practice for himself—without notable success. He handled some "heavy cases" for Kemper but couldn't make an adequate living this way.

Young Agnew next answered a newspaper advertisement and was hired as an assistant personnel manager of a growing Baltimore supermarket chain specializing in meats, with much business among the city's black population. The markets were run by four brothers named Schreiber, one of whom, Alvin, was Agnew's boss. When he quit around 1951, Agnew took over for him.

Intervening at this time, however, was the Korean War, and as a Reserve Army officer Agnew was called back to active service, although he now had three children—first-born Pam, a son, Randy, and another daughter, Susan. He was assigned to a receiving center at nearby Fort Meade and later to Fort Benning, Georgia. Within a year he was about to be shipped overseas again when the Army admitted it had made a mistake—a married man with three children was not supposed to be sent abroad. Agnew was discharged, but he was bitter; he had served his time and had been in combat in World War II, and then had been yanked unjustly from his struggle to establish some sort of career. He went back to Schreibers' and tried to take up where he had left off.

The job was not exactly the stuff of which dreams of young climbers are made. As in his earlier insurance investigator's job, Agnew was used as a cut-rate lawyer, handling matters in the store of a quasi-legal nature that were too petty for Schreiber Brothers' legal counsel, yet requiring somebody with some knowledge of the law. He was a kind of glorified store detective-judge to whom suspected shoplifters—usually caught with the goods— were brought to be "broken down" and sentenced to out-of-court restitution.

Carl Gleitsman, another Schreibers' middle-level executive who shared a tiny second-floor office with Agnew and split the interrogations with him, provides this description of Agnew at work:

"He would go about it in this manner: 'Now, you took this item. We saw you take it. We know you had it. We told you where it was and what the item was and what packet you had it in. So you know you are in trouble. Now, we're not trying to give you any trouble, all we want you to do is pay for it, give us a release and promise us you won't do it again. If you do that, why, nobody need know anything about it, except you and me. If you don't want to do that, then you're going to force me to call the police, and we'll have to put you down to the police court and you'll have to tell your side of it and we'll tell our side to the judge, and all your friends will know about it.'

"Agnew's manner was easy-going, unless once in a while you'd get a belligerent one and he could get tough with them too. It was not so much toughness as firmness: 'We have you, whether you realize it or not. Now, if you want to look for trouble for yourself, just say so and we'll get the police. We're not going to stand here and argue about it. You either say that you did it and pay for it and give us a release, or if you can't pay for it, give it back and we'll let you go. Or we're going to lock you up. Now, make your mind up [about] what you're going to do. If you won't make your mind up, I'll make your mind up for you.' Words to that effect." Gleitsman remembers that "one time I had one I couldn't break down, and Agnew lived all the way out in Lutherville, and I called him at home . . . It took him about thirty minutes to get back down, but he came all the way in to handle it."

Most of the shoplifting was petty, and some culprits were amusing in their audacity. Gleitsman remembers a thin woman in her seventies wearing a long black skirt down to her ankles "and beneath this black skirt she had a big sack. She'd just pull the zipper down from her skirt, put the stuff in and it would go down into the sack. We didn't lock her up, we just brought her up, took the merchandise away and got her to sign a paper [to protect Schreiber Brothers against later charges of false arrest] and let her go. And then there was the rich man whose wife stole. He was a friend of one of the Schreibers and he called and said, 'Look, I know my wife steals. She can't help it. Just let her go, and at the end of the month tell me what it cost and I'll send you a check.' And he did."

When Agnew first burst into national prominence, there were stories that he had been a mere clerk in the supermarket, or at best a floorwalker, bagging groceries and dressed in a white coat that said "No Tipping Please." Both Gleitsman and Eugene Schreiber, one of the brothers, deny emphatically that is so. It is true, they say, that Agnew—as all other members of the staff, the four Schreibers included—went down to the floor to help in rush periods, such as Thanksgiving and Christmas. But on such occasions they did no bagging and wore long white coats different from those the clerks had, without the no-tipping admonition.

"We had a unique system," Gleitsman recalls, "that when a person came into the store they were given a shopping card, and as they went around to the various counters the amount of their purchases was recorded on this shopping card. Many of these people would lose them on purpose because they had a large total on them. Some would even steal the cards. Quite often Agnew would check on all these things, but he was never on the produce counter. He never was a member of that union and they would have objected to that."

It also was Agnew's job to get permits for the store to stay open on Sundays to take inventory; to deal with customer complaints, accidents in the store, general public relations; and to handle minor grievances and labor troubles. He was well liked by the other employees and according to Gleitsman often took their part, although one of his jobs was to help negotiate their contracts, especially the butchers'.

The market was a family business, but one of the four brothers, Martin, was the big boss. By all accounts he was an authoritarian of the most domineering sort. One member of the family has described him as "a dictator" who had a habit of firing anybody who looked at him in a way he didn't like, and sometimes for less cause than that. "He was a tough man to work for," Gleitsman recalls, "and I had to fire many a man on his say-so, to get rid of them. With many he was exactly right, but on others I had considerable doubt." Getting along with Martin Schreiber was a tenuous undertaking for everyone, Agnew included, and the fact that Agnew was still smarting from his unwanted return to the army did not make matters easier. "The recall and being so close to going back overseas again made a terrific mark upon him, and he was still undergoing this readjustment at the time," Gleitsman says. "He often spoke to me about it and he was very bitter about the foul-up."

The breaking point came in the summer of 1952, a few days after Gleitsman had gone on vacation with his family to the seashore. That left Agnew on duty to handle alone all the shoplifting interrogations, labor problems and the rest. "One afternoon," according to Gleitsman, "I got a call from Eugene Schreiber [a nephew and the company's comptroller] requesting me to come back to Baltimore, that Agnew had left the company, that Agnew and Marty had had a difference and Agnew had left. I never knew the exact details, but a day or two later Agnew called me. He had heard I had been called back and he apologized for getting me involved in the difference he had with Martin Schreiber. I always looked upon it as not being a discharge, but Agnew never indicated what the difference was. I'm sure it was something Martin

Schreiber wanted done that was against Agnew's ethics. It happened many, many times. Agnew was more the defender of the employees than anybody had been up to that point, because everybody was scared to death of Martin."

Sam Kimmel, who joined Agnew in a law partnership shortly afterward, is more specific. "Ted [which was the name Agnew now was being called by his colleagues in the legal profession] was getting fed up with Martin. Martin felt he was overly friendly with the meat cutters, that he wasn't strong enough with them in negotiating, so Ted quit before he was fired. He was unable to take much more of it. Martin was making a target of him." And a member of the Schreiber family, speaking anonymously to preserve family peace, says, "I am completely convinced in my own mind Agnew was fired by Marty, and I'm reasonably convinced there was no good reason. He had days when if he didn't like somebody's looks, he'd fire him, and I'm sure that's what happened." Agnew says only that "Marty was pretty tough to get along with. Things got really unbearable with my personal relations with him, and I saw a chance to get into law practice, so I left—I resigned."

Agnew, of course, had not planned on spending the rest of his days as a grand inquisitor of penny-ante shoplifters. With the help of a board director at Schreibers', Judge Herman Moser, he was taken into the prosperous Baltimore law firm of Karl F. Steinman, who liked his young lawyers to specialize. He assigned Agnew to corporation taxes. "That didn't strike Ted as too exciting," Kimmel recalls, and Agnew quit to try his own law practice in Baltimore. To make some money on the side, he became a staff aide on a county committee studying a charter form of government—a development that would prove to be somewhat of a door opener to politics for him.

Agnew's friendliness with labor, which Kimmel says was his undoing at Schreibers', proved to be his salvation in private practice. The butchers at Schreibers' belonged to the Amalgamated Meat Cutters and Butcher Workmen of North America, AFL-CIO, and they always felt he had treated them fairly. Now he was asked to represent them in negotiations with Baltimore area stores. Another lawyer friend, Richard A. James, rented space to Agnew for two desks in a downtown Baltimore office building, and before long his practice was predominantly in the labor field.

Leon Schachter, district manager and organizer for the meat cutters in Maryland, Virginia and Delaware, soon had Agnew traveling through his territory handling negotiations.

One of his most successful was in Kilmarnock, Virginia, on the Chesapeake Bay, where he obtained strong contracts for an unusual community of five hundred black fishermen on boats that ply the Atlantic about six months of the year in search of huge schools of menhaden, a fish used for oil and fertilizer. The fishermen were so pleased with Agnew's work, Kimmel says, that they bought a lot for him on the waterfront and offered to build him a house if he would move down there and work exclusively for them. The owners of the boats also tried to hire him, but he declined both offers, in part because he was getting more and more interested in Baltimore County politics.

In 1955, when Lester Barrett was named a judge in Towson, he closed his Baltimore office, and Sam Kimmel, who had shared space there, moved in and took one of Agnew's two desks. For about six months they went along like that. Then, Kimmel says, "Ted and I at this time thought, 'Well, our judge is out in Towson, why don't we go out there and open an office?'" With a third friend and lawyer, George W. White, Jr., Agnew and Kimmel opened a small suite at the county seat, just across the street from the Towson courthouse.

Until that time, though Ted Agnew had been living in suburbia for about eight years, he had been a city-based man, working in the city on problems of the workingman—supermarket shopping (and stealing), contract negotiating, insurance claims and the like, heavily involving black Americans, with whom he always got on well. In 1954 and 1955, he had gone back to night school at Johns Hopkins, to study advanced accounting, with the idea, according to one friend, of selling insurance to business executives. With accounting training, he would be equipped to counsel them about which plans would be most favorable for income tax purposes. Now, with his move to Towson, he was to be introduced increasingly to an entirely different world—of something called "subdivisions" instead of "neighborhoods," of sewer and land acquisition and zoning problems, of Kiwanis and community associations and P.T.A., and—above all—of whiteness.

In many ways Towson is not unlike hundreds of other county seats throughout the land—courthouse in a center square, with the life of the county feeding out from it. But unlike other county seats, whose essentially rural character is retained in old shops that box in the courthouse on all sides of the square, Towson exudes suburban sprawl and the lawyers' windfall associated with it. The gold-domed courthouse, built in 1854, has been rendered an anachronism by the construction of modern office buildings on three sides of the square. In these buildings are housed the hundreds of lawyers representing special interests scrambling for their profits from the particular phenomenon of white America in the second half of this century—the flight from the overpopulated, overburdened, overtaxed and increasingly black inner cities. And perhaps nowhere in the United States is there a political entity whose boundaries more graphically and exactly circumscribe—and hem in—the problems of the inner city than does Baltimore County.

The county encircles, but does not include, the city of Baltimore, which in the mid-fifties had a black population of about one-third and now is more than half black. From Towson emanate the local regulations that in large measure determine who may build what, and where; and when Agnew first moved his law practice there, who might live where. In the mid-fifties Baltimore County, more than any other major suburban area outside the Deep South, was a white noose around a black inner city. (The same situation applied around Washington, thirty-five miles to the south, but there five different local governments maintained the white noose.)

Agnew also moved his family from Lutherville to Towson, to a middle-income subdivision called Loch Raven Village. His new home was part of a six-family structure, each unit with two stories and basement, in the row-house style. It made for togetherness, this sharing of walls on either side. Mrs. Edith Shane, the Agnews' next-door neighbor all the years they lived in Loch Raven, says knowledgeably of them, "They were an ideal couple. You never heard them argue. And believe me, you really get to know people when you live next door to them here. We always knew when Spiro was waiting for Judy to get ready to go out. He'd sit in the living room and play the piano. And he enjoyed playing upstairs with the girls. You could hear him chasing them around. They had a good time, but he said 'when.' He was a strong father, very disciplined. When the children were small and he said 'time for bed,' that was the end of it."

Both Ted and Judy plunged into the neighborhood community life. On Thursday nights they went bowling with the Shanes and the Wilhelms, the neighbors on the other side, and Ted became active in the P.T.A. at the Loch Raven Elementary School, which was just a few doors down from the house. Later, when the children moved on to Dumbarton Junior High School, he joined that P.T.A. and became its president. Many of the bowlers also belonged to the Loch Raven Kiwanis; he joined that too, and there his piano playing made him much in demand. He found, in fact, that playing the piano made him the life of the party wherever his new suburban friends gathered. With Judge Barrett, he wrote a tune they called "Blue Melody," and another lawyer-mentor, Albert Menchine, also a judge, recorded it for them on a home device that made wax records. Barrett and Agnew never got around to writing the lyrics, but the men often teamed up to sing three-part harmony on the popular tunes of the day.

Also in full swing by this time was a special social group of husbands and wives who met faithfully one Saturday night every month, the member couples rotating as hosts. The gatherings had begun around 1946, according to Alan Clarke, an insulation contractor, with just a few couples from the Forest Park area. Over the next several years, new couples were brought in. George White, Agnew's law partner, has been a participant, and so have Lee and John Harrison, brothers and boyhood chums of Agnew, and their wives. The group also includes a real estate man, a retired Marine Corps major, a salesman, a manager of an oil-burner-equipment company and a rentor of seashore property. ("The bowling team," one Agnew associate calls the group.)

Although one of their number now is the Vice-President of the United States, the Saturday night group still meets regularly and has met down through the years, with the Agnews seldom absent, whether he was county executive, governor or Vice-President. Nor has there been a single divorce among the eleven couples. In the early years there would be much singing and dancing. More recently it has been mostly talk—the women in the living room, the men in shirt sleeves in the kitchen, with Agnew, Scotch and soda in hand, sometimes holding forth about his latest adventures but more often joining in a general discussion about golf or tennis or football. Then as now, Agnew was an avid Colts fan and a season-ticket holder. Also, "if there was a piano in the home," Clarke says, "he would find his way to it. If you could name a song, he could play it." Often he would play old tunes and the couples would try to guess the titles. Now that the Agnews live in a hotel apartment in Washington, the couples all go down there when the Agnews' turn to play host comes around. The group also holds an annual New Year's Eve party, with Joseph Murray, the real estate man, taking home movies. "They don't forget their old friends," Clarke says—a phrase that one hears over and over again as the early years of the Agnews are traced, and it appears to be true. Even now, men with whom Agnew worked in situations perhaps better forgotten by the successful politician correspond regularly with him and can pick up the telephone and get through to him immediately.

One other thing these old friends from Baltimore and early Towson days remember about Ted Agnew: he never talked politics. Clarke says he didn't know in those first postwar years whether Agnew was a Democrat or a Republican, and even after Agnew's talks with Judge Barrett that contributed to his change in party registration, his interests seemed to be more in sports, and family matters, the P.T.A. and Kiwanis, than in politics.

Above all, as his many job changes indicated, Ted Agnew was a man determined to make something of himself—restless to do better, to break out of the series of dead ends his life had been, to climb the ladder. He obviously sought financially to escape his modest beginnings, yet he was deeply immersed in the life style of those beginnings and indeed continued to be comfortable in it. He knew and remembered the tribulations, and the foibles, of the workingman—the union member and the white-collar paper-shuffler; the honest penny-stretchers and the corner-cutters—the shoplifters. But he was now also beginning to make his move out of the rank and file of the middle class and into the elite in the pantheon of Middle America—suburbia. He was a struggling lawyer in the county seat of a mushrooming suburban area, and he did not need to have the political perception of a Mark Hanna to see what public office could do for him. Not even Hanna, of course, could have foreseen that this young man panning the political stream for a few nuggets would strike the bonanza he so quickly did. An incredible series of opportunities had to fall in place, and after all the dead ends, the first of these opportunities was now at hand.

3

◇◆◇◆◇◆◇◆◇

THE BOTTOM RUNG

ALTHOUGH Spiro Agnew, Democrat, had become Spiro Agnew, Republican, in 1946 under the guidance of Judge Barrett, he did not plunge immediately into political activity. There had been the matter of getting a career going, and it was not until the early 1950s that he finally committed himself to work in the party that eventually was to catapult him into the center of national political life.

A World War II hero, Marine Brigadier General James P. S. Devereux, a leader of the defense of Wake Island, was running for Congress as a Republican in the Baltimore area, and Agnew enlisted as a volunteer. To Devereux's best recollection, young Agnew was assigned to direct a team of coeds from Goucher College in a kind of Burma-Shave roadside drill—the girls standing one behind the other on streetcorners, each holding a sign with part of the message urging passers-by to vote for the general. Devereux was elected to his first of four terms, and later served under Agnew in the Baltimore County government.

Agnew's move to the Towson law office with Kimmel and White, and his increasing involvement in P.T.A., the Kiwanis and other service clubs, soon channeled his interest into another form of political action. Baltimore County's postwar development had been unprecedented. The antiquated commission form of government that had been good enough in the county's sleepy rural days now was incapable of grappling with the scores of new and complex problems that resulted from suburban sprawl. Reformers in both parties organized and proposed a new county charter that would streamline their government—a seven-member elected county council with an elected county executive.

Although the reform drive was bipartisan, the uncertainties involved in any new system posed a threat to the entrenched Democrats, who under an old-time boss named Michael Birmingham had ruled the county like a fiefdom. By the same token, the prospect of a new charter gave the Republicans hope of making inroads. Registration overwhelmingly favored the Democrats, about four to one, largely because the heavily populated southeastern corner of the county, notably the towns of Dundalk and Essex, abounded in blue-collar workers traditionally loyal to the party of Franklin D. Roosevelt. But elsewhere in the county that rings the city of Baltimore, the exodus of middle-class whites to suburbia offered a considerable potential for G.O.P. recruiters. Here as elsewhere across the country, demographers were finding that as blue-collar Democrats moved into the suburbs and acquired houses, lawns and fences, they often began to perceive their political self-interest in a different perspective. They did not often become card-carrying Republicans like those professional and business men whose Republicanism was hereditary and an article of faith. But they were more open than before to the exhortations of the party of the propertied.

Ted Agnew, lawyer and Kiwanian, threw himself with energy and conviction into the drive for charter reform. According to Kimmel, he worked the service-club and P.T.A. circuit tirelessly in its behalf, making numerous speeches in support of the plan to rescue the county's political structure from the inadequacies of the past. The charter was approved by the voters in 1956 with Birmingham, the last president of the old board of commissioners, automatically appointed the first county executive under a transition arrangement.

In the first election under the new charter, in 1956, Agnew wanted to run for the council. He went to one of his new Towson friends, Scott Moore, a lawyer who along with Osborne Beall, a prominent Ford dealer, ran what there was of a Republican party in the county. "We said 'No' to him," Moore recalled, "because we had another man who was more active in the party and better known." Disappointed but still a loyal soldier in the ranks, Agnew worked hard in the election, and to the great surprise of nearly everyone, his Republican party won four of the seven council seats.

It so happened that one of the innovations of the charter government was establishment of a new county board of appeals, responsible for reviewing zoning decisions. In this mushrooming suburban county, the importance of the board and the sensitive nature of its work were obvious; to guard against runaway partisan decisions, the charter stipulated that only two of the board's three members be appointed from the majority party—in this case the Republican—and one from the minority.

Having been turned down for a place on the ticket for county council, Agnew zeroed in on the Republican seats on the board of appeals. "He was interested because it was the closest thing to a judgeship," Kimmel says. "You sit as a judge on zoning cases, and I think Ted's original aspiration was for a judgeship." But Scott Moore suggests that Agnew's interest was less specific. "It was a job open for a Republican," Moore said. "He would have wanted any job. In fact, he wanted to be chairman. He was a real pusher."

"It was a prestige job to me at the time," Agnew said later. "There was a brand-new charter in effect; this was the most important appointment that the new county councilmen could make. It was really a quasi-judicial position where we actually made the record in zoning cases and other appeals for the courts, and it was good for my law practice to have the prestige connected with this."

Agnew, with his party's blessing, was named to a one-year term on the board in 1957, at a salary of $3,600. He served without major incident, winning a reputation for conscientiousness, even-handedness and honesty in a job in which a zoning decision could be worth hundreds of thousands of dollars to a developer who received a favorable ruling. Moore recalls that Agnew once ruled against one of his clients in an appeal before the board that the courts later upheld. "The son of a gun should have decided the case in my favor," Moore says, implying Agnew bent over backward excessively to avoid any appearance of favoritism.

Edgar L. Feingold, later an aide to Agnew, says of him, "He seemed to me then to be a guy of some bearing. He articulated well and carried out his office with a great deal of dignity. It seemed to me he was interested in preserving zoning laws in the interest of individual homeowners and groups."

The chairman of the appeals board was a fellow Republican named Charles Irish, a prominent Chevrolet dealer in the Baltimore area. He had been in G.O.P. politics longer than Agnew, had been a bigger contributor and was much better known. In addition, Irish was one of the three losers on the Republican slate for the county council, so he was given first crack at the appointive jobs. "It was kind of embarrassing to Agnew," Moore recalls, "as it might be for anyone who had experience with court proceedings as he did. Charlie Irish didn't follow normal procedures. Agnew saw how the rules were made under Irish and he couldn't understand how the party could let a layman work as chairman in a lawyer's job. Irish, if a lawyer before the board said something he didn't like, would tell him, 'Shut up and sit down!' With this kind of thing happening, Agnew wanted to be chairman in the worst way."

For Irish, who was foremost a businessman, the job of appeals board chairman soon lost its luster, and after about a year he decided to step down. Agnew, who had been appointed to a full three-year term in April 1958, was moved up to chairman in May. "He ran it in a lawyerlike fashion," Moore says. "And he was kind of a breath of fresh air. The [Baltimore] Sunpapers loved him and gave him a lot of favorable publicity."

Agnew the zoning board chairman did, indeed, handle the job like a lawyer—one who read the small print and acted on it. And with his thoroughness there was an unmistakable righteousness that would become one of his public trademarks later on, when he brought his legalistic outlook to the state and national scenes. In July 1958 he charged Frank H. Newell III, a Democratic state's attorney in Towson seeking re-election, with "unconscionable delay" in not prosecuting against the continued operation of a junkyard which a county zoning commissioner, the appeals board and the circuit court had found to be in violation of county codes. The junkyard owner had appealed the ruling, petitioning for a rezoning that would allow him to continue to operate the junkyard, which had existed prior to adoption of the prohibiting code.

One of the board's Democratic members, a laundry operator named Nathan Kaufman, in turn criticized Agnew. "It is highly improper for any member of the board to concern himself with any property which is the subject of an appeal pending before our board," Kaufman said. Then he added, "I have tried conscientiously to keep political considerations out of the affairs of this board, but I cannot help but feel that the issuance of this statement by Agnew was politically motivated."

Newell did not take Agnew's charge lightly. The county grand jury was sitting in Towson, and Newell announced he would bring the matter before it, since failure to prosecute a law violator could be an actionable matter by the jury. He summoned Agnew to testify, and the grand jury determined that Newell had not been derelict. In the process, Agnew and Newell exchanged barbs that underlined Agnew's strict constructionist legal thinking. "Law enforcement is not delayed because there is a mere possibility" that a change in the existing law may be under consideration, Agnew said. And when Newell replied that "a man has a right to exhaust his legal remedies before prosecution is brought which could wipe out his business," Agnew rejoined that Newell's reasoning was like refusing to prosecute a man for bigamy because he had filed papers to divorce one of his two wives. As for Kaufman's charge of politics, Agnew said his action had been "purely administrative in seeking to get court orders enforced." He said he was sorry Kaufman had implied that politics was involved and hoped the existing amicable relations among the board members would not be disturbed by the incident.

The matter was not so easily resolved, however. John A. Maguire, the junkyard owner's lawyer, called for Agnew to step aside, since the rezoning appeal might come before him. Agnew replied that Maguire was "a past master at fogging the issue," and that his own record on the zoning board was his best defense of fairness. "The absurdity of Mr. Maguire's demand that I disqualify myself can easily be seen," he said, "by the following example: If Mr. Maguire's charge of bias was logical, then no judge or quasi-judge could hear more than one case involving a particular individual. The mere fact the individual had appeared before him on another matter, however unrelated it might have been, would be enough to disqualify him."

Newell, reflecting on the incident long afterward, said it had been a considerable embarrassment to Agnew. "It was most unusual for an attorney such as he is not to know that when an appeal is pending, nothing can be done. If a man is sentenced to death and he's appealed his case, you don't say, 'Go ahead and execute him.'" As matters turned out, the board ruling was reversed on appeal and the junkyard was permitted to remain open.

Although Agnew's duties as chairman of the appeals board enabled him to function as a judge, he was not one. Still aspiring in that direction, in March 1960, against the better judgment of all his closest friends, he announced he would be a candidate for the county circuit court. The court already had three judges who were seeking re-election, including his friend Albert Menchine. Also, since the county bar association had a long-standing tradition of endorsing the re-election of sitting judges as long as they had performed satisfactorily, it would be political suicide to buck this entrenched policy, but Agnew decided to hit the tradition head-on.

"Under our judicial system," he said in announcing his plans, "judges must be elected by the people. If the intent of the people was to have justices appointed by the bar association the law would so read. Judicial decisions affect the entire electorate and it is fitting that the people decide who shall determine their problems." Besides, Agnew argued, judges often were appointed by governors who disregarded the recommendations of local bar associations. While Menchine and the other two incumbent judges were "gentlemen of ability and character," he said, "the sitting-judge principle is a cloak which can be donned or discarded depending on the severity of the weather or, more bluntly, whose ox is being gored."

As the judgeship campaign proceeded, Agnew continued to speak bluntly about the tradition that stood in the way of his aspirations. He called it "package buying" and said it "effectively delivers the re-election of judges into the hands of politicians." He charged that a committee to promote the re-election of sitting judges had "gently but firmly applied the thumbscrews to every lawyer" in Baltimore city and the surrounding counties of Baltimore and Harford. And when his friends on the Baltimore *Sun* endorsed the principle, he responded with a blistering letter to the editor which was a precursor of the later Spiro Agnew:

"Unless the sitting-judge bandwagon has a very heavy frame, it is in danger of collapsing from the weight of the politicians who have jumped aboard hoping to self-identify with the principle and thereby enjoy the obvious benefit of togetherness with your editorial position. There has been a veritable frenzy of endorsement as the vote-seekers grab for handholds on the chosen vehicle which they hope will transport them to the Valhalla where dwell all political officeholders." Agnew pointed out that when it suited the Birmingham organization, candidates were entered against sitting judges, and when that happened "nary a b'hoy [defined in *Webster's Third New International Dictionary* as "rowdy, tough, in Irish slang"] was moved to orate on the infallibility of the sitting judge principle." Two other Republican sitting judges had been "thrown to the wolves," he charged; they were "socially unacceptable to the b'hoys because each suffered from a disease of the registration glands, feared by the organization to be communicable, known as 'Republicanitis.' "

The letter was a typical example of Agnew's response to criticism in those and later days. "He was extremely sensitive, to a tremendous degree, so much so that he couldn't bear to have any unfair criticism," Mrs. Fringer, his private secretary, said. "He'd phone me from home right after I got to the office and say, 'Did you read the morning paper? Get your book and pencil. I want to give you an answer. Type it so it's ready when I get in.' I used to tell him, 'Mr. Agnew, all you're doing is keeping this alive. By stewing over it, you make it bigger than it deserves. You don't have to slap back all the time.' It was hard for him, as it is for everyone, to look in the paper and see something that is not true. But I told him, 'When you start to fight something like that, you make enemies with the press.' He agreed. Eventually, he had quite a few friends among the reporters in Towson. He's still sensitive today, but nothing like it was. Now he does make rebuttal, but he doesn't just slap back."

Agnew ran in both the Democratic and Republican primaries. He finished sixth out of seven candidates on the Democratic side, but second out of three on the Republican and thereby entered the general election as a G.O.P. candidate. In November, however, he ran dead last in a five-man field, as all three sitting judges were easily re-elected. For all of Agnew's determined opposition, the status quo remained unshaken. His friends had been right; he couldn't buck tradition. In trying, though, the name of Spiro T. Agnew as a challenger of political dragons was enhanced. In the last four years, that name had been breaking into print much more frequently than the Democratic organization liked, and it was time, its leaders decided, to dispose of this upstart before he did any real damage to the comfortable Democratic establishment. His term on the appeals board was running out; Spiro Agnew would have to go.

In January 1961, two months before his term was to expire, the word was out that the Democrats, who had just won all seven seats on the county council, intended to replace him. "Ted wanted to be reappointed," Kimmel recalls. "He really wanted it." Although the council was solidly Democratic, Agnew began a campaign to pressure its members. He rallied his friends in the Loch Raven Kiwanis, his P.T.A. friends and what semblance of a county Republican party there was. The council was bombarded with petitions, and Agnew began issuing public statements and writing to the newspapers. He made a cause célèbre of it, and soon the Baltimore *Sun* was taking up the fight as a good-government crusade. He charged that his opponents were "afraid they can't control me," and he warned them, "I'm not going to lie down and take it. I will continue to fight to retain my post because I believe this is a highly sensitive area and because above all I believe a minority appointment has no real meaning when the wishes of the minority party are ignored."

On the night of February 16 the county council met at the county office building in Towson, in a council room packed with irate citizens, mostly Republicans and homeowners prepared to do battle for Agnew against the ever-suspect real estate interests. Agnew was there to defend himself in what soon degenerated into a wild shouting match between him and Dale Anderson, chairman of the council and later Agnew's successor as county executive. Anderson had been casting around for another Republican to fill the minority slot, and shortly before the meeting he called Charles Steinbock, Jr., a Catonsville accountant who had been on the zoning board once before. "He told me, 'We're going to get rid of Ted Agnew,'" Steinbock recalls of that phone conversation. "He said, 'We want you. If you don't take it, we're going to put a political hack in there who won't be any credit to the Republican party.' So I said all right."

It was quite clearly a railroad job against Agnew, and although all seven members of the council were Democrats, two of them, Brooks Bradley, a funeral home director, and Joseph Dignan, owner of a trucking firm, would not go along. "There wasn't anything wrong with Agnew," Bradley said later. "We felt he had done a commendable job, and he was honest. They sensed he was a competent man in his job, and maybe untouchable." Agnew busily lobbied Bradley and Dignan, and the other members of the board too. A third, J. Cavendish Darrell, a Maryland trade association official, said later that "Ted called me on the phone and asked whether I would be for him. I told him, 'Ted, you need four votes, and if you can get three others, I'll be for you.' "

But Agnew couldn't get that fourth vote, and he went under by 5 to 2, with Darrell voting with the majority because, he said, "I never voted for a loser." The remark caused him regret when he uttered it and great embarrassment later; in voting against Agnew, he helped put him on the path to becoming one of Maryland's all-time political winners. Then, though, the defeat seemed for Agnew a cloud with no silver lining.

One of Agnew's more vociferous supporters jumped up after the vote and yelled at Anderson, "Castro! Castro!" The bedlam made headlines in the next day's papers. "They printed it as a goddamn dirty political deal, which it was," Darrell says. "Agnew was making a name for himself. With the influx of people from Baltimore city moving into the county, the Democrats were concerned the county might go Republican, and Agnew was getting to be Mr. Republican."

In his defeat, Agnew lashed out at those who had cut him down. "The reasons for my removal given by some of the councilmen would make a new edition of Grimm's *Fairy Tales*," he said. "They are fantastic insults to the public intelligence. Such weak, small-caliber excuses hide the real reason about as effectively as a coat of cellophane. The job was being done honestly and with reasonable efficiency. Perhaps in the minds of some, those traits require immediate extermination."

The selection of Steinbock, and Steinbock's willingness to serve, irritated Agnew particularly. "He resented this bitterly," Brooks Bradley said. "The Republican party was leading from its weakness. They should have insisted on keeping their strongest man. I told Dale Anderson sometime later, 'You thought you were so smart that night you denied Ted Agnew, but you made him Vice-President of the United States.'"

After the vote Agnew said that Steinbock "is a compromise, a shield to dull the glare of public scrutiny. I would guess that in

time the bosslets will find him just as distasteful as they found
me." But based on Steinbock's past record, Agnew said, he would
do a "fair and adequate job," so there was no reason for public
confidence in the board to be undermined by his own defeat. He
urged the voters, however, to take "a long hard look" at the five
members of the council who had done him in "and decide if those
councilmen meet the standards Baltimore County deserves in its
elected representatives." Clearly, Ted Agnew was not the kind of
man who goes to bed angry at night and wakes up the next morning forgiving and forgetting.

Nor was he the kind of man who backs off at the first sign of
adversity. The publicity generated by the Democrats' crude dis-
posal of Agnew cast him as the honest servant wronged by the
machine; he had to find some vehicle into which he could pour
this new and rich political fuel. He went to Scott Moore and advised him he wanted to run for Congress, with the election more
than a year away.

It so happened, however, that another, more prominent Republican, a gentleman farmer named J. Fife Symington, also coveted
the seat. He had, in fact, run twice for it and lost each time. But
the man who had beaten Symington, Democrat Daniel Brewster,
had decided to try for the Senate, and Symington saw the development as his chance finally to enter Congress. The news that
this upstart Agnew was thinking of challenging him was intolerable, and Symington also went to Moore. "He was furious,"
Moore recalls. "I remember he was going out of the country, and
the last thing he said was, 'Get Agnew out of there. Tell him Congress is no place for a young lawyer with a family."

While Symington was away, Moore called a meeting of fifteen
or twenty Republican leaders in the county, including Osborne
Beall and Agnew's law partner, Sam Kimmel. They acknowledged
that Agnew's reputation for honesty and hard work on the appeals
board, and the publicity generated by his unceremonious ouster,
were political chips that ought to be cashed in somewhere. With
Symington determined to make a third try for Congress, the other
possibility was to run for county executive.

On the surface, more than a year before the next election, the
chances for a Republican to be elected county executive seemed
dim in the overwhelmingly Democratic county. But developments were unfolding within Democratic ranks that began to sug-

gest otherwise. Birmingham, who after his term as the first county executive had stepped down and let his old lieutenant, Christian Kahl, run for the job, was not happy about his behavior in office. Having been elected county executive, Kahl had been under the impression he *was* county executive, but Birmingham tried to remain the power behind the scenes; increasingly Kahl resisted the efforts of Birmingham to make the political decisions in the county, as he had for so long in the past. A falling-out was distinctly in the making; some said later that Agnew knew it and that his expressed interest in running for Congress was merely a way of maneuvering Baltimore County's Republican leaders into giving him the nomination for county executive. Whether that is so or not, Spiro Agnew, who had lost in his only previous bid for elective office, suddenly found himself being asked to run for the highest post in the county government. Long shot or not, he grasped at the chance.

"It is apparent to even the most casual observer of the local political scene," Agnew said on October 24, 1961, in announcing his candidacy, "that the leadership of Baltimore County must be pried from the tired but still-greedy hands of the feuding majority party factions. . . . For nearly twenty years our citizens have been presented at the polls with the same old political 'concessionaires' and their servants. Intelligent young leadership in the Democratic party has been ruthlessly and methodically destroyed to assure continuity of power in Messrs. Birmingham and Kahl. Their satellites vary and even interchange, breaking loose from one as the patronage of the other overcomes the gravitational field of the first. A constant struggle for power is in progress, leaving no time for the many complex problems of the county government. But even worse, the financing of this private war is done through the accommodations of special interests, obviously to the great loss of the taxpayers. Having been removed from the county board of appeals at the insistence of these same special interests and despite public sentiment to the contrary, I know to what lengths the Birmingham crowd will go to accommodate them."

The aggressive thrust of Agnew's declaration of candidacy was a harbinger of the kind of campaign he would wage against the Democrats. At forty-three years of age he was established as a civic pillar and was president of the Loch Raven Kiwanis Club;

now, as his party's candidate for county executive, he would be—for the duration of his candidacy, anyway—the leader of the party in Baltimore County. The Sunpapers trumpeted him as the wronged embodiment of good government, and for the next year he sallied forth through the tidy subdivisions that bespoke white Middle America's growing affluence and comfort, spreading his promise of liberation from the oppression of the Birmingham-Kahl machine. Kiwanians and their spouses (Ki-wives), P.T.A. members, the county Republican lawyers association of which he now was director, all rallied to the side of their white knight, whose righteous indignation shone into every political dark corner where the machine's undemocratic methods long had functioned unchallenged.

On one occasion the Democratic chief clerk of the elections board called in all registrars and elections judges who were to preside over a county reregistration of voters, both Republican and Democratic. Unexpectedly, Birmingham was there to address them, and when Agnew heard of it he complained bitterly. "To use an official instruction session of election registrars and judges as a political rally," he charged, "not only is in poor taste but unquestionably out of harmony with the spirit of the election laws." Democrats in turn accused Agnew of trying "to latch on to the meeting for purely political purposes." Republican state central committee members, they said, also were introduced. But Agnew had scored a few more points for his growing Mr. Clean image.

At this time there occurred an incident that, while it did not impede Agnew's political climb, later was to cause him some embarrassment. As a practicing lawyer in the county, he was appointed by the court to defend a thirty-two-year-old man named Lester L. Grogg who, along with a teen-age boy, was accused of murdering a ninety-one-year-old woman in a robbery in her rural Baltimore County home. The boy, Robert A. L. Kelley, had pulled the trigger on a rifle and shot the woman, Katie Hoffheiser, through a screen door as Grogg was talking to her in the living room. Grogg took $28, divided it with the boy, started to run, then went home, where he was arrested the next day. Grogg pleaded not guilty, and not guilty by reason of insanity, but he was convicted and sentenced to life imprisonment, while Robert Kelley spent less than nine months in jail. The boy was released on a suspended sentence, on grounds he had been under Grogg's influence.

The case was a sticky one for Agnew; although Grogg had been in mental hospitals three times, state doctors ruled he was competent to stand trial. In an effort to ensure a sympathetic jury, Agnew asked a prospective juror, Mrs. Mildred E. Engers, wife of a milkman: "Now, in the past hundred years, do you believe that we have made great progress, some progress or little progress in the field of understanding and treating mental illness?" The state's attorney objected and the judge sustained the objection because Agnew's inquiry, apparently designed to ascertain whether the woman was biased toward psychiatry, was "too broad a question to be asked on voir dire examination." Agnew then accepted the juror, later taking exception in the judge's chambers to his ruling.

When Grogg's case came up on appeal—after Agnew had been elected county executive—the court was asked to rule that Agnew should have been allowed to ask the question, and that the lower-court judge had erred. But the appeal was thrown out. Next, Grogg filed a postconviction proceeding petition, in which the only basis for appeal was that his lawyer had been incompetent. This time the court appointed another Baltimore County lawyer, James Gede, to represent Grogg. Gede reviewed the trial transcripts and records and built his case on Agnew's failure to pursue adequately the voir dire examination of Mrs. Engers, or of subsequent prospective jurors. In defending the lower-court judge, the state had written in its brief: "Nowhere in the record do we find any explanation for [Agnew's] failure to rephrase the question in more specific terms, or to otherwise elicit the opinion of the veniremen on psychiatry, or on the defense of insanity. The trial judge did not in his ruling hold all questions on the subject to be objectionable, he merely found the one question propounded to be too broad. Appellant's counsel then abandoned the entire area of questions—and by that unexplained failure to pursue the subject with proper questions leaves himself without any proper ground on which to object to the actions of the trial court. . . . It is not difficult, we submit, for any experienced trial counsel to frame proper questions on the subject of mental illness, or on the defense of insanity. Moreover, if Appellant's counsel had reason to believe that the court would not entertain any questions in that area, he should have, for the purpose of perfecting the record, made proffers of the questions which he desired to ask, so that this Honorable Court would not be required to deal with the question in a vacuum."

Agnew was obliged to defend his performance in court, and the judge ruled against Grogg. When the matter came up on appeal in federal court, Grogg's plea once more was turned down. Agnew, by this time governor of the state, told the court he had pursued the case "as vigorously as any law case I ever had."

Reflecting on the case later, Gede said, "Ted was on the stand in that hearing for quite a good while, primarily because I was trying to bring out the fact that because of Ted running for office, he was somewhat more preoccupied with running for politics than with representation. . . . However, I wasn't able to bring this out as proof because the only thing I really established that raised maybe a question, and I don't know whether it did in the judge's mind or not, was that Ted was appointed in September of 1961 and did not visit Grogg until sometime in October, and then he visited him for a total of three times in eight and a half months. And we never established the times that he visited him but it looked like he visited him for approximately a total of no more than about three hours. And then right before the trial he did send a doctor down to examine Grogg."

Gede said that had he not been appointed by the court to take Grogg's case, he never would have pursued it. After reading the transcripts of the trial, he said, "I thought it was somewhat political that he [Agnew] was even appointed, because they knew he was a candidate running as a Republican. I've always felt that the only reason Ted was appointed to this case was to somewhat embarrass him, because a murder case, especially when you're going with a jury, takes a great deal of time to prepare, especially when you're not primarily a criminal lawyer. Ted to my knowledge prior to that, in every case I'd ever seen him, had always done a good job of trying a case. I think they were just trying to put him in a spot where he'd be a little busy. I might not have tried the case in the same manner, but he proceeded with the case in a manner which I think anybody involved in criminal law would have to proceed with. . . . The only surprise was that he didn't come back [in the voir dire examination] and narrow the question down."

Agnew did indeed have politics on his mind during this period. Not content with attacking the Democrats, and not forgetting the earlier squeeze play of Fife Symington, in February 1962 he endorsed another Republican congressional candidate, George H. C. Arrowsmith. It appeared Agnew was bent on eliminating Symington as a threat to his county party leadership, and the matter finally came to a head in a rousing verbal brawl between the two men in Scott Moore's office. Moore, the apostle of party unity, did all he could to avoid the split. "I felt Agnew should not take a position in the congressional race," he recalls. "After all, he didn't have any opposition in the primary. The correct thing, the smart thing for him to do was to stay out of the congressional race. But he wouldn't. I pleaded with him not to take a position on it, but he wouldn't listen. He was determined. That's the way he is, and you can't budge him when he gets that way."

Before the row was over, Symington had teamed up with G. Gordon Power, the county council chairman who in 1957 had appointed Agnew to the board of appeals and now was running for the State Senate, and the whole mess was thrown before the Republican county committee. Agnew got his candidate endorsed, along with an opponent to Power, W. Giles Parker, but not without opening more wounds. Symington and his allies howled in protest, but Agnew, who only two years earlier had sought to shatter the principle of party endorsement of sitting judges as a grossly undemocratic procedure, complained about the sour-grapes protests of the unendorsed Republican candidates. The theory of party endorsement, he said, was to attract good candidates who might not otherwise be able to compete in freewheeling primaries because of the cost.

Unopposed in the primary, Agnew became the party's nominee for county executive, but his men, Arrowsmith and Parker, lost to Symington and Power. As only politicians and small children can do, however, the Republicans quickly shelved their past enmity and showed a united front to the county's voters, confident that what had happened on the Democratic side had given them a rare opportunity for a G.O.P. sweep. Birmingham, who was now in his seventies and the uncertain head of a doddering political dynasty, nevertheless had enough residual power to unseat Kahl, the upstart for whom he had stepped aside and who now refused to repay the favor. The bitterness of the Democratic primary shattered party ranks and loyalties and Agnew became the beneficiary—a phenomenon that was to repeat itself only four years later when he aspired to the governorship under bizarrely similar circumstances.

In Agnew's fledgling law firm was a young attorney named Edward Hardesty, a loyal Democrat who once had so impressed Agnew with his presentation of a zoning case before Agnew's board of appeals that Agnew asked him to join the firm. By this time Hardesty also had a post in the county solicitor's office and was an active member of the Kahl faction of the Democratic party, running for the House of Delegates on that slate. When Birmingham defeated Kahl in the 1962 primary, Birmingham could have moved to heal the resultant breach by reaching out to Kahl people like Hardesty. Instead, he turned his back on them. The courts had recently ruled that malapportionment of the Maryland legislature had to be rectified by addition of seven more delegates from Baltimore County, and Hardesty as a defeated candidate on the Kahl slate was interested in being nominated as one of them. Birmingham, however, completely ignored the Kahl bloc in picking the additional slate. Agnew went forthwith to Hardesty. "He said to me," Hardesty recalls, " 'Well, they've knocked you down and now they've kicked you.' And then he said, 'I'd like to talk business.' "

The business, of course, was a bid to Hardesty to cross over into the Agnew ranks. Reluctant to leave the Democratic party but disgusted with Birmingham and friendly toward his law partner, Hardesty agreed to back Agnew, while remaining a Democrat. He thus became the first Democrat of any note in Baltimore County to sign on with Agnew. "That opened the floodgates," Hardesty says. "The gates opened and they came out of the eaves. Kahl himself was in no position to support Agnew openly . . . but he made it clear he would not punish anyone in his faction who crossed over and worked against Birmingham. Democrats went to Chris and he told them, 'You stuck with me and we lost. Now each man has to do his own arithmetic.' Well, many did, and Democrats made the difference for Agnew."

One of the more prominent early switchers was Brooks Bradley, one of the two county council members who had voted against Agnew's ouster from the board of appeals. Bradley, utterly disillusioned with the Birmingham-Kahl bloodletting, took the big step and switched party allegiance. "I believe," he said in announcing the switch, "there comes a time when reform in government, with new faces and new vigor, is more compelling than voting a straight party line." He helped spearhead the Agnew attacks on Birmingham, writing anti-Democratic press releases and going about the county proclaiming Agnew as an honest man arrived on the scene to save Baltimore County from festering machine politics.

Hardesty later was appointed deputy zoning commissioner by Agnew, after a bitter row with the Democratic county council, and Bradley was named to the county board of recreation and parks, a nonpaying job. Both men said they had agreed to back Agnew on principle, with no jobs offered or asked for. Scott Moore said later, however, of Agnew's successful race, "We made a couple of deals and got some prime Democrats. Agnew promised them jobs and he gave them to them after he won."

After Hardesty and Bradley joined Agnew, Walter J. Rasmussen, clerk of the county circuit court, also climbed aboard. "Although Mr. Birmingham is well respected and a fine gentleman, he has chosen to surround himself with people who have put a cloud over the Democratic party," Rasmussen commented. "If he wins, they will control the Democratic party in Baltimore County. I honestly believe in taking this stand, that it is the action necessary to restore the Democratic party to the greatness it once enjoyed." Other Democratic officials apparently agreed. At a bipartisan dinner for Agnew, there were nearly as many Democrats as Republicans. Recognizing their presence, Agnew observed that "each is resorting to emergency measures to cleanse his party of the festering sore of bossism." A reporter covering that dinner for the Baltimore *News-Post*, Frank DeFilippo, wrote that less altruistic motives were involved for some—that Rasmussen had been offered a $12,000 county job to support Agnew. The next morning the reporter's phone rang; it was Agnew, whom he had not known before. "He called me every name you could think of," DeFilippo recalled in Annapolis, where in 1971 he was serving as press secretary to Agnew's successor as governor of Maryland, Marvin Mandel. "He called me a liar and a phony, and why did they let me near a typewriter, I was the worst reporter in Maryland. He demanded an apology and a retraction, and I told him I didn't retract what I wrote, if he wanted to issue a denial, that was another thing. So he said, 'Let me talk to somebody down there who can write.'" DeFilippo suggested that Agnew talk with Sterling Noel, the managing editor and a staunch Agnew friend and backer. The paper ran Agnew's denial, but DeFilippo neither retracted nor apologized. After Agnew's election, one of the first appointments was the one to Rasmussen about which DeFilippo had written.

Despite the Democratic split, Agnew had to work hard to make the race. For one thing, he had very little campaign money. He and Moore together began knocking on doors; they obtained the names of past Democratic contributors and went around to see them, on the assumption that the factional fight might loosen some purse strings. They were right. Agnew also went to labor leaders, reminding them that he was a labor lawyer, and this effort produced some money. Together, Moore says, they raised $30,000. It was, by Moore's own definition, "peanuts" for such a campaign, but Agnew's past romancing with the Sunpapers produced favorable publicity for his good-government "crusade" that was worth at least that much.

Agnew also achieved a break in the labor ranks when executives of the United Steelworkers of America, who had backed the Democratic ticket, switched and endorsed him in the hope of putting an end to "Mr. Birmingham's political chicanery." Agnew called the move "a new political awareness on the part of labor," and he commended the steelworkers "for reaching objectively the conclusion that individual candidates should be judged impartially on individual merit and not on the oversimplified basis of a party label." Other labor unions, including his old butcher friends, also boarded the Agnew bandwagon.

On issues, the candidate was pointedly progressive-minded, if not wildly liberal. When Birmingham said the county council should wait to see what the state legislature would do before acting on an equal-accommodations bill, Agnew backed such a bill, promising to campaign on the issue of racial bias in public places "even though only three percent of our population in the county is colored." And he called for stronger county laws against air pollution in terms that would appeal to suburbia. "Many of our good industrial neighbors are self-policing," he said, "but unfortunately others are not. Air pollution can and must be controlled at the source by strict and practicably enforceable legislation." He also called for state legislation to make antismog devices on automobile exhaust systems mandatory.

Finally, Agnew had a sitting duck in Birmingham, who was old, a machine politician, and a private dealer rather than a public orator. Agnew continued to cast himself as the white knight and challenged Birmingham to do forensic battle on the highest plane. He said the primary results proved "there is a strong sentiment against mudslinging and character assassination, which are often the tools employed by unqualified candidates to distract attention from their own inadequacies." The voters, were "beginning to see through inept candidates who hide behind smooth, well-heeled political machines and speak only through the glib utterances of their public relations staffs."

Again and again Agnew challenged Birmingham to debate. He called on civic and service clubs to elevate the campaign by sponsoring debates. "Too often," said Spiro Agnew in words that later would take on a certain irony, "campaigns are based on the vilification of personalities or on catch phrases that divert public attention from the very real problems of the community."

Agnew tried everything, including ridicule, to get Birmingham on the stump with him (a tactic that also was to serve him well four years later, in his race for governor). When Vice-President Lyndon B. Johnson came to Pikesville for a Democratic rally in October, Agnew said Johnson's purpose was "to distract attention from the tarnished record of the Baltimore County bosses and to ensure their raising the enormous amount of money needed to camouflage a weak ticket." Of Birmingham's plans to attend the rally, Agnew predicted his opponent would be "in charge of dispensing platitudes and pleasantries under a theory that every man should be used to the full extent of his apparent ability, and that the assignment is fitting." And shortly before the election, Agnew asked, "Why doesn't somebody wind up Mr. Birmingham so that he can talk? He is an empty-chair candidate running from his obligations to talk out loud to county voters and relying on old-fashioned machine organization to pull him through."

The words were biting, but pretty much on the mark. With significant recruitment among Democrats and labor, and Chris Kahl sitting on his hands, Agnew received nearly 79,000 votes on election day to about 61,000 for Birmingham. It was a clear-cut victory over the previously entrenched but warring Democrats. And from all outward signs, anyway, it was a considerable personal victory for the white knight; his old foes but recent ticket mates, Symington and Power, lost, leaving Spiro T. Agnew the undisputed Republican leader in Baltimore County. And as the executive officer of Maryland's largest county, he also found himself the highest-ranking officeholder in the state party.

All this was not bad for a fellow who only ten years earlier had quit or been fired at Schreibers' supermarket, and had only begun to dabble in politics. Maryland, however, like Baltimore County, was solidly Democratic; it would take a party split of the proportions of the recent county dichotomy to enable Agnew to go any higher. On December 1, 1962, when he was sworn in as county executive, such a possibility was only a speck on the horizon, if indeed it was there at all. But events had a way, he was now finding out, of working for him. And he was beginning to demonstrate an unmistakable predatory style toward the people and the opportunities around him. Ted Agnew was not known particularly as a hunter, but the instincts were there. Increasingly, circumstances would offer political prey to him, and there could be no doubt of it now—he had caught the scent of bigger political game.

4

◆•◆•◆•◆•◆•◆

THE RIGHTS OF MAN

IN the last month of 1962, when Spiro Agnew took office as Baltimore County Executive, nearly nine years had passed since the Supreme Court's landmark decision requiring public school desegregation, and the movement for equal rights for black Americans finally was beginning to assert itself. The lessons of the North Carolina sit-ins in 1960 had spread to every part of the South, eroding the anachronism of separate public facilities that had been the bulwark of die-hard segregation. To those who had struggled against segregation with so little success for so long, the new climate was exhilarating and inspiring.

As a candidate for county executive, Agnew had made much of his posture as a civil libertarian who had opposed discrimination for moral, not political, reasons. He had campaigned against racial bias in public places "even though," as he pointedly said, "only three percent of our population in the county is colored." Now, at the outset of his term, he sought to outlaw racial discrimination in public accommodations in the county. Under an antiquated state constitution, any of Maryland's twenty-three counties had to get approval of the General Assembly before enacting such legislation for itself. Accordingly, the new county executive asked the solidly Democratic county delegation in Annapolis to help clear the way. But the Democrats promptly refused, advising Agnew that the county council, which now had six Democrats and only one Republican, already had the power, and that Democratic Governor J. Millard Tawes already had sent a bill to the General Assembly that would bar such discrimination throughout the state.

Some Democrats contended that Agnew knew all this beforehand, and simply was grandstanding. Agnew, for his part, came right back with a bill to make clear that the county had the power to enact an equal-accommodations law. "It is foolish," he said, "to allow artificial objections to drag this through the courts for two years. This bill would eliminate any need for a court test." But in the Democratic-dominated legislature, such a bill from an upstart Republican, predictably, got nowhere. Some Democrats said Agnew knew that would happen, too.

The new county executive's initiatives were not, of course, created in a vacuum. The pressure that was building for racial justice elsewhere in the South—and Maryland was a Southern state sentimentally as well as geographically in the early 1960's—was being exerted right up to the Mason-Dixon line and even beyond; Agnew was not exempt from it. A county citizens' group headed by Eugene L. King, Sr., of Catonsville, a black teacher of special education, called on him to establish a county human relations commission, and there was much pulling and hauling over it through Agnew's first spring in office.

To demonstrate the need for such a unit, King's group confronted Agnew with a list of areas in which discrimination existed—in housing, county employment of police, teachers and office workers, and in private industry. Agnew received the complaints, then asked the group to review them and submit specific tasks with which a human relations commission would be charged.

Meanwhile, however, Maryland civil rights activists grew increasingly impatient. A particularly irritating and symbolic holdout on the racial line was the Gwynn Oak amusement park in the northwest section of the county. Children who nine years earlier had received the Supreme Court's blessing to go to school together still could not ride the merry-go-round side by side. A biracial effort was undertaken to negotiate an end to segregation with the owners of the park, James, David and Arthur Price, but they would not budge, contending that integration would destroy their business and force them to close down. "I talked with them many times, but they were just adamant," King said. "But then the pressure began to come. Many organizations withdrew their support; the school system in Baltimore city withdrew, the Catholic schools stopped going out there, some of the unions stopped going out, all of this kind of pressure. But it really wasn't enough." In May, small, orderly demonstrations began and some arrests were made on charges of trespassing. Through all this, Agnew remained aloof, still not creating the county human relations commission the King group and others were demanding.

Finally, on May 31, 1963, with the Gwynn Oak situation obviously in mind, Agnew announced plans to present legislation to the county council creating the human relations commission, but expressing at the same time concern that the civil rights activists might undermine this effort and civil rights progress generally. "It is my earnest hope," he said, "that there will be no outbursts of demonstrations, no intemperate haste . . . no rash actions to jeopardize the advances that are possible if we exercise statesmanship and strength." The legislation could fail, he warned, if presented "under the shadow of racial violence or overwrought emotions." He urged "mature consideration of the desirability of a peaceful transition, and support for the establishment of the commission, which will be charged with acting in areas of employment, housing, education, public accommodation and other fields where intergroup relations are in question. Throughout the entire metropolitan area, I believe we need a calm and dispassionate approach to these changes lest there are setbacks to gains that are imminent."

For Agnew to talk to the black community about "intemperate haste," and the "calm and dispassionate approach" toward wrongs that had existed for years and were resented with a deep passion, was to demonstrate considerable insensitivity to the emotional underpinning of the whole civil rights movement. The integrationists informed the Price brothers in no uncertain terms that if they did not desegregate by the Fourth of July, they would face the largest biracial demonstration yet mounted in the area.

On the appointed day, no progress having been made through June, the civil rights forces were true to their word. From all over the state, and even from outside Maryland, sympathizers came to demonstrate and, if necessary, be arrested under the trespass law. Many among the white clergy who up to now had fought the battle against racial injustice from the pulpit turned out in force. Integrated groups entered the amusement park and submitted to arrest in a massive test of the law. In all, 275 individuals were removed in an orderly procedure, prearranged between King and County Police Chief Robert J. Lally. Suddenly Agnew was confronted with a crisis that he could not talk away with admonitions against "intemperate haste." He called a session of the county council and urged it to complete action on the bill creating the human relations commission.

The bill was passed, but on Sunday, July 7, their impatience undiminished by the county executive's emergency move, the demonstrators marched for a second time against Gwynn Oak. About a hundred participants were arrested and one woman injured. It was, subsequent events were to prove, a most injudicious action for any group that hoped to get sympathy and help from Spiro Agnew.

On Tuesday, Agnew appointed the eleven members of the new commission—in a way that left no doubt he considered the demonstrators ingrates who had double-crossed him. Weeks earlier, two community civil rights groups now demonstrating against Gwynn Oak—one predominantly from Catonsville headed by King and another from Towson—had combined to help Agnew write legislation establishing the new commission. He had asked them to suggest members, and they did so. "We submitted twenty-one names to him," King recalled, "and my name was the only one that was selected out of the twenty-one. We had gone through the county and picked white and black who we thought would represent the county fairly on these kinds of issues. The group itself was about ninety-five percent white, but he ignored us. It indicated that Ted Agnew was not going to do what you asked him to do."

Instead, Agnew named to the commission one of his law partners, Gus Hennegan; the former Republican county chairman who had run and lost with Symington, G. Gordon Power; and a collection of other nominees from groups other than the Catonsville-Towson civil rights coalition. Among them was a high-spirited young man named Michael G. Holofcener, whose name had been put forward by a local citizens' committee for good government. It was a selection that Agnew would soon regret, but one that would generate a controversy particularly enlightening about

the new county executive. Agnew also appointed the former reporter for the Baltimore *Sun* who had covered his days on the
appeals board, Edgar Feingold, to be executive director of the
commission.

At the same time the county executive issued a policy statement that made clear his feelings—if his snub of the civil rights
coalition had not. He acknowledged that "some useful purposes
were served" by the initial Gwynn Oak demonstration on July 4,
and that "the scope of the protest caused me to accelerate certain
programs to eliminate unlawful discrimination and to bring
about legislation to combat the racial bias."

But the July 7 demonstration, after Agnew had pushed the
county council to create the new commission, was another matter
entirely. In the manner of the disappointed father who knows
best, Agnew said of the demonstrators: "Although I am in sympathy with the goal of the demonstrators, I seriously question the
wisdom of their actions. In their impatience and resentment
against an individual property owner, the demonstrators have lost
sight of their reciprocal responsibility. They have thrown,
through hasty and immature decisions, an undeserved burden
upon the Baltimore County police force, which is sworn to uphold
existing law. They have, without benefit, and probably with great
harm to the high moral purpose of their movement, wasted the
money of the taxpayers of Baltimore County. Regrettably, fairness and restraint have lost out to ill-advised haste and emotional
self-hypnosis. The July 7 demonstrators are hardly to be commended for their failure to think now and then of what they can
do for their community in addition to concentrating on what their
community has failed to do for them."

For all his calm exterior—and Agnew made certain that in
public he always maintained an aura of imperturbability—the
words betrayed a hostility toward the civil rights leaders that was
to grow and deepen in succeeding years. It was not the cause for
which they demonstrated that so disturbed him, insiders of the
time said. "It was the use of threats as a negotiating position, and
deadlines," Feingold said. "He hated deadlines, and pressures; he
resented them. His thinking was bogged down by legal procedur-
alism, and he felt going outside the established way of doing
things was wrong. So he maintained at all costs these deified legal

procedures, and any demonstrations that carried threats and deadlines just rankled the hell out of him." The physical appearance of some of the demonstrators also offended Agnew, Feingold said. "He had this real feeling for 'ordinarism.' Any deviation from his own standards—in dress, grooming, speech, tactics, rhetoric—really offended him. Part of it was his own meticulous grooming. I walked into the county building once after vacation with a two-week beard and he saw me. An aide called me in a few minutes and told me Agnew said to shave it off."

Several days after the second demonstration, the new human relations commission met and organized. Although Hennegan and Power were more prominent politically, and Eugene King was the most experienced in civil rights and a black, young Holofcener plunged in with a gung-ho attitude, offered himself for leadership, and was elected chairman. "I didn't know the first thing about civil rights," says Holofcener, an excitable, red-haired man who now runs a ski-clothes and equipment shop in Timonium, Maryland. "But I knew I wanted to get involved, and I wanted to get involved in leadership. So I started to think, 'What would I do if I were organizing this kind of commission?' and I went to the meeting with that in mind." Hennegan, Agnew's law partner on the commission, says, "I think he volunteered and nobody else wanted the job."

Holofcener's enthusiasm obviously impressed most other members of the commission, and they let him take the lead as the group aggressively tackled its first assignment from Agnew—settlement of the Gwynn Oak controversy. The initial objective was to cool the situation, and to shift its focus from demonstrations at the park grounds to talks before the new commission. A day after Holofcener had been elected chairman, the commission made its first proposal—that demonstrations end at once, and that the Price brothers agree to integrate Gwynn Oak as of July 26, two weeks later. The demonstrators, led by the Congress of Racial Equality (CORE), readily agreed, but the park owners would not. Next, the commission proposed that the Price brothers pledge to integrate the amusement park by the next spring. This time they agreed, but the demonstrators would not. The integrationists feared that in six or eight months too much could happen to make the Price brothers' promise meaningless, and the whole painful process of mobilizing an effective demonstration would have to begin again. Principle and political reality demanded, they now felt, that the park be desegregated that summer.

The two parties were apart, but it was far from an impasse. Previously the Price brothers were saying integration would kill their business; now they were saying, "All right, but wait until next year." The only question now was agreement on when integration would occur. The commission members settled down to a second stage of tougher negotiations, buoyed by the progress they had made in a short time and by the climate of good will in which it had been made, with Agnew benignly standing aloof while they labored as his representatives.

Suddenly, without warning, Agnew jumped in on the side of the Price brothers. The spring opening had already been rejected, but now he broke his silence and urged the demonstrators to accept the offer. "Although I have remained apart from actual negotiations in the Gwynn Oak Park matter," he said, "I feel that my official responsibility obliges me to strongly urge that the integration groups accept the current settlement proposal before them. This proposition suggested by the commission and accepted by the Price brothers, that the park be integrated beginning with the 1964 season, is clearly a substantial victory for civil rights in this area. . . ."

The commission members, and Holofcener in particular, were dumfounded at the county executive's intervention, which cut the negotiating ground from under them. The demonstrators viewed the intrusion as rank betrayal, and they eyed the Agnew-appointed commission with new suspicion. "We are shocked to learn of Mr. Agnew's statement," said the Reverend Robert T. Newbold, Jr., an integration spokesman, "in view of the fact that he indicated at the beginning of the negotiations that he would not impose his will upon us, and that negotiations are still in progress. We consider it very untimely. It also lends itself to . . . [appearances of] an attempt to take the settlement of the dispute away from the commission he appointed and place it in the court of public opinion." Holofcener, who now looks back at the incident with amazement about his own political naïveté, moved without hesitation to shore up the damage to the commission's credibility. He bluntly and openly told the county executive to buzz off. "We strongly feel that any public statement made by Mr. Agnew or others at this time will be prejudicial to our mediation efforts," he said. "Considering the delicate nature of the discussions and the high feelings on both sides, we fail to see any useful purpose in such pronouncements. In fact, because of the possibility of misunderstanding, more harm than good is likely."

Young Holofcener's bold reply to Agnew gave some reassurance to the civil rights advocates, and the negotiations continued. Agnew for his part said nothing about this show of insubordination, but as his brief political history already had demonstrated and as Holofcener and the whole human relations commission were to learn before long, he was not one to let slights go unanswered forever.

Although the main leadership of the Gwynn Oak demonstrations continued to talk, an offshoot group decided there was only one way to break the impasse—resume the demonstrations. Plans went forward for another weekend protest on the park grounds, thus putting even greater pressure on the negotiators to reach agreement. In a marathon session that ran until after four o'clock in the morning, the commission hammered away at the park owners, who insisted they were not against blacks per se, but were fearful that the immediate shock of integration during the season would administer a financial blow to the park it could not sustain. "When I would ask them, 'Why don't you want to integrate?'" Holofcener recalls, "the answer was, 'It's not that we're against Negroes, but we want to keep out undesirables.' But when I asked, 'Can Ralph Bunche come into Gwynn Oak today?' the answer was, of course, 'No.'" CORE spokesmen were able to offer guarantees from white churches that they would send large groups to the park for the remainder of the regular season, which was to end on Labor Day, but the Price brothers were not persuaded. "We are in the business of selling entertainment, not holocaust," David Price argued after the meeting. Still, the brothers could see that the alternative—demonstrations for the rest of the season and probably the next year too—was unacceptable. Finally, they offered a date of September 1, just a few days before closing. The integration group rejected the offer as mere tokenism, but advanced its own July 26 date a full month, to August 26—a decision involving more face-saving than substantive difference. Rabbi Abraham

Shusterman, one of the more moderate members of the commission, said the Price brothers' offer was a "trick to the Negro. We have struggled too hard and too long for that."

For the second time and at an even more critical juncture than before, Agnew jumped in. Without a word to the chairman of the commission, the county executive met with the Price brothers and the leaders of the demonstrations and took over where the commission had left off in its long negotiation session. Later that day Holofcener got a phone call from Towson. It was Agnew, triumphant. "He told me he had a press statement to make, that he had finished the deal," Holofcener recalls. "I didn't suspect anything at that moment, but later some of the people on the commission felt we should have concluded the arrangements. But Agnew did it, and I was brought into it. I sat there while he made the announcement. I was so naïve. I was just so happy to see it settled. Nothing occurred to me then. Now I realize something political was scored there. Why had not Mr. Price settled the night before? What had happened to change it?"

It appeared to Holofcener and others that in negotiating the settlement, Agnew had simply carried the thrust of the commission's work to its logical conclusion—a compromise. The two sides, already so close, each gave a little and agreed to an integration date of August 28. It can be argued that the commission had gone as far as it could, and that it took the prestige of the county executive to move the two sides that small last distance. But some of the commission members insisted later that Agnew should have consulted with them, and he had not. Up to the point where only six days separated the demands of the two sides, King said later, Agnew's only show of interest had been a thinly veiled irritation at the integrationists for being so recalcitrant. King remembers that at one point Agnew referred to them as "a bunch of cranks"—hardly the phrase of the dedicated fighter against racial injustice he later claimed to be, in wearing the Gwynn Oak settlement as a civil rights merit badge. "Ted wasn't all that het up on integration," King says. "He was a negotiator. What he wanted to know was, 'Can we get an answer?' If the man says he's going to integrate in the spring, okay."

Discussing the episode later, Agnew called such criticism "a rather cruel attempt in my judgment to pre-empt an area where I take a great amount of credit for accomplishing something. I try not to take credit when I'm not entitled to it, but the point is that there was no possibility of a settlement in that thing until I got in it. And not only that; everybody wanted me in it. There was no one that suggested I shouldn't be in it. All this suggesting came up years later as a way to denigrate my contribution. The park owners wanted me in it; the leadership of the Negro community wanted me in it; I got in it because, first of all, it was my county and I was interested in it, and everybody wanted me to mediate it, which I tried to do. There were a few politically ambitious people who were critical, some of them my own appointees to the human relations commission. But I think if you read the record you'll see that what they were interested in doing more than anything else was getting a share of the attention for themselves. Just about everybody in the controversy requested that I be in it."

The resolution of the Gwynn Oak problem, which had spurred creation of the human relations commission, disposed of a crisis facing Agnew. But it only whetted the interest and appetite of chairman Holofcener and other commission members to speed racial integration in every other aspect of Baltimore County life. According to Scott Moore, Agnew had established the commission mainly "to get the heat off his back" on civil rights, yet Holofcener considered he had been given a mandate to push for broad social change. "I read very carefully the mandate the commission got," he recalls. "It said in effect, 'Go into all areas within your concern,' in terms of discrimination in education, housing, and so on. It was all listed. I know now Agnew had a crisis situation and he dealt with it, and that was that. But I took the mandate literally, and I acted on it."

Within weeks of the Gwynn Oak settlement, Agnew began to feel the heat again. CORE selected as its next target the county's segregated, privately operated swimming pools, and almost at once there were demonstrations and arrests. On the weekend of August 12, seven pickets were arrested for trespassing at four pools where only whites who paid a minimal "annual membership fee" could swim. Rudolph T. Jones, Baltimore County chairman of CORE, warned that others would return to the four pools by midweek if there was no progress. At first, in accordance with Agnew's specific request, no mass-arrest tactics were used, as at Gwynn Oak. The county executive complimented the integrationists for their restraint. "Ideally," he said, "I would prefer that there would be no arrests, but this is a difficult thing to accomplish." He would take up negotiations with the pool owners, but he warned the civil rights leaders: if they did resort to mass demonstrations and arrests, he not only would withdraw his personal support but also would "call upon the people of the county, the press and everyone else included to do the same." While reiterating his belief that integration was a "moral right," Agnew told the integrationists, "Peaceful picketing is the answer. It dramatizes the situation."

Once again Agnew was making it abundantly clear that he was not one to be squeezed, to be leaned on. He urged civil rights leaders to work through the human relations commission before taking to the picket line, and instead present their demands to the commission to be conveyed to the businessmen. And he suggested that the commission seek out situations of potential trouble and try to head them off before the point of confrontation was reached. In light of the Gwynn Oak affair, in which even massive demonstrations and arrests could not persuade private businessmen to desegregate without long and tortuous haggling, such proposals demonstrated Agnew's continued insensitivity to the problem. Everywhere, the head-on clash was taking place, and the safety valve of a human relations commission was no substitute for the picket line in getting the businessmen to yield. They would desegregate only if they had no viable alternative; the picket line got the message across that they no longer had one.

Holofcener was determined to have the commission be more than a go-between, a neutral mediator dealing with two sides with equally just claims. He saw its role as an implementer of racial justice; as a quasi-governmental weapon on the side of the integrationists to persuade the recalcitrant property owners to meet just demands with a minimum of trouble. Others on the commission, notably Agnew's law partner Hennegan, favored a more passive role, and when Holofcener called a meeting to put the commission strongly on record in support of the CORE drive to desegregate the swimming pools, the effort failed. Only five of the eleven members attended, and Holofcener lost his bid to have a minority of the commission adopt the position.

The volunteer county human relations committee that had recommended appointments to Agnew charged the official commission with inaction and called for its dissolution and reformation "if the commission does not take a firm stand on behalf of justice now." The volunteer group accused Agnew of loading the commission with patsies after having rejected all but one of those persons recommended. "Our brainchild, by Agnew's inappropriate appointments, has changed into a Frankenstein monster," the volunteer group charged. It accused the county executive of panicking in the face of the Gwynn Oak affair and told him it was time "to get the commission back on the track." Only Holofcener, Rabbi Shusterman and Feingold were excepted from the criticism.

Agnew stuck to his guns. "When I appointed the commission," he said, "I tried to get the people most qualified in the county, a composite group. They were my own selections, no group's recommendations. If we are going to achieve anything through negotiation, selectees of the integrationist groups would alienate people. I tried to give it balance, and I think it has balance." What he wanted, the county executive said, were independent thinkers, "not rubber stamps," and he deplored Holofcener's effort to get a prointegration statement approved. It was, he said, "a little precipitate to try to ram it through without the majority present. It reflected panic under pressure of integration groups at the meeting." In the Agnew rule book, there was only one thing to do under pressure—resist it. This was a self-imposed rule that would be tested repeatedly by crises and pressures in his future.

When a CORE representative responded by saying Baltimore County was in for "the biggest jail-in you ever saw" if there wasn't immediate action to desegregate the swimming pools, Agnew replied, "CORE would be well advised to substitute intelligent requests for demands. These pressures hold back progress and CORE defeats itself by creating an emotion-charged atmosphere. They have no evidence of anything but good faith on our part. It's an attempt on their part to obtain something by threats, and the county didn't entrust me with this position to yield to threats." After a meeting of more than two hours between Agnew and CORE leaders, CORE reaffirmed its intent to picket the pools, but a pledge was made to the county executive to limit the protest to peaceful demonstrations and to avoid the mass-arrest tactic. Agnew called the meeting "very encouraging," but, he added, "I have urged the representatives of CORE to make known to their executive committees that my active efforts to resolve the swimming facilities problem will be continued only so long as demonstrations under their control are peaceful and lawful. Should mass-arrest-precipitating techniques be employed, I will consider such tactics a repudiation of the steps thus far taken by the human relations commission and me, and shall immediately withdraw from further personal attempts to solve the dispute."

In this frame of mind, Agnew called in representatives of six segregated pools and hammered out a conditional agreement committing them to negotiate through the human relations commission. The agreement provided that the integration groups would refrain from issuing any ultimatum or threat of massive demonstrations and would agree to limited picketing under ground rules set by the commission. CORE also agreed, on one condition — that the commission report "some progress" within two days. "We are hoping that the commission and the pool owners come to an agreement to desegregate before the end of the month," Rudolph Jones said on August 14. "By Friday we expect to hear that some progress has been made. We prefer having progress to mass demonstrations, but we will demonstrate in mass this weekend if there is no progress."

As far as Agnew was concerned, that did it—Jones had gone too far; he had defied authority, he had challenged the Agnew rule by threatening. As threats go, Jones's was not much, but it was enough for the county executive.

"The statement by CORE laying down dates again for things to be accomplished, with the threat of the resumption of jail-ins," he said, "amounts substantially to a rejection of the proposed agreement. I cannot ask the pool owners to negotiate under such circumstances. . . . Accordingly, I am withdrawing from the controversy until cooler heads among the integration leaders prevail. Should the members of the integration groups reconsider their precipitate course of action I will gladly make myself available to mediate the dispute."

As soon as Agnew stepped out, Holofcener stepped in—with a declaration of independence. "The commission by its own actions must generate its authority and status," he said. "To be most effective it must be made known to one and all that we follow through in the civil rights area from beginning to end. This means Mr. Agnew should not be an appeals board from the commission nor should he be injected into matters coming before the commission. . . . In the light of the lack of action that is taking place since the successful demonstrations at Gwynn Oak, it is easier to understand why the integration groups insist their demonstrations are the most effective instrument."

For months, the wrangling continued with Agnew standing alone and no agreement on the pools controversy ever achieved. But because some other settlements were reached during his tenure as county executive, Agnew won a public reputation as a champion of civil rights. Those who were exposed to his irritability over being pressured, however, and to his response to antisegregation tactics, did not so regard him. They were suspicious of him, and they sniped at him at every opportunity. As part of the Gwynn Oak settlement, he had promised that charges against the four hundred demonstrators arrested would be dropped, and a month later CORE accused him of holding out as a threat against future demonstrations. "There should be no doubt in anyone's mind, least of all yours, as to whether the charges should be dropped," Leo W. Burroughs, Jr., and W. Maurice Holmes of CORE told him. "By whose authority do you now seek to dominate the civil rights movement in Baltimore County?"

Agnew's answer to Burroughs and Holmes—a month later—and to his pledge to have charges dropped against the demonstrators, was to write to Frank Newell, the state's attorney, not urging him to drop the charges, but to submit them to a grand jury. Agnew reminded Newell that part of the amicable settlement of the Gwynn Oak crisis was the park owners' agreement that the charges against those arrested be dropped. "At the time and in my position as mediator," Agnew wrote, "I committed myself to do everything possible to accomplish this purpose." And then he added, in words that conveyed his strictly legalistic approach to that commitment, "I would feel remiss in my responsibility if I did not send you this formal, public request that you attempt to dispose of the charges. Understandably there is a great responsibility on your part to be considered, and you are properly cognizant of your oath of office. May I suggest that you might clearly relieve yourself of your official responsibilities by bringing these cases before the current grand jury along with whatever recommendations you might make in good conscience. If the grand jury saw fit not to indict, the matter would be terminated and you could certainly not be criticized." Newell, however, elected to prosecute for disorderly conduct. He won convictions, but eventually the Supreme Court reversed them on appeal.

There were other things that Agnew said and did that undermined his position with integrationists, black and white. The Sunday after the bombing of a black church in Birmingham, Alabama, in which small children were killed, he flatly rejected an invitation to a downtown march and commemorative service for the victims organized by CORE. In a telegram to Rudolph Jones, Agnew lectured that "the demonstrations and drama at Baltimore City Hall will do nothing more than provide a forum for publicity seekers." He told the grief-stricken: "Grief needs no publicity."

All the while Agnew was demonstrating his sympathy to civil rights in these rather odd ways, young Holofcener was barreling ahead, burning with a sense of mission augmented by his power as head of the commission. He was, another commission member observed, "like a cat in a bowl of catnip." Integration of public facilities was the battleground of the day, but looming just ahead was the even more controversial and incendiary issue of open housing, and integrationists pushed for implementing legislation at every governmental level. Holofcener was convinced that this was the area in which the commission should be pressing, and he was determined to so channel its efforts.

In mid-October 1963, when Agnew said he did not think open-occupancy legislation was "an area for government action at this point" and that he would "probably not" back such a bill before either the county council or the General Assembly, Holofcener again publicly took issue with the man who had appointed him. "There are certain injustices which can only be corrected with legislation now," he said. Although Agnew had urged the commission members to concentrate on what he told them were the more pressing problems of public accommodations and equal job opportunities, Holofcener said, "I still am of the opinion that this is where the main effort should be." The commission chairman argued that wiping out discrimination in the real estate market was the best and surest way of attacking discrimination in the other areas as well.

The difference of opinion again surfaced Agnew's repugnance for public challenge and repudiation by a subordinate, and his abhorrence of pressure tactics. Beyond that, this latest clash with Holofcener brought into focus Agnew's basic commitment to the conservative dogma of personal property rights. To a letter from Baltimore Neighborhoods, Inc., charging him with soft-pedaling the commission's interest in open housing, the county executive replied, "We face a long and difficult problem in educating the general public so that changes from a segregated to an integrated neighborhood will not affect property values. These changes can best be achieved by understanding between the races. . . ."

But Holofcener was of a different mind. He pushed. Says Scott Moore, "It was an area where Agnew wanted somebody to sit down and work quietly, and Holofcener wanted to do everything in the newspapers. He was just a wild hare. He wanted to run the county." And Dutch Moore observes: "This county is very, very conservative. I don't say it's racist, but it's one step away from being racist in a lot of ways, and the human relations commission was set up as something to buck things to, primarily. If you had a sensitive racial problem, you sent it over to the human relations commission, and Holofcener used the post for publicity, that was it in a nutshell. . . . It was bad because after the battles that they had, it became almost impossible to get good people to serve on the commission, and when they got good people to serve, after they attended a few meetings their interest would just wane and you couldn't even get a quorum for a commission meeting."

According to Holofcener, there were other pressures at work. "Somebody or some group must have said to Agnew, 'Holofcener must go; he must go and the commission has to be toned down,'" Holofcener said later. "There's no question that happened. I was told by a friend who was in the building industry that I should not talk about open housing. He told me not as a threat, but as advice from a friend." Still, however, the commission chairman preached across-the-board integration. He made repeated attempts to see the county executive to remind him of the mandate and to enlist his support, "but when I finally was given an appointment," Holofcener said, "Agnew told me, 'Why don't you concern yourself with discrimination in education and the more noncontroversial areas?'"

The inevitable confrontation came one day in mid-November as Holofcener was driving toward Towson. "I was in my car when I heard it on the radio. That was when I really saw the wrath of

Ted Agnew. It came as a complete surprise. I went to Ed Feingold's office, and I was steaming. I wrote out a blistering rebuttal,
and I refused to quit. Obviously I was going too fast. The housing
interests were edgy, concerned about the economic effects. I was
pushing no more for open housing than I was for open swimming
pools. But in those days open housing was the most critical, most
sensitive area. In those days, if anyone said the words 'open housing,' it was a dirty word."

What Holofcener heard on his car radio was a report that Agnew had sent a letter to other commission members—with no
prior warning to his target—urging that the chairman be replaced. "The body as presently constituted has lost its impetus,"
Agnew wrote them, "and a reorganization would be in the best
interests of Baltimore County. . . . The leadership of the commission seems to be faltering. It expends too much energy attacking the [Agnew] administration." Holofcener had failed "to mold
the commission into a cohesive force for the accomplishment of
its purpose," and Agnew blamed the lack of interest demonstrated
by some other commission members on their chairman's "overly
aggressive attitude."

From all accounts, it was true that Holofcener's attack strategy
had rankled some other members. Only four of the eleven members had attended the most recent meeting. But it was also true
that others saw Agnew's demand for his ouster as undue interference; they rallied behind Holofcener—not so much because they
wanted him to continue as chairman as because they felt independence required that posture.

The open Agnew-Holofcener clash was big news in the county.
Television cameramen and reporters were waiting for Holofcener
when he came out of Feingold's office, and he made the most of
their presence. "I have no intention of resigning from the commission nor relinquishing the chair, where my efforts can be most
effective," he told them. At first Agnew rejoined that he wasn't
asking that Holofcener be thrown off the commission, only that
he step down as chairman because he didn't "reflect the thinking"
of the majority of the group. In amplifying his position, the
county executive made clear that open housing, as Holofcener
had charged, indeed was at the core of the matter. "I would like to
see the commission come in and sit down with me," Agnew said,
"and get to work on job opportunities and problems in the educa-

tional field, and get away from those controversial hamstringing problems such as swimming pools and equal housing. We can get action in some fields which are less controversial. As I see the failures becoming more and more acute, I realize that something must be done. All I want is a commission I can work with."

Holofcener now had the spotlight and wasn't going to let go. Expressing shock at Agnew's intrusion, he attributed the conduct to Agnew's "total lack of knowledge and understanding of the vital program we are conducting. . . . I think he is disappointed that the commission did not choose the less controversial path favoring the status quo in Baltimore County." In the face of Agnew's purge attempt, Holofcener escalated. "It is obvious that the three-point-five percent Negro population in Baltimore County is not a very potent political force," the beleaguered chairman said. "To the contrary, a politically expedient role would dictate little or no attempt to redress the grievances of the Negro in Baltimore County."

Confident of his position, Holofcener offered to resign if a majority of the eleven-member commission so voted. Hennegan and Power called for a special meeting and the battle lines formed: Agnew and his allies on one side, Holofcener and his supporters—on the commission and among the civil rights groups—on the other. Although it was a commission meeting, Agnew arrived armed with a long statement of his personal civil rights position, expressing his moral support but warning of the dangers of unlimited open housing.

The meeting took place several days after the assassination in Dallas of President John F. Kennedy. To the rancor that already existed between Agnew and the civil rights groups now was added a bitterness that he would intrude on the public grief of that shattering event with his determined effort against a strong civil rights advocate. But Agnew charged ahead, in a manner suggestive of his later postriot lecture in Baltimore, making a virtue of his attack:

"There are those who will later contend that what I am going to say should not have been said at this sad time. They will say that out of respect to our tragically departed President, controversies should be avoided; that accord and unity are now needed at all costs; that a tolerant attitude and a yielding would have smoothed troubled waters. Although I indicated my preference that this meeting be postponed for a reasonable period, I must not be tempted to equivocate the issue. Whatever differences my party had with the President's policies, I cannot desecrate the memory of a courageous man by evading controversy and pretending that very real and unpleasant problems do not exist, when in fact they do. Accordingly, I make these remarks with the firm conviction that they are fitting, beneficial and even obligatory to the proper discharge of my office."

Having thus disposed of the matter of timing, Agnew plunged into his assault on Holofcener. In a remarkable mix of castigation and condescension that warrants full presentation here for what it reveals about Agnew's thinking in that formative period, he went on:

"The greatest enemies of effective, intelligent government are opportunists who have learned that a measure of popularity can be cheaply purchased by boldly assuming oversimplified positions on highly complex, volatile issues. But the real danger lies not with these chauvinistic self-seekers, whose insincerity is sooner or later detected, but with their well-motivated but poorly informed sympathizers. These average citizens, mentally fatigued after a day in the arena of private enterprise, are quick to seize upon the simple, clearly defined opinion and all too often prefer it to the enlightened viewpoint that focuses strongly in those troublesome gray areas of doubt. But it is difficult to criticize the average citizen for not having the energy to become expert in fields not related to his vocation. Just remaining competitive in one's own work is a formidable task in our complex society. So, unfortunately, many turn to the oversimplified demi-truths of the lunatic fringes of any emotional dispute. They proudly identify themselves as 'liberals' or 'conservatives,' take predetermined stances on matters about which they have insufficient knowledge, and, when controversial issues arise, generally make it extremely difficult for those in positions of governmental responsibility."

Agnew then launched into a defense of his own position on open-occupancy legislation: "Not since the early and bloody days of the labor movement have there been more fertile soils for the malcontent opportunists than the hatreds of segregationist dogma on the one hand and the unreasonable ultimatums of some power-crazed integrationist leaders on the other. Caught up in a searing heat of deprivation by the decade, the Negro is eager to have civil equality legislated and enforced. This he is entitled to as a moral right if our system of government and our way of life is to have meaning. I repeat, so that I may never again be misunderstood; the Negro is entitled as a matter of moral right to have his civil equality legislated and enforced.

"You may then properly ask me why I am here to request a diminution of the aggressive posture favoring racial integration favored by the chairman of this commission. This is a fair question. The answer is that the chairman, and occasionally some members of this commission, have confused civil equality with social acceptance; that civil rights do not stop with a prohibition against racial discrimination but go on to protect the right of privacy, the right to own and enjoy property without government interference, the right to do business for profit and the right to seek out and prefer the company of one man to another.

"Open-occupancy legislation, the attempted crashing of private membership clubs, unlawful trespassing and unlawful demonstrating violate the civil rights of others just as clearly as segregation violates the civil rights of the Negro. Social acceptance can never be legislated because it is voluntary acceptance by one man of another as a companion, not acceptance by one race of another in casual contact.

"I take a strong position that it is wrong to tell the owner of a private dwelling place, be it single family or multiple unit, that he must offer it for rent or sale to anyone with whom he does not wish to do business. This applies whether or not he is biased and applies regardless of what his bias may embrace. If he dislikes Greeks he should not have to deal with Greeks, and the government that infringes upon his discretion in this respect abrogates his freedom of selection and disregards the intent of the Constitution of the United States. On the other hand, when an individual openly or impliedly seeks the good will and business of the general public, I believe that he thereby waives his rights to personal preference. He then becomes obligated to sell his product or render his service to all persons who present themselves as prospective customers, as long as they do not by their conduct or demeanor offend his other clientele.

"However, I cannot agree with the statement of this commission that there no longer is any basis for fears of severe economic impact when a previous segregationist policy is suddenly abandoned voluntarily. If abandoned by reason of legislation this is probably true, but it does not apply to voluntary abandonment. Although it is unfortunate, it is nevertheless factual that where competitors maintain the status quo, the suddenly integrated facility may sustain a severe loss of business. It is not my position that these public places should not be integrated; I simply mean that this commission must not shut its eyes to the economic realities in its eagerness to achieve sudden and startling gains.

"We have undertaken an arduous and difficult task. Patience is a word that has apparently lost most of its meaning in the rush to right the wrongs that have been done our Negro citizens for so many years. Yet patience is an absolute necessity if these wounds are to heal properly, from the inside out, and not become deep-lying and festering infections under superficial mending. The fact that the Negro lacks confidence in those who select the surer but less sensational path is not surprising. He looks at a history of unfulfilled promises while he is concurrently being goaded by those same self-seeking opportunists who constantly demand the sensational. When the rash conduct of others makes his position untenable, these same fair-weather friends depart for distant geographic points and leave the local Negro holding the bag. It is an obligation of this human rights commission to protect our Negro community against exploitation by politically motivated opportunists, and to see that steady progress, rather than the 'jump forward two, slip back three' type is implemented.

"As the chief elected official of this county, I have been often attacked by those who call me a pawn of the integration movement, but I have been attacked no less strongly by those who vilify me as an ardent segregationist. I state to you with sincerity that the words of this statement accurately reflect my convictions on this subject. They are offered without fear for the purpose of clarification and to make a clear permanent record.

"Finally, I think it is important that you, a commission authorized by the elected members of the county council and appointed by an elected county executive, keep in mind your obligation and responsibility to the administration and to the council. It is the county council and I who stand responsible to the voters of Baltimore County in all policy matters, and the authority that this commission is vested with comes to it through the elected officials and by virtue of the fact that the voters have reposed certain confidences in them. I charge you that a change in your leadership is essential if you are to maintain the full confidence and cooperation of the county government."

It was not exactly a reaffirmation of the commission's independence. Although some members admitted later that they were less than enchanted with Holofcener's leadership, a bare majority of the commission present at the meeting stood by him in the face of Agnew's demand and he was sustained by a 4-to-3 vote. Agnew allies Hennegan and Power were among the minority. Agnew argued that the vote was hardly a demonstration of confidence in Holofcener, but the chairman said he was going to stay on. He expressed a hope that Agnew would "relent and accept the decision of the commission, and give us a chance to operate."

It was a naïve hope. Determined not to accept defeat, Agnew took out after Holofcener. He spoke derisively of "Holofcener hysterics," and shortly after the commission meeting retaining the chairman, Agnew escalated the battle in a surprise appearance before the Baltimore County committee on good government. "I made the appointment against my better judgment and much to my woe," he told the civic group. "I have no intention of relenting in my position toward Mr. Holofcener. I am now at the point where I would like to see him off the commission—completely off the commission. . . . Now, obviously, he feels his personal leadership of the commission is more important than the welfare of the commission itself."

In the next days, Agnew made clear to the other members that as long as Holofcener stayed, the commission no longer would be regarded an employable tool in civil rights mediation. It did not take long for the message to sink in, and a meeting of the other members finally was called to decide what to do. As Rabbi Shusterman remembers the climax: "We came to the conclusion after a while that as long as Mike remained as the presiding officer, the work of the human relations commission could not go forward, could not be accomplished. . . . The commission voted to request him to resign, but Mike refused. Thereupon somebody presented a motion that he be declared no longer the chairman, and those who had voted to ask him to resign voted on Mike's side. We felt we shouldn't impeach him. So he was not thrown out by our vote, but we were all unhappy about it.

"At this point, Don Kellett invited a number of us to have lunch with him. When I went there, I found it was a kind of cross section of the committee, some other clergymen and Mr. Agnew. We sat down and in a very dignified way, Mr. Agnew raised the question that he wanted the human relations commission to succeed, to succeed in a way to keep too many scars from being opened. He wanted to keep the business people happy, but wanted the commission to move forward but not impetuously. All there agreed.

"Then somebody, not Mr. Agnew, urged that we make another appeal to Mike to resign. So King and I got him on the phone in a booth in the next room while Mr. Agnew was having lunch, and we both talked to him. We said, 'Mike, we're on your side, we voted with you but we think you should resign so the work of the commission can go forward.'"

Still Holofcener refused. Again Agnew escalated, with a public threat either to take the matter to court or to have the ordinance repealed under which the commission was created. In another open meeting, Holofcener finally told his fellow commissioners, after much wrangling with Agnew, that he was willing to step down if he could be assured that the group's progressive program would go forward. But the county executive would stand for no such ultimatum. He rejected a request for another closed-door meeting and stalked from the room. "Mr. Holofcener has demonstrated his complete unfitness to hold the chair," he said as he went. "His conduct has varied from self-deprecating obsequiousness to utter boorishness, and with that I leave."

Finally, when two Agnew allies on the commission thereupon quit, Holofcener saw that his position was untenable and in December he gave in. "I cannot remain as chairman under this cloud that has been placed on the leadership and independence of the commission," he said. "I believe the conclusion is now unmistakable [that] policies of the commission are in serious jeopardy." Holofcener stayed on as a member of the commission until mid-1964, at which time, to nobody's surprise, Agnew passed him over for reappointment.

The Holofcener affair, however, put Agnew on the defensive in the area of civil rights, although those closest to the inside acknowledged that personality as much as ideology had been at the root of the clash. Agnew appointed Francis Iglehart, a Towson lawyer and a Democrat, as the new chairman, and assured the public that "despite charges to the contrary from some areas, I do not want a soft, do-nothing policy in the civil rights area." He pledged "the full weight of this administration behind the commission to overcome through whatever means are necessary the discriminatory practices that deprive Negroes of their public rights." He emphasized, though, that an equal part of the job was "to provide a better climate for voluntary and social acceptance of the Negro through sensitive persuasion and not militant pushing."

Iglehart soon learned how Agnew reacted to what he called "militant pushing." The new chairman recalled in an interview: "The first time I noticed him to be testy was when CORE had a demonstration at a roller rink in a God-forsaken part of the county [Catonsville]. They were demonstrating every night, and it was the beginning of the sit-in tactic. Because the police were dragging them or rushing them somewhat summarily and in some cases they were being thrown somewhat solidly against the walls of the police vans, CORE charged police brutality and fired off a telegram to him. He did get a bit testy about that. He reacted very quickly and was hot about it. He didn't like that kind of charge being made. He didn't like CORE to push him like that. First he asked the commission to investigate the charges and report our finding, and then I think he realized, and it's probable he may have received a cautionary word from the police department, that he might be making us into a police review board, so he very quickly withdrew the delegation from our hands. A day or two later he issued a statement that he had investigated the whole incident and found there was no evidence of police brutality. The police command had made it clear to him immediately that they expected him to back them up, that the men in the ranks were really sore; that they were in enough trouble with demonstrators as it was, the lie-ins, the sit-ins; they had to carry them, load them into the police vans and they expected Agnew to back them up."

In that instance and thereafter, Iglehart said, Agnew demonstrated a penchant for overreaction to any threat of "militant pushing" as he called it. "He'd file a very quick statement, and some of his friends and advisers would shake their heads and say, 'He shouldn't have done that, he shouldn't have said that,' and then the problem would work itself out so that by the time of a second statement, when he could expand more on his position, he seemed to do a pretty good balancing act."

Iglehart recalled that once, toward the end of his term as chairman of the commission, the county received a phone call from the Dundalk area warning that a group of black students was going to demonstrate at the courthouse in Towson. "This was during the period they were having massive sit-ins and lie-ins and the offices of officials were being occupied, and because of that the reaction of the administration was a little rigid," Iglehart said. "I got a call from Agnew or his secretary, 'Please report to the county executive's office; some trouble is expected.' It was toward the end of the day, and I remember walking up the street from my office to the county office building, and the place was swarming with uniformed police. Every entrance was guarded; they had two police vans backed up to the elevator shaft where they could pick up the bodies that would be brought down from Agnew's office. They all assumed there would be a rush on the office and a lie-in or a sit-in. The whole place was like an armed fortress. Ted Agnew asked me to sit out front in his office to mediate before these troops stormed his office. Nothing happened. The hours went by and finally the time came to go out and we heard word, 'They're here, they're here.' And when we finally left the building there was this little group of about twelve high school kids, aged about fourteen to sixteen or seventeen, parading around in a very calm group with a few signs."

As for the "sensitive persuasion" Agnew spoke of, he made clear it required a human relations commission that functioned as a strictly impartial arbiter, not as the battering ram against racial barriers that Holofcener had sought to make it. When any member of the commission did anything that appeared to side with the integrationists, Agnew acted as if he had been betrayed. During the CORE drive to desegregate the roller rink in Catonsville, for example, Agnew diverted the charge of police brutality by countercharging that Eugene King, the black teacher on the commission, actually had "encouraged demonstrators who were in the process of being arrested to go limp and lie down." He charged that "such partisan activity, an interference with the police in the course of their duties, is obviously improper and not in keeping with the role of a commissioner." King called the charges "untrue and unfounded" and said Agnew was "telling a bald lie," but Agnew kept at him. A week later, he again criticized King for passing on to a police officer a demonstrator's complaint of police brutality because, "if he as a commissioner was unable to see any first-hand evidence of brutality, he certainly should not have made the complaint."

The commission later investigated Agnew's charges against Eugene King and ruled in King's favor, although Iglehart said later that King "was always getting out close to the scene of action and not comporting himself the way a commission member was supposed to." King would call a newspaper, Iglehart recalled, "and say, 'Meet me at a certain tavern,' and then he'd go in with a group of people who wanted to be thrown out, to demonstrate it was a segregated tavern. He wouldn't check with me or any other members of the commission and tell them this was what he intended to do. You can't have someone who is supposed to be a member of an official mediation agency, who might have to sit in judgment of a complaint of discrimination, charging around the county leading demonstrators."

Agnew further challenged King's objectivity by reporting that King once had made a $25 contribution to CORE. "It is very difficult for me to understand how this is compatible with an impartial attitude in the matter," Agnew said. The CORE contribution, King replied, actually had been made by his sons out of their allowances, but anyway, such a contribution "does not mean that the contributor condones every act, but only that he sympathizes with the overall cause of the organization." Even that position, however, apparently violated Agnew's idea of the attitude a member of a commission charged with calming racial tensions should adopt.

These were days, however, when Agnew's strict concept of "sensitive persuasion" was not enough to get the job done. Racial barriers were not crumbling of their own volition; talk too often meant equivocation and tactical delay; civil rights leaders were finding, as unfortunate as the fact might be, that words spoken by them at the negotiating table had little persuasive power unless backed by action or the threat of action in the streets. And so they continued to engage in what they called peaceful, nonviolent demonstrating—and what Spiro Agnew called "militant pushing." More confrontations between the two points of view lay ahead, but the "serendipity effect" of which his friend Jervis Finney later spoke already was injecting itself imperceptibly, turning new crises into new political opportunities Agnew himself scarcely could have imagined at the time.

5

SKIN-DEEP LIBERAL

BY the spring of 1964, for all his temporizing in the civil
rights field and his personal irritability toward the movement's leaders, Spiro Agnew was gaining a reputation in conservative Baltimore County as something of a liberal. That he was
more dragged by events than spearheading them was obscured by
a polarization taking place in the county, and the whole state of
Maryland for that matter, over the tactics of the desegregationist
forces. Agnew tried to be a man in the middle at a time when
there was less and less middle ground.

In the next three years of his county stewardship, however,
other men and events were to intrude themselves in a way to make
his moderation in a conservative environment seem liberal. Bona-
fide liberals, of course, did not so perceive him, but political circumstances cast him as an ally in hard times. It may be constructive, therefore, to examine the Spiro Agnew of the mid-1960's, and
those events that helped shape his image—but not really his philosophy—as a liberal.

At this critical juncture in Agnew's career, one man did more
than any other to make him seem a liberal—George Corley Wallace, the cocky bantam-rooster governor of Alabama. While
Agnew was being buffeted by an ever more aggressive and demanding civil rights movement in Baltimore County, Wallace
was playing on its emotional content across the country with un-

matched virtuosity. He had national ambitions, and in early 1964 he cast predatory eyes unabashedly northward, to presidential primary states where the white backlash might offer an opening to a candidate clearly identified as hostile to the pace, even the very premises, of racial desegregation in all its troublesome facets.

One of the states on which Wallace focused was Maryland, where President Lyndon B. Johnson's banner in the Democratic primary was being carried by liberal Senator Daniel J. Brewster. Both the geography and the political climate were right for a challenge from a presidential candidate who understood white fears and was not reluctant to articulate them in the bluntest terms. In Baltimore County, Agnew was becoming increasingly aware of that fact. That he did not like the militancy of the civil rights movement, and that he was especially irritated at being confronted with its demands and deadlines, had been amply demonstrated in the Gwynn Oak amusement park episode. Aside from personal pique, however, his unease was compounded by the fact black militancy put him on the defensive with influential conservative elements in the county, many within his own party, that were growing ever stronger and more agitated. It always was hard to defend the cause of racial equality before these conservatives when civil rights leaders insisted on threats couched in aggressive language; it was more so now, when Wallace was seizing on black militancy to extend his constituency northward.

After Gwynn Oak, a steady stream of other civil rights incidents in the county sharpened Agnew's irritation and bolstered his conviction that those in the forefront of the push for racial justice were opportunists preying on the inflammatory mood and circumstances of the day. Not only in Baltimore County, but throughout the state of Maryland, strident demands and civil disobedience were integral to the civil rights assault on old racial barriers. Agnew was convinced such tactics played directly into the hands of Wallace. When, for example, Mrs. Gloria Richardson and her associates disrupted the Eastern Shore community of Cambridge, out of Agnew's jurisdiction but not beyond his awareness and dismay, he sounded a dire warning. "The continuance of civil disobedience is seriously impairing the cause of civil rights," he said. "It is time for the Negro leadership to lift their horizontal crusade from the streets and convert it to an upright, lawful American appeal for decency and equality. It is time for introspection, for self-improvement, for commendation for those who fight the same battle. It is time to stop piling fuel on the fires of reaction which are now so carefully tended by the Alabama governor."

The Wallace threat so disturbed Agnew that he spoke at a testimonial dinner for Senator Brewster. "Many Marylanders have become angered by militant civil disobedience on the part of certain Negro groups," he acknowledged. "They are threatening to turn to Governor George Wallace as an expression of their displeasure. They don't want Wallace but they are sick of lie-ins, stall-ins, going limp, false accusations of police brutality, et cetera. Please, my Democratic friends, do not encourage hatred and bigotry by supporting Mr. Wallace. Your complaints may be valid but Wallace is not the answer. I urge you to support Senator Brewster in the primary. If you have to express displeasure with the Johnson Administration, you will have an opportunity to do so in November." While discrimination in the use of public facilities was "unconscionable and the basis of justified Negro complaints," Agnew told the Democrats, "most of the voices raised so far in the civil rights controversy are either militantly integrationist or militantly segregationist. There is a great need to hear from calm moderates of both races"—like, of course, Spiro Agnew.

The Republican county executive was not speaking in a vacuum. He had particular and personal reason for being sensitive to "the fires of reaction" of which he spoke. In a county his friend Dutch Moore later described as "one step away from being racist," Agnew did not escape their flames. Offensively worded handbills, distributed in the blue-collar town of Dundalk by the Maryland chapter of the National States Rights party, with headquarters in Birmingham, Alabama, linked Agnew and his administration to Communism and, for all his trouble with them, to black civil rights leaders. The John Birch Society, too, was active in the county and increasingly hostile to Agnew, particularly when he committed himself to an ambitious urban renewal program. That commitment is especially interesting; it put his views on the sanctity of individual property rights in a curiously different perspective from the one to which he seemed so wedded on matters where individual civil rights clashed with the principle of private ownership.

Urban renewal for Baltimore County—actually for the towns

of Towson and Catonsville—had been a Democratic brainchild in the previous county administration, and the voters had endorsed the general idea by a two-to-one majority in a referendum two years earlier. The term "urban renewal" as applied to a suburban county, however, was really a misnomer; it did not mean, as it customarily did in a large city, the leveling of slum dwellings and their replacement with decent housing for low-income residents, often predominantly black. Rather, it meant spurring economic growth in the county by the construction of office-building complexes, new industry, and the like. Few in the minuscule black population of this county would benefit; urban renewal in County Executive Agnew's domain constituted an elaborate government-safeguarded investment for the snake-oil salesmen of suburbia— the land developers.

In the circles in which Ted Agnew now traveled, urban renewal was perceived as a rare and most desirable mix of community do-goodism and low-risk profit. Though the profit motive is basic in the American system, its excessive and even ruthless application over the years has tended to discredit it; when profit seeking can surface in the guise of public service, that façade is a sure-fire device for rallying the hard-nosed businessman to the improvement of the common weal. Yet, in ultraconservative circles, "urban renewal" had become a dirty word, no matter what its refinements or focus. To the Wallacites and the John Birch Society, whose members guarded the ramparts against any trace of what they considered socialistic meddling with the free-enterprise system, there was no such thing as good urban renewal. So they mounted a holy crusade against Agnew, and when it took hold, others jumped in, including old-time Democrats who saw the chance to give him a political licking, and the battle was joined.

"He took that thing by the tail," Scott Moore recalls. "Because the previous referendum had won by two to one, politically it made sense, and he believed in it. I remember telling him, 'If you get through four years straightening out urban renewal, it may be the best you can do,' and he committed himself to it. He nailed all the contributors to his election campaign, got money for urban renewal and spent it for urban renewal. No politician does this— raises money for a cause and spends it for that cause, not himself. But he did it."

The harder Agnew worked, though, the harder his opponents

fought him. One day Dutch Moore was walking across the street from the county courthouse with Agnew when a prominent Democrat coming out of the building spied him and called over, "Agnew, we're going to get you on this one." That was the no-holds-barred climate that prevailed.

Agnew publicly warned that the program was being imperiled by Wallacite states rights groups motivated by unjustified racial fears. "Many of the difficulties," he said, "arise out of resistance to the entire program of integration and civil rights. . . . In many instances these groups are related to the so-called Wallace states rights groups that are charged with emotional fears about compulsory integration. These fears are being interjected into the urban renewal issue, whereas in fact they are not related." Agnew said it was not necessary for the county to have a nondiscriminatory housing code to remain eligible for federal urban renewal aid, and contrary reports "are efforts to convince some of our more gullible citizens" that urban renewal meant more integration, which it did not. "Alarmist propaganda is difficult to overcome as people are sitting with closed minds, hearts and brains," he declared.

Thus it was not as any civil rights champion that he fought for a bond issue of $3.8 million for Baltimore County's face-lifting. Yet the identity and the tactics of his opposition inevitably cast him as a liberal even as he advanced a cause dear to the hearts of the county's moneyed interests. One vehement urban renewal foe, Joshua A. Cockey, a Democratic candidate for Congress and owner of a segregated swimming pool in the county, helped build this reputation for Agnew with forensic overkill. During an anti-urban-renewal meeting at the American Legion Hall in Towson, he called urban renewal "a scheme of a few money-grabbing, land-grabbing politicians and real estate speculators," but didn't stop there. To him, it also was "a malicious, socialistic cancer," and he lamented, "It's just as if we were behind the Iron Curtain." His fullness of patriotism spilling over, Cockey topped off his tirade by castigating Agnew's chief urban renewal planner, a Lebanese named Vladimir A. Wahbe, for not having completed all steps for obtaining American citizenship. Wahbe would not be an American citizen for another week, Cockey revealed grandly. Agnew denounced the meeting, charging that "veiled threats, fear-mongering and appeals to bias seemed to be the order of the night"; Cockey had "reached a new pinnacle of bigotry when he called attention to Mr. Wahbe's ancestry. . . . I congratulate Mr. Cockey on being able to be born in the United States." Out of all this there emerged a growing image of Ted Agnew as a liberal, even while he was fighting for an issue most beneficial not to liberal interests, but to the developer barons of the suburban fiefdom over which he reigned.

To one of Agnew's most conservative and tenacious opponents, State Representative Bernard J. Medairy of Towson, it was not that Agnew was liberal, but that he was wrong. "Urban renewal was really not necessary, because the land itself was susceptible to development by private enterprise," Medairy says. "The county had doubled population in ten years, and this was the county seat. I opposed the urban renewal program because I didn't want to see the taxpayers end up paying the cost of the developers who would acquire the land at a discount. I was also opposed to the taking of private property for what I considered to be not public use. I wrote to Ted at that time and opposed the program. He wrote back and said he could see nothing wrong with it."

Medairy owned property that would have been subject to sale, and he admitted that factor was involved in his opposition. But beyond that, he said, was the basic matter of property rights. One might have thought that Medairy's argument would have appealed to a man like Agnew, who had made such a staunch defense of property rights on the issue of open housing. "I take a strong position," Agnew had said then, "that it is wrong to tell the owner of a private dwelling place, be it single-family or multiple unit, that he must offer it for rent or sale to anyone with whom he does not wish to do business." That statement, of course, was made in the context of sale by the property owner to another individual of a different ethnic or racial background, and Agnew was against forcing such a sale. In the context of urban renewal, the buyer would be ethnicless, raceless, and except to those on the inside of the slick and lucrative world of real estate development, faceless. In these circumstances, the sacrosanctity of private property obviously lost its magic for Agnew.

In the end, and to Agnew's great shock and chagrin, the voters of Baltimore County rejected his urban renewal bond issue by a clear-cut margin of three to two. The outcome left him disappointed and bitter; Scott Moore was in New York with Agnew the night the results came in, and heard him rant about the stupidity of the voters. "The next morning at the New York Hilton, the press got to him and he raised hell with the voters of Baltimore County," Moore recalls. "He thought it would be overwhelmingly passed. For two weeks after that, he was soured on the issue, and on the people who opposed him. For a couple of weeks he just blasted them, and he didn't care what they thought."

Still, ironically, out of this bitter defeat came one of the ingredients in the emerging image of Spiro Agnew that was to accelerate his political climb to national prominence. Because he fought for urban renewal, and because the rednecks and the reactionaries of Baltimore County fought him on it, he was perceived increasingly as a liberal. The Baltimore Sunpapers, which had regarded him as a "clean broom," embraced him even more enthusiastically for his urban renewal stance and his outspoken combat against the forces of reaction. It has been written, not with unfailing accuracy, that by a man's enemies you shall know him. "It's that bunch of tennis-shoe gals in Catonsville who got you," Scott Moore told Agnew after the urban renewal defeat. True or not, Agnew was to learn that in certain important political quarters, having such opposition was not the worst thing that could happen in the long run to an aspirant Republican politician in a Democratic state.

For all this, Ted Agnew was not by any means a candidate for the Americans for Democratic Action Man-of-the-Year. On the one issue that now was coming into the forefront of the civil rights crusade—an end to discriminatory practices in the rental and sale of private dwelling places—Agnew clung to a defense of individual property rights over the right of an individual to rent or buy whatever apartment or house he wished if he could pay the legitimate asking price.

In the midst of the row with Michael Holofcener, Agnew had made his position clear. "We face a long and difficult problem in educating the general public so that changes from a segregated to an integrated neighborhood will not affect property values," he wrote then. "These changes can best be achieved by understanding between the races. . . ." And after that row came his long dissertation elaborating on the same point: "Social acceptance can never be legislated because it is voluntary acceptance by one man of another as a companion, not acceptance by one race of another in casual contact. . . ."

That was the social philosophy of Spiro Agnew, and he stuck to it. Efforts in mid-1964 to get him to back even a study of open housing in Baltimore County were turned away abruptly. When the human relations commission, now under the more friendly Iglehart, unanimously passed a resolution calling on Agnew and the county council to appoint a committee to cooperate with Baltimore city on such a study, he categorically rejected it. "It has been my stated position on many occasions that I am not in favor of open-occupancy legislation," Agnew said. "In my view, housing occupancy cannot be legislated without invading the rights of privacy guaranteed in our Constitution. Consequently, I do not feel it advisable to appoint any such committee to operate in this area." The response was lauded by the more conservative elements in the community. County Councilman Wallace A. Williams called Agnew's comment "what we have been fighting for. If he sticks to this," Williams said with a prescience that probably astounded him later, "he can be elected governor. . . . Evidently Mr. Agnew seems to be realizing what I have been trying to say all along. The home is the foundation of our civilization. That's what we're trying to preserve." Those lines, too, were to have a certain relevancy to Agnew's political career later on, but in a context not even an amateur clairvoyant like Williams could have anticipated.

By this time, the right of an apartment owner to rent or sell to whom he pleased had become the high ground on which Agnew would make his stand against the inexorable push of the civil rights activists. The public-accommodations battle had been resolved in their favor at Gwynn Oak and in subsequent tests, and Agnew in fact pressed a public-accommodations bill in the county council in 1964 in return for an agreement from CORE that further picketing of segregated county facilities would be suspended. When the council postponed action, Agnew charged its members with "breaking faith" with the CORE negotiators. He noted that the agreement had kept the county free of racial demonstrations for a time, and he said to the politicians concerning the activists' restraint: "Since they have embarked on a statesmanlike action, we certainly cannot expect less from our public officials." In these and other observations, Agnew demonstrated a willingness to accommodate to change. The presence of a statewide referendum on a law barring racial discrimination in hotels and restaurants likewise won his endorsement. "It seems to me to be nothing less than justice and high principle," he told the voters, "that an antidiscrimination law should apply equally to every political subdivision in the state of Maryland." (The county public-accommodations bill squeaked through the council, but later lost in a referendum pushed by conservative groups. The statewide measure lost in the county in November 1964, in spite of Agnew's endorsement.) On the matter of open housing, however, he remained opposed.

To the advocates of civil rights, having won the public-accommodations fight on the county level at least, the question of housing became the most critical issue. In the mid-1960's, where one lived determined more than any other factor where one's children attended school; it affected job opportunities, social activities and in many cases the very quality of life a family could pursue. As Agnew clung to his "if he dislikes Greeks he should not have to deal with Greeks" philosophy, the civil rights movement hammered away at him, particularly in the context of new real estate development in the county, which went forward even without his urban renewal scheme. Why, the activists asked, should blacks not have a crack at the new housing?

After some deliberation, Agnew allowed in April 1965 that he might accept a law requiring developers to open large new subdivisions "over a certain size" to minority groups, but he emphasized he still opposed any law that would compel an individual property owner to sell to someone not of his choice. "I am very much in favor of open housing voluntarily achieved," he observed at one point; but the reality was that very little was being achieved voluntarily. In January 1966, on the recommendation of the human relations commission, he instructed the county solicitor to draft legislation making it illegal to refuse to sell a new house or rent a new apartment to anyone on racial or religious grounds. But he made clear he would back a limited open-housing bill only if it did not control a private-property owner's right to sell even in an "arbitrary" way, provided Baltimore city and Anne Arundel County (Annapolis) introduced and supported similar bills. "Whether I deplore it or not, whether I disagree or not, my neighbor, white or black, in his private life has a right to be selective, discriminatory, even arbitrary," Agnew said. "No matter how many breadmen, milkmen, laundrymen offer him a better price, he has the right to deal with the one he likes, whether for good reason or for no apparent reason. Whether he sells his hunting dog, a family heirloom or his residence, no law should make price the only criterion he may employ in selecting the purchaser. Our system of government, our basic freedoms, depend upon the individual's privilege to be free of governmental intrusion in his private life so long as he does no harm to the community."

When civil rights activists balked at this half a loaf, Agnew was ready with one of his typical father-knows-best observations. "Integrationist groups would do well to reconsider their demands for broader legislation and support this limited legislation which has a reasonable chance of success," he said. And then Agnew explained why he favored open housing covering new construction only. "First, everyone who buys there knows what to expect," he said. "Second, Negroes have historically been charged with running down neighborhoods which were run-down when they got there. These will be new neighborhoods and all can see what happens to them. It will put the best image on integrated housing possible."

Even this limited approach, however, was too much in the state of Maryland. The rural-dominated House of Delegates, which at any time could reach in and strike down county actions, blocked any kind of open-occupancy order. Yet Agnew's espousal of even a limited open-occupancy bill, like his championing of an urban renewal bill that would have benefited land developers more than the poor, augmented his image as a liberal in conservative eyes. In other areas, too—opposition to an antiloitering law that he saw as hostile to individual rights, and support of gun-control measures—he took standard liberal positions. Although he could be fiercely partisan, Agnew was not locked into blind allegiance to party dogma, and in fact one characteristic about which he boasted most was his independence.

Another was his integrity. He considered himself that rare animal in politics—the untouchable man. Several associates from his zoning-board and county-executive days recall his telling them on more than one occasion that in the booming area of suburban growth, he was in a position to get rich by making the right decisions. But he told them in the same breath that he was interested only in good government, not in lining his pockets or getting in bed with special interests.

Nevertheless, his term as county executive was not free of allegations that he sought special favors for his friends. In September 1965, Charles Steinbock (the Republican who had replaced him on the county zoning board of appeals when Agnew was ousted by the Democratic majority) charged that in 1963 Agnew had tried, for political reasons, to influence his decision in an apartment-house rezoning case. Agnew had let the board know at the time of Steinbock's appointment that he bore no malice toward his successor, but according to Scott Moore, Agnew felt strongly that Steinbock had let the Democrats off the hook by being so available as a replacement. In March 1964, in fact, as county executive Agnew had pressed the county council into removing Steinbock for another Republican of his choice. Agnew held a private dinner for the council and told them, some of them reported later, that Steinbock ruled on zoning cases "by plebescite"—that if sufficient numbers of protesters came to a meeting opposed to a rezoning application, he would knuckle under to them and deny it.

With this ill feeling as a backdrop, Steinbock charged more than a year later that Agnew as county executive had pressured him on the 1963 zoning case. While Steinbock was part of a two-man board reviewing a rezoning request for an apartment house in Pikesville, he said, "Mr. Agnew telephoned me and asked me to grant the petition. I told him I decided cases solely on the evidence present at the hearings, and that the evidence did not warrant reclassification. He then had [an associate] call me and ask me to grant the rezoning for the good of the Republican party. I told him I was not on the board for the good of any party and promptly denied the petition." The other member of the board granted the petition, but the split decision resulted in automatic denial. On appeal to the circuit court the rezoning was granted, but neighborhood people took the matter to the state court of appeals and Steinbock's denial was upheld. "This infuriated Mr. Agnew, who is very easily infuriated," Steinbock went on, and this case was the real reason Agnew had forced him off the board. "In my five years on the board, he was the only county official or employee to attempt to influence my decisions," Steinbock said.

The allegation could not be dismissed out of hand because for a

time after Agnew was thrown off the zoning board, he had represented the petitioner in the apartment-house rezoning case, resigning when he became county executive. Agnew, however,
brushed aside the charge as "a campaign of character assassination . . . simply a bitter backlash from a person who has been
passed over for reappointment." He said he had "never called Mr.
Steinbock with any such conversation at all. . . . I flatly deny
the insinuation." Such charges, Agnew warned, "might be actionable" and he might consult his lawyers about them. According to
the Baltimore *Sun*, however, charges that Agnew had called
Steinbock on the Pikesville apartment-house case had circulated
earlier, during the fight over Steinbock's ouster, and Agnew at
that time conceded he had called him. However, the *Sun* reported,
Agnew had explained that "it was simply to obtain information
about future hearing dates for the drawn-out testimony." But
Steinbock countered that it was hardly necessary to phone him at
home at midnight to obtain routine information readily available
at the appeals board office. Despite the seriousness of the allegation, the matter was dropped; no legal action was brought against
Agnew and none taken by him against Steinbock, and Agnew continued to govern as "the clean broom" the Baltimore *Sun* had proclaimed him to be. (After Agnew became Vice-President, Steinbock declined to discuss any aspect of the incident. "I'm not going
to discuss it in any manner whatsoever," he said in his office in
Catonsville. "Ted and I have agreed to call it a closed case. It was
a misinterpretation, perhaps, of what he wanted to say. Ted and I
are good friends and hope to stay that way." Accounts of the episode in the *Sun* were "distorted," Steinbock said, but when asked
to clear up any distortions he said irritably: "Why don't you just
forget it? Why bring it up at all? It's not important. It's a dead
issue.")

Later in 1965, Agnew found himself in hot water with the
Democratic county council over his previously undisclosed and
lucrative designation of three Republicans—one of them his old
Kiwanis buddy, Clarke Langrall—as insurance "brokers of
record" for the county. The matter came to light when the three
men began circulating their copies of the letter of authority,
which made them exclusive agents for a proposed multimillion-
dollar life and health-insurance plan for county and school board
employees. The designation infuriated the insurance broker in-

dustry, particularly because county open-bid specifications had gone out to sixty companies and brokers, with no mention that brokers of record existed.

According to the Democratic county council chairman, Frederick L. Dewberry, Jr., rumors of such an arrangement had circulated for some time, but when confronted with them at a private meeting of the council, Scott Moore, "speaking on behalf of the administration and Mr. Agnew, said, 'No, absolutely not.' He denied that there was any special deal cooking or anyone that was going to benefit from it. He assured us of this." Dewberry joined the insurance industry in criticizing Agnew. He called on him to repudiate "this closed political deal," and Gerald E. Mathison, a member of the Baltimore city insurance advisory board and sales representative of a large insurance company, observed, "If this isn't discrimination, nothing else is." But Agnew professed to see nothing wrong; it was only "the special interests" whining again. "The big brokers are putting the heat on the companies," he said, and he would not bow to them by rescinding the letter of authority.

When the first newspaper story on the matter broke, by Christopher Gaul in the *Sun*, Agnew was out of town. His aide, Dutch Moore, acknowledged it was a simple case of political patronage. This admission jarred Agnew's self-image as the citizen-administrator above politics, and on his return he called Gaul at home one night. "He told me I had misunderstood," Gaul recalls. "He wouldn't concede to the simple mechanism of political patronage. I don't think he ever saw himself as a politician; he saw himself as a respectable, responsible businessman, an administrator who kept the lid on. It was the bread and butter of politics to be able to respond to pressure, but he couldn't make it on that score. Any time there was aggressive questioning, he would bristle. His rhetoric was legal rhetoric, and he took refuge in his legalism. I don't think he saw it as taking refuge, but he tended to talk like that and he thought like that."

When Agnew finally gave a public explanation, the hair-splitting legalism of which Gaul spoke manifested itself. "Yes, it's patronage," the county executive conceded. "But bear in mind these are not just people picked to be the recipients of a political largesse. These are full-time insurance men." In other words, giving such authority to a Republican shoe salesman would have justified criticism, but not giving it to a Republican insurance broker. It was difficult always being right, but Agnew seemed to have no doubt that he always was, if one only looked closely enough. He acknowledged small errors, such as not having listed the brokers of record in the specifications mailed out to the industry. "Due to the press of other business" at the outset of his term, he said, he had forgotten to make the arrangement public. But on principle, he had nothing to apologize for, and much—his integrity—to defend. He called a meeting to explain the appointment and "correct the outrageous distortions and improper inferences" made by Dewberry, but specifically excluded the council chairman because "I have no intention of dignifying his charges with a personal reply."

One Democratic councilman who did attend, Dale Anderson, said the meeting "failed in its intent to clear the air. In fact, it further confused the whole issue." The *Sun* reported that when a Towson insurance consultant tried to ask Agnew critical questions, the county executive cut him off, gaveled the meeting to a close and stormed from the room. The famous Agnew back was up. "If I had it to do all over again," he told reporters after the meeting, "I'd never have appointed brokers of record. But to back off now would be tantamount to an admission of lack of integrity, and there is no impropriety here." A moralist on government, obviously, had to stick to his guns, no matter how rough the going got.

The critics were not placated, of course, by this righteous stance. Nor were they less incensed when they were reminded that one of the three designated brokers, Everett T. Hay, had headed a grand jury committee that recommended open competitive bidding on such business after having examined a county fund held by a local insurance company to pay commissions to agents. The fund had created a political stir at the time and had been used as a prime target by one candidate campaigning for reform—Spiro T. Agnew.

In the end, political muscle won out over Agnew's version of defensible patronage. Anderson said there was no doubt the Democratic council had jurisdiction over the insurance policy and would reject it if Agnew held fast. "If Mr. Agnew rescinds that letter appointing the brokers of record," he said, "we'll forget the whole thing. If he doesn't, we'll rescind it for him."

Having given his righteous indignation a good airing, Agnew buckled under, painting the council as a heartless villain in the process. Its threat, he said, "places me in a very difficult position. If I insist on maintaining a position which has been proved entirely correct I nonetheless jeopardize the welfare of three thousand eight hundred county employees who have already waited too long for these benefits. If, on the other hand, I revoke the broker-of-record letters I will be accused of attempting to bail myself out of an untenable position because of public pressure. Let me state that I consider the council's threat no idle gesture. They have already indicated a lack of sympathy for the employee benefits plan by once refusing to appropriate funds which I requested for it. It is not unreasonable to assume that the council would exercise this excuse to again delay the granting of these benefits to Baltimore County employees."

Such clashes as these demonstrated not only Agnew's unbending manner but also the way in which he unwittingly helped bring the Democrats out of their disarray of 1962, which had opened the door to Agnew's upset victory in the county. As he approached the close of his four-year term, it became clear to him that no matter what his record in office was, no matter how moderate or conservative he was, no matter how independent and hound's-tooth clean, he had no political future in Baltimore County. Despite all this, Scott Moore urged him to seek a second term. "No," Moore recalls Agnew telling him. "If I'm going to be defeated, I'd rather be defeated for governor than for county executive."

6

MOVING UP

ONE morning in mid-June of 1963, when Ted Agnew still was learning the ropes as Baltimore County's first Republican executive, he called in Scott Moore, the county solicitor and his closest political ally and adviser. "Let's go to Washington," Agnew said to him. "Why?" Moore asked. "I want to see Senator Kuchel," Agnew replied. "I'm going to back him for President."

Among those most prominently being mentioned as presidential prospects at that time, a full year before the 1964 Republican National Convention, the name of Thomas H. Kuchel of California had not been conspicuous. In fact, it had not been mentioned at all, except perhaps in liberal precincts of his own state. In mid-1963 Tommy Kuchel was the assistant minority leader of the United States Senate; bright, liberal, personable, very well liked, a favorite dinner companion in Washington social circles. But he never was regarded as a heavy, so in most appraisals he was put down as "a good senator" who had gone as far as he could go. Almost everybody who knew Tommy Kuchel would agree with that. But Ted Agnew did not know Kuchel, had never met him, and he did not agree with that. Agnew had looked over Kuchel's record and had read some of his speeches, including one made on the Senate floor condemning right-wing extremists. He concluded in the recesses of his own mind that here was the man the Republican party needed to rescue the country from the Democratic clutches of John F. Kennedy, who was of course expected to seek a second term in 1964. Agnew thereupon appointed himself as a committee of one to see to it, and with Scott Moore and his brother Dutch in tow for company, he set off for nearby Washington to so advise his unsuspecting candidate.

"Ted didn't have any qualms about going down to see a United States senator he hadn't ever seen before," Scott Moore recalls. "He just made up his mind Kuchel was the man, and that was it. Ted made a real pitch for him to be a liberal candidate. He said, 'I think you're from a state that maybe our presidential candidate has to come from. I like your views.'" Kuchel heard Agnew with pleasure and more seriousness than the mission deserved.

Agnew went back to Towson and thought about Kuchel and the shape of the Republican party. About six weeks after the meeting, he issued a statement unilaterally nominating Kuchel as the man "to lead a march of moderate Republicanism" in the image of Dwight Eisenhower and Wendell Willkie. "He's terrific," said the Agnew of 1963. "He talks like I think." The county executive expressed deep concern that the two prospective Republican candidates, Senator Barry M. Goldwater of Arizona and Governor Nelson A. Rockefeller of New York, would pull the party apart by 1964 unless a middle-road alternative was found. "The Republican party has reached a serious impasse," Agnew said. "Instead of being united behind a candidate with broad bipartisan appeal, it is nurturing within itself the seeds of its destruction, in the form of an absurd ideological struggle . . . between liberals and conservatives. Upset by labels, we Republicans are collectively suffocated by a defeatist attitude. . . . This ill-advised, nebulous struggle is getting us nowhere. This concern over a 'brand name' is utter nonsense because it is perfectly normal to be liberal on some issues and conservative on others." He called Kuchel "the courageous enemy of all political extremists" and the "leading exponent of the moderate viewpoint of Dwight Eisenhower."

Nobody, of course, rushed out and ordered "Kuchel for President" buttons on the strength of the endorsement by Baltimore County's obscure executive officer; the shortest unwritten chapter in The Making of the President, 1964, died stillborn. According to the Moores, Agnew never talked to Kuchel about it again, but his interest in the liberal Californian was noteworthy as a reflection of his political thinking at that time.

Recalling the overture, Kuchel said Agnew had "talked like a progressive Republican and linked me with Nelson Rockefeller as the kind of Republican the party needed." Apparently Agnew liked Rockefeller even then, but was looking for a stand-in who did not have quite the "brand name" that Rockefeller had.

In the next year Agnew focused much of his political activity, when he wasn't warring with the Democratic county council, on a struggle for the upper hand in county Republican affairs against his old conservative foe, Fife Symington, who wanted to deliver a Goldwater delegation to the national convention. In January 1964, Agnew urged county Republicans to avoid endorsing either Goldwater or Rockefeller because "neither represents the moderate course of progressive Republicanism"—a phrase borrowed from a letter to party leaders from the liberal Ripon Society in Cambridge. The party, he went on, needed a candidate "who shuns the liberal or conservative label [and] so far it seems that man has not entered the race for President. It is the responsibility of uncommitted Republican voters to wait until a candidate emerges who has a logical chance of commanding enthusiastic support of the majority of the electorate" before endorsing anyone.

The conservatives, trying to lock up the county delegation for Goldwater, responded sharply. "I don't think an elected official should say that the voters shouldn't make up their minds," said Eliot P. Hurd, chairman of the county branch of the state central committee. "I don't believe in this business of sitting on our hands. It's high time the Republican party in this state stand on its own two feet. Who gives a damn about what goes on in Cambridge?" Though Agnew professed to be a moderate, his interest in Kuchel and his espousal of the Ripon Society viewpoint in the quest for a 1964 candidate persuaded many conservatives that his antilabel talk was only a smoke screen to hide the fact that he really was, alas, a liberal.

Agnew, now obviously facing a drag-out fight in the conservative-dominated county committee, began to build an anti-Goldwater strategy. He and his supporters organized a $25-a-plate Agnew testimonial dinner for early May, the proceeds of which were to go to the primary fight for Republican delegates. Tickets were sold and other plans made, but the dinner was canceled when Agnew won agreement from Symington for a coalition delegation uncommitted to any candidate. Shortly afterward, however, county chairman Hurd abruptly resigned, charging that Agnew was setting up his own liberal political organization to circumvent the regular party structure in the county. Hurd estimated the canceled Agnew dinner had brought in $30,000 and he demanded to know what had become of the money. "The [party] workers want to know," he said. He charged that the money "is being used for his [Agnew's] war chest in 1966. . . . I'm not in favor of testimonial dinners to build up a treasury for that individual's use to the detriment of the party's candidates."

Agnew's endorsement of Senator Brewster as President Johnson's stand-in against George Wallace in the Democratic preferential primary put him on the winning side, but just barely, as Wallace rocked Maryland with 43 percent of the vote, his best effort among three impressive primary showings. He got 34 percent of the Democratic vote in Wisconsin and 30 percent in Indiana, and claimed long afterward that he had been denied outright victory in Maryland only by chicanery. In his 1968 third-party campaign for the Presidency, Wallace never tired of regaling crowds everywhere with his recollections of election night in the 1964 Maryland primary: "There I was ahead at about eleven o'clock and then they said they gonna re-cap-it-u-late the vote. Now, I don't know what that means, but I'll tell you, any time they say they gonna re-cap-it-u-late on you, you better watch out!"

While Wallace was sending chills up the backs of regular Democrats in Maryland and elsewhere, the Republican party nationally was cutting itself to pieces, as Agnew had predicted, in ideological combat between Goldwater and Rockefeller. In a comedy of incompetence, both candidates fell before a pickup campaign in New Hampshire in behalf of absent Henry Cabot Lodge; Rockefeller recovered somewhat with a victory in Oregon, but then lost narrowly to Goldwater in the key state of California. Meanwhile the Arizonan had also been nailing down the nonprimary states with a little-publicized but extremely effective grass-roots takeover of party caucuses. Richard Nixon, professing disinterest but fueling stop-Goldwater efforts surreptitiously in the hope the party finally would turn to him, succeeded in antagonizing everybody.

Out of all the chaos and the ashes of the Rockefeller candidacy, there finally emerged a last-ditch effort by Governor William

Scranton of Pennsylvania. Scranton had been a reluctant dragon all spring, but after Rockefeller folded, and encouraged by what he thought, erroneously, was an all-out endorsement by former President Eisenhower, he made an eleventh-hour drive to save the party from Goldwater. Agnew quickly embraced the effort. He became Maryland chairman for Scranton, who proclaimed his candidacy at the Maryland state convention and set off on one of the sorriest presidential candidacies on record. Agnew said he intended to vote for Scranton on the first ballot but would not bolt the party if Goldwater was nominated. So in August he stood in the Cow Palace in San Francisco as party conservatives interrupted Rockefeller with catcalls and serenaded Goldwater, rolling to a first-ballot nomination, with rebel yells. Scott Moore, who was standing at Agnew's side, remembers that Agnew was appalled at the treatment accorded Rockefeller and tried to get to him to tell him so, but could not get through the crush.

When Goldwater's nomination came, Agnew told reporters he would support him, but added, "We must work so that moderates can regain control of the party." And the next night, he again stood with Moore on the convention floor as Goldwater delivered his incredible invitation to party liberals to get lost, punctuated with his equally incredible invitation to party extremists to pull out all the stops: "Anyone who joins us in all sincerity we welcome. Those who do not care for our cause, we don't expect to enter our ranks in any case. . . . Extremism in the defense of liberty is no vice! . . . Moderation in the pursuit of justice is no virtue!"

Asked about the speech afterward, Agnew told reporters, "He could have gone a little further trying to ameliorate the disparate feelings of the delegates. . . . many things were excellent and well stated. It was a gung-ho sort of talk." But those who had been standing near him as Goldwater's words exploded through the frenzied convention hall heard Agnew remark after the "extremism" line, "God damn it! There goes the election. That's the ball game."

Agnew's preconvention opposition to Goldwater, and his obvious chagrin at his nomination, served to advance his own image as a liberal, or at least a moderate, within Maryland Republican ranks. As early as August 1964, speculation started about Agnew, as the highest-ranking G.O.P. officeholder in the state, running for statewide office. He said he was not interested in a candidacy for either attorney general or comptroller. Asked about the governorship, he observed: "There's always a possibility in politics. . . . [But] much remains to be done in Baltimore County, and in the two years just past we've made but a bare beginning."

By the end of 1964, however, Agnew's future in the county looked dim. His urban renewal program had failed, despite a knockdown fight; his public-accommodations bill barely got by the county council and was facing a referendum (which it eventually lost); integrationists were on him for going too slow and segregationists were on him for going too fast; a campaign to replace the county's three land-fill dumps with incinerators had encountered sharp neighborhood protests in all three areas involved; his efforts to have the state give local subdivisions the right to levy a local income tax had the taxpayers grousing. On top of all this, the county was still heavily Democratic in registration, and Mike Birmingham had died, easing the intraparty split among the Democrats. Again, as in the past, Agnew began to think about the possibilities of a judgeship. A leading Democrat in the state even went to Governor J. Millard Tawes, a Democrat, and suggested to him that if Agnew were appointed to the bench, Agnew would not run for governor—to which Tawes reportedly replied, "Who's Agnew?"

As Agnew persevered through the remainder of his term, he preached party unity at every turn, aware of what the Goldwater split had done in the county, the state and the nation. The party was down, but it was not out, and when Republican John V. Lindsay won the race for mayor in New York City, in one of the few 1965 races with national implications, Agnew shared the general rejoicing. There was, however, one ominous element that he deplored—the opposition candidacy waged against Lindsay on the Conservative ticket by another Republican, columnist William F. Buckley, Jr. That example might lead to other split campaigns among Republicans, he feared. "But if the candidate can surmount the difficulties the way Lindsay did," said Agnew, the man who in 1970 was to help engineer the defeat of Republican Senator Charles E. Goodell of New York by Bill Buckley's brother Jim, "it will quickly go out of favor."

In August of 1965, according to Dutch Moore, Agnew discussed the possibilities of running for governor with two Democrats, Harry Dundore, the head of a large machine shop and a wealthy man who much impressed Agnew, and Chris Kahl, the old Democratic party power in Baltimore County. They told him the prospects of a tough Democratic primary were good, thus enhancing the chances of any respectable Republican challenger. "Scott tried to talk him out of it, that it was too quick after being elected county executive, but there just wasn't anybody else," Dutch Moore said. Agnew began a series of meetings with G.O.P. committees around the state, with the state's national committeeman and committeewoman, D. Eldred Rinehart and Kitty Massenburg, as key contacts. About $4,500 was spent on a series of dinners at which Agnew was introduced to G.O.P. leaders and for incidental expenses, and that was all the nomination cost him, Dutch Moore said.

On the advice of Democratic friends, Agnew had also contacted Irvin Kovens, a Baltimore clothier, sportsman and long-time Democratic money raiser. Kovens had met Agnew a few times socially, and went to lunch with him at The Tail of the Fox, a popular Baltimore County restaurant, to hear him out. Agnew told Kovens he believed he could get the Republican nomination without a primary fight and Kovens agreed to raise money for him. Just why this prominent Democrat would fill this role for a Republican he hardly knew never has been adequately explained. Kovens himself said in an interview it simply was because he felt Agnew had done a good job as county executive. But skeptics noted that Kovens became an owner of a Charlestown, West Virginia, race track in September 1965, and a Maryland governor could be helpful in making sure racing dates in Maryland did not conflict with those in West Virginia. Kovens denied this factor had anything to do with his efforts for Agnew, noting that Charlestown has flat racing at night, and that the lights for it were installed before he bought a share of the track, which he has since sold. Flat racing in Maryland—at Pimlico, Bowie and Laurel—is all in the daytime, though Maryland does have harness racing at night.

Eventually Kovens became one of nine fund raisers who met with Agnew through 1966 at the Chesapeake Building in Towson to consider campaign money matters. The others were Harry Dundore; Clarke Langrall, one of the insurance brokers of record in the earlier county insurance plan controversy; J. Walter Jones, a wealthy Towson real estate man who became one of Agnew's chief private advisers in Annapolis and a partner in a land deal that later hatched another controversy; George White, Agnew's lawyer; I. H. "Bud" Hammerman, another real estate man and old friend; Tilton Dobbin, president of the Maryland National Bank and the campaign treasurer; Paul Hampshire, a subcontractor; and Gus Constantine, a one-time variety-store owner and ultimately an Agnew aide in Washington. Kovens became particularly helpful among Democrats unhappy about the candidate their party primary eventually produced.

At a September meeting of Republican leaders Agnew received assurances that he would have the party endorsement, almost by default, if he ran for governor. After the meeting Agnew told the press he would "seriously consider" the race if a Democratic primary battle appeared imminent by the early part of 1966. "I am holding myself for the possibility of running for governor, of running for county executive again, and for the possibility of not running for anything." But those who knew the political realities, and the man, were convinced now it would be the first option, and it was.

In Agnew's interest in the State House, the work of one Republican governor stood out in his mind above all others to emulate—Nelson Rockefeller. Although Agnew had regarded Rockefeller as an unmarketable alternative to Goldwater in 1964, he had come to change his mind, partly as a result of an exposure to the New York governor at a meeting on water pollution in 1965. "Ted liked the way Rockefeller got things done," Scott Moore recalls. "He sent me to New York to go over his complete legislative record. From then on he was really hung up on Rocky." While Agnew was still county executive, Dutch Moore says, he had begun to think of Rockefeller as the party's next national candidate. After the Goldwater debacle, he says, "Ted wanted to be in there backing a liberal who had a chance of winning."

Around this time Agnew also wrote to Richard Nixon to sound him out on his political plans, although he didn't know Nixon either. "He wrote him about November and didn't get an answer until maybe January or February," Dutch Moore recalls. "This was when Nixon was in his law firm. I can remember Ted yet, saying, 'That damn Nixon, he won't even answer your letters. No wonder he can't get elected.' "

What Nixon eventually wrote to Agnew, Moore says he does not know. But by this time, the winter of 1965–66, Agnew had resolved whatever doubts he may have had about running for governor. He began to shop around for the prime requisite of the unknown but moneyed candidate—a good advertising agency. Many of his associates were high on a young eager beaver named Robert Goodman, a sharp, imaginative fellow who in both style and appearance was Baltimore's answer to Madison Avenue. In 1959 Bob Goodman had taken a timeworn downtown Baltimore house and converted it into a tasteful, swinging adman's office, whence he now sallies forth, leather-coated and brimful of inspirations, hops into a sleek foreign sports car and darts around town and country selling his ideas and his clients. He is a smaller version of Hollywood's "Derek Flint," James Coburn; his zest and the same faintly demoniac grin make him seem at times more like a featured player in a stereotyped movie about the advertising business than the real thing. But Bob Goodman is the real thing, as Agnew and the voters of Maryland soon came to realize.

Up to that time, the Goodman Agency had not done much political advertising. In fact, one of its most recent efforts had been a losing one in behalf of Chris Kahl, Agnew's predecessor as county executive, in Kahl's primary fight against Mike Birmingham in 1962. Bills went unpaid and a bad aftertaste lingered. At the time, Goodman had already received a feeler from State Attorney General Tom Finan, who was going to be the regular Democratic organization candidate for governor. Goodman was not impressed with Finan as a candidate, so the next day he phoned Agnew, whom he had met only once, in the office of former Baltimore Mayor Theodore McKeldin. Goodman and two assistants were invited, with some reluctance it seemed, to make a presentation to Agnew in competition with several other agencies. No sooner had one of Goodman's associates, Dick Zeinog, begun the presentation than Agnew broke in and asked about the Kahl account. He said he had heard something about "padded bills." Zeinog, who had been busy trying to collect on campaign expenses paid by the agency, made a heated defense. "Agnew got red from his neck up, and he gave me that look," Zeinog recalls. "Bob joined in too, and when we were finished we shook hands all around and left. Agnew was very cool, and we didn't particularly care either—we figured we had the Finan account in the bank back in the office."

Shortly afterward, Agnew called Goodman and told him his agency had been selected. Goodman's first brainchild was to use a motto, "Think Big," and put giant posters of Agnew all over the state. But he soon thought little of his own idea and scrapped it. Instead, he came up with an approach that, more than anything else, was credited with boosting Agnew's low-recognition factor. He wrote new lyrics to the Jimmy Van Heusen–Sammy Cahn song "My Kind of Town, Chicago Is" and saturated the airwaves with "My Kind of Man, Ted Agnew Is."

"We didn't know who we were going to fight in the general election," Goodman said later, "so the 'My Kind of Man' theme just seemed right for us then, because he could be any kind of man you wanted him to be. We decided we'd hang loose until we saw who our opponent was going to be; we would try to get some name recognition built up for our candidate, and a certain kind of image, so that by September after the primary was over and we knew who we were fighting, we would at least be equal in terms of recognition and could go on from there. And of course we did go on from there with what you might call a fear campaign, where we screamed to the world, 'Come to the aid of Maryland!' "

To sell Agnew on the "My Kind of Man" theme, Goodman took Frank Sinatra's best-selling, swinging rendition of the song to Agnew's home and played it for him, showing him the new lyrics at the same time. Agnew bought the concept enthusiastically, and to make the campaign song similar to the zestful Sinatra style, Goodman hired a New York singer, Jack Carroll, to record it. "It really was great," Goodman associate Ron Wilner recalls. "But we got more complaints about a man singing 'My Kind of Man.' Everywhere I went people complained to me. At a rally, somebody came up and said, 'Hey, how can you do that to Agnew? You're killing him with a man singing that song.' So we had to get a gal to sing it." Stella Stevens, a New Yorker who specializes in commercials—her gravel-voiced "The closer you shave, the more you need Noxzema" was a recent favorite—got the job, and her voice boomed out all over Maryland throughout 1966.

The words were as noncommittal as Goodman could make them:

> *My kind of man, Ted Agnew is;*
> *My kind of man, Ted Agnew is;*
> *A bright light shining, Ted Agnew is;*

That new day dawning, Ted Agnew is;
A time to move Maryland
With our kind of man.

Against the musical background of the song, a man's voice
came on with a narration that said as much as the lyric did: "Just
a song. But we say that Ted Agnew is your kind of man for governor of Maryland, because he's the kind of down-to-earth, get-
things-done, nothing-short-of-excellence leader we had always
hoped for. Let's not miss this chance we have with Ted Agnew. If
there's work, let's do it. If there's a song, let's sing it. This is just
the beginning."

On April 17, 1966, Ted Agnew officially entered the race. He
had no serious primary opposition, but nevertheless mounted an
active, media-oriented campaign, hoping to use the primary election spotlight to get himself better known around the state. Under
Goodman's guidance, he bombarded every available radio and television outlet during the primary period, which stretched into
September. Spots presented him saying little, and looking sincere
and hard-working while saying it. One pictured him at work in
his office, jacket off, shirt sleeves rolled up, tie loosened. Few who
saw him in those days, however, have that recollection of him. He
was then, as he is now, fastidious in his appearance. But image-
making had to be served, even for a no-nonsense public servant
like Spiro Agnew. Because there would not be sufficient time to
mount an effective campaign from a standing start in September,
Agnew ran against the Democratic field all spring and summer,
until the voters of the opposition party had worked their will and
selected a single target for him.

Not in his wildest dreams could he have imagined the Democratic electorate would be so good to him. Two major candidates
were considered to be in contention in the Democratic primary—
State Attorney General Tom Finan, the party loyalist endorsed by
the regulars and by retiring Governor Tawes, and Congressman-
at-large Carleton R. Sickles, a bona-fide liberal with strong support in Baltimore and the Maryland suburbs of Washington.
Finan was rated the favorite, but the presence of a third candidate, an ultraconservative perennial named George P. Mahoney,
could conceivably drain off some redneck votes from Finan and
help Sickles. Mahoney, however, was an old political horse who
had gone around the track too often—or so everybody thought.

He had run and lost in seven statewide races and his candidacy had taken on the aspect of a local joke. George Mahoney, however, had two things going for him. One was money—he was a wealthy paving contractor who had no reluctance to spend freely. The other was the white backlash. The same rich lode of racial prejudice and fear that George Wallace had mined so blatantly and effectively two years earlier still was coursing through the subterranean body politic of Maryland, and George Mahoney was just the man to extract it to fuel his campaign.

He adopted a slogan of which George Wallace himself could have been proud: "Your Home Is Your Castle—Protect It!" The motto needed no translation for the liberals and moderates who deplored it as a naked appeal to white fears of integrated neighborhoods, nor for the conservatives and outright segregationists who embraced it as a rallying cry and a simple return to sanity. The Democratic liberals, backing Sickles, and the moderates and party regulars, supporting Finan, made the fatal political mistake of underestimation, and they happily went at one another while Mahoney resolutely tapped the ugly lode. Talk about open housing finally reached scare proportions, but by that time the lines were drawn. The liberal-moderate vote irreconcilably split between Sickles and Finan, and to the utter shock of the "good people" of Maryland, Mahoney squeezed through with the nomination by less than 2,000 votes over Sickles. And in Maryland, the Democratic nomination nearly always was the ball game.

The jolt of the Mahoney nomination was particularly jarring because of the lateness of the primary. Now it was mid-September; only eight weeks separated the state from the shocking but real prospect that it would be led by a totally inexperienced, die-hard segregationist. It was shocking and yet it was happening, and not only in Maryland but in three other Southern states where the white backlash had turned politics upside down. In Arkansas, rabid segregationist Jim Johnson was the Democratic nominee; in Alabama it was Lurleen Wallace, wife of the master-backlasher himself; in Georgia it was Lester Maddox, whose earlier answer to integration was the brandished ax handle. This motley field caused Richard Nixon, playing his usual role as volunteer clairvoyant for anyone listening, to write in a syndicated column: "While my optimism about national Republican prospects has sharply increased, my prediction in the South must be revised—

downward. The reason is that the Democratic Party—in a desperate throw of the dice—has gambled upon racism, demagogy and the backlash to win for it what the caliber of its candidates cannot. The gamble will pay off in some backwaters of the South. But the Democratic Party has made a fatal mistake. It has risked the next generation, just to win this next election."

Maryland, however, hardly considered itself one of the "backwaters of the South," nor should it have. The contemplation of a Governor Mahoney provided a catalyst in the political community that no amount of Madison Avenue issue-making could have generated. All at once Ted Agnew, whose nomination on the Republican ticket had gone without serious challenge, found himself the beneficiary. Liberal and moderate Democrats fell over each other in the rush to appropriate Agnew as a vehicle for averting the disaster of a Mahoney administration. Victory for Mahoney would mean they would have to deliver up not only their state but also their party—for some an even more catastrophic contemplation.

Agnew had come through the primary in good shape, weathering at least two sticky disclosures that raised more questions about his sense of propriety than about his integrity and honesty. Against either Finan or Sickles these disclosures might have destroyed what little chance he had to win the governorship; against Mahoney they were lost in the holy crusade the gubernatorial campaign became. Yet they are of interest for the insight they provide into the narrow legalism of Agnew's approach to what is proper conduct, above criticism, for a man in public life—at least when *he* is that man.

The first concerned a private war Agnew was waging against gambling. Almost from the outset of his term as county executive, he had been at odds with the county council, which had a six-to-one Democratic majority. He had started by announcing grand plans to meet regularly with the council to inform the members of his legislative plans, but the council rejected his first major appointment, of former law associate Edward Hardesty to be deputy zoning commissioner. In short order, Agnew was dispatching Scott Moore to deal with the council. Unlike Agnew's Republican counterpart in Anne Arundel County (Annapolis), Joseph Alton, who established such rapport with his council members that he ran on a slate with five of them who were Democrats, the Baltimore County executive dealt with his council as an adversary, not as a partner. And in no case was this arrangement more divisive than in a fight he waged over pinball machines.

For years Agnew had been a righteous foe of pinballs, labeling them the scourge of youth and adolescence, calling on Governor Tawes to outlaw them throughout the state, warning that schoolchildren were going without lunch in order to play the machines. To tavern owners in the county, however, they were an attraction to customers and a source of income, and an effective lobby labored in support of them. In the spring of 1966, after the council had turned back the latest Agnew attempt to outlaw pinballs, he introduced a proposal to raise the annual license fee from $125 a machine to $2,500, far more than its cost. When the council rejected that, too, Agnew publicly charged that it was "under complete domination of the gambling fraternity"—though his friend and the only Republican on the council, Jervis Finney, had voted with the Democrats. County police officials, including Agnew's friend Robert Lally, were called by the council and asked for their knowledge of any link between the pinball operation and organized crime, but none was produced. Council president Francis A. Dewberry called Agnew's charge "shocking and scurrilous," and said "such low-grade political smear tactics against a group of public officials should be below a member of the Maryland bar and candidate for the highest office in this state."

Later the same year, when Scott Moore ran for county executive against Democrat Dale Anderson to succeed Agnew, John Bartenfelder, a prominent pinball-machine distributor, signed an affidavit saying he had made a $1,000 contribution to Agnew's campaign in 1962. Agnew called the charge "absolutely false. I have never solicited or received any contribution from the pinball interests," he said. "As a matter of fact if I were beholden to these interests I would not have made three strong efforts to rid the county of these machines." However, Dutch Moore said later in an interview, "The truth of the matter was Scott [Moore] got a $1,000 contribution during Ted's campaign for county executive and probably hedged on Ted a little bit [informing him about it]." Later, when Agnew was governor, a grand jury called him in on the matter, but took no action. Dutch Moore observed, "I think today he'd say, 'Yes, I got it. Scott's told me that I got it.' "

In August 1966, a month before the gubernatorial primary, a story broke alleging that Mahoney had been offered a huge bribe by the slot-machine interests. Mahoney immediately denied it. But Agnew, possibly sensing political gain, revealed in an interview that he had been offered $200,000 in the form of campaign contributions by slot-machine interests if he would promise not to veto legislation extending the life of slot machines. A bill had been passed in 1963 phasing out all slot machines in four southern Maryland counties by mid-1968. "On three separate occasions," Agnew reported, "I was approached with deals involving the slot machines. The offer at first was twenty thousand dollars, then went to seventy-five thousand dollars and not two weeks ago it jumped to two hundred thousand dollars. All I had to do was agree not to oppose or veto legislation which might pass the General Assembly extending the life of the machines. I told those who approached me on the deals that I didn't even want to talk to the slot people."

Agnew's revelation was a bombshell, though he didn't seem to be particularly impressed with its ramifications. When Frank Newell, the Baltimore County state's attorney, insisted Agnew had "a public duty" to provide the full facts on the bribe attempt, Agnew said flatly he had "no intention" of revealing the names of the persons who had contacted him. He did not believe, he said, "there was any criminal act unless a definite offer is made by the person who is making the bribe." He had been approached "by an innocent person" acting as an intermediary relaying the information "second or third hand." But Newell rejoined that if a "genuine offer" was made it constituted an "attempted bribe," and Agnew was "compounding the action by remaining silent." To this, Agnew said, "Literally hundreds of people come up with similar suggestions during a campaign. I'm sure they've been made to every candidate." But Mahoney had denied he had been approached. The $200,000 figure, Agnew said, had been mentioned to him "on the basis that if I were at all interested, someone would be in touch with me."

Agnew agreed to meet with Newell but was adamant. "Unless someone can show me that a crime was committed I am not going to reveal his name," he said of the man who had approached him. There was no "illegality" in the offer, Agnew insisted. "Nobody sat down in front of me with a suitcase full of money." And he used the occasion to renew his war on pinball machines. "The thing that makes this politically unacceptable is that it involves slot people," Agnew was quoted as saying. Although he was "one hundred percent against slot machines," he said, "their backers are being discriminated against. Pinball machines operate legally throughout the state because they carry a federal gambling stamp. Those people live a charmed life." Agnew never did disclose the name of the person who he said had approached him.

The second charge involving Agnew in the 1966 campaign was one that received a later, nationwide airing in the 1968 presidential campaign—that he had bought land near the shore of Chesapeake Bay in anticipation of construction of a second bridge crossing the bay onto the Eastern Shore of Maryland. The General Assembly had approved construction parallel to an existing bridge, but advocates of a more northern site were forcing a statewide referendum on the issue.

Although friends of Agnew, including J. Walter Jones, said later that Agnew had purposely revealed the transaction as part of a full disclosure of his assets, according to Jerome Kelly, a reporter for the Baltimore *Evening Sun*, that was not the case. Interviewing Agnew for a profile in early July, Kelly asked him where he stood on the second bridge location. Agnew casually volunteered that he owned some land near the existing bay bridge, and that he held the land with eight partners, including Jones and two other fellow directors of the Chesapeake National Bank in Towson, Harry Dundore and Leonard C. Gerber. (Agnew had become a director of the bank early in his term as county executive. Later, when he became governor, his new title was placed prominently under his name at the head of the list of directors on the bank's letterhead. This association, like the bay-bridge land deal, was to be challenged later, in Agnew's 1968 race for the Vice-Presidency.) He said he owned a one-ninth interest in the 107 acres of property, valued at $267,000 and located about two miles from the existing bay bridge. Records showed the group had bought the land in June 1965, about six months after Governor Tawes first introduced plans for a parallel span at the same location.

Before Kelly's interview, an independent candidate for governor, Baltimore City Comptroller Hyman A. Pressman, and Democratic Congressman Clarence Long had been hounding Agnew to sign a petition favoring a more northern crossing. Agnew had said he would add his signature "in my own time," but he told

Kelly he had "never gotten around" to signing the petition. "This is why I haven't taken a position on the bridge," he said. "The only thing I can do is disclose my holding and say I'm awfully glad it (the bridge site decision) is going to referendum." There was no conflict of interest involved, Agnew insisted, because the land was not in Baltimore County. "I see no impropriety of any kind," he said, "in holding property outside my jurisdiction. . . . I will certainly sell it if I am elected." Agnew said he had paid $5,000 in cash in the deal, and that mortgages and a personal loan brought his total investment to $34,200. "I feel that this disclosure was complete and timely," he said. "I don't expect you to believe it but when this transaction was being worked out, not one of us said anything about the parallel bridge. It didn't occur to us." Agnew said he had been "looking around for a good investment and I had been prohibited from buying in Baltimore County," so went outside the county.

But if there was no legal conflict of interest, there certainly was a question about the propriety of the county executive going into such a major business deal with men, particularly Jones, who did so much business with the county. It was disclosed, for instance, that Jones had received more than $24,000 for county land-appraisal work in the previous two years, said to be about half the county's total payments for such work. Others in the deal were W. Ernest Issel, like Gerber an official of McCormick and Company; Robert O. Crampton, president of the Schilling spice firm of San Francisco, a McCormick affiliate; Harry T. Solomon, a Westinghouse Corporation executive; Lester Matz and John C. Childs, members of Matz, Childs and Associates, a consulting engineering firm that had done a great deal of work for the county; and Allen C. Jackson, then advertising director of the Annapolis *Evening Capital*.

Discussing the deal much later in his Annapolis office, Jones gave this version: "I ordinarily don't take partners, but there was a piece of land in Anne Arundel County and Agnew, being county executive in Baltimore County, could not or would not get involved in any investment that had to do with Baltimore County, because as county executive he might have to pass on public works or something like this. Well, I'd gotten a call from this fellow over in Anne Arundel County who said this piece of land was available . . . The property was located, I'd guess, several miles from the bay bridge and Revell Highway. . . . I happened to be over in Annapolis one time and ran into him and he said, 'I'd like you to take a look at this land.' . . . We drove by, and it was a piece of land, anybody could have bought it, it was for sale for years and years and the sign was very, very rusty. [Since] there was some financing involved . . . I talked to some of my friends who had not been investing with me but were friends in other areas, and I talked with County Executive Agnew—'This is a piece of land in Anne Arundel County that would give you no conflict or anything else.' So I got nine people together; Agnew was one of the nine. . . . This was long before Agnew even thought about running for governor, and you would have to assume that he knew he was going to run for governor and that he could get a bridge across. They were talking about four or five alternatives for the bridge and there was tremendous resistance to the bridge. But, you see, there was already a bridge. The value of this land didn't relate to a bridge going from the Western Shore to the Eastern Shore. The future value of this land had to do with the fact it was near Annapolis, Washington and Baltimore. Going to the Eastern Shore, there just wasn't that much activity there. The bridge didn't even enter the picture at all. But even if it had, what did that have to do with a man who had never thought about running for governor?"

Pressman and Congressman Long, however, thought it had a lot to do with a man who since the purchase had decided to run. The fact that he had held the property without disclosure for more than a year, Long charged, "raises the question of his fitness to make a sound decision on the bridge location if elected governor." (There is reason to believe, according to Kelly, that foes of the parallel-bridge site were about to expose Agnew's land purchase, and that fear of such disclosure led Agnew to reveal the deal. When Kelly brought up the subject of the second bay bridge in a general way, Agnew volunteered the information about his land deal, immediately producing supporting documents. That night Kelly encountered Christopher Pfrommer, an aide to Congressman Long, and told him about Agnew's disclosure. Pfrommer blurted out an expletive and said he had been looking into ownership of land by Agnew in Anne Arundel County.)

Dutch Moore, himself a real estate man, said later there was "no credibility at all to the fact that they bought the land hoping that a second bay bridge went into that area; it wasn't close enough to the approaches so that it would be taken by the state. The industrial impact around that bridge," he said, "is already there. The second bay bridge doesn't change the picture as far as industry going into the area." The profit, he said, would have been in getting the land rezoned from agricultural to industrial use and thus increasing the value of the property. "The whole thing bad about the deal—and I never saw it brought out if anybody wanted to criticize the deal—it was because Ted was in a deal with Walter Jones, who was doing business with the county. . . . Strictly from the viewpoint of two men, Lester Matz and Walter Jones . . . Ted could call the shots on the contracts with respect to the type of business these two men do. Walter does appraising business, and it's a type of patronage. In other words, any professional appraiser can come into the county and request business. It's up to the county to decide . . . and obviously the department heads look to the administrative officer or the county executive for some guidance in who to select. . . . Previous county commissioners were in land speculation deals here in the county. . . . I give Ted credit for at least going out of the county if he was going to do any land speculation. The irony of it is, they didn't get their zoning, even after Ted got out of this thing. . . . It was speculation all the way."

Agnew, according to Jones, was "very upset" about the furor because "of course he had never been involved in a situation where anybody ever questioned his integrity." A day or two after the disclosure, Agnew said he was "very seriously thinking of disposing of the land. The transaction," he insisted, "was above reproach but it seems my opponents want to foist political implications on it. I want to give this a day or two of thought before I take any action. . . . My name was the first on the deed and the land records are open to the public. There obviously was no conflict with my public duties, since the land is not in Baltimore County."

The same day, Agnew announced he had decided to sell the land at cost—but not before turning the matter into an attack on his critics. The charges by Pressman and Long, he said, were "consistent with their often-demonstrated philosophy of government that calls for personal political gain at any price." In other words, evil sees as evil does. The land, he said, "has an excellent industrial potential and I purchased my share as proven investment for my family's future." But despite the "excellent industrial potential" of which Agnew spoke, when Agnew's share of the land was put up for auction along with Jones's a year later, there was only one bid—from the remaining seven partners, who bought it for $13,200 over the original cost to Agnew.

Agnew also delivered one other parting shot. No other public officials or candidates had divulged their finances, he noted; he called on all of them to reveal their land interests. But he would be bigger about the matter than his critics were, Agnew promised. "If such disclosures should indicate recently purchased investment property within one's own political bailiwick and near a government installation about which he is in a position to have superior knowledge," he said, "I assure you I shall not do as he did and attempt to make a cheap political issue out of it."

The next day, however, Agnew publicly charged that Long had bought a 112-acre farm in Harford County, Maryland, one month before the state roads commission began buying up adjacent rights-of-way for a proposed northern throughway. The transaction, Agnew said, was "an unusual coincidence." Long replied that he had paid $118,000 for the farm and had publicized the purchase when it was made, in June 1965. Of his day-old promise, Agnew said, "I previously said I would not make a political issue of such a thing as this, but this purchase of Mr. Long's is such a flagrant conflict of interest that I had to speak out. Mr. Long's characterization of his land deal as 'a long-term investment' just won't bear scrutiny. A more likely explanation would be that Mr. Long's property would make an ideal motel or restaurant site, once the northern throughway has been completed, to house the many relatives and friends of servicemen visiting the Aberdeen Proving Grounds from out of state." In this case, obviously, it was good sees as evil does. Long pointed out that his land was thirty miles from the proposed throughway. Reflecting on the incident later, Long said, "That's Agnew. He manufactures an opponent in order to hit him. He's very good at it. He came up to me one day and said, 'Look, both of us have good images. Let's stop this.' He's really a full-time public relations man."

Shortly afterward Agnew made a full disclosure of his financial assets, totaling about $86,000. They included joint ownership with his wife of their Towson home, with an equity of about $15,-000 and a mortgage indebtedness of about $23,000; bank accounts of $21,200, of which more than half, he said, was money left to him by his parents; $11,000 in stock left to him by his father; $3,240 in stock purchased himself in the Mount Vernon Mills Textile Company of Baltimore; $1,650 in a piece of property in the Virgin Islands; a row house in Baltimore left to him by his parents, estimated at $15,000, in which his Aunt Teddy still lived; accumulated pension savings of about $5,000 in the Baltimore County employees retirement system; two Buicks valued at about $2,500; $50,000 in life insurance, including GI insurance, with a cash surrender value of $7,000. "And that is all," Agnew said, "except my interest in the Revell Highway property and my two most valuable assets, a wonderful wife and four fine children, and the good name I enjoyed before all this adverse publicity."

There was, of course, more than one kind of publicity. All the while the people of Maryland were hearing the Agnew name linked to the pinball, slot-machine and bay-bridge controversies, they also were hearing it float unspecifically and innocuously on the airwaves across the state, in Bob Goodman's theme song. Commenting on the "My Kind of Man" ditty a few days before the September 13 primary, Agnew observed: "Some people hate it, some like it. But they don't forget the name and that's the purpose. When the primary is over, we'll get down to serious discussion of issues. I'm not going to push the show business aspect. I intend to campaign on very positive issues and not scratch the surface such as they [the Democrats] have done in superficial position papers that I have seen thus far."

Others in the Agnew campaign, however, had other plans, especially since the opposition turned out to be George Mahoney. "Of course we did go on from there," as Bob Goodman testified later, "with what you might call a fear campaign." But it was a fear campaign based on a widespread concern among moderates and liberals that Maryland was going the way of racism and bigotry. The "good people" of Maryland were too preoccupied with that fear to worry that in the tactics of their new Republican knight in shining armor, there might be more than a modicum of the excess that so frightened them in Mahoney.

7

THE HOLY LIBERAL CRUSADE

FOUR weeks after Ted Agnew won the Republican gubernatorial primary and pledged to talk issues to the voters of
Maryland, and four weeks before the voters would decide between
him and Democrat George P. Mahoney, the Agnew campaign was
traveling the high road. Position papers were spun out and issue-
oriented speeches delivered by the candidate with all the dignity
and reserve that his status as the citizen-politician demanded. But
according to Edgar Feingold, Agnew's former human relations
commission aide and chief public relations adviser in the 1966
campaign, Ted Agnew was a crashing bore.

"The great crunch arose," Feingold recalls, "because Ted was so
deadly dull. He was getting no press coverage; he was fooling
around with these large conceptual things and getting nowhere.
We had polls taken that showed what he had to do. He had to
reach out to the liberals and the blacks in Baltimore City and
County." An analysis of more than sixty pages based on extensive
public opinion polling was prepared, and a memorandum went to
the candidate. It began:

TO: Spiro T. Agnew
FROM: Edgar L. Feingold
RE: The Politics of This Election

The election is four weeks away—it is time to shift the emphasis of the campaign from the cerebral to the visceral. During the preceding months, you have proposed and presented details of your program for the state. It is acknowledged that you are thoughtful about the issues, articulate about the problems and well-briefed about the specifics.

Against that background, it is critical now to begin an emotional appeal to the voter, to arouse and spark his interest, to compel his attention, and to bring him to the polls out of a sense of urgency and commitment.

This is not to say that you forego future discussion of issues or cut back the issuance of position papers or statements on the issues. But, the central theme of the campaign should shift from one oriented exclusively to the issues to one focused on attracting Democratic voters to your side. . . .

At the Goodman Agency, the same thinking prevailed. An internal memorandum was prepared entitled "Points to Stress with Mr. Agnew," and it began:

> He has waged a constructive campaign. He has laid the groundwork of a strong, intelligent well-thought-out treatment of the many issues in this campaign.
>
> We are facing an opponent who has an emotional issue and we agree that the best way that we can overcome it is with an even stronger, longer, deeper, wider, even more emotional campaign than that of this opponent. This issue is that of the KKK [Ku Klux Klan] and the fanatical extremists who are supporting the candidacy of this opponent. We would like to bring the campaign together in a unified climax as it is closing, so that the voters will see a clear choice. . . . This entire approach does not preclude appealing to the higher and more refined instincts of the voters on an inspirational level, such as employing the words "Crusade for Conscience" to counterbalance the more emotional issue.

In the jargon of Madison Avenue, Agnew had run his good-government banner up the flagpole, and nobody was saluting. In fact, in at least one instance, his issue talk was getting him into hot water with the blacks and liberals he needed. He had started off in August by telling a black group, "I deplore the silence on the part of many candidates, who feel safer dodging the issues of civil rights. . . . Open housing, for example, is an issue very much on people's minds. Is it enough just to say 'I'm for it' or 'I'm against it'? This is a period of major transition for the civil rights movement. Transition sometimes brings with it temporary confusion and profound impatience. I can understand this impatience at a time when the movement is groping for new directions. In this period of uncertainty and change, friends are mistaken for enemies. Let there be no mistake on this: I am your friend." A month later, however, Agnew told a group of newsmen: "If an open-housing bill affecting the right of the individual homeowner to sell to whomever he wishes is passed, I would veto it."

This observation was taken among influential blacks as a rollback on his previous support of limited open housing. Agnew compared to Mahoney was a radical on integration, but also in the field as an independent was the liberal Hyman Pressman; if Pressman siphoned off enough votes from Agnew, Mahoney could win. Agnew aides passed the word to the blacks that their man was sorry he had phrased his answer on open housing the way he had. But at the same time he did not want to become the identifiable black man's candidate and thus feel the whip of the white backlash. "The word 'veto,' " he told a group of 150 Montgomery County Democrats a few days later, "may have been somewhat strong. I would be inclined to leave the question of constitutionality to the courts." He would accept open-housing legislation applying to existing private homes, he said, "if it were passed by a strong vote and if there were public sentiment for it." Another staff memo warned of the same pitfall:

> Discussion of the open-housing issue should NOT be initiated by Mr. Agnew. If questioned, he should answer that his position has been stated and restated, and that he stands on what he has said. He can turn any questions in this area to his advantage by observing that there are no quick and easy solutions to the problem, but with him in the State House the problem will be considered and resolved in a reasonable way. On the other hand, the Mahoney position can only bring turmoil in the state.

That was the emerging strategy—make the issue Mahoney, pure and simple. Another section of the same memo urged:

> Mr. Agnew should underscore and stress his moderate stance. He should draw a comparison between himself as a qualified, able and sensible candidate and Mahoney as a reactionary, inept, unqualified candidate whose only experience is that he has been a candidate

seven times. Mahoney should be exposed as a man who will not only retard the growth of progress of the state but will drag it back fifty years. Pressman should be exposed as a political opportunist whose programs and bleatings are impractical, unworkable and expedient.

In other words, the mission was for Agnew to be an emotional voice of reason. It was not an easy assignment, and from the tone of the introductory observations in some of the memos, the counselors of the citizen-politician apparently felt the need to butter him up a bit for his profundity before asking him to descend into the pit of political hand-to-hand combat. (One of the private polls, categorizing Maryland candidates with other politicians as they were perceived on the political spectrum, placed Spiro Agnew squarely in the "moderate" group with George Romney, Millard Tawes and the average voter. George Mahoney was in a group called "conservative with moderate leanings"—with Richard Nixon. But shortly before the election, Nixon issued a statement of support for his fellow Republican, whom he had never met. "Mahoney is exploiting and trying to gain on the race issue," Nixon said. "But he is not going to win. Ted Agnew will win over Mahoney because Ted is superbly qualified and the other fellow isn't.")

Mahoney himself had been in the pit all along, characterizing both Agnew and Pressman as "those two nuts" and Agnew as "that big slob." Agnew played it casually at first. "When I came down to breakfast this morning," he reported, "my kids said, 'Here comes that big slob.' It's pretty hard to live with at home." He was content with dignified dismissals of Mahoney as an "unseated king in his paper castle," and he expressed confidence the voters would "ultimately reject the vulgarity of this opportunistic politician." He spoke about the environment when it was not yet a politically profitable issue—and his staff groaned. "At one of the biggest rallies," Bob Goodman recalls, "he talked about pollution—pollution was a nothing issue then. We screamed about that pollution speech. It was after that speech that I took care of the speech writing. I couldn't stand it any more. He was still on unemotional subjects. It was only the advertising that aroused the fear syndrome. . . ."

Others were concerned too in October about the bland tone of Agnew's stump campaign. A Republican who shelled out $100 at an Agnew fund-raising dinner was overheard to say, "I can step outside and tell air pollution is bad, but when we pay $100 for a roast-beef dinner we want to hear something that will inspire us to go out and lick Mahoney." James B. Rowland, writing in the Washington *Star*, reported that "some Republicans in their party's upper echelons are distressed at what appears to be a lecture-hall campaign approach by Agnew." He quoted one Republican veteran as saying, " 'We need some good razzle-dazzle, crowd-jumping campaigning.' " And another: " 'To beat Mahoney we need a John Lindsay- or Kennedy-type candidate with a lot of dash personifying the aggressive man-on-the-go.' " All the right endorsements were coming in: the Baltimore *Afro-American*, the *New York Times*, even the Baltimore chapter of the Americans for Democratic Action. But the spark was missing.

Even when the objective was clear, Feingold recalls, "it was hard to get Ted moving. We had to take him by the hand and lead him into the black community. The Sickles liberals moved in and imposed themselves on the established campaign, and that had some impact on him. The fright of Mahoney became so great, Agnew became the knight in shining armor. He became the salvation. And eventually he himself began to get swept along. For the first time he thought maybe he would become governor."

What Agnew's other advisers may not have known, as Feingold did from his Baltimore County days, was their man's zest for the attack, when aroused. Mahoney gave Agnew a peg when his supporters rammed through the Democratic state convention a plank that specifically incorporated the Mahoney campaign slogan:

> We oppose any form of racism or bigotry. We hold, however, to the undeniable right of all men and women of all creeds and races to acquire, own, manage, rent, sell or otherwise dispose of private homes without governmental interference or dictation beyond the laws of zoning and essential health regulations. We, therefore, are opposed to any law which takes away the right of the individual homeowner to sell his home to whomever he chooses, and we will hold to one of the most basic and respected precepts which we have; that a man's home is his castle, his own, to live in as he chooses, without fear of search and seizure, with whom he chooses, for any reason he chooses.

Slowly, Agnew warmed to the attack. He called Mahoney "an embarrassment." He had tried to dismiss the man as a bad joke,

Agnew said, "but I am afraid of encroaching Maddoxism across the country." And he asked, "Wouldn't it be terrible if my opponent won?" He called on his audience at a rally to imagine its embarrassment "as you watched this man make a complete idiot of himself before the country" on television. Mahoney's slogan, he said, had no more relevance to practicality than such catch phrases as "Fly the Friendly Skies of United."

The next day Agnew escalated, charging that Mahoney had "put his party to shame" and had shocked "decent men and women in the state by ramrodding his anti-open housing slogan into the Democratic party platform." More than Mahoney's slogan "is the way in which the emotional overtones of this slogan have been exploited and used to inflame."

Now, finally, Agnew was off and running. Opening a "Democrats for Agnew" headquarters in Prince George's County, he castigated Mahoney for refusing to debate with him, charging that his refusal was leading to a "yellow, skulking, slinky campaign." A better slogan for Mahoney, Agnew said, would be the toothpaste line: "I wonder where the yellow went." All Mahoney could think of, he said, was slogans. "If they asked him about transportation he would probably say, 'Take a bus and leave the driving to us.'" Noting that the British Broadcasting Company was covering the campaign, Agnew said, "When they come all the way over from Europe to see if we are still swinging from the trees, Maryland is in a bad way." And for the benefit of the Democrats present, he quoted President Kennedy as saying, "'Sometimes party loyalty demands too much.'" (The Feingold memo had advised Agnew: "I would recommend that you appear at such functions where the audience is predominantly Democratic to begin to develop the idea that your strength is heavily bipartisan, and your appeal cuts across traditional party lines. Often, as you know, the voter will get his impression of a candidate or a political development on what it appears to him to be, not necessarily what it actually is." And the memo provided this specific pitch to Democrats: "There are times when party loyalty conflicts with principle, when party clashes with conscience. The gubernatorial election of 1966 is such a time. The question we must ask is this: Is our first consideration to party loyalty or to political responsibility? It has been answered for us by John F. Kennedy. 'Sometimes,' he said, 'party loyalty asks too much.'") Four years later, when Republican Senator Charles E. Goodell of New York made the same observation about policies of the Nixon-Agnew Administration, Agnew was dispatched to New York to purge him.

From then on, Agnew needed no encouragement. In a speech in the town of Hancock, he called the Mahoney slogan "a veil of voodoo . . . we simply cannot run into our homes and close the door . . . 'Your Home Is Your Castle—Protect It' is an attempt to frighten people into walling themselves in from social responsibility." Agnew jumped on Mahoney, too, when he cursed reporter Frank DeFilippo, threatened to run him out of the state, and told another Democratic rally that the press "have had a pipeline, but it's going to be discontinued when I get to Annapolis." Said Agnew, "He is against free speech. He is against free press. He is against the right of the public to know what is going on in government. Now we know that the man who talks about guarding castles doesn't really care about individual rights and constitutional protections."

When Mahoney's campaign manager, Paul Reed, predicted his man would win the election by 80,000 to 100,000 votes, Agnew let him have it too. "I wonder where he gets his LSD," he asked.

Part of the strategy, obviously, was to get the politically undisciplined Mahoney to lose his composure completely. Agnew ridiculed him about his refusal to debate. He would show up at a television studio and then debate with Pressman over Mahoney's unwillingness to join them. One night in late October, DeFilippo and Jerry Kelly of the *Evening Sun*, covering a dinner at a Baltimore County synagogue, informed Agnew that Mahoney would be arriving shortly. When Mahoney came in, the two reporters signaled Agnew, who walked over to shake Mahoney's hand. Mahoney tried to ignore him at first, then finally stuck out his hand and said, "How are you, Mr. Agnew?"

"Fine, George, how are you?" Agnew replied.

"This is certainly a relief from campaigning, isn't it?" said Mahoney, and off he walked, circulating through the room.

Agnew went after him, finally catching up. "Let's talk about the issues, George," he said. "There are reporters here. Let's hold a press conference and discuss the issues. We can talk about education, taxes and other important problems facing the people."

Mahoney looked peeved and impatient with Agnew's persistence. "Let's talk about your friends in New York who are giving you all that money," Mahoney shot back—a reference to Greek-American backers of Agnew.

"Come on, George, I finally caught up with you," Agnew said. "You can't keep running away from me forever. People want to know whether or not you're qualified to even be governor."

It was a rare opportunity for Agnew, and he was making the most of it. He turned to the crowd that now had gathered and asked: "Why is this man afraid to talk about the issues?"

Mahoney was fuming now. "You run your campaign and I'll run mine," he snapped as an aide pulled him away.

Later Agnew apologized to the organizers of the dinner. "I am sorry, but this is getting frustrating," he said. "I am just going to spend the last two weeks before election day questioning Mr. Mahoney's competence." As Agnew was leaving, he met DeFilippo in the parking lot. "I really feel terrible," Agnew told him. "I don't want to come out and be mean to this guy, but I've got to. I've got to hit him for his incompetence. I cannot let this guy win, or the state's going to go."

Importantly involved in the attack on Mahoney's competence, Feingold says, was Robert Daly, a radio specialist who insisted that Agnew must go all out—not only on Mahoney's qualifications but also on the nature of his support. Agnew made much of a widely publicized Ku Klux Klan rally at which Mahoney stickers were seen everywhere. At the same time, Feingold says, Agnew was receiving more and more threatening calls. "He began to get radicalized. He began to stump with fire, campaigning before liberals and blacks and wowing them. He became emotional and animated. He began to concentrate on the racism issue. The campaign picked up overnight." Goodman agrees. "He had a sense of timing on the campaign. He thought he would go to the attack only in the last three weeks. It was a very ugly campaign. When you're running against an extremist, terrible things happen. I mean, crosses weren't burned on his lawn, but threat letters, hate mail, vulgarity in phone calls; he was a besieged guy in terms of ugliness and threats, but it never bothered him. One quality is lack of physical fear; it never gets to him; he laughs it off and says, 'Let's go,' just like Kennedy did. I think his biggest fear, maybe, is embarrassment to his peers—feeling sensitive in a personal way; if there is any fear in Ted Agnew, I think he hates to be embarrassed among the bowling team. I think if he put a ball down the gutter, that would really upset him. But if somebody threw a bowling ball at him, that would not frighten him."

Agnew certainly campaigned as the fearless candidate from then on. Radio spots were aired in key areas bringing "the fear syndrome," as Goodman candidly called it, to a peak. One television spot had Agnew intoning: "We here in Maryland are at a time of crisis. It has happened in the last few weeks, and even in the last few days of this campaign. They are here—in Maryland. The extremists. The robed figures. The faceless men. This election has attracted all the elements of hate, prejudice and bigotry that still operate in this United States. These are the fright peddlers, the fearmongers—the people who either for power, for money or for some sort of destructive fanaticism—will attempt to exploit a people to their own ends. The literature is despicable, the threats are inflammatory and the attacks upon liberty and our basic constitutional freedoms are being made as if no Constitution and no Bill of Rights ever existed. I don't have to tell you that the fanatics are rallying to this election, because you can see their pictures in the newspaper. The hooded Klansmen and the straw hats with my opponent's name on them are seen side by side. And no one needs to tell *me* who's at work in this campaign. My family and I are getting the threatening letters and phone calls that are typical of the extremist technique. They don't scare me. And, as far as I'm concerned, they just help to identify the kind of people who have entered this campaign. What has happened is that these people have seized upon my opponent's weakness—his desire for public office no matter what the cost. I don't believe—at least I don't *want* to believe—that he directs them. But I know he cannot reject them, for without the fright peddlers he cannot win."

On the stump, Agnew now hit the fear theme with abandon: "Why were these Ku Klux Klanners wearing Mahoney hats at their rally two weeks ago? You remember all those cars with Mahoney bumper stickers on them when the National States Rights party nearly caused a riot in Patterson Park last summer. Well, it was all deliberate. It is nothing but bigotry that this man is appealing to." And in another speech: "It's not what he says, it is what he doesn't say that is tacitly giving comfort to the forces of evil. . . . Everyone believes and knows that your home is your castle, but it won't do any good to have a castle if the community is so insecure that you will build a fence around your castle and be afraid to go out. The type of philosophy this man is expressing won't make this community secure or the state and the nation either."

To the Baltimore Kiwanis he said, "Unless decency, integrity and responsibility set off a spark that sets the entire state ablaze we are lost. For other forces are setting fires—fires of hatred, fear and uncertainty." And in another speech the same day: "There is no middle ground in this election. The electorate of Maryland must choose between the bright, pure, courageous flame of right-eousness or the evil of a fiery cross. Voters impassioned by a slo-gan which exploits fear and uncertainty consider reacting through their vote. . . . Backlash is the personification of tangi-ble terror." He called regular Democratic leaders "political vul-tures circling greedily about the Democratic candidate waiting to pick clean the bones on the carcass of state government." He charged they "see a last glimmer of hope and flock like moths to the flame of the fiery cross."

In a speech at the Baltimore Civic Center, Mahoney gave a re-buttal to Agnew's KKK charge: "My opponent has reached the lowest of the low in the history of Maryland politics, but I feel sorry for this man. I shall pray for him." But Agnew was not turned aside by such solicitudes. "We must all go out and work," he told a rally at the same place, "to halt this festering, creeping, grasping Maddoxism."

In his late-hour abandon, Agnew did not spare Pressman either. "I am really annoyed to hear you call yourself a Democrat," he said to Pressman at a Salisbury meeting. "I think you're just an opportunist as far as running for office is concerned." And he re-minded Tawes, trying to stay out of the line of fire, that the Dem-ocratic governor once had branded Mahoney "unfit for public office."

In the town of Frostburg, Agnew outdid himself. He called Ma-honey's platform "a two-pronged pitchfork based on incompe-tency and bigotry which he brandishes about while laughing to himself and waiting to pick bare the bones of Maryland. This man is a menace." And he added about his closing campaign drive, "I have no apologies to make. I have presented my views on the issues repeatedly but people didn't realize how bad he [Ma-honey] was. Until a few days ago I did not really believe he was a bigot, but he proved it." In Essex, outside Baltimore, a week before the election, Agnew said his only goal in life was "to expose George P. Mahoney for the fraud he is." His voice hoarse and emotional, Agnew warned, "This state must not be controlled by a devil that sits holding a two-pronged pitchfork of bigotry and hatred." Ron Wilner, Goodman's associate, said he went out to hear Agnew speak and was appalled at some of the things he heard his own candidate say. "It was mean, a mean type of thing," he recalled. "I was standing in the lobby and some people walked out. One man said, 'I didn't come here to hear that.'"

The next day Agnew said he was sorry he had called Mahoney a devil, but he explained that "a devil is a tempter of mankind" and Mahoney was "trying to tempt mankind to yield to its baser impulses." Mahoney's use of his slogan, Agnew argued, "is devilish. He would have man retreat into himself and forget his responsibilities to his fellow-men and his community." But he allowed that Mahoney "is not a force of evil—he is misguided." Then, quoting news reports of Mahoney's use of a racial accent in some of his speeches, Agnew glared at his audience and asked bitterly, "Whose accent will he use next?"

In the final week Agnew added the secret right-wing Minutemen organization to the KKK as supporters of Mahoney, producing a copy of Minutemen literature he said he had received, apparently in a mass mailing, that implored Maryland voters: "Don't let George do it alone." The flyer went on: "George P. Mahoney won the primary election. Now all these groups are disowning George because he is a bigot. You know of course that if you are against forced housing you automatically become a bigot. . . . Don't buy that—Don't let that prevent you from voting for what is best for you and yours. . . . Let Hymie Pressman and Spiro seek the liberal and Negro vote. Let them fight like two jealous women over it. Neither of them are concerned with the property rights of you and yours."

In striking back at Agnew, Mahoney only helped him. In a television appearance near the end, he accused Agnew of injecting racism into the campaign. "I tell you," he said, "that his outright appeals to the Negro population with promise after promise are a deliberate and calculated appeal to them to base their vote on the color of their skin, and this is racism in its broadest form." And then Mahoney was off. To an all-white audience he said: "I'll take care of those birds. Who do they think they are? The audacity of these people. They think they can go along and do anything they want. . . . Police departments have been told to treat certain people with kid gloves—cautioned not to do anything to them except as a last resort. Well, I'll change all that. Police will be told to hit first, fire first." And at a dinner rally: "Police are told not to protect themselves. . . . They say to the police, 'Take anything, wait until you are shot before you move.' " Baltimore was so crime-ridden, Mahoney said, "that you're even afraid to go to church on Sundays. I'm sick and disgusted and tired of people being raped on the streets. We've got to light up the streets, get sufficient police, else there will be no protection from these people. . . . When I am governor I am going to talk to those judges who give out small sentences for rape. I say that is destroying this state. If it happens when I am governor, I'll talk to the judge. I'll tell him—"

For all of Agnew's own vitriolic words, none served him better than such diatribes from Mahoney. On the night before the election, now that it was just about over, Agnew expressed regrets about the personal attacks he had inflicted with such bitterness and zeal on Mahoney in the final weeks of the campaign. They were necessary, he told a TV audience, to jar the electorate out of its lethargy. (Just prior to Agnew's appearance, Mahoney gave a prerecorded talk on television. Agnew watched it coolly, took a few notes, and then went on live. "I'm not reading from any idiot card," he said, in an obvious parting shot at his opponent.)

On election night, November 8, Agnew had a steak dinner with his family in the Oak Room of his headquarters hotel, the Lord Baltimore. Then he went to the Florentine Room to watch television and take telephone reports from lieutenants around the state, while one floor below, a Montgomery County high school band belted out "My Kind of Man." Charlie Bresler, who ran unsuccessfully for state comptroller on the Agnew ticket, concluded from the early returns that Agnew had won, and so informed him, but Agnew preferred to wait before claiming victory. Before long, however, even Agnew was persuaded he was a winner. Amid the merrymaking, Bresler recalled, Agnew began to talk with his aides about setting up a gubernatorial staff and taking over from a Democratic administration. Eventually, he went downstairs and joined the victory party. "That new day dawning, Ted Agnew is," the theme song said, and for him it was a prediction far beyond even his expectations.

When all the votes were in, Spiro T. Agnew had been elected Governor of Maryland over Mahoney by 81,775 votes, or 49.5 percent of the total in the three-man race. The regular Republicans, the liberal Democrats, the black voters in Baltimore and the Jewish voters there and in suburbia all had come through for Agnew. Later, when he was Vice-President, he acknowledged that the anti-Mahoney vote had been critical for him, including as it did liberals who probably wouldn't have supported him had they had a chance to vote for Sickles, defeated by Mahoney in the primary. "On the other hand," Agnew said, "I'm not at all sure that I wouldn't have beaten Sickles by putting together the people who voted for Mahoney with the Republicans." Mahoney's problem was that "he demagogued it up a bit in the campaign in an obvious way. To be candid, he didn't bear the scrutiny of a campaign. He didn't expose himself to the debates and what-not. There was a great amount of fear that George Mahoney was prejudiced, that he was a bigoted man. I'm not sure he is or isn't; I don't know him that well. But that's the way he came across in the campaign."

The next day, Agnew's forty-eighth birthday, he appeared smiling, triumphant, yet humble, at a press conference. "I wouldn't want to say that my election has national significance," he remarked. "I have difficulty imagining myself as a national leader, and sometimes I have difficulty imagining myself as a state leader." But at a luncheon later in his honor, his old friend Bud Hammerman presented him as a man who someday would be introduced "as President of the United States." The line drew good-natured grins and applause. After all Ted Agnew had been through, no doubt he could stand some good-natured, even preposterous humoring, now that he had reached what few really doubted would be the pinnacle of his career.

8

❖•❖•❖•❖•❖•❖

ANNAPOLIS

THE night before his inauguration as governor of Maryland, Spiro T. Agnew drove with his wife, Judy, from their Towson home to the Charterhouse Motel just outside Annapolis. The next morning he appeared at the State House in top hat and morning coat and was sworn in as the fifth Republican of fifty-five governors of the state. Then he greeted well-wishers in the old Senate chamber where George Washington resigned his commission in 1783. Asked why he hadn't driven down directly from Towson that morning, the new governor replied, "Have you ever tried sitting for a long ride on these tails?"

The sense of tidiness characterized by that comment soon came to mark the Agnew administration in Annapolis. Callers on the new governor in his spacious office often remarked afterward that Ted Agnew kept a clean desk and, as well as he could arrange it, a clean slate. "He didn't like to get up early in the morning," one Democratic legislative leader who saw him frequently recalls. "He often would get in about ten A.M. You could walk in and there wouldn't be a paper on his desk. He built up a shield around him. He was a pleasant fellow, but for some reason he just liked to be aloof from the daily work of government." A reporter who covered the State House said Agnew told him at the outset of his term that he intended to be a "nine-to-five governor" who took two afternoons off a week to play golf and didn't work weekends. Different men have different work habits that best suit them, of course, but apparently it was true that the impression, valid or not, soon grew among most state legislators that the new man in the State House was unusually proper, orderly and detached.

There were those who also insisted he came to Annapolis with a rather clean mind concerning the duties and prerogatives of the office to which he had been elected. Before his inauguration in January 1967, Agnew had invited Democrat Marvin Mandel, then Speaker of the House of Delegates, to dinner to discuss how they might work together. They talked generally for a while about matters to be brought before the Democratic-controlled legislature, and then Agnew brought up a specific. "One thing I'd like above all," he told Mandel. "I'd like the legislature to approve my nomination for state treasurer." Mandel was stunned. "Ted, that's not your job," he told the governor-elect. "That's for the state legislature to name. You're not going to get a Democratic legislature to put in a Republican." The man Agnew wanted was Tilton Dobbin, treasurer of his gubernatorial campaign and president of the Maryland National Bank. In spite of Mandel's counsel, Agnew went ahead anyway and the General Assembly predictably rebuffed him, reappointing the Democrat already in the job.

Veteran legislators who soon learned about Mandel's conversation with Agnew were appalled, not so much by the new governor's effort to get his man appointed as by his failure to know that the job was not his to fill. There were other instances of the same ilk, and it soon became common scuttlebutt that the low-keyed, pipe-puffing but extremely influential Mandel was giving Agnew unofficial on-the-job training. Many observers of the Annapolis scene, reflecting on those early and subsequent days of the Agnew administration, assign Mandel a large share of credit for whatever legislative achievements were attained. He functioned, some say, in much the same benevolent style as U.S. Senate Majority Leader Lyndon B. Johnson did during the two administrations of Dwight D. Eisenhower, guiding the Republican President's acceptable programs through the Senate. "It was a constant trading game," one of Agnew's chief Annapolis aides says. "The Democrats had the votes. They could withstand the public pressure of newspapers and things of this nature. . . . It was a trade-off constantly."

The cornerstone of Governor Agnew's 1967 legislative program was a $127 million tax reform package, including a graduated state income tax, a state property tax increase and authority for the state's counties and Baltimore city to impose new "piggyback" local taxes to be collected at the state level. As a new governor, he offered no comprehensive program in his first year, submitting instead a caretaker budget of about $1 billion and a pledge to propose individual bills strictly on a basis of priority. Eventually Agnew won enactment of his tax reform plan, but only after several court challenges required legislative revisions.

As an administrator, Agnew reorganized the executive office and created a series of program directors with whom, the legislators soon learned, they were supposed to do business. Except to the leadership—men like Mandel and State Senate President William S. James—the governor was a distant figure, both in space and mood. "He didn't like meetings," one veteran legislator recalls. "He didn't like to be in crowds. In his office, if he had to meet people he couldn't wait until he got them out. He turned down most public appearances. He told me he never was really happy as governor or county executive. He told me several times he didn't think he'd run again. The few people who were close to him, people he liked to have around, were always businessmen." One of them, J. Walter Jones, a connoisseur of wines, built Agnew a wine cellar in the governor's mansion and he and other friends stocked it.

The access of such people to the governor always made him suspect concerning "deals" such as the land purchase near the bay bridge. "Ted was an honest guy," one of his Annapolis associates says, "but there always seemed to be people around him who were in business. Being governor, you didn't have to do anything, you just had to be there. Having it known you were close to him was enough." And another says, "He wasn't corrupt, but he allowed himself to be used by the people around him."

Assessing Agnew as a freshman governor depends a great deal, of course, on one's perspective. To Jones, Agnew was not so much stand-offish as selective in asserting himself. When he went to a legislative hearing he would be sure he knew "as much as anybody in that room and probably collectively more," Jones says, and "when he had some hell-raising to do, he didn't send close associates in to do it. He would bring the committee to the mansion for dinner or breakfast and give them hell himself. He is his own man and he does his own homework and he has confounded many people because of this approach. He does this today. He's got a unique mind. You may think sometimes when you talk to him, he's almost going to sleep on you. Then he starts to talk about what you were talking about and you know he wasn't sleeping at all."

Some less partisan observers also give Agnew high grades as governor. One of them, Richard Homan of the Washington *Post,* says that Agnew, "after Tawes's Democratic fiefdom, set Maryland state government on a different course. He brought in men who had expertise in their fields rather than the proper political antecedents. The Democrats didn't feel at home with them. They couldn't work out the usual shortcuts for their constituents. Agnew's reforms weren't always the best, but he imposed a new system on an old system. It would have been interesting to see how it would have turned out after four years."

If Agnew's remote attitude did not make for backslapping camaraderie around the State House, neither did it produce the kind of excessive partisan sniping that had marked his administrative days in Baltimore County. He had early run-ins with Louis L. Goldstein, the Democratic state comptroller, over the tax program, and with Francis Burch, the Democratic attorney general, over a request for a legal opinion on a state strike law, but they were more in the nature of isolated skirmishes than an interparty war. There were conflicts over the tax plan, including a warning from Agnew that he would call the General Assembly back into special session if it quit before enacting his reforms, but these were not unusual in a government of split responsibilities.

More than any specific program submitted, what grated on the Democratic leadership was Agnew's inexperience, and his choices for key top-echelon department heads to whom he delegated much power. For instance, rather than relying on the Maryland career budget experts who were familiar with the process, he brought in a new budget chief from New York State; when the year's budget projections fell short, the Democrats howled that Agnew's inexperience and his selection of the out-of-state budget chief were at fault. Agnew was obliged to ask the legislature for supplemental appropriations.

In his first month in office, Agnew told newsmen he wanted to abolish the state board of motion picture censors, an anachronism that only Maryland among the states still had. But he thought he could do it simply by deleting funds from the budget, when in fact the board was mandated by the legislature. Similarly, later on, he got into hot water with the General Assembly when he tried to change an important program of state scholarships to state loans, when in fact the grants were mandated. Such moves gave the Democrats ammunition with which to criticize the new governor not only as a greenhorn but also as one who did not do his homework and failed to surround himself with aides knowledgeable about Maryland's legislative process.

Nor had Agnew heard the last of suspicions about his purchase of land near the bay bridge. After having been in office only a month, he called on the General Assembly to authorize three new bridge sites across the Chesapeake Bay and to start acquiring land for all three, one of which would be parallel to the existing bridge —though that plan had been rejected by the voters in the November referendum. The state would need all three eventually, he said, and meanwhile, land costs were soaring, adding to the ultimate cost of these projects. The state roads commission could decide on construction priorities later. His old foe, Congressman Long, called the move "a transparent attempt" to advance the parallel bridge. "Whom does Governor Agnew think he is kidding?" Long asked. "If this bill were passed, it would be followed by another parade of experts, well-paid to give the priority recommendations expected of them—namely, for a parallel bridge." Eventually that site was selected and the bridge begun, after Agnew had disposed of his share of the land.

Throughout Agnew's first year and into his second, another matter drew much attention away from the freshman governor: the calling of a convention to revise the state's antiquated constitution, which embodied, among other things, the excessive dependence on state legislative action for local reforms. Agnew signed the bill providing the machinery for the convention in March of 1967, after a two-year study by a twenty-five-member committee appointed by former Governor Tawes. The draft constitution proposed to strengthen the role of the governor and of local governments, reaffirm the rights of individuals, and revamp the judicial system. Agnew supported the new constitution and participated in efforts to make appointive the important elective posts of attorney general and comptroller, held by the Democrats, but the convention balked. Instead it voted to retain an elected attorney general and comptroller, but to strip the comptroller of much of his power. Of the intensive lobbying that went on to maintain these two offices as they had been, the new governor said, "We are witnessing an effort to protect the jobs of elected officeholders at the expense of establishing an effective branch of government. It is indeed unfortunate that the convention's recent deliberations have been more involved in present-day politics and personalities than in drafting of a sound, workable document of government for future generations."

Such righteous commentaries grated on the Democrats, who saw in Agnew's own actions more than a speck of old-fashioned politicking. Philip H. Dorsey, a Democratic leader in the House of Delegates, said he did not go to the convention "to participate in the coronation of Spiro the First." The characterization, to many who were cooled by Agnew's regal, aloof manner, seemed an apt one, and later, when his old supporter, the Baltimore *Sun*, turned against him, cartoons appeared showing him in kingly robes labeled with that title.

When the new 14,000-word constitution finally was completed, Agnew dubbed it "superb" and said it was "without parallel in the nation." But the voters of Maryland apparently disagreed. In May of 1968, they rejected it by a three-to-two majority, in one of the major disappointments of the Agnew administration.

By and large, however, Agnew was getting high grades from many observers in Annapolis. After the governor had been in office two months, Jack Eisen of the Washington *Post* noted that the legislature had given Agnew "more legislation, and money to pay for it, than has any session in memory." And after six months Eisen wrote: "The 48-year-old Agnew has been a quiet, strong-willed and often impatient administrator, ready to take and willing to run political risks to achieve his objectives. He much more closely resembles a political career city manager, a technician of law and administration, than a political officeholder." On Agnew's first anniversary as governor, Eisen observed that Agnew remained "the possessor of an untarnished good-guy image. The big question now is how long he can keep it." Legislators generally saw Agnew as a good manager who kept politics to a minimum, the *Post* reporter wrote; while he was criticized for shooting from the hip and for being too insulated by his staff, "for now at least, Agnew remains a good guy who wears a white hat that has barely begun to get dusty."

That image continued through the first months of 1968, as Agnew unveiled his first comprehensive legislative program bearing his own stamp. It contained fifteen points, including a new $100 million anti-water-pollution program, and ambitious programs in the fields of mental health, alcoholism, housing and highways. He proposed creation of a state housing authority and virtual abolition of the death penalty in capital crimes, a proposal that had been rejected by the legislature in 1967. He promised there would be no further income tax increase for the three years remaining of his term.

The no-tax promise, however, contributed to a growing financial bind the state was facing. To cope with it, the governor announced a 10 percent cut in medical aid to the indigent, which meant 27,000 persons between twenty-one and sixty-five would be cut from the rolls. However, when the medical community and members of the legislature applied public pressure, he backed off.

Agnew described the state budget of $1.15 billion as "preshrunk and tight"; one legislator, Delegate (later Congressman) Paul Sarbanes, called it "an austerity budget in a time of prosperity." In an unusual twenty-two-page analysis of Agnew's spending proposal, Sarbanes criticized planned tax relief for business at the expense of education needs, and called it "the East Coast version of the Ronald Reagan budget." For his impudence, the young legislator got a curt dismissal from the governor, who called the detailed analysis "a Sarbanality." Yet, for all the verbal games, the legislature finally passed the Agnew budget with slight cuts, giving the state $96 million more to spend than it had in the previous year.

By mid-February 1968, however, it was clear that the aloofness and partisan jibes of the governor finally were taking their toll. Eisen, who had heretofore been fulsome in his praise of Agnew's performance, wrote in the Washington *Post* that "a lack of sense of urgency and increased feelings of partisanship have cast a shadow over Agnew's legislative program." And shortly afterward his *Post* colleague, Richard Homan, wrote that Agnew was "finding himself virtually ignored by a Maryland General Assembly preoccupied with crime, riots, politics and impending constitutional change." At the end of March, Agnew insisted he was pleased that the legislature had passed nearly half his proposals, especially the anti-water-pollution plan. It was patterned after Nelson Rockefeller's and was regarded by friend and foe alike as one of Agnew's major contributions to Maryland's well-being. "I find that this year my relationships with the [legislative] leadership are better than they were last year," the governor observed. "They have been much closer; there's been a freer interchange with less reservation between [the Democratic leaders] and me than ever before." Also: "One thing that has to be thoroughly recognized is that a governor of a minority party working with a legislature cannot go around beating his breast and throwing his weight around."

That statement was made on March 28, 1968, while Charlie Bresler was at Bowie State looking into the complaints of the protesting students there. Of that situation, Agnew said, "We are going to help in any way we can. But one thing I am completely aware of is this: students always have objections to the way colleges are run. I doubt if we'll ever change that. Our problem is to make certain that we properly assess their objections and make changes where they are indicated, but don't overreact. I don't think we're going to overreact in this case." The comment indicating his disinclination for breast-beating and weight-throwing also came just two weeks before Agnew's postriot meeting with Baltimore moderate black leaders.

Many of those leaders, including a good number who had supported him for governor against Mahoney, had been observing Agnew with increasing interest. For although he was occupied with matters of the legislature, one social issue continued as in the past to intrude on his political career: civil rights. In his first weeks in office, he had appointed a thirteen-member committee on human rights and proposed that all civil rights legislation be screened by it. At that time he still clung to his limited espousal of open-housing legislation that would apply only to new housing and new apartment units; he still defended the right of the individual owner of any existing home to sell it to a buyer of his choosing, and to deny sale to anyone, even on grounds of race.

In February 1967, when his advisory committee approved a broader bill, Agnew tried to side-step the issue by saying he didn't think it could pass. "I am not hostile to the bill," he said, "but to me it's not politically salable. I'd like to put my weight behind a bill that I think has more than a fair chance of succeeding." If it were confined to his more limited position, he said, "I will immediately throw my weight behind it." The proposed legislation was to cover all apartment buildings of five or more units and all existing homes unless the homeowner gave "expressed written instructions" to his real estate agent to sell the house on a discriminatory basis.

Many Democrats, of course, also shared Agnew's view, and the bill was quickly watered down in the legislature. Maneuvering even reached a point where the legislation faced a weakening beyond what Agnew himself wanted, and he stepped in and lobbied against the gutting. Sponsors credited the governor with swinging six important votes for the bill. Agnew sent a statement to the State Senate calling the legislation "an important and significant start." Civil rights advocates, though, were critical. "It's quite a pill to swallow, watching the emasculation of something desperately needed in this state," said State Senator Meyer M. Emanuel. Senator James Clark added, "When the bill goes into effect, it would not make one dwelling available at once. All we are handing out to the people is a little hope." Within ten days, the bill was passed by both houses of the General Assembly and shortly signed into law—the first open-housing legislation in Maryland history and the first enacted below the Mason-Dixon line. It had been rolled back to Agnew's position—applying only to new apartment buildings of twelve or more units and homes in new subdivisions. Also, it exempted homes built under permits applied for before June 1, 1967—a two-month grace period—and completed by a year from then. An important feature, however, was a provision barring racial discrimination by banks or other lending agencies in the approval of home loans and mortgages. "To those who would decry the limitations of this bill," Agnew said, "I remind them that it is a solid achievement, not another legislative defeat, and I predict it will win the acceptance of the general public instead of generating more controversy and conflict."

Controversy and conflict—it seemed to Agnew the two always were present when civil rights was at issue, and he made no secret of his severe reservations about the wisdom and tactics of the civil rights leadership. During the legislative fight over open housing, national civil rights leaders had begun to speak out more forcefully than before against the Vietnam war, perceived in the black community as the black man's burden. Agnew warned that such antiwar comment by men like Dr. Martin Luther King, Jr., Floyd McKissick and Stokely Carmichael was hurting the chances for open-housing legislation in Maryland "and doing grave violence" to their movement by alienating legislators whose support they otherwise would have. When Dr. King announced a summer campaign against the war, Agnew proclaimed in a press conference that he had completely lost confidence in King. And, he said, since he never had had any in Carmichael, "I really haven't lost any." The Interdenominational Alliance wired Agnew that his "intemperate and inconsistent pronouncements constitute an affront and a disservice to a cross section of the Maryland community which supported you in your bid for office when extremism was close to victory."

Thus, though it was true that under Agnew, Maryland had passed the first open-housing bill south of the Mason-Dixon line, in the black community suspicions mounted about the depth of his understanding of the civil rights cause and his commitment to it. He made it very clear that in his view the leadership in the black community should rest with the old-line moderates. In late July 1967 he invited one of them, Roy Wilkins, the respected executive secretary of the National Association for the Advancement of Colored People, to discuss the racial picture. After their meeting Agnew announced he was considering an executive order ending all discrimination in state jobs. In the midst of a summer many had feared would be racially explosive in the big cities, he reported confidently, "Everything I have seen shows that I have no cause for unrest. . . . I don't have any reason to believe Baltimore is close to an explosion."

Just four days later, the governor suddenly had ample cause for concern, not in Baltimore, but in the small, racially torn Eastern Shore town of Cambridge, still scarred by the severe riots that had struck it four summers before. There, on the night of July 24, discontent within the town's black population of about 4,000 (out of a 13,000 total population), burst wide open in a nightmare of burning and gunfire. H. Rap Brown, successor to Carmichael as leader of the Student Nonviolent Coordinating Committee and the leading exponent of the black-power rallying cry, had been invited to Cambridge by the town's Black Action Federation. He came and delivered a bitter, vitriolic, antiwhite speech to an audience of several hundred, mostly teen-agers and young adults. Whether or not, as Agnew and the federal government later charged, Brown was responsible for inciting a riot, his words were clearly inflammatory. According to the Washington *Post,* Brown told his cheering listeners " 'to get your guns . . . if you gotta die, wherever you go, take some of them with you. I don't care if we have to burn him down or run him out, you gotta take over these stores, gotta take your freedom.' " The *Post* reported that Brown pointed at the local black elementary school and said, " 'You all should have burned that school long ago, you should have burned it down to the ground, Brother.' " And later: " 'If America don't come around, we're going to burn America down.' "

Brown harangued the crowd for about forty minutes, concluding shortly before ten o'clock, when all but about 125 to 150 teen-agers and young adults dispersed. After some milling about, Brown led a march of about forty blacks toward Race Street, where local police wearing riot helmets and armed with shotguns awaited them. According to the state's attorney for Dorchester County, William Yates 2nd, police fired while the marchers still were some distance off, and the march broke up. Brown was hit in the head by a shotgun pellet, but the wound was superficial; he was treated and released, and he promptly disappeared. A twenty-seven-year-old patrolman, Russell Wroten, was hit in the neck and hands by pellets as he drove into the black section in response to a call. Incidents of rock-throwing at cars, and buckshot fired from them, kept the situation tense as about a hundred state troopers and the local police force of twenty-two men patrolled the streets into the early morning hours.

Then, at about two-fifteen, fire broke out in the black school. The all-white fire department refused to respond, giving as the reason fear of sniper fire in the black section of town. Police Chief Bruce G. Kinnamon held all fire trucks out of the area for about seventy-five minutes, while the fires spread and individual black homeowners tried to water down their houses with garden hoses. As the fires crept toward the white business section the fire companies took up posts there, and when a crowd of blacks went to the police station to plead for help, Kinnamon said: "We've had a policeman shot there tonight. We can't go fight any fire." Emerson Stafford, a local black, told him: "We don't want the fire department. Just give us hoses." Blacks offered to provide escort for the white firemen, jumping on the trucks to encourage them, but to no avail. "They don't care if we all die," said Elaine Adams, chairwoman of the local Black Action Federation. "This is what they do. They won't help us." Finally Attorney General Burch climbed aboard a fire truck and urged it into the burning area. By five o'clock that morning the fire was brought under control.

Before daybreak Agnew, who had been in communication with Colonel Lally, arrived in Cambridge. He surveyed the damage and flatly blamed it on Brown. "I hope they pick him up soon, put him away and throw away the key," the governor said. "Intelligent citizens of both races, I am sure, share my grief and perplexity at this senseless destruction precipitated by a professional agitator." Agnew gave orders for Brown's arrest. He was charged with "inciting a riot" and "inciting to burn," and in a few days was picked up by the FBI at Washington National Airport as a "fugitive felon." Released on bond, Brown praised Cambridge blacks for "their offensive action," then disappeared again.

But in or out of custody, Brown was prominent in Agnew's thoughts during the months ahead. Several days after the riot the governor declared that "it shall now be the policy of this state to immediately arrest any person inciting a riot and not to allow that person to finish his vicious speech." What such a policy might mean to constitutional guarantees of free speech, and how one was to determine in advance which public statements were to be permitted and which not, Agnew did not indicate. (Three weeks later, after much criticism of his first statement, Agnew sent a letter to Lally cautioning the state police, in stopping speeches inciting violence and destruction, not to "abridge anyone's right to speak on any subject that he wants." But Agnew also cited Supreme Court rulings to remind Lally that "the right of free speech is not absolute at all times and under all circumstances.")

The governor said he supported "legitimate pressure on those in authority to break the senseless and artificial barriers of racial discrimination." He made clear, though, that by legitimate pressure he meant "the power of the vote, the power of organized political, economic and social action." Such action, he said, "does not give any person or group a license to commit crimes. Burning, looting and sniping, even under the banner of civil rights, are still arson, larceny and murder." Nor, he added, would acts of violence be "later forgiven just because the criminal after a while adopts a more reasonable attitude. The violent cannot be allowed to sneak unnoticed from the war dance to the problem-solving meeting," which "must be reserved for those who shun lawlessness, who win their places at the conference table by leadership that builds rather than destroys." Again Agnew was specific—he meant "the Wilkinses, Kings, [Whitney] Youngs and [A. Philip] Randolphs—not the Carmichaels, Joneses [presumably Rudolph T. Jones of Baltimore CORE] and Browns." He commended members of both races who acted with restraint and expressed pity for the "confused and weak who seek to excuse, appease and rationalize for the criminals who threaten our society."

In the next months, efforts went forward with Agnew's blessing to improve harmony between blacks and whites in Cambridge. But always there was the admonition that Agnew's type of leader —the Wilkinses, Kings, Youngs and Randolphs—should represent the black community. The memory of Brown stuck in Agnew's mind and craw. When General Gelston suggested to a congressional investigating committee that had Cambridge officials listened to the grievances of local blacks, Brown might never have been invited to speak, Agnew told an Annapolis press conference, "I feel that Brown was a lot more important to the violence in Cambridge than General Gelston seems to think he was. I think H. Rap Brown was a major, direct and contributing factor to that violence." Moderate black leaders who called on the governor in the fall and winter of 1967 reported receiving sermons from him about Brown. "It drove him crazy," Ed Feingold recalls. "He had a tape of Brown's speech in his office and he would keep playing it to black ministers who came in. 'Listen to that,' he would say. 'Isn't that incitement? Isn't it?' "

At the same time Agnew sought always to stress that it was not progress in civil rights he opposed, but some of the methods and people involved. His successor in Annapolis, Governor Mandel, says, "I don't think there's a prejudiced bone in his body. . . . I never knew him to be prejudiced about anybody or anything." When a county circuit judge, William B. Bowie, used a racial slur while sentencing a black woman in the fatal stabbing of her common-law husband, Agnew quickly denounced him. Bowie had ignored prosecution and defense recommendations for probation and had said: "If they want to live like animals, let them stay in a pen." And later: "White people don't go around doing that, and

Negroes do." Agnew called the statements "a most unfortunate incident which undercuts efforts to promote understanding among the races." Later on television, Agnew called Bowie's slur "a very careless statement, an overgeneralization which inflamed the Negro community and, I think, rightly inflamed them. However, I don't think the matter is one that could not have been put to rest had the man that made the statement forthrightly admitted that it was an uncircumspect statement and apologized for it." Then the Republican governor whose own righteousness by now had become a personal trademark added: "We get so bound up in our desire to protect ourselves from ever making a mistake that we can't say we're wrong." (When Agnew was criticized for not taking any action against Judge Bowie, he noted he had referred the matter to the state judicial disabilities commission. "I did not appoint Judge Bowie to the bench," he said. "I feel no personal responsibility for his actions.")

In Agnew's 1968 legislative program, with Cambridge clearly a catalyst, the governor backed bills to give his office more powers in riot situations. To charges that the bills' purpose was "intimidation," Agnew told a press conference: "The word intimidation, if you're going to apply it to lawbreakers, is one I would subscribe to. Yes, I hope it will intimidate anyone who decides he's going to take the law in his own hands. As far as intimidation against citizens who wish to use a legitimate right of protest in demonstrating within the law, these bills are not intended for that purpose and couldn't have any effect on that kind of exercise of civil protest. But I'm going to do everything I can to intimidate those who would break our laws, and I don't mind this word in that context. And if a person comes in with efforts to incite people to break the law, which is clearly breaking of the law itself, yes, it is intended to intimidate."

By the spring of 1968, there was one thing about which Spiro Agnew had made up his mind concerning the fight against racial injustice and inequality—the fight had to be made on his terms. He wanted laws that would intimidate potential lawbreakers, and for his own part, he was not going to be intimidated by those who pushed him too hard, threatened him or made demands on him. It was in this frame of mind that the Bowie State boycott and eventual capitol sit-in caught him in late March 1968.

Dr. Samuel L. Myers, the college's president, was sympathetic toward the students from the start, and tried to prevail on Agnew to come to the campus and hear what Myers considered to be their just grievances. Myers was told unequivocally, however, that under the circumstances, a personal visit to the campus was out of the question. "He thought that it would be to disparage the office of governor, to weaken that, to yield under pressure," Myers says. "We tried to get a number of people on the side who were close to him to try to get him to see whether he would see these people. But he was quite persistent. He did say, however, he would send his aide down here."

The aide Agnew sent, as noted earlier, was Charles Bresler—a highly successful real estate developer and former state legislator who even his friends say makes up in brass what he lacks in tact. By his own testimony, he has "a tendency to jump to a conclusion and move very quickly," in contrast to Agnew, who in Bresler's view has "a lawyer's syndrome—that every *i* should be dotted and every *t* should be crossed and all your facts should be a thousand percent correct—and then he will logically come to that end conclusion." Short, stocky, self-assured, Charlie Bresler comes on strong, and he came on strong that day at Bowie State, with incendiary result.

To Dr. Myers, student president Roland Smith and most others on the campus, the unrest at Bowie State was homegrown, out of long-smoldering complaints about on-campus matters. Smith said later that except for the group which came early from Howard, all the student participants in the boycott and what happened afterward were from Bowie. The visitors from Howard, he said, were thanked for their concern and asked to leave, which they did. But to Bresler, armed with state and FBI intelligence reports, the trouble at Bowie was one of a series of related incidents on predominantly black campuses that went back to Orangeburg, where three students had been killed and twenty-seven others injured by trigger-happy police at South Carolina State College seven weeks earlier.

"The Bowie incident," one Agnew aide said later, "was one of a series of instances that were coming up . . . an outside thing that moved from one place to another, the same organizers, the same people. I'm not saying it was a plot, and I'm not defending the fact that there weren't things wrong. If there's not something wrong, you get nobody to respond to you."

Bowie had been neglected, this aide acknowledged, but he said the fault originally had been with the Democrats in power, who had let the place wither. When Agnew took over, he said, the education system was revamped, Bowie State was raised from the status of a teachers college to a state college and given a large budget increase. The growth of the predominantly white Belair section of Bowie, a Levitt community, put pressures on both the physical facilities and the social climate of Bowie State. Also, this Agnew aide said, "The problem you had in many of these black institutions was that those who controlled them, the professors and the faculty, were paternalistic, were plantation types—I hate to use that term—but they did not relate to the youngsters. They liked the status quo and they had their nice little house and these sorts of things. Agnew was very much aware of that."

With this Agnew-administration view of the Bowie discontent in mind, Bresler met in a small classroom for two hours with leaders of the campus boycott. He tried to explain the state's budgeting process and the limitations on gubernatorial action, but to Roland Smith and his fellow students it all added up to an elaborate stall. Campus authorities took Bresler on a tour of the facilities, during which he saw flaking paint, missing tiles on the floors, dripping faucets, and cracks and holes in the walls. As he walked around, about two hundred students crowded into Tubman Hall, an old, high-ceilinged, paneled room once used as a dining area. Bresler's challenge to them to burn down the campus— with his cigarette lighter—and his lecture on how that action would save the state of Maryland millions of dollars in education costs predictably inflamed rather than pacified the campus.

On the same day, Agnew held his regular Thursday press conference in Annapolis and told reporters he had no intention of "overreactioning" to the Bowie boycott. Recourse for the students' grievances, he said, lay with the state colleges board of trustees.

On Friday, March 29, Smith and the other campus leaders held an eight-hour meeting with Dr. Myers, while their followers continued the sit-in in the corridors. Dr. Myers promised to act on a list of twenty-seven grievances submitted to him, and at first it seemed that a tentative agreement had been reached. "But these were small things," Smith said later. "The buildings were the big things, and the big things were up to Agnew." The visit by Bresler had solidified their demand that Agnew demonstrate his concern by coming to the campus himself, and nothing short of that would now suffice.

Threatening talk at Bowie also contributed to the intransigence in Annapolis. A regional NAACP youth leader named Kenneth Brown came in and counseled the students—unwisely, many thought—to disrupt the routine of the campus even more by letting all water faucets run open and by tying up administration phone lines with long-distance calls. According to Smith and Dr. Myers, the advice was rejected, but its substance was printed in the next day's news stories read in Annapolis, thereby stiffening the governor's resolve, if indeed any further stiffening was needed, not to "surrender" to pressure.

Assuming that the long meeting with the students had calmed matters, Dr. Myers went off to Baltimore Friday night to make a speech. While he was in the city, however, aides called to tell him that the students finally had gone all the way—they had taken over the campus, including the administration building and his own office. Myers raced back to Bowie full of apprehension. "When I got back, though," he said later, "it really was not a serious takeover. From one point of view, this was a very peaceful, orderly, responsible and legal way of the students sitting in—orderly and magnificent in every way. From another point of view, because of what this fellow Brown had said about turning on the water and making long-distance phone calls, it appeared to be a situation, from the outside, in which some militants had taken over a campus and were ravaging it." Looking at the evolving crisis in this latter light as Agnew did, Myers said, it was understandable that he responded as he did.

Myers telephoned Agnew over the governor's private line several times that night and early morning, talking first to press secretary Herb Thompson and eventually to Agnew himself. Myers urged him to come personally to the campus, but to no avail. "I went to the students," Myers recalls, "and said to them, 'You can't issue an ultimatum to the governor. He feels that if he yields under pressure here, this is going to stimulate other groups to put pressure on him, and thereby will be a whole situation in which his office will be overwhelmed with pressure from various groups.' I wanted to tell them, 'Now, if you can just let this whole thing bog down, and then within a couple of weeks, the governor will see you.' But he would not even permit me, even though this was the clear understanding, to present it to the people as a deal, even to promise that he would see them."

Instead, according to Myers, Agnew informed the state colleges board of trustees that as a contingency he was alerting the state police. The next morning, Saturday, State Attorney General Francis Burch was dispatched to Bowie to hear the students' demands and to confer with Myers, and after more phone calls to the governor, Agnew ordered the troops in. About 150 troopers arrived shortly after noon, stepping over the students still sitting in the corridors reading books and singing protest songs. Like the students, the troopers conducted themselves in a restrained and responsible way, while the talks proceeded in Myers' office. Through Burch, Agnew passed the word that the protesting students would have to leave or be thrown out. At one point, according to Myers, "they [Agnew and Burch] said that I as president could declare the college closed at five o'clock, and if I declared it closed, the students then could be arrested for trespassing if they stayed there. I said no, it was quite obvious I had been with the students all along, and I was very sympathetic with what they were doing, so I could not do this. . . . The governor said that he could recognize my position among the students and that he could not encourage or even ask me to issue such an order, and he did not. I have to respect the man who sees my position and sees I can't do something and therefore does not order me to do it."

At about two o'clock Agnew himself issued a statement putting the squeeze on the students. He told them that unless they got out of the school buildings by five o'clock "and revert to their status as students, they will be removed from the buildings by whatever means are necessary. . . . Negotiations are impossible in this sort of atmosphere." Agnew expressed hope that "the responsible students of the college will allow the campus to revert to its normal condition so that their grievances may be handled in a proper fashion. The activities of publicity-conscious outsiders can only injure the cause of higher education in the state of Maryland." There it was, the conspiracy theory working again in Agnew's view.

The appearance of law-enforcement officers on the campus had a telling effect. Negotiations in Dr. Myers' office finally produced a settlement that was read and overwhelmingly accepted by the students. Burch promised to seek prompt action on their demands, and while no specific commitments were made, the attorney general agreed to tour the campus the next Monday with state legislators involved in taxation and fiscal matters. Both Burch and the student leaders expressed a hope that Agnew would meet with the students by the following Wednesday. But in another statement after the settlement, the governor emphasized that he had made "no commitments or promises to anyone. . . . After the students have returned to normal campus life . . . then and only then will I consider discussing their grievances with them." From the start, he warned them that he had been "prepared to issue a proclamation closing down the college indefinitely, had that become necessary." Brown told reporters that if there were no concrete action about the grievances by the following Wednesday, the students would "close the college forever." But on Saturday night they carried their blankets and mattresses out of the administration building, and it appeared the worst was over.

The first four days of the next week were quiet. Monday classes were canceled by Dr. Myers to permit a further cooling off, while Burch and the legislative committee members made their tour in a calm atmosphere. Campus hopes climbed when members of the committee labeled conditions at Bowie "atrocious" and promised they would try to discuss them with Agnew. On Tuesday, as classes resumed, the state colleges board of trustees met with student leaders for two hours in Baltimore, and trustee Samuel Hopkins said the board would back a crash program of rehabilitation —but could not commit any money for it immediately.

All this time, for all the outward calm, rumors were floating through the Bowie student body. The student leaders had pressed Attorney General Burch to come up with concrete answers by Wednesday, and when he did not, tension mounted again. On Thursday came the erroneous report that Agnew, after having refused to come to Bowie, was going to predominantly white Towson State College to listen to grievances. That did it; the students climbed into buses and cars and descended on the state capitol. By nightfall, 227 students had been arrested and Bowie State closed down. The same night, Martin Luther King, Jr., was assassinated; two nights later Baltimore was in flames.

At first it was thought that the Baltimore police could handle the situation, but by Saturday afternoon City Police Commissioner Pomerleau had asked Colonel Lally for help. Nearly five hundred state police were moved into the city as the looting and burning spread. The primary targets were stores in the black ghettos, both black- and white-owned, but the fires seemed to be everywhere. By seven o'clock that night, according to Lally, "it was clear the situation had grown beyond the capability of the state police." A high-level meeting was summoned, attended by Mayor D'Alesandro, Pomerleau, Lally, Gelston, commander of the Maryland National Guard, and State Attorney General Burch. They concluded that the National Guard had to be called in and recommended that step to Agnew, who issued the order. By now the rioting was in full swing. Agnew sat tight in a riot command post in Annapolis, maintaining what one aide called "an outward calm" that bolstered his staff through the crisis.

Meanwhile, the moderate leaders of Baltimore's large black community took to the streets to try by sheer persuasion to smother the fire of anger, despair and vengeance that had been ignited by King's assassination. "Many of them were out on the street trying to cool things," Lally said afterward. "I can recall many of the black political people like [State] Senator Clarence Mitchell and many black civil rights leaders who went around trying to get them to quit." But it was no use. By the time Agnew came up to the National Guard armory in Baltimore early Sunday morning, it was clear that still another step was necessary. Around noon the governor called the White House to ask that federal troops be placed on stand-by alert. He was referred to the office of Attorney General Ramsey Clark, who made the necessary arrangements and dispatched a representative to Baltimore. That afternoon Agnew toured the city by car with Lally and Gelston and decided to request that federal troops be brought in. They had been flown to Fort Meade, just south of the city, and by eleven o'clock they were on the streets. By now the worst was over, but the worst was bad: six deaths, seven hundred persons injured and five thousand arrested.

Dr. King was buried in Atlanta on April 9. Sometime earlier, Agnew had dispatched invitations to about a hundred of Baltimore's most prominent and most moderate black community leaders to meet with him downtown on Thursday, April 11, in the legislative council room of the State Office Building.

While Agnew was upstairs conferring with his law-enforcement chiefs, the black leaders began to arrive at the designated meeting place on the eighth floor. The tight security, and the battery of television cameras, persuaded the blacks something was amiss, and they had that impression confirmed when reporters in the room, who had been given advance copies of Agnew's speech, showed it to some of them. What they read primed them for Agnew's appearance and they complained among themselves about the remarks. But even the words in cold print did not prepare them fully for the scene that was about to unfold.

In the midst of the patronizing lecture by Bresler about humble beginnings and bootstraps, in strode Agnew with his phalanx of uniformed enforcers around him and General Gelston's riding crop catching every eye. Then, before they could protest, they were being told like so many schoolchildren that they had misbehaved—nay, had retreated like cowards before bullying elements of their own race. "*And you ran,*" Agnew intoned to those who by Colonel Lally's later admission had sought to be moderating influences in Baltimore's streets during the burning and looting. Now it was clear: Spiro Agnew had chosen to have it out, once and for all, with the civil rights leadership that ever since his entry into public life had been pushing, demanding, threatening—while, in his view, temporizing on black extremism.

From then on, Agnew was both more defensive about his civil rights record and more rigid on the broad issue of law and order. Bob Goodman, who had been read a draft of the April 11 speech several days before its delivery and thought it had not sounded overly abrasive, was out of town the day of the meeting. Returning to Friendship Airport at about one o'clock the next morning, he read the story in the *Sun* about the black walkout and stayed up the rest of the night writing what amounted to a retraction of the speech. Then he raced to Annapolis to give it to Agnew. "I woke the governor up and he read over what I had written," Goodman recalls. "His mail by this time was running overwhelmingly in his favor, something like twelve hundred and fifty telegrams, letters and calls to eleven against. And he was shaken. He wasn't very happy the mail was in his favor; he was visibly shaken, terribly distressed, and surprised that the blacks had turned on him this way. (Ed Feingold, however, recalls that Agnew said, "I know I should apologize to Clarence Mitchell, but look at this stack of telegrams in support of what I said. The white community needs someone to speak for them.") The speech to the blacks had two parts. One was, 'God damn it, we can't let this go on again, and you're part of the problem.' The second thing was, 'All right, let's let bygones be bygones and let's really go out and do something together.' A lot of people question whether if he reversed the two parts of the speech it would have been different." But at any rate, Goodman added, Agnew did not want to make any retraction, and Goodman's all-night effort was filed and forgotten.

In Agnew's first press conference after that, he said he was "profoundly grateful" for the mail reaction. "In response to the emotional charges that I am a bigot," he said, "I need only to cite my record of unprecedented action through executive appointments, executive order and new laws to assure equal rights and equal opportunities for all citizens. This record stands and it cannot be obliterated or obscured by reckless accusations." Again he called on the black community to work with him, "but in beginning such an effort, we must reaffirm our allegiance to only lawful means and reassert our support of only lawful control and command. . . . I hope that leaders of the Negro community that I met with are willing to dedicate themselves to such an exclusively lawful effort." Already, Agnew said, he had been "taking steps to re-establish communication with those who will work exclusively within the law. I look forward to the response, to resuming the dialogue and to getting down to work." But after the April 11 castigation, that dialogue never would be resumed in any atmosphere of mutual trust. Many who got postmeeting letters from Agnew threw them away or kept them as collectors' items and never bothered to answer.

Agnew did not stop trying to reopen the dialogue, but to little avail. A couple of weeks after the Bowie State episode, he had Bresler call Roland Smith, the leader of the student protest there. The atmosphere was calm on campus again and Bresler told Smith the governor now was ready to meet with him. Smith and about five other students went to Agnew's office in Annapolis where, according to Smith, "he delivered a few little platitudes about how we had conducted ourselves. He said, 'I refuse to knuckle under to the demands of students no matter how justified they are.' He said he would not bend to students when they were pressuring him thus. He repeated the Bresler line that there was nothing wrong with Bowie that paint and plaster wouldn't fix, and that there had been 'outside agitators' at the school. We told him

Bowie State was a small college and we knew all the students, but he brushed that aside.

"He said he was going to try to get some mobile homes onto the campus until the dorms were repaired. He was calm until I asked him to make the commitment public. Then he said we were questioning his integrity by asking that. For the last twenty-five minutes of the meeting, he tried to feel us out on what we were going to tell the press. He said, 'I guess we better figure out what we're going to say to the press.' We made no agreement, but we didn't say much. We were a little sick of the whole thing by then. And we realized we were still under threat of prosecution, and some of us were seniors. I had the feeling all through the meeting, if Bowie students were to make themselves more vocal, there could be repercussions in the courtroom."

Out of that meeting, however, did come a public statement of Agnew's willingness to try to improve conditions at Bowie. The school by then had been reopened; eventually the charges against Smith and the other Annapolis sit-ins were dropped, and by summer some mobile homes were brought to the campus. But Smith's negative view of Agnew's conduct remained unchanged.

A month later, when campus demonstrations erupted at yet another predominantly black school, Maryland State College at Princess Anne, Agnew responded in a manner entirely contrary to his aloof posture in the Bowie State episode. Discrimination against students by a town restaurant was the immediate catalyst for the demonstrations, but the protest soon broadened. Learning of the trouble, Agnew immediately took the initiative and invited representatives of the student body to Annapolis. Obviously aware of the contrast with his Bowie State conduct and never one who wanted to appear inconsistent or to appear to be giving in to "intimidation," Agnew repeatedly stressed that he was not acting under duress. He dispatched his human relations aide, Gilbert Ware, to the scene—not Charlie Bresler—and called the president of the college to advise him of the invitation.

"I want to emphasize," Agnew told reporters, "that this meeting is at my own initiative and is brought about by a fervent hope that the attitudes at the college have not crystallized to the point that we cannot, in a dispassionate and objective fashion, discuss the problems that have caused the outbreak of the demonstrations there in the last few days." Asked whether he would term the

Maryland State trouble "a Bowie State type of situation," Agnew replied, "No, I wouldn't term it that at this stage because this demonstration was triggered by a non-college-oriented incident more than by bringing to fruition grievances within the college, whereas the Bowie situation arose within the college itself." He also noted that several months prior to these demonstrations, he had held good talks with Maryland State alumni and student leaders and "there have been no complaints, there have been no demands that the governor go and meet with the students, or that the students will take any affirmative action with regards to the college administrators or faculty. The students' participation is in an exterior sense, in the march in the community, and there has been no move against Maryland State itself."

This time Agnew even offered to provide transportation to bring the college representatives to Annapolis. "I was so encouraged because of the other meeting I had with the alumni and the way they presented the situation," he said, "I felt that I should make an overture to try to reach the same constructive result that was reached at that time."

Again the legalism of Spiro Agnew was drawing what he considered to be a clear and justifiable line between "making an overture" in the Maryland State situation and "refusing to knuckle under" in the Bowie State case. Asked whether his latest decision reflected "any second thoughts on the way you handled the Bowie situation," Agnew unhesitatingly replied, "Not at all. I'd do the same thing over again in the Bowie situation, and as a matter of fact, if there are outbreaks of violence followed by demands for meetings in this situation, I will not respond to them at all."

By now, few doubted that the governor meant what he said. In less than two months' time he had established himself as a hardline law-and-order man. And, increasingly, the focus of his hard line was the black protest. In late spring, when the Poor People's March on Washington created Resurrection City near the Lincoln Memorial, Agnew unleashed his biting rhetoric against them. He labeled the protesters "lobbyists for opportunism." Asked whether he saw anything wrong in lobbying for poor people, he replied: "Not if it's a frank lobby, or the kind that they have here in Annapolis when they register and admit they're getting paid well for being advocates, and that they're not living examples of the conditions that they are attempting to portray. But I think there is something a little incongruous about people who are relatively affluent living in shacks, marching through mud, traveling by jet all over the country and making statements. I think they should admit what they are."

To those who did not know the early Agnew, and had perceived him chiefly as the white knight who had saved Maryland from George Mahoney, his "transformation" into a hard-liner came as a severe jolt. But to those who did know the early Agnew, his conduct was not surprising. "He didn't change," J. Walter Jones said later. "If he changed he would have had to change overnight. Why people can't see it—it's as clear as can be. The difference between the reasonable Agnew and the unreasonable Agnew, the liberal Agnew and the conservative Agnew, had to do with one speech. The day before he gave that speech when they burned his city down he was the Agnew who had run on the liberal thing, and the day after he was a racist. And of course Agnew didn't change. The circumstances changed.

"The night before, we were sitting on my boat in the harbor in Annapolis, talking about it. He was very much concerned about it, and he was angry. He knew the black leadership in Annapolis had been with the extremists, and while they didn't concur with the burn-baby-burn thing, they did not denounce it. They were more concerned about their position being threatened. I think they were caught with their hands in the cookie jar. He could have acquiesced to it, remained silent, or he could have done what he did."

Agnew wrote the speech himself, Jones said, and read it to friends, including Jones, before delivering it. "The next day he was the same Agnew. The only difference was that speech. Now suddenly is he an archconservative, a racist?"

To Bob Goodman, too, Agnew's conduct over this period was an affirmation of the man, not evidence of a transformation. "As county executive he ran against the tide for the sake of liberalism and for the sake of reform," the Baltimore ad man observed. "When the cities burned in '68, he then felt somebody had to stand up for a society that he thought was being threatened by emotionalism and chaos and bad people and bad ideas, with no substance behind them. And hence he became the boy at the dike. That was his attitude; he didn't change his views. If you check his civil rights record or anything in terms of fair play for minority groups, you'll see the most consistent record in politics, still. Yet he thought he had to articulate the idea that the society was worth keeping and that this couldn't be destroyed by—children. And the thing that prompted that meeting in Baltimore was his disillusionment with the elected blacks. He thought they were as Uncle Tom as many of their own people did. He thought they were Uncle Toms because, God damn it, they wouldn't speak out against any of their own kind, even if it was a Stokely Carmichael or a Rap Brown who was threatening to wreak havoc."

Agnew himself balked at the interpretation that he somehow had changed. Concerning "the speculations and oversimplifications that I have read about my apparent shift in opinion from a liberal to a conservative," he said at the time of his observations on the Poor People's March, "I have never felt more liberal . . . If you ask me specific questions aimed at trying to develop an inconsistency in my philosophy between the time that I was elected and today, you can't find any inconsistency. If anything, I have moved more to the liberal side." He said he now favored "unqualified" open housing, that in spite of his earlier objections based on individual property rights, the public interest in open housing "transcends this. . . . the situation in this country does demand that there must be a lack of emphasis on race."

When Agnew was Vice-President, he was asked in an interview what had led him to relent in 1968 and favor unconditional open housing—the only instance he acknowledges to be a change in position since his Baltimore County days. His answer again revealed his restrictively legalistic approach to problem solving. "I took the original position," he said, "because legally I couldn't convince myself that open housing all the way across the board really was not interfering with the constitutional rights of other people. I felt that a man who owned a house, if he wanted to be selective in who he sold it to, out of any reason, however bigoted or arbitrary or personal—maybe he didn't like the persons who came, didn't think they'd be good for his neighbors—I thought he had a right to say, 'No, I'm not going to sell it to you.' And I didn't think it was government's business how he made that decision.

"Yet I thought that the integration of communities, particularly where social and economic compatibility was there, should take place, and there shouldn't be racial segregation. So I came up with the next-best thing I could think of to push the integration of communities, without interfering with this right I thought the individual had who owned the house to sell it to whom he wanted. And that was to say a builder or developer does not have those same personal interests that an owner has, and it's all right to tell him that he must sell to anybody that applies, because after all, his only motive is a profit motive. An owner might have some kind of agreement with his neighbor that 'if I ever sell the house, I'll give it to you at such-and-such a price, or I'll give it to your cousin who wants to move next to you,' whatever the case may be. I couldn't see any of these personal considerations affecting a builder or a developer, so I went with an open housing affecting these structures.

"I also thought it was logical that people who came into a new development together had a much better chance of making an integrated neighborhood work, than an individual Negro family that might move into an established neighborhood where there are all sorts of cliques already in existence, and that made sense to me. I still feel legally that's probably the only correct position.

"But then after I became governor I began to see that this wasn't going to happen, because basically the developer or the builder, unless he would be faced with an open situation everywhere, was not going to get the financing, was not going to build such a community when he didn't have to. So finally, after a great amount of agonizing personally over the legality of the position, because I do try to be consistent in my positions, I came to the conclusion—even though I couldn't justify it legally, on moral grounds it almost had to be more far-reaching—that perhaps the right of this owner was not as important as the overall objective of breaking down these barriers, senseless barriers, that I think exist where people totally compatible in an economic sense and in a social sense aren't able even to find out that they like each other, because of these prejudices.

"That's when I changed my position to support open housing, and I made clear at that time that it was a change in position that had come about after a great amount of thought and a great amount of agonizing. This is the only issue that I can think of where I've actually changed a stated political position. It's the only one, and I don't think it's a radical change; it's a change in degree. So when people say to me, 'Why have you suddenly become a conservative?' I always say to them, 'Well, you can call me

Nixonites, and to grasp the degrees of luck and finesse required, it is necessary next to examine the political realities that existed about Nelson Rockefeller—and the political fantasies that were nurtured—in the period before the great Agnew "transformation" took place.

9

THE COURTSHIP OF
NELSON ROCKEFELLER

NELSON ROCKEFELLER first met Spiro Agnew in 1965, when Agnew was Baltimore county executive and chairman of a nationwide county officers' organization. Rockefeller remembers going to a motel in Maryland to talk about New York State's pioneer anti-water-pollution program, financed by a billion-dollar bond issue. "He was a very friendly, gracious person," according to Rockefeller, "and he was very enthusiastic about the program." But Rockefeller did not see Agnew again until he appeared at a Republican governors conference as the chief executive of Maryland.

Agnew, however, did not forget that first encounter with Rockefeller and his anti-water-pollution program. He was deeply impressed by Rockefeller personally, and by his high-powered entourage that collected and served up facts, figures and innovative ideas with a thoroughness Agnew had not seen before in government. It was an impression shared by most of the Republican governors, who, when ideology was put aside, frankly regarded Rockefeller as the class of their league. He was a man who was on top of his job, who had the biggest problems, who wrestled with them more aggressively and who got more results than any other man sitting in an American state house.

"I think he's a tremendous man," Agnew said later, when he was Vice-President and had been through his own personally vexing experience with the New York governor. "I always have, and I have a great respect for him. We had some very good governors, but Nelson had a way of always being very prepared, and of course he has a tremendous access to staff work that probably no other governor has. If he doesn't get it in his budget he goes and gets it anyhow. This is not to take away from his ability, but just to say that he was always better prepared than most governors. And they respected him as a leader; he's a charismatic man; he makes friends easily."

But the ideology—that was the problem. Nelson Rockefeller was—there was no other way to put it—a liberal. He saw government not merely as a caretaker, nor as a fire-fighting apparatus against social conflagration, but as an aggressive instrument for anticipating and meeting the people's needs. While many of his Republican colleagues gnashed their teeth over the phenomenon of an ever bigger and more powerful federal establishment, Rockefeller argued that only if state government fulfilled its responsibilities and grasped its opportunities with vision and daring could the encroachments of federal power be stemmed. Long before Richard Nixon as President began to speak of a "new federalism" in which state governments would assume a greater share of the burden of meeting public needs, Nelson Rockefeller was preaching that very slogan—and living it as governor of New York. In the fields of civil rights and labor, particularly, Rockefeller initiated programs that not only ran ahead of federal reforms but also undercut the traditional Democratic liberal base in his state. They gave him that rare potential among Republicans—the prospect of making serious inroads into the vote of big-city blue-collar workers and blacks. That potential could be a great asset to a Republican presidential candidate.

But first, alas for Rockefeller, it was necessary to get the Republican nomination, and such are the ideological bloodlines in the Grand Old Party that a candidate's appeal to independents and Democrats seldom carries great weight. In the party, the True Believer in recent years has taken precedence over the Ideological Revisionist; Rockefeller had found that out in 1960, when the party chose Richard Nixon, and in 1964, when—incredibly to the outside world, but inevitably to the party faithful—it picked

Barry Goldwater over him. These two experiences, especially the latter, soured Rockefeller on presidential politicking; although he wanted to be President and was confident in his own mind that he was better equipped than any other Republican to handle the job, he vowed after the 1964 debacle to abandon the chase.

Because his primary contests against Goldwater in 1964 had been so divisive, and because he had declined after the convention to campaign for Goldwater, Rockefeller was saddled within the G.O.P. with a large share of the blame for Goldwater's disastrous loss. Nixon, circling over the remains, ingratiated himself among the beaten Goldwaterites and other party loyalists by singling out Rockefeller as a "spoilsport" and a "party divider"— characterizations that inspired columnist Murray Kempton to observe that Nixon sought "to bind up the wounds of the Republican Party with a tourniquet around the neck of Nelson Rockefeller."

Rockefeller, for his part, undoubtedly felt the squeeze. In deep trouble in his own state in 1965 as a result of a heavy tax load he had imposed to finance his ambitious reforms, he was rated a near-certain loser should he try for a third term as governor in 1966. Part of his trouble also was his demonstrated presidential ambition. Twice now he had made a pass at national power while occupying the State House in Albany. In 1960 he had tested his prospects before pulling back, then sniped at Nixon as an undeclared but available alternative. In 1964, after divorcing his first wife and marrying a divorcee with four children, he had made an open race against Goldwater, had lost in two of three primaries and had nearly been hooted out of the Cow Palace in San Francisco. If he wanted a third term in Albany, his advisers told him, he would have to make an unconditional pledge that he would not seek the Presidency again.

Rockefeller made the promise in 1965, and by dint of a punishing and costly campaign and the luck of drawing an ineffective and disorganized opponent, Queens County District Attorney Frank O'Connor, he won a third term. O'Connor was a very likable product of the regular Democratic organization, but he lacked the ability to project a star quality—important in a large state where television plays a major campaign role. His candidacy, though a losing one, was responsible for an addition to American political folklore that doubtless will live far beyond memory of the candidate himself. City Comptroller Mario Procaccino, later the Democratic candidate for mayor of New York, speaking at a Manhattan dinner in O'Connor's behalf, told the audience that the candidate was not the kind of man who immediately inspired people. But after a while Procaccino said with all solemnity, "he grows on you—like a cancer." With opponents like that, Rockefeller didn't need friends. (After that, Procaccinoisms knew no bounds. In his own campaign for mayor in 1969, Procaccino told one Harlem audience that "except for an accident of birth, I would be black," and another that "I may be white, but in my heart I'm just as black as you are.")

Down in Maryland, however, Nelson Rockefeller had a better friend than he realized. While other Republican eyes turned to Richard Nixon—who had predicted a massive off-year party comeback in 1966, had labored tirelessly for party candidates and had emerged as both prophet and healer—Agnew looked toward Rockefeller. Agnew believed strongly that if the governors formed a bloc they could be a major force in the choice of the nominee, and he talked to others, notably James Rhodes of Ohio, along these lines. In April 1967, brushing aside Rockefeller's 1965 pledge that he would not run for the Presidency again in 1968, Agnew announced at the Yale Republican Club that he planned to ask Rockefeller to do so.

Rockefeller already had thrown in with Republican Governor George Romney of Michigan and was providing personal financial backing estimated by one source at $400,000. Romney, himself re-elected resoundingly in November 1966 and the G.O.P. front runner in the major national polls, had set out early in 1967 to acquire the national exposure some of his aides felt was necessary to build a national candidacy. Romney was no Frank O'Connor; he was a rugged, handsome man with a definite "presidential look": square, set jaw, broad, winning smile, a silvering mane—and an evangelical stump style.

But, alas for Romney, if there was little O'Connor in him, there was some Procaccino. At a luncheon in Idaho, for instance, while Mrs. Romney and the wife of then Republican Governor Don Samuelson sat nearby, he said of Samuelson, "He and I share a common asset—our wives." And Romney was given too often to more serious attacks of foot-in-mouth. He criticized President Lyndon Johnson for being "locked in" on the Vietnam war, then a day or two later said Johnson was ambivalent on the war, talking peace one day and escalating the fighting the next. He forever was saying something and then "clarifying" it, and eventually he was to make the observation that he had received "the greatest brain-washing that anybody can get" in an earlier visit to Vietnam. That remark proved to be the final straw against him, but until then and even for months afterward, Rockefeller stood steadfastly behind Romney, with both moral and financial support.

There were those—and Agnew may have been among them—who believed that Rockefeller merely was using Romney as a stalking horse through 1967. Mrs. Romney, for one, made no secret later of her suspicions and bitterness at Rockefeller's eventual entry into the race. But there is strong evidence that Rockefeller's support of Romney was genuine; that if he did not see Romney as the ideal leader of Western civilization, he did see him as a decent exponent of moderate Republicanism, and preferable, certainly, to his old foe Nixon. And in the spring of 1967 at least, Rockefeller was saying repeatedly that he had had his flirtations with the Presidency and had put them behind him; that he had promised the voters of New York he would not seek the office again, and he intended to keep that promise.

Such was the state of affairs in moderate Republicanism and in Rockefeller's own mind when Agnew announced his intentions at Yale. "I think he can win,'" Agnew said. "He's a tremendously able person and he's done a job that's been greatly underrated." Agnew said he had nothing against Romney "but it just so happens that I'm tremendously impressed with Governor Rockefeller. I think that if he wants to run, he ought to get into the race now and not wait like Bill Scranton [in 1964]." Rockefeller's remarriage, which had helped do him in politically in 1964, "will not have any effect," Agnew said; Rockefeller's easy re-election to a third term in Albany had proved that.

Agnew was not alone in his interest in Rockefeller as a presidential candidate. In the key primary state of Oregon, Governor Tom McCall, among the most liberal and outspoken of the Republicans, was trying to keep the door open. He wrote a letter to fellow Republican governors urging them to delay endorsing anyone until they could act in concert, and on Rockefeller's copy he added a postscript urging the New Yorker to reconsider. "I'm out of it," Rockefeller replied. "If we moderates want to preserve any chance of nominating a candidate who can win, we'd better stay united behind George Romney." Rockefeller noted that for all of Romney's troubles he still was running 10 percentage points ahead of Johnson in the national polls. "Any move to undercut him or proliferate the moderate support or even to consult with a view to looking to other candidates will, in my humble opinion, simply deliver the nomination to the other side on a silver platter." Rockefeller didn't identify "the other side," but to all who understood G.O.P. politics and the particular chemistry of personalities, it was clear he meant Richard Nixon. To both McCall and Agnew, Rockefeller spelled it out once again: "I am not a candidate, and under no circumstances will I run."

But Agnew was just as adamant. He reiterated that he intended to take the case directly to Rockefeller. "I have a feeling Governor Rockefeller could be persuaded if there is substantial evidence of a wave in his direction," Agnew said. If on the other hand Rockefeller convinced him he would not be a candidate under any circumstances, he said, "I would be rather foolish to continue."

On May 1, 1967, Rockefeller agreed to see Agnew. For ninety minutes they talked in Rockefeller's Manhattan office, which Rockefeller preferred to the confining political climate of Albany. Rockefeller did not budge an inch, nor did he leave the door open to a candidacy even a crack. "I am disappointed," Agnew told awaiting reporters. "I feel a tremendous sense of need to have a candidate of the Rockefeller type."

In the next months, even as Romney continued to reel downward, Rockefeller held firmly to his position. Although some may have expected that Romney's misfortunes would pull Rockefeller inexorably from that position, those misfortunes actually worked on him the other way. The more Romney slipped, the more bolstering and moral support he needed; the more others turned away from Romney, the more it was incumbent on Rockefeller to stay with him. This was so not only for Romney's sake but also for the sake of Rockefeller's own credibility as a man who had given his word and intended to keep it. Once, riding through Manhattan's frantic rush hour with him in his limousine, a reporter asked Rockefeller what he would do if Romney did falter and the party turned to him. "I frankly feel that what you say is impossible," he replied. "I'm just not going to knock myself out thinking about it." Why, then, did he think his name kept resurfacing in all the speculation? "I'll be darned if I know," he said, the expressive line in his forehead deepening for an instant. "All I know is these people weren't speaking that way last time when I was working like hell for it."

At a meeting of Western governors at West Yellowstone, Montana, in late June, Romney agents descended with a desperate, ill-advised effort to nail down commitments from G.O.P. moderates. Two primary targets, McCall and David F. Cargo of New Mexico, already sizing up Romney as a loser, made it known that they would have no part of the scheme. Romney's campaign, said McCall with customary candor, "is lying dead in the water."

Immediately after the West Yellowstone meeting, the Western Republicans crossed the border to Jackson Hole, Wyoming, for the semiannual gathering of all G.O.P. governors, then twenty-five in number. Agnew was among them, and although he had been a governor only six months, his presence, confidence and good fellowship already had made him a favorite colleague. The governors as a group are lovers of golf, and they always have the foresight to schedule their conferences within a chip shot of an excellent course. Agnew, though later prone to well-publicized embarrassments as a golfer, could hold his own with most, and he soon was accepted as one of the clique's sportsmen.

When it came to President-making, however, the consensus among his colleagues was that Ted Agnew was a duffer. The reality was that Nelson Rockefeller couldn't get the Republican nomination even when he had fought for it. So how could he get it now, when he wouldn't, and when the party was so down on him for having tried so hard, and having caused so much damage, the last time? At a reception at the outset of the Jackson Hole conference, Rockefeller told political reporters he was just as solidly as ever for Romney. He tried to disabuse them of the idea that the Romney camp was trying to obtain firm pledges. "This isn't a fraternity," he cracked. The denial was, of course, a ploy to minimize the dimensions of the failure at West Yellowstone and Jackson Hole to get the Romney candidacy off the ground. But Agnew held firm. "I'm not encouraged by what Governor Rockefeller is saying," he said. "I've detected no softening in his attitude, but nonetheless I'm not giving up any effort to persuade him to run."

One wondered by this time what it would take to convince Agnew, and so did Rockefeller. When advised of Agnew's position, he asked with some distress, "How can you do more than say you are not going to be a candidate under any circumstances?" Rockefeller aides set about undercutting the Maryland governor; one told reporters that Agnew must be "smoking opium" if he thought Rockefeller could be persuaded to run. Agnew conceded that his position was "sort of out on the end of the ice floe. At some time," he said, "I'll have to admit it's the point of no return." Then—in July 1967—he did not know how prophetic those words would prove to be.

Agnew went back to Maryland—and to Rap Brown and the Cambridge riots—but he was not giving up. At still another gathering of the clan, the Southern Governors Conference in Asheville, North Carolina, he tried another tack—a Rockefeller-Reagan unity ticket. By now Romney had made his "brainwashing" remark, and Rockefeller, Agnew said, "cannot help but be impressed" by the increasing clamor for some other moderate-liberal Republican to replace him. Though Reagan lacked the experience to be President, Agnew said, he would make a strong "copilot," and together they would be "without question the strongest ticket the party could offer."

To the political pros, including the Nixon operatives who were quietly but efficiently cementing their man's base in the party, the idea was a ludicrous pipe dream. Nevertheless, a few weeks later, when the ever-junketing state executives gathered again, this time on the decks of the S. S. *Independence* for the first floating governors conference, pictures of Rockefeller and Reagan graced the cover of *Time* magazine. News photographers aboard drove them together with the mixture of cajolery and bullying that works so effectively for them with meek and mighty alike, and the resultant pictures kept the "dream ticket" talk alive.

A short time out of New York harbor en route to the Virgin Islands and the land-based portion of the conference, three reporters intercepted Rockefeller on the ship's sun deck and asked him what he thought about the Rockefeller-Reagan cover of *Time*. "I wouldn't be human if I didn't appreciate a nice remark," he said, "but I'm not a candidate, I'm not going to be a candidate, and *I don't want to be President*." Was he saying flatly he not only wasn't running but didn't want the job? "You heard me loud and clear," he said. Well—if nominated, would he turn down the nomination? "I *said*"—this time with an edge in his voice—"I don't want to be President."

The disavowal was the most categorical Rockefeller had uttered to date. Later, aides insisted privately he had made the statement on purpose, to shore up the sagging Romney, who meanwhile had gone to him on the *Independence* and offered to step aside. But the spontaneous way the question was raised, and the way Rockefeller blurted out the answer, suggested otherwise.

In any event, word of Rockefeller's remark soon swept through the ship and reached the official passenger from Maryland, Ted Agnew. "That's pretty definite," he said. "But I still say, if he's drafted it would take a pretty emphatic individual to turn down a genuine draft. Indeed, I can't conceive of it." Maybe the whole incident was no more than an exercise in semantics, but it did underline one thing: Ted Agnew was a man who didn't give up easily. It would take something more, obviously, than even a flat statement that his man didn't want the highest office in the land to convince him to desist.

While Rockefeller thus was trying to hold firm for Romney, and Agnew was holding his own personal and solitary line for Rockefeller, Nixon agents aboard the *Independence* were quietly sounding out the other governors. Former Republican Governor of Oklahoma Henry Bellmon, chairman of the "Nixon for President" committee, and Nixon political operative John Sears softsold the G.O.P. governors on the virtue of staying uncommitted.

Several weeks later, when the Republican governors met again, this time in Palm Beach, Florida (governors never meet, for some reason, in Newark or Buffalo), Nixon agents John Sears and Robert Ellsworth began to drive the final nails into Romney's political coffin. They persuaded Governor Tim Babcock of Montana, a conservative who had been considered a Reagan man but secretly had been in the Nixon camp for at least two months, to say he was perfectly willing to accept Nixon if he won the first two 1968 primaries; if that happened, Babcock would take no part in a stop-Nixon drive. Other governors concurred that they would not join any stop-Nixon effort if he showed he could be a winner. Sears and Ellsworth talked to Agnew, said they were aware he was for Rockefeller, but told him the Nixonites fully expected their man to be nominated and wanted to keep friendly relations with everyone in the interest of a unified party. Agnew told them he had nothing against Nixon and would support him if nominated. "It's beginning to look like we'll have to reconcile ourselves emotionally and ideologically to Nixon," McCall said, and Cargo added, "There's no fight. There's nobody who will get up and say we've got to get behind Romney."

Rockefeller kept up a positive, optimistic front by calling Romney, who by then was a declared candidate, "one of the great campaigners" who could salvage his campaign by "going to the people of New Hampshire in an exciting way." But then Rockefeller himself helped fasten the lid on Romney. He told reporters that while a Rockefeller draft was not a possibility in his mind, he would "have to face it" if it occurred. For the first time in many months, Agnew was able to take heart from something his unwilling noncandidate had said. Rockefeller clearly was the man most of the governors wanted, Agnew said, if only he would offer himself.

During the meeting, the influential Governor Jim Rhodes of Ohio pulled Agnew and McCall aside, linked arms with them and said grandly and conspiratorially, "Boys, let's put this one together for Rockefeller." But Romney was the stumbling block. As long as he stayed in, Rockefeller would stay out. Asked whether he would have to re-evaluate his backing of Romney if a genuine draft occurred, Rockefeller told newsmen, "If what you're saying happens, it would only happen if Romney isn't there." Also, there was the risk of tearing the party apart again, after all the rebuilding. Rockefeller wanted no part of that, and Agnew knew it. "If he can become the nominee before becoming the candidate," Agnew said after Palm Beach, "I think he'll do it"—meaning if he could avoid divisive primaries. But that called for the Republican party to dismiss the winner of the primaries and then in effect coronate Rockefeller. That scenario never was realistic, and if Agnew didn't know it, Richard Nixon did. He laid careful plans for the primaries—and waited.

Romney, throwing all he had into New Hampshire, started campaigning there early in January 1968, hoping by dint of sheer effort and personality to overcome his image as an ineffectual bumbler. Actually, his organization and strategy were much better than generally recognized. An old Rockefeller aide, John

Deardourff, and David Goldberg, who had helped engineer the 1964 write-in victory for Henry Cabot Lodge, established a network of "home headquarters" around the state; Romney visited several a day, meeting and talking with neighbors in a homey, living-room format. In such surroundings, he was at his most effective. But by now, after all that had happened before he came to New Hampshire, he simply was not being taken seriously. His slogan—"George Romney Fights Moral Decay"—made him sound, as one staff aide put it, "like a toothpaste." And as often occurs with a politician saddled with a negative image, things kept happening to underline and magnify his shortcomings. One day he walked into a bowling alley, shook some hands, then tried his luck at duckpins. In a demonstration of the same kind of embarrassing doggedness that marked his bid for the Presidency, Romney failed to knock down all the pins with his first ball, and also with his second, and with his third, and with his fourth. As a crowd gathered, he dug in, refusing to quit. Finally, after his thirty-fourth attempt, the last pin fell. That, more than one voter no doubt felt, was poor old George for you.

From Annapolis, Agnew observed Romney's general ineptitude with mounting hope that it would force Rockefeller's hand. Although Rockefeller held his ground, his chief political adviser, George Hinman, was keeping tabs on pro-Rockefeller sentiment around the country. In Oregon, scene of Rockefeller's only 1964 primary victory, McCall was involved in a massive petition drive to persuade Rockefeller to run. At one point McCall met Hinman secretly at the San Francisco airport for three hours to discuss the Oregon picture. The site of the meeting was as interesting as what was said; it indicated the care Hinman took not to generate reports that Rockefeller really was interested in running in Oregon and hence was playing games with Romney, using him as a stalking horse. From all available evidence, Rockefeller still was hoping to ride out the year behind Romney, but the pressure was mounting on him.

In this uncertain atmosphere, early in January Rockefeller filed a statement of noncandidacy in Oregon as required by law to keep his name off the ballot in the May presidential primary. But the wording he used was interpreted by some as falling short of the flat disavowal of candidacy the law demanded. Agnew called the development "sort of a left-handed encouragement," but said he was "encouraged much more by the tremendous amount of public pressure that is being put on the governor to revise his position." He didn't see, Agnew told reporters in Annapolis, "how a man as sensitive as Governor Rockefeller can fail to be impressed by the groundswell of desire for his candidacy. I think that we are going to find that as the pressures mount, he may revise his position." Agnew announced that he was going ahead with a "draft Rockefeller" organization in Maryland, and hoped the effort would spread to other states. In early February he reported that fifty-eight leading Baltimore businessmen and bankers had been signed on, headed by L. Mercer Smith, vice-president of the Chesapeake and Potomac Telephone Company of Maryland, and also including Agnew's old friend and investment mentor, J. Walter Jones.

Meanwhile, back in snowy New Hampshire, George Romney was coming face to face with the futility of his year-long pilgrimage to nowhere. Surveys by his trusted Detroit pollster, Fred Currier, indicated that for all the effort and thrashing about, not only was Romney not climbing, he still was struggling with a basic identity and recognition problem among New Hampshirites. On top of that, a local college professor, a rank amateur in presidential politics, was revving up a write-in for Rockefeller. As amateurish as it was—and the Rockefeller camp wanted no part of it—there was a distinct possibility that the write-in could produce more votes for Rockefeller than Romney's professional operation might generate for the hapless Michigan governor. Rockefeller had even made a trip to New Hampshire to urge his old backers to get behind Romney, but it hadn't done much good. "We haven't moved, George," Romney's campaign manager, former Republican National Chairman Leonard Hall, told him in a meeting in a New Hampshire motel. "And we have this Rockefeller problem. We have to consider the possibility of getting creamed." If the trend continued, Hall told Romney, "we'll have to consider whether we want to pull out to avoid complete humiliation." This was not the sort of thing one ordinarily would suggest to the proud and stubborn Romney, but he took it, surprisingly, with a nod.

A few weeks later, when further polling confirmed the bleakness of the outlook, Romney jolted the political world—and sent Ted Agnew's hopes for Rockefeller soaring—by acting on the dismaying counsel he had received in that New Hampshire motel room. On February 28 he abruptly announced he was withdrawing from the presidential race, two weeks before the nation's first presidential primary.

At first the Nixon camp was chagrined that its candidate thus was deprived of a clear-cut victory. Nixon himself suspected that the pull-out had been programed as part of a scheme to bring Rockefeller into the race. But Nixon's sources of political intelligence in New Hampshire and around the country quickly put that suspicion to rest. Rockefeller had been caught as unaware as anyone else; he was left high and dry, with neither a plan nor an organization. It soon dawned on the Nixon operatives that their man had just scored the first technical knockout in American presidential primary annals, and with one blow not only had put George Romney on the canvas but also had flattened a more dangerous barrier to the Nixon political comeback—Nixon's own haunting "loser image." Now, suddenly, he was a winner, and so overwhelmingly a winner that his opponent had been chased out of the ring.

Rockefeller's conduct in the days immediately preceding Romney's decision to quit had been viewed with deep suspicion by Romney and some of his aides. Four days earlier, at a fund-raising luncheon for Romney in Detroit, Rockefeller had lauded the Michigan governor at length, but then, in response to the inevitable question about a draft for himself, conceded he would accept it if it came. As usual, he discounted that possibility and repeated his backing of Romney, but the disclaimer was lost in the headlines highlighting his availability. In an interview much later, Rockefeller said he was committed to Romney to the very end, and in fact had hoped Romney would have stayed in the New Hampshire primary all the way. But Romney later told Robert J. Donovan of the Los Angeles *Times* that Rockefeller's Detroit remarks had "cut the ground out from under me, and consequently there was no possibility of my winning the nomination." And that was "the decisive factor" in his withdrawal, Romney insisted. Others involved said, however, that Currier's poll, indicating not only defeat but humiliation for Romney, was the critical element. If the cause of moderate-liberal Republicanism was to be salvaged, Romney had to step aside and let somebody else—obviously Rockefeller—take over.

The development was precisely the sort that Agnew had been saying could occur to bring his favorite candidate into the race. About ten days before Romney withdrew, Agnew talked in his Baltimore office about his fledgling "draft Rockefeller" organization in Maryland, and about his hopes to extend it beyond his own state. Agnew acknowledged that he had been keeping in touch with Hinman, and through him had been keeping Rockefeller thoroughly advised about what he was doing. "He doesn't say no," Agnew said with new optimism. "I just tell him how many people are interested, and he indicates it's very flattering." But Agnew also went out of his way to stress that he was not in the business of organizing a stop-Nixon movement. "I like Nixon," he said near the close of the interview. "If Rockefeller can't be brought in, he may well be my choice."

Only a few weeks before, Agnew had had his first real exposure to Nixon. A mutual political associate, State Senator Louise Gore of Maryland, arranged without the advance knowledge of either man for Nixon and Agnew to drop by a women's Republican reception in New York. They immediately fell into deep private discussion. Nixon launched a long dissertation on the capture of the *Pueblo*, the American spy ship just seized with its full crew by the North Koreans. Nixon and Agnew talked for an hour or more, not on presidential politics but on issues. Each man left much impressed with the other; Nixon told Louise Gore that she ought to get her governor to speak out more on foreign policy matters. "The two men hit it off," one observer says, "because they're very much alike. They're both very sincere, they're both very dedicated, they're both very aware, they both have a tremendous concept of the problems of government, and they've both been through the mill. . . . They understood what each was saying. . . . They related to each other. They could look each other in the eye and discuss on an intelligent level." It was after that meeting that Agnew took pains always to say his pro-Rockefeller efforts were not to be construed in any way as anti-Nixon. The meeting, however, did not figure at all in early Nixon calculations, according to one Nixon lieutenant. "We had pretty well kissed Agnew off through the time Rockefeller got out," he said. "We had no reason not to. He was openly and strongly for Rockefeller."

When the Romney bombshell hit, even Agnew was momentarily immobilized. Romney had timed his announcement for the opening of a Republican governors meeting in Washington, and Agnew, reached there, said he didn't think it was quite the time "to start a Rockefeller bandwagon." The Republican governors, he said, ought to have "a decent interval" to check sentiment back in their states. He said he would favor a special meeting, perhaps in the next month, to see if a consensus of the governors was possible on another candidate. (Romney, seething over what he perceived as Rockefeller's "betrayal" of him, deleted from his text prepared by an aide a call for the other governors to rally behind Rockefeller. In fact, Romney wanted to hold a press conference to denounce Rockefeller, but was dissuaded by cooler heads.)

Meanwhile, Agnew met with Rockefeller again and reported that the New Yorker had agreed to run if "there is a broad base of support for him." But Rockefeller had stressed, Agnew said, that he didn't want to be tossed into the breach simply as a stop-Nixon candidate, creating a schism in the party as in 1964. Agnew, of course, did not want that either, now that he had met Nixon and had been so impressed by him. In fact, according to one aide, Agnew specifically went up to New York around this time to tell Nixon he was going to run a draft effort for Rockefeller in Maryland. Agnew told Nixon, this aide says, that he admired him highly but was backing Rockefeller because he thought he could win the Presidency.

On March 1, 1968, Rockefeller conferred with other governors and then spelled out his position. "The party must decide who it feels can best represent it and who it thinks can best command the confidence of the American people and best serve the country," he said. The Republican party "wants to nominate someone who can get enough independent and Democratic votes to get elected. I am not going to create dissension within the Republican party by contending for the nomination, but I am ready and willing to serve the American people if called."

That was good enough for Agnew. He intensified his efforts, while Rockefeller and his immediate inner circle—including George Hinman, Bob Douglas, Hugh Morrow, and publicist and long-time confidant Ted Braun of Los Angeles—began three weeks of intensive research and political soul-searching. The big question, as always with professional politicians, was whether it was "do-able"—whether, considering the lateness of the political season, Nixon's organizational start across the country and his certain triumph in New Hampshire, Rockefeller had any realistic chance for the nomination. With the memory of the 1964 split fresh in his mind, and particularly his own role in it and the giant's share of the blame he incurred, Nelson Rockefeller didn't want to go through all that again. Meanwhile, though, the Romney pull-out had generated a great deal of pressure from around the country and considerable offers of help. It was decided there had to be some sort of organization to drain off this activity—to keep support in a holding pattern until Rockefeller made up his mind. If the answer was going to be yes, this grass-roots interest could be put to good use. As noted earlier, former Governor Scranton was to be the front man for this holding operation, but when he balked, and when the suggestion of J. Irwin Miller was brushed aside, Agnew was approached—not knowing he was the third choice. An office was opened in Annapolis under Al Abrahams, and at the same time Agnew worked to mobilize influential Republicans to urge an open candidacy on Rockefeller.

McCall in Oregon also was interested again. A large contingent of Oregonians came east specifically to urge Rockefeller to enter the Oregon primary, whose deadline for filing was fast approaching. In Annapolis, Abrahams swung into action. He hired help, opened local bank accounts, all with Rockefeller money, and by March 6 the phone calls and mail that had been smothering Hinman were being routed to Annapolis. Within another few days Abrahams had put together for Agnew the first national "Rockefeller for President" meeting in nearby Washington. Republicans from seventeen states heard a pep talk from Agnew, who now had begun to look less like a foolish neophyte in national political affairs and more like a prophet. There were some important fat cats in the group, notably Stewart Mott III, the young auto heir and political philanthropist who often ran ads in the *New York Times* offering to match public campaign contributions for liberal candidates.

But if Agnew and the others were revved up for a presidential campaign, Abrahams was not. "We were dancing until it was decided whether we were going to bed," he said later. Hinman had told him at the very start that the three-week exploratory period was exactly that. It would take considerable grass-roots support to enable Rockefeller to end-run the hostile party machinery, and it was already late, with the first presidential primary all but completed and filing dates on others closed. Hinman had told Abrahams that in light of all this, Rockefeller's decision was "a close thing—no better than a fifty-fifty chance." Abrahams had passed on this word to Agnew at their first meeting, but the freshman governor, who had sustained himself on much less than that for a year, remained optimistic that the answer would be affirmative.

On a Sunday afternoon in early March, an impressive company of Republican governors and other party leaders, Agnew among them, met for several hours with Rockefeller in his Fifth Avenue apartment. They came away expressing confidence that Rockefeller would run.

Within the inner circle, however, to which Agnew never was privy, a very lively debate was going on. The immediate focus was the filing deadline for the Oregon primary, March 22. If there was one place on the primary trail where Rockefeller might beat Nixon, it was Oregon. Rockefeller's foot-dragging had dissipated some of the enthusiasm for him there, and had made life difficult politically for McCall, but as the man who in 1964 "cared enough to come" to the Oregon primary when Goldwater did not, Rockefeller still figured to have a reservoir of support. Hinman led the forces who argued for entry into the Oregon primary. Braun led the opposition, which stressed the divisive potential in a head-to-head contest against Nixon. Rockefeller himself and particularly his wife, Happy, wanted to avoid a repetition of the bitterness generated in the 1964 primary contests, in which their marriage had been an issue, both spoken and unspoken. Finally, if Rockefeller was to enter the Oregon primary, precise timing was important. The filing deadline for the Nebraska primary was March 15, and everyone agreed that Rockefeller ought to avoid Nebraska—a sure thing for Nixon. Thus, Rockefeller would have to declare his candidacy after March 15 but before March 22.

While the inner circle debated the matter, fresh polls were taken in Oregon, and according to Hinman later, they were "not as encouraging" as the Rockefeller camp had expected. Also, on the Democratic side, another soul-searching New Yorker, Senator Robert F. Kennedy, was reassessing his own candidacy at precisely the same time, and the Nebraska deadline suddenly became fluid. Kennedy decided he wanted to enter Nebraska, and state officials were persuaded that their deadline did not apply to presidential candidates. Knowing Rockefeller's decision was due shortly, that deadline was left open; thus, if Rockefeller went into Oregon, he would be placed on the ballot in Nebraska as well. "A statement going into both primaries was actually drafted," one Rockefeller aide said later. "But Nelson finally decided against it because this [Nebraska] was playing in Nixon's room." If he was to be nominated, Rockefeller finally concluded, it would have to be outside the divisive primary route. (Agnew shared the concern of other Rockefeller supporters about the Nebraska primary. He told reporters he hoped Rockefeller would not be forced into it because Nebraska was "probably the top state for Nixon in the whole country." Rockefeller himself brushed the matter aside. "The world isn't going to be made or broken on one primary," he said.)

As late as March 18, however, three days before he was scheduled to make his plans known in a televised press conference, Rockefeller was still exploring. He went to Washington for an evening meeting with advisers at his Foxhall Road home, and a breakfast meeting the next morning with Republican senators. Before going out to Foxhall Road, he was met at the Page Airways terminal at National Airport and taken to a dinner of the Order of Ahepa. The dinner gave Agnew a last opportunity to make his case to Rockefeller and to make his own assessment of what the decision would be. The New Yorker was mobbed by well-wishers; invited to a private VIP reception, Rockefeller instead asked to be taken to the general reception because "there are more voters there." Rockefeller said later he had advised Agnew that night not to get out on a limb about his candidacy. But Agnew looked at and listened to the public acclaim at that dinner and Rockefeller's smiling, eager response to it, and drew his own conclusion. "Agnew apparently came away with a rosier picture than I had been led to believe existed," Abrahams recalled later. "If anything, I was hearing it might go the other way. Happy [Mrs. Rockefeller] was against him running, for one thing. And after talking to Hinman and others in New York I felt more and more that Rocky wouldn't go. But Agnew apparently convinced himself he was going to."

At the breakfast with the G.O.P. senators the next morning, according to Hinman, Rockefeller "was rather chilled by their approach to the whole thing. Their idea was, 'Why, sure, go in and give Nixon a race. It will help him.' That wasn't exactly what the governor was looking for."

Rockefeller returned to New York. The next day the *New York Times,* in a front-page story, said he was going to announce that he would run. It is this story that Rockefeller said later had been planted, presumably by foes at City Hall, and was the reason he decided not to advise anyone, including Agnew, of his no-go decision in advance of his March 21 press conference.

Some others, however, were told. At about eleven-thirty on the morning of Rockefeller's big announcement, Abrahams was in the Annapolis office when the phone rang. It was Hinman. "Close down," he said flatly. "He's not going."

Abrahams took the news with chagrin but no great surprise, after what he had been hearing. "I've got one question for you, George," he replied. "Has anybody told Agnew?"

"The governor talked to him this morning," Hinman said. "He had six calls to make and Agnew was one of them."

"Are you sure?" Abrahams asked.

"Yes," Hinman replied. But, as things turned out, Hinman had no basis for his certainty.

Thus Abrahams, sitting only a short walk from Agnew in his office at the State House, knew more than an hour before Rockefeller's TV appearance what was going to happen—and said nothing. "If I had known Agnew hadn't been informed, obviously I would have raced up Main Street to tell him," he said later. "But I knew how disappointed Ted would be. It would have been a bit presumptuous for me to go busting into his office at such a time; it was between Nelson and him."

Meanwhile, at the State House, Agnew's lieutenants were proceeding blissfully on the assumption that Rockefeller was about to make their boss a clairvoyant. It was a nice touch for Agnew to hold his regular press conference just before the Rockefeller appearance on television; that way the reporters would be there to record Agnew's moment of glory and get his comments for Maryland readers and evening TV watchers. "If I had known he was going to hold a press conference, with the television set in there," Abrahams said later, "I would have run up there and smashed the set."

Ironically, one Republican governor who, compared to Agnew, had been a late recruit to the idea of a Rockefeller candidacy—Harold LeVander of Minnesota—did get advance warning. It saved him from holding a press conference in St. Paul similar to the one in Annapolis that proved to be so humiliating to Agnew. An aide to LeVander, Jerry Olson, was working for Rockefeller in New York. About fifteen minutes before Rockefeller was to announce his decision, Olson called LeVander and warned him to hold off saying anything until he had watched Rockefeller on television.

None of the foregoing was known by Agnew, still a Rockefeller outsider for all his long and tenacious support, as the Maryland governor sat in Annapolis, a television set in front of him and the Maryland State House press standing in a wide arc around him. Thus, when Rockefeller announced that he had decided "to reiterate unequivocally that I am not a candidate campaigning directly or indirectly for the Presidency of the United States," Agnew suddenly and most unexpectedly was face to face with that "point of no return" to which he had alluded nine months earlier.

Although he had been the staunchest, most public Rockefeller fan in view, Agnew was not moved to resist or try to reverse the noncandidate's judgment. He told reporters he would comply with Rockefeller's wishes and close down the "draft Rockefeller" shop—which Abrahams already had been instructed by Hinman to do. One thing was certain: Spiro Agnew had been badly used, and how he now responded was to become an important factor in determining who would be the next Vice-President of the United States.

10

THE SWITCH TO RICHARD NIXON

A T first, although Ted Agnew was publicly humiliated and privately crushed by the cavalier way he had been handled by Rockefeller, he continued to speak of the New Yorker as the best man for the Presidency. Asked shortly after Rockefeller's decision whether he had "jumped off the Rockefeller scooter," Agnew said, "Well, a scooter is a two-wheel device that can't remain upright unless it's running, and this scooter seems to have stopped for the moment. It's pretty difficult to remain on that scooter. Whether the scooter will resume its momentum and I will jump back on it or not is a question to be seen. I will say this—I *still* think Nelson Rockefeller is the best candidate the Republican party could offer to the electorate in November. But having someone who is not willing to become a candidate be the best candidate is certainly no way to elect anybody, so I'm in the process of revising and watching and waiting to see what's going to happen. I don't have anyone who's running at the moment that I can support."

Agnew said he would decide later what to do about the "draft Rockefeller" organizations set up in Baltimore and Washington, but he obviously was demoralized. "I question the ability of the volunteer groups to hold the enthusiasm that's pouring out all over the country in the face of his announcement," he said. As for Nixon, Agnew reiterated that "I am not against Mr. Nixon. He may—may—even be my number-two choice."

In Maryland especially, the Rockefeller decision put Agnew on the spot. He now was faced with the possibility that his state's delegation would go one way and he another—or, more accurately, nowhere. Maryland Representative Rogers C. B. Morton already was in the Nixon camp, and Agnew somehow had to reassert his party leadership. (Later in 1968, during the general-election campaign, Agnew told the editors of the *New York Times* of his feelings about Rockefeller's decision, "I was heavily involved in the effort [to draft him]. I had personally persuaded many centers of influence—influential people who had never taken a position before a convention on a candidate, some of whom were Democratic who supported me, to go with Mr. Rockefeller. They had publicly announced their position. This was my political base and my strength. . . . It's not personal rancor, it's like hitting you where you work. This was an incursion into my political acceptability, and, after all, what does a politician have but his credibility? And when I told these people the man was going to become a candidate and they announced, and then he didn't, it had a very bad effect on me in the eyes of my influential constituency.")

The alert Nixon camp wasted no time moving in. John Sears, the young and astute political operative from Nixon's New York law firm, was in Alaska wooing Governor Walter Hickel when Rockefeller made his announcement. Sears immediately called Nixon and urged that an emissary be sent to Annapolis to get to Agnew while he was still warm. Bob Ellsworth was dispatched forthwith and a meeting was arranged between Agnew and Nixon in New York on March 29. For more than two hours they talked politics and issues. Agnew came out still saying he thought Rockefeller would be the party's best candidate but acknowledging he was "discouraged" and was taking a good look at Nixon. "I am not ready to announce any support of Mr. Nixon at this time," Agnew said, but he added, "I have high regard for him. He's the front runner." As for Nixon, aides recalled later that he was very impressed by Agnew's "strength." There is some belief among Nixon's lieutenants of the time that the meeting caught Agnew at precisely the right moment, and that in his bitterness he really unburdened himself about Rockefeller being an ingrate. "What may have happened was that Agnew was so boiled about his treatment at Rockefeller's hands that he had some vengeance in him that he talked about," one lieutenant theorized later. "You know, Agnew is a strong, forceful fellow when he gets something on his mind."

From then on, the Nixon camp pursued Agnew avidly. "The effect of Nixon and Agnew even being seen together after Rockefeller said he wasn't going into the primaries," a Nixon hand said, "was to cause some people who had been behind Rockefeller to think twice before they started back on that path, and at least buy some time. I don't think any of us thought, even when Rockefeller made that declaration, that he wasn't going to be a factor by the time the convention came around, or indeed wouldn't be known as a candidate by that time. But it bought us some time, and anybody we could be seen talking to, or pick off or get out of that camp would do a lot to help us lick Rockefeller in the end. So politically it was an impressive thing for people who had been in the Rockefeller camp to see Nixon and Agnew together the very next week. It would take that much more conversation with them in the future to get them back in Rockefeller's bag."

Nixon himself thereafter would call the Maryland governor occasionally, inform him of his latest political moves and "ask" his advice—a patented Nixon tactic for making a potential supporter feel he was a valued counselor. It went beyond that, though. The Nixon staff picked up some of Agnew's own ideas on such things as the new town concept, welfare reform and job training; John Ehrlichman and Dr. Martin Anderson, two key Nixon aides, visited Agnew to discuss issues with him. Beyond that, a personal rapport developed almost immediately between Nixon and Agnew.

In their humble beginnings, one the son of a grocer, the other of a small restaurant operator, in their middle-class values and their quick political climbs, the two men had much in common. Through adolescence and into adulthood each had pressed his nose against the window of the good life, and had "made it" with a healthy assist from the Grand Old Party. And as Agnew's governorship suddenly became enmeshed in racial turmoil and civil unrest, his hard-line response met with sympathetic interest from Nixon. Pat Buchanan, the St. Louis newspaperman who became a Nixon speech writer and conservative ideologist in inner-circle debates, collected articles about Agnew's tribulations in March and April, and how he coped with them, and funneled the clippings to Nixon. "The boss thought this guy was a very tough guy," an aide recalled. "This all in Nixon's mind was another indication that his first impression at the luncheon was a valid one; that here was a real strong fellow who exuded this strength even in a touchy situation like this, and was not beleaguered by what people viewed as the politics of his past. After that meeting, as long as we did the right things, we thought we could get him [Agnew], and it wasn't an unpredictable course we had to follow to get him."

Rockefeller, meanwhile, was having second thoughts. Still another cataclysmic political event had occurred, this time on the Democratic side. The New Hampshire primary that had given Nixon his technical knockout over Romney also had seen a severely damaging blow administered to President Johnson. Senator Eugene J. McCarthy of Minnesota, accepting the leadership of a growing body of dissent against the Vietnam war within the Democratic party, had declared his candidacy in what most considered a quixotic bid to unseat an incumbent President. By dint of an effective low-key campaign, mounting anti-Johnson sentiment and incredible bungling by the President's local agents in New Hampshire, McCarthy jolted his party and the nation by winning 42.2 percent of the votes and twenty of twenty-four convention delegates. When Republican write-ins were added, McCarthy fell only 230 votes short of beating Johnson outright. The performance not only shook the White House but also brought into the open a deep agonizing on the part of Robert Kennedy; after having turned aside the bid of the anti-Johnson irregulars to lead their political insurgency, Kennedy now decided that he too would make the challenge.

The prospect for the Democratic President—having to face not only McCarthy but also his bitter foe, young Kennedy, brother of the man Johnson had succeeded in the White House—precipitated early 1968's biggest surprise. On the night of March 31, Johnson told a startled television audience that "I shall not seek, and I will not accept, the nomination of my party for another term as your President. . . ." Johnson later said the political competition and outlook had nothing to do with his decision not to run; actually, he said, the decision had been made much earlier, and he simply had been waiting for the proper time to disclose it. But the elaborate efforts in his behalf in the New Hampshire and Wisconsin primaries, including the dispatch of ranking cabinet members to campaign for him in the latter, suggested otherwise.

In any event, Johnson's announcement broke the presidential sweepstakes wide open. It clearly would bring Vice-President Hubert H. Humphrey into the race for the Democratic nomination, and with Kennedy and McCarthy also in the field, the prospects for a Republican candidate looked even brighter than before. And if the Democratic nominee turned out to be Kennedy, many liberal Republicans argued, only one man in their party could beat him—Nelson Rockefeller.

There is some evidence, and Rockefeller himself took the position, that his March 21 announcement that he would not contest for the nomination slammed the door on his candidacy more tightly than he had intended. The strategic problem facing him was the remaining primaries, and he had determined he would have to stay out of them. But now that Johnson was out, perhaps there was another way. Perhaps if the party could be convinced that only a man who had appeal to Democrats and independents could win, it would turn away from Nixon.

When Rockefeller had announced his no-go decision, not all of his supporters reacted as Agnew had. Some, like New York publishers and financiers Walter Thayer and Jock Whitney, Thomas McCabe and former Secretary of Defense Thomas Gates of Philadelphia, and Ralph Lazarus of Cincinnati, had reported within two or three days that an unusual response was swelling among moneyed liberal Republicans around the country. They were refusing, these backers said, to accept Rockefeller's decision and were pledging assistance if only he would change his mind. George Hinman, on the basis of this interest, called Al Abrahams, who was closing down the "Rockefeller for President" office in Annapolis, and advised him that all was not over, after all. Abrahams shifted the operation to Whitney's offices in the Time-Life Building in New York. (On April 11, the day Agnew called Baltimore's black leaders on the carpet, Senator Thruston Morton of Kentucky announced in Washington the formation of a new national "draft Rockefeller" committee. Its chairman would be none other than J. Irwin Miller, the Columbus, Indiana, industrialist who had "lost" the job to Agnew the first time around.)

A new strategy emerged, wherein Rockefeller would play "outside Nixon's room"—in the country at large, rather than among Republicans. The plan was simple, straightforward, and expensive—a mass-communications and personal blitz by Rockefeller in key population centers and among voting groups that offered the best prospects for improving his standing in the national polls. If he could come into the Republican convention clearly established as the only Republican who could beat the Democrats—and conversely, if Nixon could be shown to be a loser—then the party would pick Rockefeller, no matter what happened in the primaries. Or so the Rockefeller camp persuaded itself.

And so, on April 30 in Albany, the governor of New York entered the race. "I do this," he said, "because the dramatic and unpecedented events of the past weeks have revealed in most serious terms the gravity of the crisis that we face as a people. . . . In the new circumstances that confront the nation I frankly find that to comment from the sidelines is not an effective way to present the alternatives. . . ."

One of the first orders of business for the Rockefeller camp, obviously, was to try to woo Agnew back into line. Rockefeller himself recognized the affront he had administered to Agnew, and he had moved immediately after the March 21 debacle to make amends. He had phoned Agnew that afternoon but got nowhere. "He was very upset," Rockefeller said later. "I couldn't blame him for it. He was very upset because I hadn't told him, because, you see, he had gone out on a limb. I pointed out to him that I'd warned him not to take it for granted, and not to make any assumptions, but he was so sure that he didn't pay any attention to what I said."

Did Agnew attempt then to change his mind about running? "No," Rockefeller said. "No, that was it."

And, without doubt, that *was* it. In the next weeks, other approaches were tried to win Agnew back, all to no avail. Nelson Rockefeller's banker brother, David, went to Annapolis to see him, and also to get at him through J. Walter Jones, but as far as Agnew was concerned, it was all over between him and Nelson Rockefeller. George Hinman tried his luck too. "I was very friendly with Ted and I was very sorry circumstances didn't permit him to have fuller notice," Hinman says. "He was really entitled in fairness to fuller notice of it. I was embarrassed about that, I think we all were, and chagrined. I talked with him myself and tried to explain. He was friendly but obviously down deep he was hurt. He didn't talk much about it, he just didn't come along either." Stewart Mott sent Agnew a telegram telling him Rockefeller interest remained high and his help was needed, but Agnew wired back that he wasn't interested. He regarded Mott's move as a stop-Nixon ploy and wanted no part of it.

Importantly, Rockefeller's antics were not taking place in a vacuum. There had been, as already noted, Agnew's close-up discovery of Richard Nixon and the ardent courtship that followed immediately on Rockefeller's first decision against running. Beyond that, there now also had been the Bowie State sit-in and arrests, the assassination of Dr. Martin Luther King, the resultant Baltimore riots and finally Agnew's confrontation with the black moderates. Not only had the political climate changed; Spiro Agnew now was looking at the American scene through a more aggravated focus, and the more he looked at it and at the Republican field, the better Richard Nixon looked to him—both politically and ideologically.

When Rockefeller finally decided to follow the advice to run that Agnew had given him more than a year earlier, Agnew's reaction was decidedly cool. "I think it is very good for the Republican party that we have two candidates," he said. "Certainly Governor Rockefeller, as I said on many occasions, is a highly qualified person and may very well provide a formidable candidacy for the election in November." But then came the hooker: "I do think a lot of things have happened since his withdrawal . . . and I think it's a new ball game. I think I've got to take another look at this situation."

Asked whether he was "less enthusiastic" now for Rockefeller's candidacy, Agnew replied, "No, I'm not a bit less enthusiastic for Governor Rockefeller's candidacy, but I'm much more enthusiastic for Mr. Nixon's candidacy than I was before." The answer confirmed the spadework the Nixon camp had done.

Agnew would not say that he favored Nixon over Rockefeller, but he indicated that at the request of the Republican state central committee, he was leaning toward becoming a favorite-son candidate. That move in itself would fit into the Nixon strategy, which was to encourage leading state figures around the country to tie up their delegations if they were not disposed to come out immediately for Nixon. The thinking was that once Nixon had swept through the primaries—and there was nobody in sight now to block him—the favorite sons would see the inevitable and fall in line. Some favorite sons, of course, like Senator John Tower of Texas, were brought into the Nixon camp early and were just waiting for the proper time to crumble. Agnew was not yet in that category, but he clearly was vulnerable now.

"The situation in this country in the past month has made some very dramatic changes," he observed. "I sense a change and a concern in the electorate. I sense that the candidates are responsive to this change because of the very important statements that are being issued one on top of another. I feel compelled to look very carefully at these statements before I make a decision as to where I am going to throw whatever influence I can have in this election."

It was only May, but already some in the Annapolis press corps thought they could see an emerging strategy. "Governor," a reporter asked, "do you still maintain that you have no ambitions at all on the national scene?"

"No, I have no personal ambitions on the national scene."

"Governor, on reflection of the one-time Rockefeller situation, that he was available for a draft, are you available for a draft for the second place?"

"Well, as the governor [Rockefeller] himself said, I don't consider myself stand-by equipment. Very seriously, no, I think it would be the height of temerity for me to suggest that coming from a state that never had a Vice-President possibility and being only a little over a year in office, that this is something serious enough for me to consider at this time."

That observation was made on May 3. Two weeks later, David Broder of the Washington *Post* interviewed Nixon and reported that among those he was considering for Vice-President was Spiro T. Agnew. The high regard of other Republican governors for the freshman from Maryland, and his opinions on urban affairs (the subject of a recent meeting between Nixon and Agnew), were mentioned by Nixon as important considerations in Agnew's favor. The next day, another veteran Nixon-watcher, Don Irwin of the Los Angeles *Times*, listed leading Republicans being surveyed by Nixon and included "a man who has gained ground in recent months because of his strong stand on the cities—Governor Agnew of Maryland." The governor said he was "very flattered" to be considered as a possible running mate by Nixon and had phoned Nixon to tell him so. He also announced he definitely would be Maryland's favorite-son candidate. Asked by reporters whether he would make the same kind of disclaimer that Governor Mills Godwin of Virginia had made ("I would rather be Governor of Virginia than Vice-President"), Agnew said he considered the Vice-Presidency "a very high office and a great challenge in itself." Then he went out and made a speech advancing "black capitalism" as the Republican party's "answer to the despair of the ghetto"—a Nixon proposal. Race riots in recent weeks, Agnew said, were caused "not just by evil conditions but by evil men. . . . Our solution is not black power, but green power—the power of the purse—Negro enterprise and industry."

In this period, too, Agnew repeatedly sent out other signals, intentionally or not, that he was moving into the Nixon camp. Sometimes the signals were light-hearted, such as the time he heard Democratic Senator Joseph Tydings tell a Maryland rally on the state constitution that "the road is rocky for state reform." Agnew interjected, "Some here say nix on that rocky road." But more often the signals were cold and heavy. In mid-May, Rockefeller, with several other Republican governors serving on a party platform task force, came into Friendship Airport in Baltimore and held a joint press conference with Agnew. As the two men sat stiff and embarrassed beside each other, Rockefeller suddenly blurted out an apology to the Maryland governor for "having gone the wrong way at the psychological moment" in March. Agnew clearly was startled. "No apology is necessary," he said awkwardly. "I don't accept the apology, as I don't think it's necessary at all. I don't think many people realize what a candidate for President has to go through."

Later, a sumptuous reception in Rockefeller's honor—and at his expense—was held for Maryland Republicans at the home of party stalwart Kingdon Gould, by arrangement of liberal Republican Senator Charles "Mac" Mathias, Jr. The purpose, obviously, was to bring Rockefeller and Agnew together and, hopefully, heal the breach. Most of the evening, however, Agnew studiously avoided the guest of honor. "Ted kept circulating in the back rooms of the house," one participant, aware of the reception's purpose, observed. "He went into every corner of Gould's manse he could find, both indoors and out. I kept looking for Ted, and he was nowhere to be found. Then I would see him; he would be talking to some little old lady, and ordinarily he wouldn't be caught dead talking to a little old lady. But it was better than talking to Rocky and Mathias." During the affair, Rockefeller addressed the crowd on the back lawn and made a fervid, even embarrassingly impassioned, plea for forgiveness, going out of his way to admit error and praise Agnew. But when it was Agnew's time to speak, he confined his remarks to diplomatic niceties and generalities.

Rockefeller got the message but maintained a brave front. "I don't blame Ted Agnew," he told a questioner on ABC's *Issues and Answers*. "It was really a very unfortunate situation. He had gone all out for me and then I didn't come out, and he was very upset, and I don't blame him. I don't blame his followers. It was a very embarrassing situation. I was just trying to pick the right timing, frankly, and I think I did." Then Rockefeller the irrepressible optimist spoke: "I was down there in Maryland the last few days and I think we are beginning to re-establish the ties again, and he understands."

It was, for Rockefeller, a time of frenetic travel, political fence-mending and Madison Avenue magic-making. Having by-passed the primaries, he had given Nixon a clear path to use them in that key aspect of his campaign, the dispelling of his nagging "loser" image. Romney's abrupt pull-out in New Hampshire had been most fortuitous; on top of it, the refusal of Rockefeller or any other Republican to do battle with Nixon in Wisconsin, Nebraska and Oregon—the three "must" primaries of 1968—enabled Nixon to amass impressive votes in each state. Ronald Reagan, playing the favorite-son game in California, allowed his name to stay on the ballot in each of these states, and a documentary film glorifying him was shown on television. But he did not campaign in person and never made a serious dent in Nixon's display of strength. For all practical purposes, the ball game was over after Oregon, and the Nixon entourage repaired to Key Biscayne, Florida, to plot convention strategy and the course of the general election campaign beyond. Nelson Rockefeller, however, refused to believe Nixon was in. Pursuing his basic strategy of boosting himself in the national polls by stumping the country and flooding key states with mass television, radio and newspaper advertising, he hoped to come into the convention as the people's choice and thus the only sensible choice for a party that wanted to win.

On June 5, at about thirteen minutes past midnight, an event occurred in the Ambassador Hotel in Los Angeles that again shattered the politics of 1968—and brought the nation and the world to shock and grief. Robert Kennedy, after Democratic primary victories in Indiana, Nebraska and the District of Columbia and his first loss in Oregon, had come roaring back in a feverish one-week campaign in California, and had just acknowledged the raucous acclaim of his followers in a victory speech in the Ambassador ballroom. His nomination still seemed improbable, but he was exuberant and optimistic. He had thanked his campaign workers, told them "On to Chicago!" and then headed out in the usual crush through a pantry area toward the press room to answer questions. As the world now knows, he never got there; a disgruntled Jordanian youth named Sirhan Bishara Sirhan shot him down in a wild and bizarre moment of madness that at once robbed the 1968 campaign of excitement and focus, and deprived the American scene of a vibrant and urgent voice.

While Robert Kennedy lived, there remained at least the prospect that Richard Nixon would have to confront openly and candidly the issue of the war in Vietnam in the general election; indeed, as the Democratic nominee Kennedy undoubtedly would have made the fall campaign a referendum on the war. In his absence, the war became a shadow issue, with neither the Democratic nor the Republican nominee willing to grapple with it head-on. When life went out of Robert Kennedy, it also seemed to pass from the Democratic party for the rest of 1968; what happened thereafter, in Chicago and in the general campaign, stirred tempers and emotions but no forward movement. In a spring of continuous political upheaval and shock, this blow finally was too much for a rational citizenry to bear. By the millions, Americans appeared to tune out politics, and for all the millions of words with which they were assaulted by the remaining candidates, they seemed not to pay much attention any more. When the time came to cast their votes, millions arrested the traditional upward trend and stayed home.

Spiro Agnew was not untouched by the shock of Kennedy's

death. "This veneer we call civilization," he said, "is being worn thin by the acids of hate and violence in our society. At no time have we had the bitterness and reaction that we seem to have today." He called Kennedy's assassination "an unmistakable sign that violence cannot be encouraged without reaping the horrible product. All those who are disciples of hate, who spew forth exhortations to burn and kill, must bear the responsibility for the deranged few who cross the line from talk to action." He spoke just two weeks after yet another racial outbreak in Maryland had intruded on his involvement in presidential politics. A twenty-two-year-old black, a deaf-mute, was shot by a white policeman as a burglary suspect in the Eastern Shore town of Salisbury, precipitating two days of violence. Agnew declared a state of "public crisis, emergency and civil disturbance" and called in state police and the National Guard.

With Robert Kennedy gone, Nelson Rockefeller moved quickly to offer the electorate a compassionate substitute. His campaigning and his oratory took on a new note of urgency, echoing the call of the two slain Kennedys to get the country moving again. But Agnew for one was not impressed. He chided Rockefeller's obvious bid for Kennedy backers, noting "he has been very benign in his attitudes toward the opposite party."

At a Republican governors meeting in Tulsa, where Rockefeller made another direct pitch to his one-time supporter, Agnew came away cooler than ever. "I read Nelson's statement on Vietnam," he told reporters, "and I don't know what it says." He said he also was "puzzled by his lack of views" in the field of civil disorders, and that Nixon's "firm" position "may provide the best solution." Even on the question of which candidate was the strongest vote-getter, Agnew said, his "gut reaction" was that polls showing Rockefeller the stronger were wrong. He was impressed by "a tremendous surge to Nixon after the King assassination and the subsequent riots" and "an overwhelming turnabout" in public opinion. A conservative mood had developed in part from "fear of change," as manifested in such things as the rejection by Maryland voters of the proposed new state constitution.

In a late-night chat with four or five reporters in his suite at Tulsa's Camelot Inn, Agnew twirled a bottle of Michelob in an ice bucket and elaborated on his concern, and on his reading of the public mood. "That Poor People's campaign is out of hand," he said. "Did you see the Cadillacs parked around Resurrection City? I tell you, things are changing in this country. When I told those black leaders in Baltimore that I felt they were responsible by not reading the riot act [to black extremists], you should have seen the mail I got, not only in Maryland, but from all over the country. . . . People are fed up with the riots. I've tried to be liberal, but at some point you have to stop leading the people and start following them."

Six days later Agnew went to New York for another private meeting with Nixon in his Fifth Avenue apartment. Aides reported later the two men had talked of civil disorders and demonstrators, but on Agnew's return to Annapolis he held his regular Thursday press conference without mentioning that he had just seen Nixon. Significantly, however, he proceeded to hit the law-and-order theme hard in his answers. He said he thought Nixon would be more forceful than President Johnson had been in dealing with civil disobedience "because I think he's concerned, as are most of the people in this country right now, that there is a wave of permissiveness that has been allowed to prosper and flourish, and the people really don't know when the politicians—the people in government—are going to actually have the courage to put their foot down and say no to some of these unreasonable requests. I think Mr. Nixon has made it perfectly clear that while he advocates the causes of civil rights and equality of opportunity, he distinguishes between those factors and the broad generalizations of economic improvement without effort which seem to come so frequently from the people you are referring to."

As for Rockefeller, Agnew said he and the New York governor were "not hostile to each other in any fashion. I've simply made a judgment for reasons that I've previously explained and he understands. . . . I'm calling my analysis on the basis of personal conviction and a feeling that the general tempo and the tenor of thought in this country is against this permissive wave, is against the oversimplifications that I've mentioned, the misconstructions, the verbiage."

Even without the knowledge that Agnew had just seen Nixon, the Annapolis reporters had no difficulty recognizing what now was an all but headlong plunge by Agnew into Nixon's arms.

Reporter: "Governor, you are speaking out more and more on

national issues; are you pledged to serve the full four years as governor?"

Agnew: "I was elected to serve four full years, and I would say this just to give you a hint: we don't have a lieutenant governor here, and under the [state] constitution I suppose what happens if I would move to the national scene is that we would have a Democratic governor very quickly. Now, that doesn't sound very likely to you, does it?"

Reporter: "Are you then saying that you're pledging yourself to serve four years?"

Agnew: "You'll have to draw the conclusions that you wish to draw. I am not anticipating any move out of the governor's office at this moment. I'll put it that way."

Reporter: "Would it be fair to conclude that you would seriously consider any offer at the national level that you might get after the November election?"

Agnew: "Well, I think it would be fair to say that I would consider it, yes. But I do feel a heavy obligation to the party in Maryland and to the people who elected me to serve this four years. And in spite of the fact that it is very flattering to be discussed as a potential candidate and to be discussed as a potential recipient of some appointed position, I would feel a responsibility to complete the major portion of this term. So, I'd say it is unlikely that I would attempt to move into the national scene at this time."

Two days later, when the state party met to pick its convention delegation, the membership, though weighted with Nixon backers, remained committed to Agnew as a favorite son. He held to his own uncommitted status and promised this time that he would not "under any circumstances" accept the vice-presidential nomination nor any appointed job before the conclusion of his term as governor. A week later, at his next press conference, he said flatly: "I intend to serve out the four years."

Reporter: "No matter what?"

Agnew: "No matter what. As long as I'm alive, that is."

Spiro Theodore Agnew, after more than a year of chasing the phantom of Nelson Rockefeller's candidacy and after a spring of domestic turbulence that had stiffened his back and turned him inexorably toward Richard Nixon, was now very much alive. On July 30, a few days before departing for the Republican National

Convention in Miami Beach, Agnew lashed out at the Kerner Commission for blaming "white racism" for civil disorders.

"This masochistic group guilt for white racism which pervades the Kerner report and to a large extent preoccupies the mind of our nation excuses individual responsibility altogether. . . . If one wants to pinpoint the cause of riots, it would be this permissive climate and the misguided compassion of public opinion." Agnew said the nation had "embarked upon a national whining catharsis. . . . We've followed this negative moribund course to its natural dead end, and it's time to play a new game called 'What's right with the United States.' " Agnew called "the agonizing of a police officer who could not bring himself to kill a looter over a pair of shoes" an example of the "insidious relativism that has crept into our thinking." The guilt of a looter, he said, could not be determined by the value of property stolen. "Where does this line of reasoning end?" he asked. "Do you kill a thief over a pair of boots? A diamond ring? When a person is looting another's property, can his depth of involvement be measured by the monetary or material value of his loot?"

The speech, in New York, created such a stir that on his return to Annapolis, Agnew called in reporters to clarify his position. "I don't think that looters should ever be shot," he said. "First of all I think they should surrender when challenged and apprehended by the police. . . . But a policeman trying to apprehend a fugitive has no way of knowing what kind of crime has been committed. And when that fugitive runs in the face of an order of halt, I think the policeman is justified in using the severest means to stop him. So the question is not really shooting looters. It's should people who are facing justice where the policeman doesn't know the severity of the crime be stopped by any means available? And I say yes, they should. . . . When you try to arrest somebody and he runs, the policeman has to stop him by any means available—and if that includes shooting him, he has to shoot him. If the general public gets used to the idea that if you can outleg the police officer you can get away scot-free, the whole system of law and order will break down. Nobody will ever submit to arrest if they believe nothing will happen if they run."

Agnew then produced a year-old press release to show that his views on crime "are nothing new." Crime would be a major issue in the approaching presidential campaign, he predicted. "You can see the candidates flocking to it in droves because they're now conversant with the fact that the people of this country are just not going to put up with a soft line on crime any longer."

Meanwhile, in isolation at Montauk Point, Long Island, Richard Nixon, the new object of Ted Agnew's political affection, was confidently absorbed in two tasks. The first, we are told, was the writing of his acceptance speech. The second was the sorting out of hundreds of views he had solicited from Republican leaders around the country on the kind of man he should choose to be his running mate. It is not known how many, if in fact any, of those solicited letters mentioned Spiro T. Agnew. But speeches like the one in New York on the care and treatment of looters were being funneled to Nixon's attention by the conservative Buchanan, and were not going unnoticed.

SPIRO WHO?

FOR at least two months before the Republican National Convention opened in Miami Beach in August, Richard M. Nixon had been weighing the matter of a running mate. His unopposed sweep through the primaries, the disorganization of his liberal Republican foes, and his pre-empting of much of the old Goldwater conservative base gave him the luxury of time in which to consider all the options. After his unopposed Oregon victory at the end of May, while Nelson Rockefeller chased his illusions around the country and Ronald Reagan treaded water in California, Nixon made a pilgrimage to Barry Goldwater in Phoenix, John Tower in Dallas and Strom Thurmond in Atlanta—all valued lieutenants in denying the South to Reagan. Then he settled in at Key Biscayne to plot his convention and fall campaign strategies. The convention plan had already been decided; a string of favorite-son candidates who had been holding the line for him would announce their support one by one and break the back of any movement for Rockefeller on the left or Reagan on the right. Nixon was, as he always was fond of saying, "a centrist" in the Republican party, and although he wanted a first-ballot victory, the strength of his position was that a movement by the convention at almost any time either to the left or the right would drive many at the opposite pole onto his centrist ground.

In the selection of his running mate, Nixon eventually came

around to the viewpoint that the man also ought to be someone who, while not necessarily popular with either the right or left wing of the party, was acceptable to both. Within the Nixon staff, however, there had been a running debate through the spring focused more on offsetting the centrist Nixon candidacy with either a liberal or a conservative; Nixon himself would hold the broad center, and the vice-presidential candidate might help deliver more votes on one end of the political spectrum or the other. Nixon said little, heard out his aides and kept his own counsel. The liberal-moderate viewpoint was espoused by men like Ray Price, a young speech writer from the old New York *Herald Tribune,* who argued that the ticket needed a running mate attractive to the industrial North, like Mayor John Lindsay or Senator Charles Percy, whose strength would offset expected losses to George Wallace, now a declared third-party candidate, in the South. The conservative position was put forward by aides like Pat Buchanan, who felt Reagan could cut deeply and directly into Wallace strength in Dixie and free Nixon to campaign in the North. Price and Buchanan debated the matter heatedly, as did other members of the staff, and there is no evidence that the name Spiro T. Agnew was ever seriously injected into any of those early staff evaluations. At one point Buchanan sent a memo to Nixon advancing the pro-Reagan thinking, but he did so at a time when Hubert Humphrey, as the prospective Democratic candidate, was leading Nixon by about 6 percentage points in the major polls and Wallace was holding at about 18 percent. It appeared then that Nixon would have to gamble on a running mate who might hurt him but who could also help him. Later in the spring, however, as the Democratic party's troubles mounted and Nixon moved ahead, Buchanan and the like-minded conservatives abandoned their case for Reagan, recognizing his inclusion on a Nixon ticket as part of a "high-risk strategy" that no longer seemed necessary or wise.

Through all this, Nixon said little to his staff aides to indicate his own preference for any individual. By mid-June, however, they were able to surmise certain guidelines that were governing his thinking. "He got very afraid, after everybody on the staff had had his say about the Vice-Presidency," one insider said later, "that by picking either on the conservative side or on the liberal side he might provoke another split in the party. Nobody ever suggested Agnew, and he wouldn't mention anybody when we'd talk about it. He'd just listen. But it was sometime in around there that he got down to trying to figure out who could stand in the middle with him and avoid the problem of bringing the convention to blows about its factions. And he never said that, really. It just became more and more apparent that he wasn't seriously considering anybody who was readily identifiable on either side. As we got down to the convention, it seemed from various things that he was doing, that he no longer had in mind a Lindsay or a Percy, or a Reagan on the other side. And once you got beyond Reagan on the other side, I don't think he had anybody else in mind. So by the process of elimination you just had to figure, thinking to yourself, it had to be someone in the middle there someplace."

Other clues also helped in the process of elimination, if not in arriving at an assessment of Nixon's positive thinking on the matter. It was clear to all, for instance, that foreign policy was Nixon's strong suit and he could handle that area alone in the campaign, so it was likely his running mate would have domestic affairs as his strength, and that suggested the possibility of a governor. Also, Nixon told Buchanan and others that it never was good for a presidential candidate to have a "superstar" on his ticket who might upstage him in the campaign or be hard to handle in office later, if the ticket won. That took care of Rockefeller, Reagan, Lindsay and several others. Nixon had talked much and loftily about the role of the Vice-President, but when it came down to one of his own, he wanted a man who would do as he was told.

In 1960, presidential nominee Nixon had selected Henry Cabot Lodge, the American Ambassador to the United Nations and a prestigious figure, and had lived to regret it. Lodge had treated his campaign for the Vice-Presidency like a casual autumn tour of the countryside, rationing his public appearances, going his own leisurely way and—on at least one occasion, when he promised that Nixon would name a black to his Cabinet—overstepping his bounds, with poor political judgment to boot. According to a very close Nixon aide, the relationship was so cool that Nixon and Lodge did not get together to talk for more than two years after their 1960 loss. When they did, in Lodge's office in Saigon when he was ambassador to South Vietnam, Lodge said, "You know, Dick, all those stories about how I took a nap every afternoon in the 1960 campaign? They weren't true." According to the aide who was present, Nixon just looked at Lodge and said nothing for an embarrassingly long time—a most unusual reaction for Nixon, who abhors a conversational vacuum. In 1968, another aide says, "it had to be strictly a second-liner."

Adding to the difficulty this time were polls indicating that none of the prospective running mates being mentioned helped Nixon; in fact, he ran worse with any of them than he did alone. The polls supported the orthodox political theory, to which Nixon subscribed, that a vice-presidential candidate can't help the ticket; he can only hurt it. "Actually, we wanted to run without a Vice-President," one aide observed. But that wasn't possible, so Nixon had to look for the next best thing—a harmless nobody.

Some members of the staff continued to think about or argue for one or more of the more glamorous Republicans, but many long shots eventually figured in the speculation: George Romney, Nixon's TKO victim in New Hampshire; Governor Dan Evans of Washington; freshman Senator Howard Baker of Tennessee; Senator John Tower and Congressman George Bush of Texas; Congressman Rogers Morton; Governor John Volpe of Massachusetts; even former Secretary of Health, Education and Welfare John W. Gardner, put forward through Buchanan, to Nixon's astonishment, by conservative columnist William F. Buckley, Jr.

In late July, prior to the opening of the convention, Nixon had gone to Montauk Point with only a few aides. As already noted, he went ostensibly to write his acceptance speech and to examine the hundreds of letters he had solicited from party leaders on selecting a running mate. But the acceptance speech turned out to be largely a repackaging of old themes and phrases, and the letters were essentially intraparty public relations. "Any time you see R.N. polling people," an aide said later concerning the letters, "you can be pretty sure he's not seeking their opinion. He just wants to substantiate his own views. He's not the kind of man who comes to a situation without an opinion. In spite of all this searching and consultation, the fact we got who we did proves he wasn't coming at it with an open mind." And another said: "Of course he had no intention of taking that advice when he asked for it. That's just Dick's way of making people feel they're involved in important decisions. It doesn't cost anything, and some people eat it up."

One night during this period, Nixon was Agnew's guest for dinner at the governor's mansion in Annapolis. Before leaving, he told the other guests: "If I'm elected, I assure you there will be two piano players in the White House." The dinner for Nixon brought to light the existence of a special fund for Agnew collected by J. Walter Jones and others. Called "the Executive Assembly," it drew $1,000 each from wealthy contributors in Maryland to help finance the governor's political expenses. The first—and only—payoff to the donors was dinner in the governor's mansion with the front-running Republican candidate. One report indicated that there was $35,000 in the kitty at the time. Joseph Dukert, then the G.O.P. state chairman, said there would be no public disclosure of the members of the fund because "we consider this information in the same way the military does classified data—it could be of help to the other side to release it." About a month later Dukert reported that the fund had been disbanded and the balance turned over to the state party.

According to one close Nixon lieutenant, the candidate may have decided on Agnew as early as June. "I say that not because he really told anybody that he decided on that, but it was not like Nixon to go down to the convention and wait until the night before to have in mind who he wanted as Vice-President. If one is writing an acceptance speech, he's pretty sure he's got the nomination, and I think he came to the convention figuring who he wanted, and that was Agnew. Just at what point back into June he decided that, I don't know. But it was along toward the end of June that he stopped thinking in terms of taking someone from the liberal or conservative wing of the party and started thinking of taking someone who hopefully would have a foot in each camp, to keep the whole thing together."

Proof that Nixon had a middle-road running mate clearly in mind before his own nomination, according to one insider, came when he told various state delegations prior to the presidential balloting at the convention that he would not pick anyone who would be divisive. The meetings with the delegations were private, but somehow the Miami *Herald* acquired a tape recording of one of the Southern meetings. The transcript quoted Nixon as denying "some cockeyed stories that Nixon has made a deal" on his running mate, and he assured his audience, "I am not going to take, I can assure you, anybody that is going to divide this party."

That meant, to his Southern listeners, no Rockefeller, Lindsay, Percy or Senator Mark Hatfield. But it also meant no Reagan, whose selection could have precipitated a liberal Republican walkout. "He solemnly pledged in there that he would not pick someone who was offensive to a lot of the conservative delegates, and although not in as strong terms, he did much the same thing with groups from New York and Pennsylvania or any of the states we were just going through the motions with," this same insider said. "He was smart enough not to put himself on the horns of that dilemma if indeed after the fact his choice would have been a Lindsay or a Reagan, which obviously would have made his statements a lie."

If all this, however, provided clues to who was not in the running, it was not much help in divining who was. Still, there were some hints to anyone who was privy to Nixon's thinking—and his personality. He liked strong men, and he liked the notion that he was able to "discover" people—to see in them political value that others might not perceive. "A lot of people were mentioned as possibilities, and Nixon had some kind of a feeling one way or another about most of them," another insider mused later. "He had been around politics long enough that he had an impression of Reagan, of Volpe, of Lindsay just from living in New York, and anybody else you could mention. And here all of a sudden was a guy out of nowhere who he had never even thought of. The timing of their personal contact was such that in Nixon's mind he was able to form his impression of Agnew, against this background of personalities that he had some feeling about from the past, with a pretty fresh outlook. His personal contact with him started fairly early to enforce this idea that here was a good, strong, tough guy that maybe nobody had thought of."

Just before the convention opened in August, while Nixon thus consulted with himself, another unexpected development drained the drama from what little real uncertainty remained about the presidential nomination, and focused interest on the vice-presidential question. Rockefeller was coming into the convention with his hopes pegged entirely on a strong showing in the national polls; not simply an edge over Nixon, but a margin so wide that no matter what their personal sympathies, delegates would have to choose between losing the Presidency with Nixon or winning it with Rockefeller. That had been the objective of all Rockefeller's efforts since he belatedly entered the race three months earlier; Rockefeller advance men in Miami Beach proclaimed the theme with huge searchlights that played the legend ROCKY CAN WIN on the sides of major convention hotels each night. But on Monday morning, July 29, before most delegates had arrived and as party platform hearings were to begin, the Miami *Herald* ran the preconvention results of the final Gallup poll. After all of Rockefeller's poll-oriented efforts, Gallup showed that Rockefeller, "the people's choice," only ran even against Humphrey, and that Nixon, "the candidate of the politicians," actually ran two points ahead of him! For Rockefeller it was a case of being destroyed with his own weapon, and although the ROCKY CAN WIN slogan continued to be flashed on the convention hotels each night, from then on it was more a mockery than a prediction.

Agnew came into Miami Beach on August 2, still publicly uncommitted to any candidate and still holding out the Maryland delegation as its favorite son. But he also came with one piece of private information that gave the Nixonites supreme confidence that they had him—and gave Agnew some reason to think he was in the vice-presidential sweepstakes. As Agnew revealed later, he had been approached in mid-July about placing the name of Richard Nixon in nomination for President. "That was one of the tip-offs that Agnew was probably in the running," a Nixon staffer noted. "Once I saw Agnew in there [as nominator] I figured he was in the finals. A lot of people thought, 'Well, that just showed he was being thrown a bone,' but he didn't need any bones. He never had been a man to require that kind of egotistical massaging. Agnew was not holding out his delegation to have any bones thrown at him. You can safely say we would have been greatly disappointed by the time he went down to the convention if he hadn't stopped being a favorite son and supported us. I thought, Agnew must be in there to raise a little publicity for himself and have the convention take a look at him."

Actually, Agnew had considerable doubts about whether it was politically wise to make the nominating speech for Nixon. Important members of the Maryland delegation were still for Rockefeller, and he was concerned that he might unduly offend them by nominating Nixon, after having abandoned Rockefeller. Before leaving for Miami Beach, Agnew had sought counsel from, of all people, Democratic Speaker Marvin Mandel, who told him that if he was convinced Nixon was going to be the nominee, he had better not slight him by refusing. It was a piece of advice over which Mandel—his successor as governor—often mused later, as Agnew's serendipitous career soared.

The confidence in the Nixon camp that Agnew would fold his favorite-son status at the proper time was not misplaced. When Agnew arrived in Miami Beach, it was with the greatest political irony. He had in his hands the key to squeezing the last breath of life out of the Rockefeller candidacy, and Rockefeller knew it. Rockefeller met privately with Agnew, who again remained non-committal. In previous weeks Agnew had been huddling with two other favorite-son governors from large states, George Romney of Michigan (48 delegates) and Jim Rhodes of Ohio (58 delegates) who together with Agnew and Maryland's 26 delegates appeared to represent enough votes to block a first-ballot Nixon nomination. Romney and Rhodes held fast, but on August 3 Agnew called an hour-long private caucus of the Maryland delegation and announced he was bowing out as a favorite son and endorsing Nixon. Rogers Morton had already salted away at least sixteen Maryland delegates for Nixon, and pressure from Agnew helped bring in two more, including Republican national committeeman D. Eldred Rinehart, once one of Rockefeller's staunchest supporters. To Agnew's chagrin, eight Rockefeller backers held the line. They had a petition ready asking Agnew not to quit as a favorite son, but decided against offering it, one pro-Rockefeller delegate said later, because the group felt Agnew would simply disregard it. A verbal appeal in the same vein was gaveled down by State Chairman Joseph Dukert, who then hustled Agnew out the door.

As matters turned out, Nixon got only 24 votes from the Agnew-Romney-Rhodes triumvirate of states—Maryland (18), Michigan (4) and Ohio (2). Since he exceeded the 667 votes needed for nomination by 25 votes on the first ballot, he still would have been nominated, even if the three governors had denied Nixon all the votes in their states. In terms of sheer arithmetic, Spiro Agnew thus had nothing to do with Nixon's nomination; yet in terms of the psychology of the convention—the creation of an atmosphere of inexorable movement and an inevitability that Nixon would win—Agnew's timely abandonment of his favorite-son status was important.

Agnew announced after the caucus that he was "vigorously"

endorsing Nixon, with whom he shared "deep ideological bonds." He refused, however, to say how many Maryland votes he could deliver for Nixon beyond indicating that his move could cinch the nomination. And in response to a question, Agnew said it was "not in the cards" for him to be Nixon's running mate.

Four nights later, Spiro Agnew stood before the Republican National Convention and nominated Richard Nixon to be its candidate for President. According to several close associates, he had a splitting headache at the time but rose to the occasion, so much so that Frank DeFilippo of the Baltimore *News-American* (formerly *News-Post*), never hesitant about criticizing the governor in the past, wrote the next day:

> Agnew's speech placing Nixon's name in nomination was considered by many convention listeners as ordinary, but its delivery style added a second dimension to the governor's usual one-dimension speaking manner. Ordinarily flat, nasal and containing the chipped edge of Baltimore, Agnew's voice graveled and thinned alternately as it choked through two octaves for dramatic impact on his national television audience. Marylanders accustomed to seeing Agnew grip the rostrum sides with white-knuckled discomfort detected the governor's flailing finger stabs, clenched fists and hand-waving gestures of emphasis.

In content, however, the speech by most yardsticks was a standard nominating address—chronicling the nation's ills, extolling the virtues and experience of the candidate to cope with them. It was, notably, heavy in the rhetoric of law and order. "We are a nation in crisis, victimized by crime and conflict, frustrated by fear and failure. A nation torn by war wants a restoration of peace. A nation plagued by disorder wants a renewal of order. A nation haunted by crime wants a respect for the law. A nation wrenched by division wants a rebirth of unity." And while the Nixon team was busy dressing its man in the image of a winner, Agnew reminded the convention that Nixon had been a loser waiting in the wings. The voters would cast their ballots in November, he predicted, "for a man who had the courage to rise up from the depths of defeat six years ago. . . . When a nation is in crisis, and when history speaks firmly to that nation that it needs a man to match the times—you don't create such a man; you don't discover such a man; you recognize such a man."

Nominating speeches, of course, seldom make any difference

in the way a convention votes, and this one was no exception. If it was intended to start a buzz of vice-presidential speculation whispering through the convention hall, it had little impact on that score either.

The next night, to the surprise of nobody, the 1968 convention nominated Richard M. Nixon on the first ballot. Nixon watched the roll call on television in his plush $300-a-day Hilton Plaza suite, took the restrained congratulations of his inner circle and family and a pro-forma phone call from Rockefeller, and settled in for a long night of deliberations on the matter of his running mate. The roll call had not been completed until about two o'clock in the morning of August 8, and it was almost three o'clock by the time this selection process got started. In 1960, Nixon had performed the same ritual in Chicago, asking all the party bigwigs for their recommendations and then picking Lodge. On that occasion it had been easy because Lodge, like Nixon, was regarded as a "centrist," a prestigious addition to the ticket as a nationally known figure, and high on nearly everybody's list. There was little doubt then, too, that Nixon went into those deliberations with his mind made up on Lodge and was simply going through the motions for the sake of party good will.

This time it was much the same, except that Nixon was much less certain how his choice would be accepted and he set out, in three separate post-nomination meetings with his staff and chief supporters, to test it on them. He did not throw the choice open, nor did he use the meetings as a unity forum, since the sessions were notably barren of the liberal wing best represented by Rockefeller, Lindsay, Hatfield and Percy. "The meetings," an aide said later, "were like the letters," referring to those on the No. 2 choice he had solicited prior to the convention. "To make everyone feel he was in on it"—everyone who had been with him, that is.

For the first session, more than two dozen ranking staff aides and regional leaders, most of whom later were to become prominent in the Nixon Administration, were called in.* Agnew was

---

* They included John Mitchell, Bob Haldeman, Bob Ellsworth, Dick Kleindienst, Peter Flanigan, Leonard Garment, Frank Shakespeare, Herb Klein, Maurice Stans, John Sears, Pat Buchanan, Charlie McWhorter, Rose Mary Woods, Wayne Hood, Dick Moore, Glen Olds, Linwood Holton, "Bo" Callaway, Fred LaRue, Governors Wally Hickel and Tim Babcock, Congressman Clark MacGregor, Senator Roman Hruska, Mrs. Pat Hitt and Ed Nixon, the nominee's brother.

not invited, but the omission of the man who had placed Nixon's name in nomination apparently caused no stir. Unlike Agnew, the only two governors there, Walter Hickel and Tim Babcock, had been early enlistees in the Nixon cause.

Of the three meetings, the first necessarily would be more attuned than the others to the trend of Nixon's own thoughts on a running mate. Many in that first session had taken part in the spring staff debates that first had considered the relative merits of liberals and conservatives, then had moved into the middle ground as they became aware that was where Nixon was looking. Now they talked about middle-ground prospects, but not—according to several participants—about Spiro Agnew until Nixon himself, who had been waiting patiently, casually asked, "How about Agnew? That was a hell of a nominating speech he made." Those who had heard the speech may have agreed, but apparently nobody said so. "The only reason Nixon said that," a participant later observed, "was to give the guy a credential." Nixon then let the conversation go on, finally winding it up, as he often did—summarizing what had been said but announcing no decision—by saying, "So your general advice is that I pick a centrist." Thus spoke Richard Nixon, centrist, who had spent the four years since 1964 preaching party unity and needed nobody to tell him what kind of man he required to preserve what he had built.

A slightly smaller group was ushered in next, mostly members of Congress and old party stalwarts.* According to one account, Nixon opened the meeting by listing some of the names mentioned in the first meeting, nine or ten in all, but he made no recommendation this time, either. The gesture was taken partly as a way to get the discussion rolling, partly as a harmless way to soothe feelings and let important Republicans think they were under consideration, whether or not they actually were; Nixon knew, of course, that word of which names were mentioned would soon filter out to the party faithful, if not to the public at large. Agnew was on the list, but apparently his name generated

---

* Senators Karl Mundt, Paul Fannin, Hiram Fong, Jack Miller and Strom Thurmond, and Congressmen Leslie Arends, Don Rumsfeld, Sam Devine, Bill Brock and John Rhodes—and also presidential losers Barry Goldwater and Thomas E. Dewey; Governors Jim Rhodes and Louie Nunn; Herb Brownell; Dick Ogilvie of Illinois; state party leaders Harry Dent of South Carolina, Bill Murfin of Florida and John Andrews of Ohio; and sidekicks Bob Finch, Lieutenant Governor of California, and Billy Graham.

no outpouring of support this time, either, even when Nixon himself, again casually, asked about him and that outstanding nominating speech. Billy Graham, a surprise participant, in one of his less effective sermons, is said to have tossed out Mark Hatfield's name, and Barry Goldwater reportedly suggested Bill Scranton, whereupon Nixon indicated he had looked into that possibility and Scranton had said he wasn't interested. When this meeting broke up at about five-thirty, Goldwater reported later, Nixon walked to the door with him. "He put his arm around me," Goldwater recalled. " 'Could you live with Agnew?' he asked. 'Hell, yes,' I told him, 'he's the best man you could have. He's been firm, and so what if he's not known? No vice-presidential candidate ever is.' " (In that advice, Goldwater certainly could not be accused of not knowing whereof he spoke; he had selected the forgettable William E. Miller of Lockport, New York, as his running mate just four years earlier.)

By this time Nixon obviously had persuaded himself that his thinking about a centrist running mate was valid. However, the lack of enthusiasm for Agnew, according to one insider, gave him pause. Nixon rested for an hour, then called the third meeting for about nine o'clock. This group of party leaders was even smaller.* The talk here also was of a middle-ground candidate, with Nixon mentioning John Volpe, Howard Baker and—Agnew. Again, the fact that Agnew's name had not emerged amid a roar of enthusiastic support troubled Nixon. One more meeting, unannounced at first, would have to be held. This was the decisive one, with only six insiders invited: John Mitchell, the campaign manager; Bob Haldeman, the chief of staff; Rogers Morton, the convention-floor manager; Bob Ellsworth, the chief delegate-hunter; John Tower, the guardian of the Southern flank; Bob Finch, close friend and trusted adviser.

Various reports of this meeting suggest that as many as five names still were in contention: Volpe, Agnew and Baker, and as alternatives, two participants of that meeting, Morton and Finch. Baker was eliminated as too inexperienced; Morton was only a congressman; Finch only a lieutenant governor and a clearly

---

* Senate Minority Leader Everett Dirksen, House Minority Leader Gerald Ford, Rog Morton, Tower, Finch again, Senator George Murphy and Congressman Bob Wilson of California, national party chairman Ray Bliss, and state leaders Peter O'Donnell of Texas and Ody Fish of Wisconsin.

identifiable Nixon crony as well. As an Italian Catholic, Volpe had strong ethnic appeal but he couldn't win even his own state's primary against a Rockefeller write-in, and even a Nixon-Volpe ticket would be a long shot in Massachusetts. That, it seemed, left Agnew. "Well," Nixon asked, according to one participant, "who should I take?"

One of the group, on the spur of the moment and seeing that moment slipping by, decided to make one last pitch. "I think it should be Finch," he said. "You know him, you know you can trust him, you know he can handle himself. And he doesn't have to be built up nationally." But Mitchell wouldn't hear of it. "You can't do it. It's nepotism," he told Nixon. With that, Finch, greatly agitated, jumped to his feet. "No, I won't do it!" he said. "I won't put myself through it!" He recounted personal family stresses and said he could not go through a national campaign. Nixon got up too. "Bob, come in here," he said to Finch, taking him into an anteroom. There they talked privately for a few minutes and then came back, Finch calmed and Nixon behind him. The nominee turned to Morton and said, "Call Agnew."

One Nixon intimate later said he was not convinced that Nixon had ever seriously meant to choose Finch. "After he'd been through all these meetings and had been shaken a little bit about his original feeling about Agnew, and having been through all the other names, he began to wonder, 'What the hell should I do now?' But there was no other name. He was just sort of casting around for some other suggestion at that point. His own instinct would never have allowed him seriously to take that step." In addition to the fact that Finch was regarded as a liberal, and that his selection might personally offend his California superior in state government, Reagan, the cronyism argument was a very strong one. "It would be like Nixon picking himself to run for Vice-President," this intimate remarked. There are those who said later, of course, that he had done precisely that in selecting Agnew, but at the time Nixon acted, several insiders confirmed, he regarded Agnew as a moderate who had established his credentials in the civil rights field and had only reacted understandably to the militancy and crises that later broke around him. (Nelson Rockefeller said later of the Agnew selection, "I talked to Strom Thurmond that night, and he was describing how they had picked. He said the basis of the selection of Mr. Agnew was that he was the least worst of the candidates that were proposed by Mr. Nixon. That was his description.")

Through the long night and morning of deliberations, Agnew was in his suite at the Eden Roc, down Collins Avenue. With the man he had backed safely nominated, he and Judy had planned to go over to Freeport with the Walter Joneses in Jones's private plane, to play golf and swim. At dinner two nights before, after Agnew had placed Nixon's name in nomination, the two friends had discussed the excursion to Grand Bahama. "We were to leave for the airport at eight o'clock in the morning," Jones recalled, "but I got a call from the governor. He said he was still one of the group of about ten being considered [for the vice-presidential nomination] and he said he was going to hang around for a while. And then he called again and said, 'I'm one of four.' The second time I called the pilot and told him to cancel it, and we went down to his [Agnew's] apartment. That was about nine-thirty. We never would have made reservations if there had been any arrangement or agreement that he was a serious candidate."

It was shortly after noon when Morton's call came. Agnew took the phone from aide Stanley Blair and heard Morton say, "Ted, are you sitting down?" "Yes," Agnew replied. "Good, because you'd better," Morton said. "I've got a man who wants to talk to you," and he put Nixon on to break the news. The conversation was short; Agnew accepted and said he was greatly honored, then turned to his wife and said, "I'm it." Unwittingly, the simple observation was a fair commentary on the manner in which much of the abuse of the 1968 campaign and the Republican Administration beyond would be heaped on him. But at that moment Spiro T. Agnew, son of an immigrant restaurateur, was coping for the first time with the realization that he was only a few steps away from the Vice-Presidency of the United States.

Nixon gave the news to the country in a brief press conference that caught the reporters, waiting in the American Scene Room at the Hilton Plaza, with their jaws open. He milked the moment for all he could. "All of you know, from having covered me since the early days in New Hampshire," he said as the newsmen hung on every word, "the emphasis I put on the Vice-Presidency and the need for selecting a man who was, first, qualified to be President; second, one who could campaign effectively; and, third, one who could assume the new responsibilities that I will give the new Vice-

President, particularly in the area of the problems of the states and the cities. . . ." Nixon was drawing it out with obvious relish. Finally he concluded, "I have made a decision. I shall recommend to the convention that they nominate for Vice-President on the Republican ticket Governor Agnew of Maryland."

An audible gasp went up in the room, and not only from the press; Nixon aides standing at the rear joined the chorus of disbelief. The reaction obviously pleased the presidential candidate. As soon as he got the name out, he strode, smiling, off the platform and out of the room, leaving the newsmen to recover and await the arrival of the chosen one. The words "Spiro Who?" immediately began to circulate through the room, then out into the hotel corridors, down Collins Avenue and over into Miami and the world beyond.

Agnew watched Nixon's press conference on television, then went over to the nominee's suite with his press secretary, Herb Thompson. Nixon greeted his selected running mate warmly, discussed the vice-presidential nominating procedure with him, then asked him to go downstairs to hold a press conference of his own.

Agnew walked into the conference room beaming, admitted he was "stunned," expressed his gratification and pledged to do his best for Nixon and the party. He immediately encountered a barrage of questions about his civil rights posture. "I am on record with many, many statements on civil rights," he said. "I am pro-civil rights. I am for the implementation of civil rights, not just the elaborate programing and distribution of money which is intended to bring about the equal opportunity and the justice that everyone talks about. On the other hand, I expect fully that no civil rights can be realistically achieved without the restoration of order, without the abandonment of the condoning of civil disobedience." Agnew said he would "welcome the chance" to campaign in big-city ghettos to help the ticket. Asked what strength he added, he replied, "I can't analyze any strength I bring, and I agree with you that the name of Spiro Agnew is not a household name. I certainly hope that it will become one within the next couple of months." That, of course, was one wish he would realize beyond all expectation.

The choice of Agnew jolted the party's liberals, many of whom regarded him as a turncoat and viewed his selection as a crass payoff for his switch from Rockefeller to Nixon. Romney, for one, said his delegation was upset about what the choice would do to Republican hopes to recapture some of the black vote lost in the Goldwater debacle of 1964. On the conservative side, though, it was all roses. Reagan called Agnew "a darn good man"; Thurmond said he was acceptable "because he stands for the principles of the Constitution, and he stands very strong on what I think is going to be the number-one issue of the campaign—law and order." And Harry Dent, speaking for the Dixie Republican pols: "We're for him—we think he's great."

The sharp reaction was unnerving to the Nixon camp. Nixon had turned to Agnew precisely because he wanted to avoid such a liberal-conservative dichotomy, and because he regarded Agnew as a middle-roader who would be acceptable to both sides. The consternation grew when the word spread that a group of rebelling liberals was trying to get John Lindsay to seek the second spot in a direct convention challenge to Nixon. Rockefeller wanted no part of it. He went to the convention floor and congratulated Nixon without a reference to Agnew. Meanwhile, Agnew had repaired to John Mitchell's suite at the Hilton Plaza to discuss with his own staff and such Nixon aides as Ray Price and Peter Flanigan the question of Agnew's nominators. Marylander Morton would nominate him; for seconders, between Percy and Lindsay on the liberal side, he chose Lindsay first, and called him personally. Lindsay could see the challenge to Agnew as a fool's errand and so, when Agnew asked him to second his nomination, the New Yorker seized the offer. It was a haven, and an opportunity to demonstrate party regularity as well. Lindsay managed to second Agnew's nomination without saying anything much about him. Percy also was asked to second, and agreed. The rebels, led by Nevada state chairman George Abbott, Massachusetts Congressman Silvio Conte, and a few others, quickly turned to Romney and somehow persuaded him to put his neck in the noose. Why Romney, who had pulled out of the New Hampshire presidential primary to avoid humiliation, would willingly permit the convention to administer such a predictable blow to him for a lesser job, was one of the bigger mysteries of a perplexing political year. But he did so and was snowed under. Agnew swept to a first-ballot victory, with 1,120 votes to only 186 for the hapless Romney, 10 for Lindsay and one each for Senator Edward Brooke of Massachusetts and Governor Jim Rhodes, the would-be king-maker who left the convention as he had come into it—sitting on Ohio's fat bloc of votes.

Later that night, before Richard Nixon delivered his accept-ance speech in which he conjured up the image of himself as a humble child inspired by train whistles in the night, Ted Agnew cut himself a slice of humility in his own acceptance remarks. "I stand here with a deep sense of the improbability of this mo-ment," he said, in the understatement of the convention. But he was as serious as he had ever been. He knew, he told his fellow Republicans, "that more important than words in this campaign and in the next Administration will be action, the kind of action that flows from involvement in the problems, and from the closest kind of relationship with the people who are involved in the prob-lems."

Then, referring to the dump-Agnew effort that had just failed, he said extemporaneously: "As a political animal and a relatively sensitive individual who hopes he will never lose his sensitivity, I am not unaware of what took place in this convention hall to-night. I am aware that the reasons that motivated it were not di-rected at me in any personal sense and were merely responsive of the opinions of those that took part in the nomination of that great governor of Michigan, whom I consider my personal friend, Governor Romney. Those motives were simply to provide the strongest ticket for the Republican party in November. I also rec-ognize that a vice-presidential nominee does not come to the suc-cessful fruition of his nomination by virtue of his personality or his attractiveness or his ability to generate a wave of enthusiasm on his own. He comes here because he is the selection of the man who does all those things on his own, the presidential nominee. I am privileged that that great future President of the United States, Richard M. Nixon, has seen fit to invest in me his confi-dence to do the job. But I will not be satisfied, ladies and gentle-men, I will not be satisfied under any circumstances until I prove to you that I am capable of doing a job for the Republican party and the American people in November."

These were words, clearly, of a proud man—not a clown, not a buffoon. When the vice-presidential nominee of the Republican party had said the previous day that he hoped Spiro Agnew soon would become a household name, he meant it, and his intention was that his name be known in time with respect. But before those approaching months of which he spoke would end, the manner in which Spiro Agnew would become part of the American idiom would not be at all to his liking.

12

❖·❖·❖·❖·❖·❖

THE ROAD TO RIDICULE

THE day after the 1968 Republican National Convention endorsed Richard M. Nixon's selection of Spiro T. Agnew,
Nixon held a press party at his Key Biscayne hideaway. He was in
an amiable and expansive mood, and the talk got around to the
big surprise of the convention, his choice of Agnew. "There is a
mysticism about men," Nixon said in the way he had of playing
the politician's professional, sharing his insights on humankind
with the hoi polloi. "There is a quiet confidence. You look a man
in the eye and you know he's got it—brains. This guy has got it. If
he doesn't, Nixon has made a bum choice."

For the next three months, largely as a result of a string of
incredible and revealing faux pas by Agnew, that last comment
seemed prophecy. Nixon himself had reminded his own aides
that "a Vice-President can't help you, he can only hurt you," and
already, on the basis of Agnew's first press conference as Nixon's
choice, it appeared he was hurting. Although Agnew handled
himself well in that conference (Nixon later remarked that Agnew had demonstrated "poise under pressure"), the presidential
nominee was somewhat surprised at the intensity of the negative
press reaction to the man. Nixon obviously regarded Agnew as a
moderate, and here in his first exposure the press had perceived
him as a right-winger. Agnew too expressed concern about the
reaction in an interview the next day. In his Eden Roc suite, he

fretted that "it's being made to appear that I'm a little to the right of King Lear," who, he said, "reserved to himself the right to behead people, and by my definition that's a rightist position."

Agnew then launched into a long defense of his civil rights record, not at Nixon's instruction, he emphasized, but on his own. "This is hard to take for a guy who passed the first local public-accommodation legislation south of the Mason-Dixon line," he said. "For the son of an immigrant who felt the sting of discrimination, it's hard to be referred to as a bigot. I think it should be completely obvious that if my civil rights position were what has been depicted, John Lindsay would never have seconded my nomination and neither would Chuck Percy. And since Mr. Nixon sees my role in the cities as vital during the campaign, I would never be effective in those areas. But this doesn't mean that I condone violence."

Agnew expressed dismay at those who saw him as "one of the hard-liners who thinks people should be shot, who thinks property is more valuable than lives. I want to show you how ridiculous that is. When someone breaks and enters, the police officer doesn't know whether someone has stolen a diamond ring, a loaf of bread, murdered the storekeeper or raped his wife. So, the policeman says 'Halt' or 'Stop' and at that point the man runs away, and the police officer has to decide whether to stop him by whatever force is necessary, or not to stop him. The officer doesn't know what crime has been committed. If the law officer sees a grocery front broken and sees a ten-year-old kid with a bag of candy, he's not going to shoot him. I think it would be a tremendous deterrent if everyone who ran from arrest thought the police officer was going to decide it was a serious crime and that he's going to get shot."

That kind of "clarification," of course, did little to dispel the notion that Agnew was, in his words, "a hard-liner." It revealed instead a marked insensitivity to the interpretation that easily could be placed on his words. In a postnomination assessment of Agnew, Richard Homan of the Washington *Post* had written: "A bit more stubborn, a bit proud, more than a bit thin-skinned, Agnew invariably opens his regular Annapolis press conferences with a statement intended to 'clarify' some earlier statement that he feels has been misunderstood." It is a common malady of politicians that they make statements subject to interpretations other than they intend, and then complain that they have been misunderstood. That lament was to be heard from Agnew throughout his campaign for the Vice-Presidency and beyond. Agnew is, as Homan noted, a proud man, and inevitably, as his faux pas brought him public ridicule, his chagrin and his bitterness toward the press deepened. No man likes to be called a bigot, as Agnew himself observed, but as much as that, no proud man likes to be called a buffoon, and before long Ted Agnew's utterances would be yielding him that reputation. It was an unwise assessment, and one that later led many of his critics to dismiss him out of hand as a serious political force—a dismissal they later would regret.

In examining Spiro Agnew as a national figure, it is important to underline that the errors he was to make in the 1968 campaign distressed him for personal as well as political reasons. A few months before the convention he had had little reason to suspect that Nixon would pick him to be his running mate, and when he was selected he obviously did not want to be a drag on his benefactor. His friends attest that if Agnew has one characteristic that equals his pride, it is his loyalty. Nixon himself told aides in the spring of 1968 that he admired Agnew's loyalty to Rockefeller, even in those difficult days immediately after Rockefeller had snubbed him. Agnew clearly was not one to transfer loyalty easily or quickly, but when he finally did switch his allegiance to Nixon, it was wholehearted. And when the man rewarded him with the nomination, Agnew determined he would justify that decision, and so informed the convention. In the next three months, he would say things that would bring into question not only his own judgment but Nixon's in selecting him. For all these reasons, the woes of the 1968 campaign were a particular trial for him. Even the eventual victory, which would take him off the political hook, would not grant him complete personal relief, as many in politics, in the press and among the public continued to regard him with derision.

From the convention, Nixon and Agnew flew west to Texas for a foreign policy briefing with President Johnson at his ranch, and then on to San Diego, where the Nixon organization had established a planning base at a nearby resort called Mission Bay.

About two months earlier, at Key Biscayne, substantial planning had already been completed concerning the vice-presidential arm of the fall campaign. In light of the disastrous Lodge experience of 1960, Nixon had insisted on much closer communication between the presidential and vice-presidential entourages. (That insistence had nothing to do with Agnew, who, of course, had not yet been selected.) Just before going to Key Biscayne, Nixon had given an interview in Portland in which he outlined his campaign strategy. At one point he acknowledged: "Haunting this campaign is the specter of 1960." It doubtless was true; he wanted to make sure this time that if there were any flaps by his running mate, Nixon could get to him at once and coordinate the response. As part of the determination, political adviser John Sears was assigned in June to be the liaison between "the mother plane" (the *Tricia*, for the candidate's elder daughter) and the vice-presidential party, no matter who the No. 2 man on the ticket would be. The original thinking was that Sears would shuttle between the two arms of the campaign, conveying information and assessments. But events, and what soon came to be known as Agnewisms, forced a change in plan, and Sears rode shotgun all the way on the *Michelle Ann II*, the Agnew jet named after the governor's granddaughter. At first Agnew appeared to regard Sears with some wariness, but they soon became easy friends. Though Sears still was in his late twenties, he had a pragmatic political mind and a diplomatic touch with Agnew, and was able to exert a positive influence.

Mission Bay for Agnew was a time of catching up. He had to familiarize himself with national issues with which he had not been particularly conversant, and with Nixon's own stands on them. Also, the campaign strategy had to be adjusted somewhat to make maximum use of his appeal. Though Nixon was concerned that Agnew was being perceived as a right-winger, there was no hesitation—after a few weeks in the North to take the curse off—to schedule Agnew into the southern and border states, where this perception could benefit the ticket. "We always knew," said one Nixon strategist later, "that it would depend on whether the number-two man was a little to the left or a fellow who was to the right, as to how we'd use him. We wound up with a fellow who, by that time anyway, was beginning to appear to be more and more a fellow of the right, even though he had this background of how he had come to office. So things like schedule were re-evaluated, and he started right out of the box viewed as a fellow who could be used to hold the party together in its conservative wing, and helpful against Wallace."

Much of the vice-presidential schedule, of course, was determined by the same basic consideration that traditionally has governed use of the No. 2 man: he would go where the No. 1 man could not or would not go, either because he did not have the time or the appeal. The tradition was followed with one important exception; there were places neither Nixon nor Agnew would go, because certain parts of the electorate were considered to be unreachable. The most notable of these was black ghetto America. Though Agnew had said at the press conference immediately after his selection that he would "welcome the chance" to campaign there, he and Nixon avoided the slums like the political plague they were, and the strategy was destined eventually to give birth to one of Agnew's more quotable campaign blunders.

From the outset Agnew found himself personally on the defensive within what had been planned by the Nixon brain trust to be an offensive campaign against the Democratic "ins." Nixon was best on the attack, and so for that matter was Agnew. But wherever Agnew went he found himself defending his reputation, insisting he had not changed, painting himself as a moderate, "clarifying" what he had said—or what the press had said he said. Even on his return to Baltimore to attend to some state business before joining the campaign in mid-August, Agnew felt the need to explain to a welcoming crowd what he had meant by the "shoot the looters" remark.

Also greeting him was an embarrassing resignation from Dr. Gilbert Ware, the only black on his personal staff, whose appointment upon Agnew's election to the governorship had been hailed as a racial breakthrough. Ware said he could "no longer accept an association, however peripheral, with positions to which I have fundamental objections." Finally, the fact that Maryland had no lieutenant governor also threw Agnew on the defensive. Democrats instituted a suit against him, arguing that his vice-presidential campaigning constituted a vacancy in the chief state office.

Returning to San Diego, the same monkey—Agnew's image as a reactionary—clung to his back. The campaign staff, combating it, issued position papers on his civil rights achievements and arranged a meeting for him with about thirty city and county officials. After it was over, Sam Harris, director of the National Negro Business League, told reporters that Agnew had done a good job, and he urged Agnew to do "what he did today: repeat over and over again his views on social justice and equality." If he could start talking, like Nixon, about black capitalism "and talk positively about what he is going to do to implement some of these ideas," Harris counseled, "then he will stop using code words like law and order."

At a postmeeting press conference, though, it was more of the same old routine for Agnew—hard questions on where he stood on civil rights, and the same answers defending his record and past rhetoric. Agnew conceded he was concerned about the unchanging line of interrogation. "Wouldn't you be concerned if the only questions you got at a press conference were this?" he asked.

From these circumstances, the Nixon strategists determined that the first thing Agnew had to do was repair his credentials as a "centrist." And so, on his first major campaign swing, into the Midwest on August 21, he accentuated the positive. At the 69th Annual Veterans of Foreign Wars Convention in Detroit, where a predominantly white audience of fifteen hundred sat expecting a gung-ho pro-Vietnam speech, he spoke about social injustice at home. "You know how strongly I feel about the absolute necessity for respect of law," he said, "but that's not the whole answer. With law and order must come justice and equal opportunity. Law and order must mean to all of our people the protection of the innocent—not, to some, the cracking of black skulls." Also, in words that in an earlier context might have been an admonition to Spiro Agnew for his remarks to the Baltimore black leaders, he said: "In our frailty and human selfishness, we have too often shut our minds and our consciences to our black countrymen. We need to respond to conscience rather than react to violence. We must aggressively move for progress—not out of fear of reprisal, but out of certain faith that it is right."

For the next two weeks Agnew played this same theme with variations, intertwining it with some of his substantive ideas, such as the federalization of public welfare and the establishment of integrated satellite cities in the suburbs that would help relieve the inner-city ghettos. But the heavier themes were lost in the press's focus on Agnew's obvious efforts to achieve a more balanced public perception of his civil rights position.

In set speeches, Agnew was safe; it was the extemporaneous comment, as with most politicians, that posed the pitfalls. A sample of what was to come cropped up on September 4 on a farm in Cedar Rapids, Iowa, when he was taken to see some pigs. The Democrats had just nominated Humphrey and Senator Edmund S. Muskie of Maine in their chaotic convention, and in a lame attempt at humor, Agnew said of the pigs that he "thought they came from Chicago," where a yippy group had nominated a pig as its presidential candidate. Then, addressing one of the pigs, he said, "Hello, Alice." Later, apparently worried how that remark would be taken by all the human Alices, he explained that he had used the first name that had come to him. "It could just as well have been Mabel," he added.

Early in September, Agnew began to shift noticeably from his defensive stance onto the offensive. With the Democratic convention aftermath still on the front pages, he zeroed in on its young protesters, blaming their conduct on an "overly permissive society" and calling them part of an "unconscious anarchy" in the country. "I wanted to do a lot of silly things when I was that age, too, but my parents wouldn't let me," he said. "It was that simple. . . . If you tell me the hippies and the yippies are going to be able to do the job of helping America, I'll tell you this: They can't run a bus, they can't serve in a government office, they can't run a lathe in a factory. All they can do is lay [*sic*] down in the park and sleep, or kick policemen." In New York on September 6, Agnew escalated by saying he saw a "definite link" between campus revolt and the Communists, and he intended to expose the rebelling students during the campaign. The links should be investigated, he said, but not in a way that would revive "events in our recent past"—an apparent allusion to the late Senator Joseph R. McCarthy, whose free-wheeling, unproved charges of Communist infiltration in the 1950s had earned him the reputation of classic political witch-hunter. On television's *Meet the Press* on September 8, Agnew repeated his charge that youth leaders were conspiring with foreign Communist powers and were "under control of the Communist Party U.S.A. or of Moscow." Finally, he met with reporters in Washington and took that one step that goes beyond mere aggressive attack and converts it to smear.

Democratic candidate Humphrey had said a number of things in recent days that had irritated Agnew. Humphrey had labeled Nixon "a cold warrior"; he had claimed, erroneously, that troop withdrawals from Vietnam already were under way; he had proclaimed that had he been nominated on the so-called "dove" plank in Chicago, he could have run on it. At the first opportunity, a meeting with reporters in Washington on September 10, Agnew went after Humphrey. Asked by one newsman whether he thought Humphrey was trying to pin a "hard line" label on Nixon, Agnew replied, "If you've been soft on inflation, soft on Communism, and soft on law and order over the years, I guess other people look hard, I don't know." To ears sensitive to the slogans of the McCarthy era, the "soft on Communism" phrase jumped out. But Agnew went on, "When you see the similarities between now and before the war, Humphrey is beginning to look a lot like Neville Chamberlain [signer of the Munich Pact with Hitler]. Maybe that makes Mr. Nixon look more like Winston Churchill."

These were particularly strong words, and when pressed by his interviewers about the "soft on Communism" line, Agnew accused the press of trying to "build these catch phrases into something they don't mean." He told the reporters they had put "collateral emphasis" on phrases he used in his campaign speeches; he didn't stop, he said, to weigh the impact of some of the words he used on memories of past controversial utterances; to do so would inhibit his free expression. And then he said, "I have no desire to go back to the Joe McCarthy witch-hunting days. But the reaction to the Joe McCarthy days has been an overreaction. When you see Communist involvement all over the world, it is pretty unrealistic to say it can't happen here. A certain measure of it is happening here."

This outburst caused such a furor in Washington that later the same day Agnew held an open press conference. He would not back down. He said Humphrey seemed to be for "peace at any price" (a soft-on-Hitler catch phrase out of the 1930's) and in calling Nixon a "cold warrior" had mistaken "firmness for inflexibility." He and Nixon, Agnew said, were "not going to be squishy soft as this Administration has been" on the issues of crime and of "knowing your enemies." Of his own words, Agnew said, "I guess by nature I'm a counterpuncher. You can't hit my team in the groin and expect me to stand here and smile about it."

To Spiro T. Agnew, what he said may have been a ringing defense of his boss, but in the Nixon inner circle, word of his "squishy soft on Communism" performance set off alarms. Not only did it signal a running mate off the leash, as with Lodge in 1960, but it also threatened to resurrect a skeleton in the Nixon camp that at all costs had to be kept closeted. The skeleton had a popular name: "the old Nixon," and it meant many things to those who recognized and used the label. But above all else it meant the free-swinging young Red-hunter who accused Secretary of State Dean Acheson of "color blindness—a form of pink eye toward the Communist threat"; who called Acheson, Truman and Adlai Stevenson "traitors to the high principles" of their party; who won election to the House of Representatives on an anti-Communist wave of innuendo against his opponent and rode the same wave into the Senate. Nixon had worked overtime in the intervening years to make the public forget "the old Nixon." Fresh versions had emerged periodically, labeled "the new Nixon" or even "the new, new Nixon." Now the newest and most benign of all the Nixons was on display in his second and probably, if he failed, last run for the Presidency. It would not do to have "the new, new Nixon" and the "old Nixon"—Spiro Agnew as surrogate —running on the same ticket. But already the critics were sniping; Mary McGrory of the Washington *Star* wrote, for example, that "the governor of Maryland has been attempting to prove that the old Richard Nixon is alive and well in Spiro T. Agnew," and others soon would join in. It had to stop.

In Annapolis on September 11, Agnew kept up his theme about resurgent Communist influence in the United States, but neither added to nor detracted from his observations on Humphrey. He denied emphatically to reporters that he had been assigned by Nixon to take a hard-line tack on Communism. "Don't get left with the impression that my campaign is going to be a Communist hunt," he told them. He said he was "not trying to raise a big Communist scare" and was "not attempting to attract the support of those with whom such fear tactics have been successful in the past." But over in Washington, two important Republican leaders appeared concerned that he was doing just that, and they pointedly took issue with him. Senate Minority Leader Everett McKinley Dirksen and House Minority Leader Gerald R. Ford said they knew of "no evidence" to substantiate Agnew's charge that

Humphrey was "soft on Communism." Ford argued that the Republicans had enough other issues to use, and Dirksen, asked if he agreed with Agnew's accusation, said: "I don't know whether I could say that. I'm not aware of any evidence. I'm rather restrained in the statements I make."

According to insiders in his entourage, Agnew was bewildered by the reaction to what he had said. "He couldn't understand why there was so much controversy over the use of this language," one aide recalls. "He hadn't meant to convey any idea that it was reminiscent of McCarthy days or accuse Humphrey of being a Communist sympathizer. He either wasn't aware of the connotation, and it was an unfortunate phrase that lurked somewhere in the back of his mind, or he certainly wasn't aware that people were still apt to bring up the connotation twenty years after the fact. He was amazed, and extremely upset."

Contrary to the general assumption that the Nixon headquarters or Nixon himself immediately jumped in, nothing was heard from the mother plane. During the postconvention meetings at Mission Bay, Nixon had told Agnew categorically that he would not have to worry about the presidential candidate watching over his shoulder and second-guessing him. There would be mistakes and bloopers, Nixon told his inexperienced running mate, but they were to be expected, and no matter what happened, Nixon would stand behind him. Nixon himself well knew how it felt to be a vice-presidential candidate deserted by his ticket mate; in 1952, when the story of Nixon's special California fund broke and led to the famous Checkers speech, Nixon had had to scramble desperately and fiercely, with his wits and his guts, to outfox the men around Dwight Eisenhower who had wanted to throw Nixon over the side. And even when he had outfoxed them it had taken an agonizingly long time for Eisenhower to reassure Nixon. Now Nixon, in Eisenhower's shoes, was not going to treat his partner that shabbily. It was an attitude, though not enunciated in those terms to the Maryland governor, that would sustain Agnew through his most difficult hours in the campaign ahead—and later, as Vice-President, when the first "dump Agnew" stories started. "Nixon would call Agnew from time to time in the campaign," an aide says, "and tell him, 'Don't sweat it, you're doing a fine job.' "

With no instructions from the mother plane concerning the

"squishy soft" comment, at first Agnew sought to muddle through. The next day, September 12, in Portland, Maine, he showed no contrition. He had called Humphrey soft, he said, because of what the Vice-President had called Nixon, and he asked: "Is it fair to call a man a hard-liner and unfair to call a man soft?" But by the time Agnew had reached Rochester, New York, he was deeply distressed. In his motel room he discussed the situation with George White and with Sears, who advised him to make an apology and put an end to the whole flap once and for all. It was obvious the thing was getting out of hand. Agnew called a press conference, and for one of the very few times in his public career, he ate crow—in his fashion. Sears had advised him not to back away so far that he was calling himself a liar, but to state affirmatively that Humphrey was a decent American. That was what he did.

"The remarks I made that have been widely quoted concerning Vice-President Humphrey must be examined in the context that they were offered," Agnew said. "If you recall the day before those remarks were made, the Vice-President characterized Mr. Nixon as being a cold warrior, as being a hard-liner, and my observations and the use of the word 'soft' when I referred to the Vice-President were merely a comparison that I was offering in response to the attacks that he made on Mr. Nixon previously. I want to make one thing completely clear. If I left the impression that I think the Vice-President was not a loyal American, I want to rectify that. I think he is a man of great integrity and I have high respect for him." Then Agnew went on: "I don't agree with him on every issue, and the use of the comparison to Mr. Chamberlain and Mr. Churchill I think is a completely valid comparison. I think Mr. Chamberlain considered himself to be a very loyal Englishman. There were many people in England at the time he made his cry for peace at any price that believed this was a proper cry to make. He made it in good conscience and I think the comparison stands."

When he used the expression "soft on Communism," was he cognizant of the fact it had a history in American politics? "No, I was not," Agnew replied. "And of course I want to be completely candid, gentlemen—it's the only way I know to be in politics— had I ever realized the effect that this expression would have, I would have shunned it like the plague. My record is not one of sympathy to inquisitorial procedures. I have never been a particular admirer of former Senator Joseph McCarthy. I did not approve of the witch hunts at that time. I still don't approve of them. Had I known that my remark was to be related in some way to cast me as the Joe McCarthy of 1968, I would have turned five somersaults to avoid saying it."

Agnew insisted that the remarks were not part of any hard-line campaign strategy. "Had it been part of the grand strategy it would have been hedged and protected far better, I assure you," he said. He had heard nothing from Nixon nor any of his aides about the matter, he said, nor did he have "any reason to believe that there is any desire for me to retract or soft-pedal anything I have said." He wasn't under any tight discipline, Agnew said. One of the reasons Nixon had selected him "was because he thought I had sufficient inherent good judgment and tact and decency to avoid these things. Now, I have never been one to go the low road in politics. I want to get off the low road. And if I may offer one little bit of humor to a very staid gathering, it would seem to me that there's been too much attention to the line they call the 'wormy' side of this campaign. I said 'squishy soft' and I am not proud of it. The Vice-President said 'wiggly and wobbly' [in describing Nixon positions], and I doubt if he is proud of that. So we are going to try to get off of these catch phrases—as far as I am concerned we are going to get off of them—and move to the substantive issues of this campaign. . . ."

The idea that a candidate for the Vice-Presidency of the United States could not have known the political history of "soft on Communism" was incredible on the face of it. When Agnew used the phrase he was forty-nine years old; in the heyday of Joe McCarthy he was a practicing lawyer in his mid-thirties who had demonstrated an active interest in politics by working in the congressional campaigns of General Devereux. Only a few days before he called Humphrey soft on Communism, Agnew had said he wanted investigations into links between campus protesters and Communists conducted in a way that would not revive "events in our recent past." Later, immediately after he had used the phrase, he told the press he had "no desire to go back to the Joe McCarthy witch-hunting days." And reporters who covered the Rochester press conference said Agnew seemed sincere and genuinely contrite. One member of the Agnew entourage, who has since left, said later it was a fact that the candidate "had no knowledge 'soft on Communism' was a code word for McCarthyism. It showed more than anything else that Agnew has no sense of history." Another says, "He had heard that phrase twenty years before as Joe Citizen. He didn't put it together now in a political sense with what he was doing. It's the kind of problem guys have who move quickly onto the national scene. But his actual feelings about it showed a lot of character. They belied a lack of politics, which was sort of refreshing in a guy running for Vice-President."

Even as Agnew was pleading ignorance on his "squishy soft" remark, and saying he never approved of "witch hunts" or the "inquisitional processes" used by McCarthy, the suspicion was growing that he not only talked like McCarthy but also was beginning to act like him. A week earlier, in charging that some student leaders had received instruction in Moscow, Hanoi and Havana, Agnew had hinted he would expose them during the campaign. Subsequently the Baltimore *Sun* quoted him as saying he was obtaining the names of sixty-two youth leaders with suspected Communist leanings—reminiscent of McCarthy's infamous "I have in my hand" speech claiming to have knowledge of fifty-seven Communists in the State Department. Now, though, Agnew said he never intended to expose anyone, had made no such statement and was demanding a retraction from the *Sun*. He conceded that the youth leaders, while given to "anarchy and disruption," perhaps weren't Communists.

But Agnew's contrition was limited. Concerning the Chamberlain comparison from which he refused to back down, he was asked what evidence he had that Humphrey wanted "peace at any price." Humphrey's expression of hope that American units could start leaving Vietnam in early 1969, he said, would amount to that if Humphrey "fully expected to achieve those ends without a move by North Vietnam to protect the integrity of our forces." In 1969, of course, American units did start leaving Vietnam without any such move by Hanoi—as part of the Nixon-Agnew Administration's Vietnamization policy.

The night of the public pull-back in Rochester, a phone call finally did come to Sears from the Nixon entourage. It was Bob Haldeman, Nixon's chief of staff, but before Haldeman could open the subject of Agnew's misstep, Sears told him the matter already had been disposed of. Nothing more was said of it.

In any event, Agnew had opened a can of worms with his "squishy soft" charge and he wanted to close it. "Let's drop the Communist thing—put it to bed," he said the next day, September 13, in a press conference in Chicago. Just a few questions later, though, he opened another can. A reporter observed that there hadn't been many Negroes in the crowds greeting Agnew, and asked him whether that fact caused him concern. "No, I don't— that hasn't occurred to me," Agnew replied. "Very frankly, when I am moving in a crowd, I don't look and say, 'Well, there's a Negro, there's an Italian, and there's a Greek and there's a *Polack*.' I'm just trying to meet the people and I'm just glad that they're there and that they're friendly."

Agnew knew at once that he had misspoken, and in the privacy of his entourage he shook his head in chagrin and braced himself for the reaction. At first, however, the remark went by almost unnoticed—and unreported. Robert Shogan of *Newsweek* wasn't sure he had heard right, so he asked colleagues about it. "It was so unbelievable some weren't sure he'd said it," Shogan recalls. "And if he did, was he kidding? How do you handle a thing like that? Nobody knew how to handle it. But here it came right on the heels of 'squishy soft.' It started to ooze out. It was a thrill a minute. This was a guy, we suddenly realized, who was saying anything that came into his head. And because there were no issues to speak of, we started to look for this kind of thing. It said something about him."

Most reporters with Agnew wrote nothing at first about the "Polack" remark. Most focused on the fact that Agnew, after steady use of the phrase "law and order" to the outspoken chagrin of Senator Edward Brooke and other liberal Republican leaders, had begun to temper it with references to "justice." He said he would not "retreat" from the phrase "law and order," but then observed that "the real issues that we're talking about can't be summarized in a catch phrase." Yet as far as the public perception of the Agnew campaign was concerned, the paramount issue was becoming the candidate's semantics. Later that same night Agnew went to a reception for about a thousand young Republicans, as the guest of Senator Dirksen. At the end of a short pep talk, he said the G.O.P. was sure to win the election with the aid of all the young people "in Illi-noise." Boos and catcalls greeted this gaffe in pronunciation. "Slips like that," he apologized, "come late in the day"—and, for the hapless Agnew, early in the day and at mid-day. The next day, September 14, on a television panel interview in Chicago, after having condemned all kinds of civil disobedi-ence, he was asked whether it was not true that "Jesus, Mahatma Gandhi, Henry Thoreau and Dr. Martin Luther King" had all practiced it. "Let me distinguish between those cases," Agnew re-plied. "The people you have mentioned did not operate in a free society." And so it went.

It was becoming increasingly clear to Agnew aides, and to the candidate himself, that his nemesis was the extemporaneous re-mark. Yet it was obvious that Agnew disliked speaking from a text. He had a flat, dull delivery that tapered off, often wasting the best lines; he sounded like, even looked like, an unfunny W. C. Fields. Nor was he much given to gestures and histrionics as he read. In an off-the-cuff situation he was better, because the ex-change engaged him, much as it did Nixon, and he had a firm and confident dexterity with words. But syntax seldom was his trouble; it was content.

On the law-and-order issue particularly, no matter how he phrased his views, they came out hard-line. So, after the Chicago TV panel interview, he went to his hotel suite and spent several hours writing his next speech, carefully balancing his views on the limits of protest and dissent with assurances that free-speech guarantees should be protected. "We shall open the channels of redress so government can respond with speed and strength to legitimate grievances," he wrote. "We are ready to put all the in-fluence and resources of our society on the line for the man who for too long has had society's foot on his neck. And we are not going to allow any man to prey upon passion or prejudice to de-stroy our society." Then he went out and delivered it in the con-tiguous suburb of Norridge, where Dr. King two years earlier had dodged bricks and bottles in an open-housing march. As deliv-ered, however, the speech came out as a stern warning that a Nixon Administration would not tolerate unlimited dissent. "We shall establish clear and unequivocal guidelines as to what consti-tutes peaceful confrontation and what is deliberate provocation," he told his solidly white blue-collar audience. And Spiro Agnew left Chicago perceived as he had come—a hard-liner.

Even prior to the stormy week just concluded, there had been staff discussions about the pitfalls of Agnew's off-the-cuff style. A central principle of the Nixon campaign, with the polls showing the Republican ticket far ahead of the faction-ridden Democrats, was to avoid the hazards of spontaneity. Nixon himself usually limited his day to one prepared speech, plus the release of innocuous position papers and perhaps a television panel with local citizens or local reporters who asked questions he had answered many times before. For Nixon, that strategy was working very well. Meanwhile, though, over on the "B" team, Agnew was campaigning like the Dick Nixon of 1960—sticking his neck out, swinging at every bad pitch that came his way. If the axiom about a Vice-President never helping, only hurting, was true, it followed obviously that he too ought to stay out of the line of fire —even more so.

Agnew returned to Annapolis after the Chicago visit, and before he headed out again on September 17, an old Nixon speech writer came aboard. He was Stephen Hess, a veteran of the Eisenhower Administration, of Nixon's presidential campaign of 1960 and of his losing California gubernatorial bid of 1962. Hess had been working on a book as a fellow at the Kennedy Institute of Politics at Harvard when he got a call from Nixon headquarters in late August. Agnew needed a speech writer, and because Hess knew Nixon and his thinking, he would be an ideal man. What speech writing there was up to that time was being handled by several people, including Cynthia Rosenwald, the Baltimore housewife who had written for Agnew in Maryland; Bill Prendergast, a highly professional former research director at the Republican National Committee; Jim Howard, a Cleveland and New York advertising man; and Bob Goodman, the "My Kind of Man" ad man from Baltimore. But Mrs. Rosenwald could not travel extensively, and the others weren't primarily speech writers.

Hess had been brought into Washington over Labor Day to talk briefly with Agnew, and at greater length with George White, Agnew's lawyer-friend and campaign manager. It was agreed that Hess should join the entourage in about two weeks, when he had finished his book project. It was in that period, however, that the "squishy soft" and "Polack" troubles descended on Agnew, and so when Hess joined the staff his arrival had all the appearances of a muzzling operation from the mother plane. Agnew himself knew it wasn't so, but the circumstances did not make for a happy or comfortable beginning of the Agnew-Hess relationship. Sears, who got along well with Agnew, had talked to him about the virtues of using a standard set speech, and although Agnew preferred speaking off the cuff, or writing his own speeches, he didn't resist. After all he had said to the press about being his own man, though, he wanted to avoid appearances that the "A" team was putting him on a leash.

On the day Hess joined Agnew, columnists Rowland Evans and Robert Novak, who had learned about the assignment, wrote that Hess was going aboard to bail out the foundering vice-presidential candidate. The story did nothing to smooth the way for Hess. The first speech he wrote for Agnew, opening an eight-day Western tour in Fort Worth, was read by the candidate without incident—except for a mention by *New York Times* reporter Homer Bigart that Agnew had used a text, and that it was "peppered with light banter aimed at Vice-President Humphrey" that might "indicate the influence of" Hess, the Nixon man. That was the last Hess speech Agnew gave. Hess continued to write the texts for a while, and they were released to the press, but Agnew went back to talking off the cuff, though he did develop a kind of standard speech of his own. Hess busied himself writing erudite position papers that were issued over Agnew's name. "I would send them up to him in the forward cabin and he would send them back approved," Hess recalls. "I doubt if he ever read them." Nor did Hess ever have a depth talk on issues with the man for whom he was writing. For all of that, Hess says, his relationship with Agnew was always "very civil, but it was a rocky relationship. He couldn't fire me and I wasn't going to quit. He was probably disappointed with me because I was not a rock-'em, sock-'em speech writer of the kind he wanted." Later on in the campaign, another Nixon speech writer who fit that description, the conservative Pat Buchanan, volunteered for duty with Agnew, and he had much more success—and much better personal rapport—with the candidate than Hess did.

The Agnew entourage was divided basically between the old Agnew associates—the "Maryland Mafia" of George White, Herb Thompson, Charlie Bresler, Art Sohmer—and the "outsiders"—Steve Hess, John Sears and Bob Smalley, a long-time Republican public relations man in Washington who worked with Thompson. There was no real friction between the two groups, and when

Hess and Sears thought the Marylanders' political judgment was bad, they told them. But the old Agnew hands had the major access to the candidate, who spent most of his time on the plane in his own compartment up front, reading, talking with his family and playing cards with his friends.

Candidate Agnew seldom walked to the back of the plane where the press sat, possibly because on the rare occasions when he did, both he and the reporters felt ill at ease. "We didn't know what to do," Bob Shogan recalls, "and he didn't know what to do." The press contingent was dominated by Maryland reporters, many of whom had covered Agnew in Annapolis, but even they seldom had much to say to him, or he to them. His aloofness was a continuation of the attitude toward the press that had existed in Towson and Annapolis, and as the reporters began to focus on Agnew's faux pas, suspicion and tension mounted.

Once, when he did stroll back, the conversation turned to airline food and the difficulty of staying in shape. Since Honolulu was one of the scheduled stops later on, someone asked Agnew whether he would go swimming there. The candidate, pinching a roll of fat on each side of his waist, said he didn't want to reveal his "love handles." It was not at all the kind of remark those who heard it would have expected from the stand-offish governor. Accordingly, it only served to increase the feeling of uneasiness for some, rather than relieve it.

On other campaign planes, with other candidates, the atmosphere often was relaxed and jovial in the press compartment; a candidate could walk back frequently and engage in playful banter without worrying that he would be quoted. It was all part of the easy relationship, born of trust and cordiality, that usually existed on a campaign plane. But on the Agnew plane it did not exist, and so Agnew did not walk back often; when next he did, two mornings after the Fort Worth stop, he was to regret it deeply, and part of what was about to happen resulted from the absence of that usual easy rapport. The candidate, who was determined to make Spiro Agnew a household name, was about to introduce another name into the lexicon of national politics, to his everlasting regret.

13

◇•◇•◇•◇•◇•◇

THE "FAT JAP" FLAP

THE exciting thing about a political campaign, and the treacherous thing from the viewpoint of the candidate, is that potential disaster is always around the next corner. Occasionally a negative incident occurs that in itself seems trivial but is magnified by the publicity it receives into a happening more memorable and crucial than anything substantive the candidate has said and done. For Agnew, such an event took place aboard his plane just west of Carson City, Nevada, on the morning of September 20, and it soon was to dominate all discussion in and about his campaign. Trivial as the episode appeared to be, it offered in fact a unique case study of the pitfalls—for candidate and press—of a continuing atmosphere of mutual mistrust.

The Agnew entourage had just completed stops at Casper, Wyoming, and Billings, Montana, and then turned south and spent the night in Las Vegas, where the governor made a speech and held a press conference. The staff and press stayed at Caesar's Palace—an ornately grotesque monstrosity full of Roman statues and fountains and quick-buck operators—and spent much of the night gambling or watching others do the same. Agnew, however, under siege from a group of Marylanders doing the town, took welcome refuge in an invitation from Republican Governor Paul Laxalt of Nevada, and flew to Carson City for the night.

Among the traveling reporters who tried his luck at the tables was Gene Oishi of the Baltimore *Sun*, the native-born Japanese-American who had covered Agnew in Baltimore and Annapolis. Oishi stayed up late, as did most others in the party, and was bushed when the members of the entourage piled aboard the *Michelle Ann II* early the next morning to fly the 350 miles north to pick up the candidate. He took his seat in the rear section of the plane and dozed off, with Dick Homan of the Washington *Post* in the seat next to him, Frank DeFilippo and Mike Weiss of the Baltimore papers, and Bob Shogan of *Newsweek* across the way. When the plane landed, Agnew climbed aboard, and after takeoff and after talking a few minutes with aides in the front compartment, he ambled back into the press compartment drinking coffee. It was a rare incursion, and most of the reporters looked up, but Oishi kept dozing. Agnew came by, looked at him, and said to Homan, "What's the matter with the fat Jap?" Homan, surprised, says he replied, "He was up all night in the casino." About then Oishi awoke, and says he observed to the candidate, "That was a wicked city you took us to, Mr. Agnew."

After a few pleasantries Agnew walked off. Weiss turned to Homan. "Did he say what I thought he said?"

"Yes."

"That's a hell of a thing he said." Weiss turned to DeFilippo and asked whether he had heard. DeFilippo said he had, and so did Shogan. They asked Oishi, who really was not particularly fat, only stocky, if that was what he was called in Annapolis, and Oishi said it was not.

The matter at first became the cause of considerable bantering among the press and with the Agnew staff. The reporters chided Oishi about his weight and told him he ought to spend less time at the Las Vegas free lunches and more time trying to become "the flat Jap." At one point somebody sent a note to the Agnew compartment that said: "Agnew is a thin-skinned, squishy-soft Greek with love handles." Among the newsmen, there were some who wanted to write about the incident, feeling it was particularly revealing about Agnew. But Oishi wanted to let the whole thing slide. He regarded the remark as no more than a bumbling attempt to be friendly with the reporters. For the time being it was left that way, but the inside workings of the competitive press were destined before long to take those seven simple words Agnew had uttered and make them tactically the most critical to come out of his mouth up to that point in the campaign.

The flight landed in Los Angeles, and for the next two days there and in San Francisco, the "fat Jap" remark was superseded in the reporters' immediate interest by other matters. The phrase that Agnew had used to describe Gene Oishi remained, however, a subject of some concern in the press contingent. The *Time* correspondent, Charlie Eisendrath, telephoned Shogan in his room at the St. Francis Hotel and asked whether he was going to write anything about the incident. Shogan, knowing Oishi's disinclination to get into the news himself and doubtful about the propriety of such a story, said he was not. But in the meantime Oishi had phoned his wife and mentioned the remark, and she was furious. Several reporters were still pressing him about printing it, and finally he said he would not object. Eisendrath called Shogan and said he was going to report the incident to *Time*, and also told Homan, who then decided he'd better make sure the Washington *Post* had it. "My feeling was, coming on top of the Baltimore speech and the Polack remark, this indicated at the least an insensitivity toward minorities," Homan said later. "I decided, to protect myself, I'd put it in the next story I wrote."

The campaign plane took the party the next day, Sunday, to Honolulu, and that afternoon Homan dispatched a story about Agnew backing away from a claim he had made in San Francisco that the Republican ticket had a plan for ending the war. In the very last paragraph, which ran near the bottom of page five in the paper, he wrote: "Earlier, Agnew had astonished newsmen traveling with him when he made a rare visit to their section of his airplane, pointed at a sleeping reporter of Japanese descent who is, like Agnew, a second-generation American, and asked, 'What's the matter with the fat Jap?' "

That was it; that was all the story said; no indication one way or the other whether Agnew was kidding or serious. But considering the impact of this one lone sentence, it might have been bannered across every front page in the country. One of the Honolulu papers, in fact, a subscriber to the Los Angeles *Times*–Washington *Post* News Service, picked up the story and gave it page-one play.

The news hit the Agnew camp like the recurrence of a bad dream. With the elapsed time of four days since the remark was made, and all the bantering back and forth, it had been assumed by the staff that nothing would be written of the incident. The remark, after all, had been made in jest and in the privacy of the plane, where good fellowship and an unwritten code of privileged comment existed. Or did they?

That was where the Agnew staff had miscalculated. There never had been much fellowship with the press, and that fact in itself made it more likely that no unwritten code of off-the-record would be observed by some of the reporters. Most of them aboard, it was later noted both by the staff and veteran reporters, were relatively new to covering a national candidate; some staffers referred to the press contingent as "second-stringers" pressed into service because the first-stringers were covering the presidential candidates. That may have been true to some extent, but such old pros as Homer Bigart of the *New York Times*, Bob Clark of ABC, Charles Quinn of NBC and others were in the press party. Some of the old pros held, in retrospect, that it was bush-league to report a casual remark the candidate had made in jest in the back of the plane. But what Agnew had said did appear to some to be part of an emerging pattern that said something important about him; and besides—"the competition" might write it. The latter hardly was a consideration of professional ethics, but it was a reality that moved some more than others to act.

The appearance of the story greatly distressed Agnew. He felt wronged in every way. He could see how the remark could be taken as offensive, but, first, he really had said it in jest, and second, he never dreamed it would be reported. According to one very well-placed source in the Agnew entourage, the candidate sincerely did believe Oishi was commonly called "the fat Jap." "He hadn't known that Gene was not referred to in that context on a day-to-day basis back in Annapolis," this source insisted. "Frankly, he had heard that expression from members of his own Annapolis staff, going back for a couple of years. They were telling other reporters after it happened that Gene had been called that around the State House. So when Gene came forward and said he never had been called that, they were in a tough position. I don't think they conveyed that to their boss."

Some Agnew aides continued to insist long afterward that Oishi was indeed called "the fat Jap," and one of them later provided still another version of the incident that presented Agnew not as a man speaking in jest—which the candidate himself said he was—but as a man speaking out of deep concern for Oishi's health. Of all the defenses for the remark offered later by Agnew's friends, this one warrants repeating, play-by-play:

In Las Vegas that night (this Agnew associate said) he was shooting craps at Caesar's Palace, and doing very well, when Oishi came up to watch. Unfamiliar with the game, Oishi began to ask about the jargon of crap-shooting, and the aide explained the game to the reporter. "So I go away and Gene's at the crap table. I come back and I look, and it's two o'clock now, and Gene's in the bag now for about hundred and fifty bucks. . . . So, I showed him what to do, and I got him out of the hole, and I said, 'Now, go to bed, Gene.' . . . I come down at five o'clock in the morning and who's at the crap table but Oishi. He's still there. I said, 'My God, Gene, get yourself going. We're going to have a bust. Do you have luggage out?' He says, 'No, I've never been to my room.' . . . So I said, 'Okay, you better be ready to go because, you know, we don't wait.' . . . So we come back and the bus loads up and Oishi still isn't there. He's at the crap table. I go in and physically grab him out and put him in the bus.

"We get to the plane, get on the plane, Oishi sits down in the chair and—whish—flakes out. Well, you know how you get when you're tired and under a stress. You get a pale, wan look. You ever see an Oriental who did that? Neither did I. He turns green. I mean, not green-green, but sort of a very—like a dead guy. And Oishi's sitting there like this, flaked out just like this in the chair, and I got scared to death, because I never saw anybody that color before. . . . But we carry a doctor, so I said, 'Emmett Queen. Emmett, come on with me. Come up and look at this man. Something's wrong with him.' So he's lying out there and Emmett takes his pulse and I said, 'Emmett, I've never seen anybody like that, that color, in my life.' Emmett looks at him and he says, 'He's all right. He's just overtired.' I said, 'Emmett, you're a doctor. I don't disagree with you.' I said, 'Man, look at the color on that man.' He says, 'That's the way he gets. When he gets pale, he gets an ashen.' I said, 'Emmett, you sure?' He says, 'Sure.' So we take off and there's Oishi, flaked out."

When Agnew walked back to the press section, the aide continued, ". . . he looks over here, and there's Oishi. And he looks at Oishi, he says, 'My God, what's the matter with the fat Jap?

. . . That man is sick. Get Emmett up here.' I said, 'Governor, we've been through this once before.' He says, 'Don't you tell me that. Get Emmett.' So Emmett comes over . . . Emmett says, 'There's nothing wrong with this man.' He [Agnew] was seriously concerned."

The reporters who were sitting around Oishi, however, and Oishi himself, all told me they remembered no such exchange. "He looked tired," Bob Shogan said, "but he didn't look green or sick. No doctor came back. Nobody came back."

The incident, whatever the details, was pivotal both for the press and for Agnew in their perception of each other. The reporters, whether they wrote about it or not, saw in the "fat Jap" remark at the very least a political insensitivity, if not a personal insensitivity, on Agnew's part. The newsmen thought they saw a pattern emerging; some who had never considered writing about the "Polack" comment now did. They reached back, not only to that but to "squishy soft," and from then on they were attuned to anything that might appear to reveal Agnew's "insensitivity." Like the celebrated "brainwash" remark of George Romney became a kind of shorthand expression that said he was a lightweight, "the fat Jap" became a code phrase of sorts that said Spiro T. Agnew was a clod. (Actually, Steve Hess reasoned later, the ethnic remarks revealed that Agnew was apolitical. "A political hack in the Daley machine wouldn't say that," Hess said. "That's mother's milk to them.")

Agnew, for his part, saw in the incident a press that went out of its way to make mountains out of molehills, that was unfair, that didn't even play according to its own rules, that kicked a man when he was down, not just by writing what he had just said but by resurrecting a lot of old turkeys to make him look bad. Once a man made a mistake he was branded with it, whether or not it was an innocent one, or whether he was sorry and apologized. And if there were a number of mistakes, they always were mentioned; anything constructive he had to say was lost in the constant striving to make a jackass of him. If he hadn't realized it fully before, Ted Agnew came to feel now that the press held all the trump cards—in a stacked deck. Or so it seemed increasingly to him.

"It was right there," an aide said later, "that he started having a strong reaction toward the press, with everything coming together like that." And it wounded him where he lived—in his pride. "It got to be a matter of concern to him," this aide recalled, "because with more frequency he individually would start to get compared with Muskie . . . the press was saying all those grand things about Muskie, and on the other side they were saying things that he thought were unfair about him. Later on, in mid-October, a poll was taken between Muskie and Agnew, and that offended him, that people were doing that to begin with. It showed him way behind. He traced that to the fact the press was making Muskie look very good and he was being made to look very bad. Ergo, 'There are good guys and bad guys to the press, and I seem to be a bad guy.'"

Finally, in his loyalty, Agnew was concerned that these incidents were hurting Nixon, and in fact that some of what was written about him was the press trying to get at Nixon through him. But Nixon would call him every once in a while to tell him not to worry. Hess said later: "Agnew wasn't sophisticated enough to say, 'Look, fellows, the voters can't vote for Nixon and Muskie.' Or that he was a lightning rod who made Nixon look good." Also, Hess noted, "as a candidate, you don't have a batter's average, you have a fielder's average. You only need one boo-boo to get hurt."

The timing of the "fat Jap" story could not have been worse for Agnew. There he was in Hawaii—a state heavily populated with Japanese-Americans and others of Asian backgrounds, a fact brought home to him—as if he needed any reminding—by Democratic Representative Spark M. Matsunaga, a Japanese-American from the Islands. Agnew should be told, he said in a speech on the House floor, "that one does not win friends by insulting people of other racial backgrounds, particularly through the mouthings of racial prejudice." There were suspicions among some Agnew aides that Homan intentionally had held off reporting the story until the party had reached Honolulu—"fat Jap country," one of them called it—but the suspicions were unwarranted.

The immediate reaction to Homan's story raised some question whether Agnew should proceed with his schedule, which called for some island-hopping the next day. Sears recommended that he do so, and when Agnew agreed, Sears called Bob Ellsworth in the Nixon entourage to so advise him. Again there had been no directive from the mother plane or from the presidential candidate.

The next morning Agnew, a few aides and the press boarded a smaller plane for the day's tour. Almost everyone took the same seat locations, and the candidate again walked back. He saw Oishi sitting there and said to him, incredibly, "How's the fat Jap this morning?" Apparently it was Agnew's way of indicating that he had meant the crack as a gag, hence there was nothing wrong in repeating it. But by now the matter clearly had gone past the point of levity. Agnew leaned over to Homan. "He asked me if I thought he had been serious and was trying to be insulting when he said it the first time," Homan recalls. "I told him I thought he had demonstrated insensitivity. He wasn't angry, he was hurt. He thought he had been misunderstood."

Other reporters too thought Agnew was deeply wounded by the incident. The matter of the Polack remark came up, and Agnew told Shogan, "Until the articles were written I had no idea it was a derogatory term." Polish-Americans he knew, he said, "often kidded among themselves by calling each other 'Polacks.'" And without a trace of humor Agnew observed at one point to another reporter that "some of my best friends are Jewish." At takeoff, Agnew returned to his seat to work on a speech. As the plane climbed over Honolulu, the pilot noted on the loudspeaker that they were passing over Pearl Harbor. Oishi leaned forward, close to the ear of an Agnew aide sitting in the seat ahead of him, and cried: "Bombs away!"

In Kahului, on the island of Maui, members of the Agnew party were guests at a lavish luau in a large hut. There, with deep seriousness, the candidate delivered what many later said was the best speech of his campaign:

"A funny thing happened on the way to Hawaii. Maybe it wasn't so funny after all. Those of you who read your local papers are going to find that this vice-presidential candidate, this son of a Greek immigrant, is being accused of an insensitivity to the national pride and heritage of other peoples. I submit to you that this is a rather ridiculous charge to make to a man who grew up in a neighborhood where his family was the only Greek family, a man who saw his father come home dead tired in the afternoon and climb down off a vegetable truck to be ridiculed by certain people who referred to us as 'those Greeks on the block.' Yes, we were sensitive in those days, but thank God the United States has passed that point where we're drawn up so tight that we can't communicate with each other, and where our sense of humor is beginning to disappear.

"On the plane a reporter, whom I consider a friend of mine— because I never jest with my enemies—who happens to be Japanese, was asleep. I referred to him in certain slang, similar to the slang that people on athletic teams use affectionately among themselves, some of which wouldn't bear repeating. I don't think I said anything quite that harmful to my friend, Gene Oishi, and I don't think Gene Oishi took what I said in any sense of downgrading him. But coming on the heels of another amplified statement that occurred a week ago in the campaign, where in designating certain ethnic groups—as I feel I have a right to do because I am part of one, and a very big part of one—I inadvertently used a slang expression for another ethnic group, and I confess ignorance because my Polish friends had never apprised me of the fact that when they called each other by this appellation it was not in the friendliest context.

"It's pretty hard for Zorba the Greek, or Zorba the Veep, whichever you prefer, to really understand how the humor that's pervaded American life, that permits us as people of wide backgrounds to be free and easy in our expressions with each other, gets caught into such a desperate clutch that we must watch every expression we use.

"Ladies and gentlemen, I am sick of sloganeering. I'm sick of people reading something different into law and order than what law and order really means. I'm sick of people attempting to put my thoughts into a context that they didn't exist in when I spoke them. And I say to you that when you stop and consider, how utterly ridiculous it is to think that a person who had felt the sting of unkind remarks that *were* uttered harshly in an ethnic or racial sense could say something that callous without meaning it in fun and jest. It just doesn't make sense to me.

"I'm not going to apologize for the spirit in which I said what I said to Gene Oishi. I *am* going to apologize to any who might have read in my words an insult to their Japanese ancestry, or to any who might have read into my words an insult to their Polish ancestry. And I would say that ninety percent of the people who are born of immigrant parents understand probably better than most how important it is that we, the United States of America, one of the few countries in the world where it's safe to laugh, don't lose our senses of humor.

"I am sorry that the remarks I had prepared for today must be laid aside because what I'm saying has to be said. And in the spirit of Ted Makalena, your great touring golf pro, whom you lost so tragically so recently, let me ask that the camaraderie that exists among men, which allows them to insult one another in a friendly fashion, be not abolished in favor of the terrible and intense guarded atmosphere that seems to abound so freely in the dictatorships of the world. This is America—this is the melting pot of America! And if we are so ashamed of our background that a single word sets us into orbit, then the purpose of America, my friends, is beginning to fail.

"Yes, I remember when my father first came here from Greece the word Greek was considered to be an epithet. Those very sensitive people, who were sensitive because they did not know how they were going to be received in the United States, because they were sensitive in that they didn't realize that this really was a free country, and that they were most insecure, resented the use of the word Greek. They preferred to be called Grecians or people of Hellenic descent. But they got over that. They got over that because they moved up the line to where they had a sense of dignity and achievement and sophistication and assurance—just as the Japanese-Americans, just as the Korean-Americans and the Chinese-Americans and the Polish-Americans and everyone else—because the United States is now reaching a point where your ancestry is simply an interesting point of conversation, not a slur, and we won't stop until we find that in this country of America, Negro-Americans who have been so long discriminated against can feel the same way.

"If I have inadvertently offended anyone I am sorry—I am truly sorry. To those of you who have misread my words, I only say you've misread my heart."

Homan wrote the next day: "At the end of his speech, Agnew's voice was choking with emotion and he dabbed his eyes with a napkin." He drew standing applause and many there said Agnew appeared deeply moved and they had been moved by him. But in the traveling press there were of course some who retained their professional or personal skepticism. One reporter recalled that many spicy and exotic foods were served at the luau. Of Agnew's welling eyes, he observed, "I think it may have been the onions." And another said, "It was his Checkers speech."

The whole episode had, quite obviously, compounded the ill feeling between Agnew and the traveling reporters. The staff decided that Agnew should hold a small fence-mending party for them. It started off as a rather reserved sparring session but soon disintegrated into a debate over dissent, the war and journalistic ethics. Agnew made a long defense of his position that calling Oishi "the fat Jap" was no more than the kind of playful banter and good fellowship he had often heard in the Baltimore Colts' locker room. To which Homer Bigart, himself an imposing presence, wagged a finger at the candidate and intoned, "Governor Agnew, one thing you must remember. Locker-room humor should never be equated with running for Vice-President of the United States."

The conversation turned to an attack Agnew had made in San Francisco on Eldridge Cleaver, the Black Panther leader and writer. Agnew had argued against the appointment of Cleaver, an ex-convict, as part-time lecturer at the University of California, and when Shogan asked him how he justified that position, Agnew replied, "The man's a criminal. A convicted criminal. I'm disappointed in you, Bob."

"Governor," Shogan asked, "don't you feel he's paid his debt to society?"

But Agnew repeated that Cleaver was a "criminal." When Cleaver's influential book, *Soul on Ice*, was mentioned, Agnew snapped, "I'll never read it." Didn't he make any exceptions for talent? "No, he's a criminal," Agnew said. Well, someone inquired, what about Oscar Wilde? "What did he do?" Agnew asked. A reporter said Wilde was a homosexual. "Oh, say, fella," Agnew replied, laughing it off. And how about Jean Genet? another reporter asked. "I've never heard of the man," Agnew said, "but if he's a pervert or a jailbird, I have no use for him."

Some of the reporters said nothing or very little during the party, and some said later they suspected the conversation was being taped; that was the state of press relations by then. Homan, whose one paragraph had started it all, recalls that he sat next to Agnew on a sofa "but I don't think he said a word to me all night." At one point Bob Clark of ABC took it upon himself to apologize to

Agnew for the "fat Jap" incident and the way some in the press party had handled it. He had been on other campaigns where politically damaging remarks were made in the privacy of the campaign plane, he said, and never were reported. Others agreed with Clark on that point but didn't feel an apology at length was in order.

Among those who were in no mood to apologize was, of course, Oishi. He was more offended at the suggestion that he always had been called "the fat Jap" around Annapolis than at the original remark by Agnew, and his resentment deepened when Agnew's aides continued to use that alibi, even after he had pointedly told them it was not true. When Agnew himself used it in a speech, to Oishi's great distress, the reporter sent word to him. "I wasn't aware of any State House joke," he said later. "I called Herb Thompson and said I thought that explanation was offensive, not the remark. Herb said he would convey the message. But in Milwaukee about a month later, on a TV show, Agnew repeated it. I wrote him a memo in which I said I was not offended by the original remark, because he, being an Easterner, couldn't know the implication on the West Coast, where I grew up. It was the same as nigger or kike, and I resented the statement that I would accept a nickname like that. I gave the note to Herb (on the campaign plane). Shortly somebody came back and said, 'Governor Agnew wants to see you.' I walked up and Agnew said to me, 'I didn't know you felt that strongly about it. I'll never say that again.' He kept his word. He never did."

For a while after the "fat Jap" incident, Agnew tried to laugh away his troubles. He told the National Press Club, "Since the press has speculated so much already on the Nixon-Agnew strategy, I have Dick's permission to reveal my secret role in our battle plans: I'm assigned the task of insulting all groups equally." Actually, though, the vice-presidential candidate was being relied on more and more to go after one particular target. His name was George Wallace, and as the campaign moved into late September, he was posing a kind of threat to the Nixon candidacy that required as a political antidote the particular style and message the tough-talking Ted Agnew could deliver. For the harassed Agnew, the Wallace threat was an opportunity—to go on the attack and, hopefully, to put behind him the bloopers and the image of buffoonery they had generated.

14

MUDDLING THROUGH

I N the Nixon-Agnew strategy, countering the appeal of George
Wallace in the South with a strong law-and-order theme always had been planned. As the campaign progressed toward the
end of September, however, the former Alabama governor not
only was holding well in the segregationist South but also was
demonstrating a broad and strong appeal in the vital Border
States and even in part of the industrial North, where blue-collar
white voters were responding to the export version of his Dixie
racism and barely veiled hatemongering. More anti-Wallace effort
was required by the Republican ticket not simply in the South but
in the Border and Northern blue-collar strongholds, and Spiro Agnew was thrown into the breach.

Through late September and well into October, Agnew took his
law-and-order theme into places and situations where it might pry
loose Wallace support. In Milwaukee's South Side he attacked
student protesters as "spoiled brats who never have had a good
spanking" and who "take their tactics from Gandhi and money
from Daddy"; in Toledo, he told construction workers near a "Go
Wallace" sign that "we're very much for the working man"; in
Chicago, he said Humphrey's conditional proposal for a bombing
halt in Vietnam "strengthened the hand of Hanoi"; in Cape
Girardeau, Missouri, he urged Americans not to waste their vote
on a man (Wallace) who could not govern if elected.

In Portland, Oregon, on October 3, Agnew took care of his first hecklers by saying after they had walked out, "Now that the delegation from Hanoi has left . . ."; in Spokane, he challenged Wallace's selection of retired Air Force General Curtis LeMay as his running mate and dismissed more heckling as the "thoughtless frivolity of the flower children"; in Anchorage, Alaska, where Agnew flew just to make a thirty-minute speech at a high school, he expressed nervousness about LeMay's views on use of nuclear weapons; in Raleigh, North Carolina, and Jacksonville, Florida, he warned that votes for Wallace, by denying them to Nixon, could make Humphrey President. It was clear that Agnew, who had been selected by Nixon as a "centrist" like himself, now was regarded in the Nixon entourage as clearly right of center and the ideal man to cut into the Wallace strength, which was hanging on stubbornly in the national polls at a time Humphrey finally was righting his own stumbling campaign and beginning to gain.

In the process of going after the Wallace vote, Agnew was able for the first time to really get away from the inhibiting impact of his early campaign bloopers, and to start carving out a positive image for himself. The heckling by protesters along the way toughened his resolve and his rhetoric, and he began to emerge with what Ben A. Franklin of the *New York Times* called "a stern father image." Marylanders long had had this perception of the man; now it was being seen and recognized all over the country. On a national television panel he criticized Muskie for having once watched while youths burned their draft cards, and he called such conduct "inherent in the total permissive atmosphere that is sweeping the country; the atmosphere that allows irresponsible protest." And in Indianapolis on October 15, he said to the poor and to dissenting youth: "We will listen to your complaints. You may give us your symptoms [but] we will make the diagnosis and we, the establishment, for which I make no apologies for being a part of, will implement the cure."

In Pittsburgh the next day, it was more of the same. Asked at a brunch with the traveling reporters why, if he was the urban specialist he said he was, he wasn't going into any big-city ghettos, Agnew said he didn't feel "there's any particular gain to be made by debating on streetcorners. . . . You don't learn from people suffering from poverty, but from experts who have studied the problem." And two days later, in a Detroit TV appearance, he said on the subject of his failure to campaign in ghettos: "I've been into many of them and, to some extent, I'd have to say this: If you've seen one city slum, you've seen them all. . . . I don't think it is imperative that I conduct showboat appearances through ghetto areas to prove I know something about the problems of the cities." What he meant, obviously, was that as a city-bred youth and as an urban official he was familiar with problems of the slums. But in the context of all that had gone before, the remark sounded to many like a callous dismissal of the urban poor. On the day Nixon selected him to be his running mate, Agnew had said, after all, that he would "welcome the chance" to run in ghetto areas in the North. But then was then, and now was now.

Actually, though Agnew probably did not have to visit more slums to see what they were like, that wasn't the reason he didn't. It now was near the end of October, less than two weeks before the election, and he was following the same game plan being observed by Nixon—"pulling in the sails and riding it out," as one aide later put it. The brunch in Pittsburgh had been Agnew's first news session with the traveling reporters in nearly four weeks, and attempts by them to gain access to him for questioning after that were largely futile. Nor did the public see much of the candidate either. Before long his staff aides were being accused by the traveling press of playing "Hide the Greek"; the implication was that Agnew's campaign bloopers finally had led Nixon to order him underground. Actually, the bloopers had very little to do with it. Nixon's strength had leveled off at about 43 percent in the major polls; Humphrey was rising and Wallace was beginning to slip. The strategy—after the hard pitch for the Wallace vote—was for both Nixon and Agnew to go into what Agnew's friends on the Baltimore Colts would have called "a prevent defense." The idea was to fall back, play it safe and avoid doing anything to hand the opposition a quick, long gain. "We sort of got locked in at this point," a campaign strategist said later, "to just try to ride it out; not do anything flashy, appear under very controlled circumstances, and let the Democrats do what they pleased."

The swing that had started in Pittsburgh had been typical: Agnew arrived at the Pittsburgh Hilton, spent the night there, canceled a tour that had been set for the next day, and stayed indoors all day. The word was passed that Agnew was busy with "staff work," but it was just a façade. "We sat all day in the hotel until night," one aide said later, "then got into a motorcade and motored way out of town to a rally. Then we came back, we went to bed, and the next morning left and arrived in the early part of the afternoon at the Detroit airport, where we made a fast move in the cars, a distance of about five hundred yards over to the airport motel, where we sat until night; then went to Cobo Hall for a rally, gave a speech, got out and came back. We spent the night and then flew home for the weekend on Thursday—to take some rest."

The Pittsburgh *Post-Gazette* described Agnew's visit as a "nonday," and the traveling reporters besieged Herb Thompson to produce the candidate, isolated in his curtained-off compartment up front on the plane. It got so that Thompson practically was in hiding from the reporters; assistant press aide Bob Smalley spent much of his time trying to appease them. Finally, as the party made ready to go to Corpus Christi, Texas, for a leisurely weekend at which the candidate would be out of sight most of the time, reporters demanded that Thompson set up a press conference with Agnew. When Thompson so informed one of the senior staff aides, who was well aware of the dictated strategy of the near-invisible profile, he was told, "Herb, you go tell those bastards that if they want to come along with us, there's good food and drink on the plane, and we'll drop down once in a while and get a night's sleep at a good hotel. Tell them we've got a nice weekend planned in Corpus Christi. They'll have a nice fishing trip planned for them in the morning, and a picnic in the afternoon, and on Monday we may make a speech. Tell them that after the next stop we're going to get up in that plane and just fly around. If they want to come with the next Vice-President of the United States, okay. Tell them we'll land after a while and then we'll all go into town and take a nap."

The press was not mollified by such jesting counsel, but could do nothing about it. So the reporters ate the good food, drank the good drink and continued to write that Agnew was in hiding. In the long hours aboard the plane, or in the bar of this or that watering hole, they took refuge in the time-honored occupation of the campaign reporter—the writing of parodies about the candidate. Chuck Quinn of ABC was the chief author of one that was recorded and played over the plane's loudspeaker. Agnew and Company did not think it was very funny. It went, to the tune of "Love and Marriage":

> *Law and Order, Law and Order,*
> *Can't find Justice on my tape recorder.*
> *I believe in let live,*
> *But please don't let it be permissive.*
>
> *Japs and Polacks, Japs and Polacks,*
> *Want to keep them on their own blocks.*
> *Then the press grows shrewish,*
> *Though some of my best friends are Jewish.*
>
> *We don't go into the ghettos,*
> *They're not part of the nation.*
> *Besides, who ever heard of letting*
> *The patient do the operation?*
>
> *Phony intellectuals, phony intellectuals,*
> *Hand the country to the ineffectuals.*
> *No more can we afford her,*
> > *You can't have Truth,*
> > *You can't have Peace,*
> > *You can't have Law,*
> *Without the Order.*

Meanwhile, back in the Nixon entourage, the other big football fan on the Republican ticket was in his own prevent defense. His tactics inspired accompanying reporters to write a Nixon theme song that also reflected the Agnew saga. To the chorus of "Can't Take My Eyes Off of You," it had Nixon singing:

> *They're saying Nixon's the One;*
> *When this campaigning is done,*
> *If I wind up in first place,*
> *Then we'll use payrolls, not mace.*
> *As long as Hubert can't say*
> *What Lyndon's thinking today*
> *We can be perfectly vague*
> *And treat the poor like the plague . . .*
>
> *We'll slick our way 'cross the land,*
> *With issues opaque and bland;*
> *We'll do our best to impress,*
> *And tell the citizens less.*
> *We've got the formula pat,*
> *We just won't go to the mat;*
> *And when the country awakes,*
> *They'll have elected two fakes.*

And then the upbeat chorus:

> *Squishy-soft on Communism,*
> *Without much room for realism;*
> *Ted Agnew's got a way with words*
> *That Cabot Lodge did not.*
> *I need you, Spyro, for putting Hubert down;*
> *Keep swinging, Spyro, I'll try to calm them down;*
> *You take the low road, I'll keep my moratoriums high.*
> *But cool it, Spyro; don't knock the Polack vote,*
> *And let the Jap sleep, he just got off the boat. . . .*

The line about not going "to the mat" was apropos of both the Nixon and Agnew campaigns, though the two candidates continued to crisscross the country—Monday to Friday, that is. In the resolute political wisdom of campaign manager and Nixon law partner John Mitchell, the Nixon-Agnew ticket was far ahead, and simply had to hold on. As late as mid-October, that reading had been an accurate one, but now, as the campaign entered its final days, things were happening to erode it, though Mitchell seemed unaware of them. While he continued to tell fretting associates that the G.O.P. ticket would win by five million votes, the polls were beginning to indicate otherwise, and the fertile political mind of Lyndon B. Johnson was hatching a move that ultimately would turn a sure thing for Nixon and Agnew into a near-disaster.

If there was one thing that could happen before the election that might yet vindicate Johnson's foreign policy and pull Humphrey's campaign chestnuts out of the fire, it was some important breakthrough in the Vietnam impasse. Johnson had been under severe pressure within his party to halt the bombing of North Vietnam altogether as a prelude to fruitful negotiations with Hanoi—meaning acceptance by Hanoi of the Saigon government at the bargaining table. For weeks Johnson had labored to bring about such a deal, and now it appeared he was on the verge of success. He was, in fact, keeping Nixon and Wallace as well as Democrat Humphrey posted on the progress of these efforts. On October 16, Nixon was in Kansas City, about to make a speech at the Union Station, when he was summoned to the phone. It was President Johnson with the news that a breakthrough was near.

The warning—Nixon aides always expressed bafflement that the shrewd Johnson would give it to them—enabled the Nixon camp to take steps to soften the political blow. The next day in Johnstown, Pennsylvania, Nixon went out of his way to try to neutralize the expected advantage to Humphrey by embracing the new initiative, but only if it would not endanger American lives. That proviso gave Nixon an out, should he later choose to criticize any arrangement that brought great political capital to Humphrey, or that was vulnerable to attack. Nixon well knew that a President has the wherewithal to affect public opinion mightily by what he says or does, and it was one of his gnawing fears that Johnson would come up with something like this in the closing days of the campaign that would undo the Republicans.

During the next week, while Nixon and Agnew waited for the other diplomatic shoe to drop, nothing happened. It turned out later that Johnson was having trouble with an intransigent President Nguyen Van Thieu in Saigon. The closer a dramatic announcement might come to Election Day, the greater its likely impact—except, of course, if it looked too transparently like a self-serving domestic political move. On October 24, President Johnson scheduled a press conference, and Agnew drew his own conclusions. "It's fully expected," he told a midmorning rally of about eight hundred Republican women in St. Louis, "some breakthrough in the Paris peace talks may be reflected either today or tomorrow." And shortly afterward, to a street crowd, he talked of "progress at the peace table which we hope will culminate, if all goes well, in some de-escalation of the bombing."

But Johnson's press conference came and went with no such announcement. Agnew immediately was asked by reporters: Had his prediction possibly upset "delicate diplomatic procedures?" Agnew bristled. "How could I upset it? All I said was, from what I read, I believed a breakthrough was coming. I was simply reflecting an impression from what I've read. . . . I knew President Johnson had called a press conference for this morning. It was simply speculative on my part." Agnew said he was still hopeful "that things are beginning to improve, and I appreciate the President's reluctance to say too much at this point. As he points out," said the man who earlier in the day had given the matter considerable publicity, "if anything can upset a diplomatic procedure, it is too much publicity on it."

By now the early complacency in the Nixon-Agnew camp was in full retreat. The latest Gallup poll indicated Humphrey finally was getting himself untracked; from a 43 to 31 percent deficit in mid-October, he had closed the gap to 44–36 near month's end, and still was gaining. Wallace's disastrous selection of LeMay as his running mate, coupled with a massive effort in Humphrey's behalf by organized labor, was bringing many wayward blue-collar voters in the industrial North back home to the Democratic party. A sudden peace breakthrough could complete the miracle and push Humphrey into the White House. The word went to all hands from Nixon headquarters: hunker down, and sweat it out.

At this juncture, however, there occurred a totally unrelated development that enabled Agnew to play a most unaccustomed yet welcome role—the wronged innocent. Through much of the campaign, reporters from various news organizations, including the *New York Times*, had been beating the bushes in Baltimore, Towson and Annapolis to find out whether there were any damaging answers to the favorite 1968 question of "Spiro Who?" Here, suddenly, was a candidate for the second highest office in the land, and nobody seemed to know much about him. There were, inevitably, plenty of rumors, and newsmen on the trail just as inevitably came across all the old charges, including Charles Steinbock's accusation of influence by Agnew in a zoning case, the bay-bridge land purchase and Agnew's directorship in the Chesapeake National Bank. But the best they could do was to recount the old charges with a few flourishes here and there. On October 22, the *Times* ran a story from Towson by Ben Franklin that merely confirmed this—that the news sleuths were out with their magnifying glasses, but had not come up with much. "Old Issues Revived As Investigators Study Agnew's Past," the headline said over the story on a deep inside page.

Four days later, however, the *Times* broke new ground by printing a very accusatory editorial based on the Franklin story. It said:

> Richard M. Nixon, who prides himself on his investigative abilities, appears not to have done much checking into the background and associations of Spiro T. Agnew before choosing him as his Vice Presidential running mate. It now develops that as a zoning board member, as Chief Executive of Baltimore County and as Governor of Maryland, Mr. Agnew has been the political ally and financial partner of a group of wealthy land speculators. These businessmen

have made sizable fortunes out of developing land in suburban Baltimore over the past fifteen years, in part because of favorable zoning and government decisions, and Mr. Agnew's financial net worth has also risen sharply.

In 1965 Mr. Agnew joined with these businessmen in purchasing a tract of land on the probable approach route of a new, parallel span of the Chesapeake Bay Bridge. As Governor, he approved this route. In response to public criticism, Governor Agnew later sold his share of the land. With several of these same businessmen, Governor Agnew is still partner in a Virgin Islands land venture and in a bank. His association with the Chesapeake National Bank involves clear and repeated conflicts of interest. The name of Spiro T. Agnew, identified as "Governor, State of Maryland," heads the list of directors on the letterhead of this bank. Since Governor Agnew is responsible for the enforcement of the state banking laws and the state has public funds on deposit with this bank, it would seem highly improper for the Governor to continue as a director and stockholder. The same relationship existed from 1964 to 1966 when Mr. Agnew, as County Executive, voted to deposit county funds in the bank.

In his gubernatorial campaign two years ago, Mr. Agnew explained that he inherited this bank stock from his father. It subsequently was learned that his father had died a year before the bank opened and that, in fact, Mr. Agnew had purchased the shares. In his obtuse behavior as a public official in Maryland as well as in his egregious comments in this campaign, Mr. Agnew has demonstrated that he is not fit to stand one step away from the Presidency.

The charges were, as Franklin had noted in his earlier story, old hat; Agnew, so long on the defensive for real or alleged campaign bloopers, saw an opportunity to reverse his role. "The *Times* was off-base," Hess said later. "The Agnew people felt, 'We've got them by the short hairs.' " It was decided Agnew would go all out to convert the *Times*'s criticism into an eleventh-hour asset—and diversion.

The editorial came at a time the Nixon-Agnew camp felt the hot breath of Lyndon Johnson on its neck. It now seemed clear that Johnson's Vietnam negotiations deal was all but set; the Republicans needed something to stem the political tide that a peace breakthrough would generate in Humphrey's behalf. On Sunday night, October 27, on CBS's *Face the Nation*, Nixon set the stage. He accused the *Times* of "the lowest kind of gutter politics that a great newspaper could possibly engage in" for printing "stale" and "inaccurate" charges, and warned that a retraction would be demanded "legally." Nixon said he was sure the retraction would be "printed in the *Times* back with the corset ads or the classifieds toward the end of the week when nobody will pay any attention." He asked why the *Times* had waited until the closing days of the campaign to bring up the charges, and he called the paper's action "below-the-belt politicking."

The next day Agnew followed through in Houston with a biting and detailed statement that refuted the five specific charges and accused the *Times* "of having pulled the major blooper of the campaign."

"Everyone knows that the *Times* endorsed Vice-President Humphrey," he said, "and is actively supporting him. The fact that the *Times* waited until a week before the election to distort the facts and make its inaccurate charges against me compounds the libel." Then he set about answering the charges.

Agnew labeled "absolutely false" the inference that his financial worth had "risen sharply" as a result of favorable treatment given to his friends while he was governor. He had given them no improper advantage, he said; if $35,000 to $40,000 received from his parents were eliminated from his net worth, the total would be only $74,000. As for the bay-bridge land purchase, he said he had "voluntarily disclosed" it before his election as governor and had deeded his interest in an irrevocable trust; later the interest was "sold at public auction . . . after proper public notification of the auction by newspaper advertisement." The bay-bridge route was approved and recommended by the state roads commission under the previous Democratic administration. He did have a $1,600 interest in a Virgin Islands condominium venture "which to date has shown a loss," he said, and he had later purchased a vacation apartment in the condominium. His directorship in the Chesapeake National Bank was well known, he said, and as governor he did not have jurisdiction over it because it is a national, not a state, bank. Of the charge that as county executive he voted to deposit funds in the bank, Agnew said selection of banks for deposits was "determined" by the county director of finances "originally appointed by the previous Democratic administration," who would verify that Agnew "adopted his recommendations in entirety." (Agnew did not mention that he had reappointed the man or that he had the power to instruct him on which banks would get how much in deposits.) A certificate of deposit the state owned had been bought while Tawes was governor, he noted, and none other was purchased during his own term. Finally, concerning the charge that he had said he inherited bank stock from his father, when in fact the bank did not exist at the time of his father's death, Agnew charged that the *Times* had misquoted him. What had happened, and what he had said, was that he had bought the stock with the inheritance money. Agnew noted that the *Times* editorial had promised a retraction if it was wrong, and he demanded it.

The next morning the *Times* reprinted the original editorial and repeated its contention that Agnew was not fit to be Vice-President. It acknowledged that "some, if not all, of these issues were indeed raised prior to the present campaign; but that fact makes them not one whit the less valid, nor less pertinent to a judgment on Mr. Agnew's fitness. . . ." The editorial also pointed out that although Agnew may have placed the bay-bridge tract in trust before becoming governor, it was not sold until after he became governor, and that the only bidder was his old partners' lawyer, acting for them.

From Staunton, Virginia, Agnew responded by sending his attorney, George White, to New York "to see if they are big enough at the *Times* to swallow their pride and accept their wrong. . . . Newspapers expect politicians to admit their mistakes—and I'm ready and willing to admit mine—but some of them just can't stand to admit when they blunder and are caught in error. . . . We all say a few things that need correction from time to time. The way you separate the men from the boys is when a man admits his mistakes, while a boy might try to find an easier way out. I say to the editorial board of the *Times*: 'Act with decency, act like men, act with intellectual honesty, let in the fresh air.'" Agnew thanked two leading Maryland Democrats, State Treasurer John A. Leuktemeyer and Baltimore County Executive Dale Anderson, for saying the *Times* was all wrong in its charges against him.

As the campaign moved into its last weekend, Agnew continued his role as the wronged innocent. "I haven't decided what I'm going to do about it yet," he said in a St. Petersburg, Florida, television appearance. ". . . I'm not the kind of person who goes around looking for every imagined grievance." As he spoke, the

Times had printed a third editorial backing away somewhat. It said that "nowhere in our [earlier] editorial comment did we accuse him [Agnew] of violating the law." George White visited Harding F. Bancroft, the *Times*'s executive vice-president, and said later that while the meeting had gone "very poorly," the editors had made an indirect concession that the paper had erred in charging "clear and repeated conflicts of interest." After the meeting Bancroft said rather lamely that "we tried to point out to him [White] that conflict of interest was a situation and that we did not, in fact, mean that anyone had taken advantage of it for personal gain." To White's demand for a retraction, Bancroft said, "My answer was that we had gone very thoroughly into all his statements and were not willing to make a retraction." White responded, "Now we have the ridiculous situation of the *Times* publishing a third editorial saying it never claimed Governor Agnew did anything 'unlawful,' that it was merely talking about a 'potential conflict of interest.' A clear admission by the *Times* that it made an error would have been more refreshing." He said he would recommend a libel suit to Agnew. And the candidate, with his talent for directness, reduced the *Times* editorials to the charge that "Agnew is not a crook, but might become one."

The controversy dragged on through the election, with the *Times* running a long story on the Saturday before the voting headlined "POINTS IN THE AGNEW-TIMES DISPUTE ARE CLARIFIED." It admitted that its charge that Agnew had "voted" to deposit funds in the Chesapeake National Bank was "erroneous." But the paper defended its statement that Agnew had said he inherited bank stock from his father, on the grounds that the Baltimore *Sun* had quoted him as saying so. Though Agnew aides had later described the *Sun* account as "mistaken," the article went on, Agnew had sent a letter to the editor of the *Sun* correcting another part of the *Sun* story "but did not challenge the same article's statement attributing to him the explanation that he had inherited the bank stock from his father." It was an elaborate exercise in nit-picking, with all the earmarks of a libel lawyer's determination to establish that what had been printed had appeared in good faith and without malice.

A final round was fired on the day before the election, when the Agnew camp ran a newspaper advertisement attacking the editorials. The paper replied with still another editorial, accusing "the forces behind" Agnew of carrying "to its climax in this campaign one of the oldest political strategies: when criticized, deny everything, cry 'Foul,' capitalize on a posture of injured innocence and denounce your critic in the wildest terms." The *Times* again refuted Agnew's "misrepresentations" on the bay-bridge deal, noting that he had helped push approval of the bridge route through the 1967 legislature and that the land subsequently was rezoned "to the enhancement of its value and of [the] investment" of his old partners. (At the time this editorial was written, it was true that a county hearing examiner had approved a request for rezoning from farm to industrial use. However, the county board of appeals reversed the ruling in March 1970, and the county circuit court in October 1970 upheld the reversal.) It pointed out that as a member of the state board of public works, Agnew had voted approval of the engineering and design contracts for the bridge approach road. "The fundamental issue is not over the details of shades of meaning," the *Times* said. "The fundamental issue is Mr. Agnew's apparent failure to comprehend the importance of the special standards of propriety that are rightly demanded of any holder of public office. It is his insensitivity to this problem of ethics of public servants that now stands revealed and reinforces our belief that he is a poor choice to be placed one step away from the Presidency of the United States."

While this side skirmish proceeded, Agnew was making a final effort to pry loose the Wallace vote in the South and, along with Nixon, harvest wavering segments of Wallace support elsewhere, as the deadening impact of LeMay and the reality that Wallace could not win sunk in from coast to coast. In Charleston and St. Petersburg, Agnew warned that Wallace was "not electable"; in Staunton he charged that Wallace and LeMay "offer no alternative" to Johnson in showing proper restraint in the use of nuclear weapons; in Detroit he compared an invitation to Humphrey from the Economic Club to "asking Eldridge Cleaver to speak on law and order." Strom Thurmond welcomed Agnew to Charleston and heard the candidate praise him as "an outstanding senator with the courage of his convictions." Thurmond and Goldwater had been working diligently for the Nixon-Agnew ticket not only in the Deep South but also in the Border States, whose vote would prove to be pivotal; the importance of their efforts, in tandem with Agnew's, generally was overlooked at the time.

On Thursday night, October 31, after much wrangling with Saigon, Johnson finally dropped the other diplomatic shoe and announced to the country—and a joyous Humphrey—that a negotiations breakthrough had been achieved. Agnew was in New York to make one of his rare joint appearances with Nixon, at a massive party rally in Madison Square Garden. Nixon was working on his speech for later that night when, at about six o'clock, Johnson called him. It was a conference call also involving Humphrey and Wallace; Hanoi had agreed to include Saigon and the National Liberation Front in the talks. The President would announce the news shortly, and the broadened talks would begin the next Wednesday—the day after the American election. Accordingly, a total U.S. bombing halt would start in a few hours, on Friday morning—just four days before the nation would go to the polls.

As already noted, Nixon had been laboring for two weeks to minimize or neutralize the political blow, by supporting the halt with patriotic rhetoric while constructing a political escape hatch in the event the talks collapsed. Shortly after the conference call, Johnson went on nationwide television and told the American people the news. He didn't say precisely that a deal had been struck with Hanoi, but he did say that in light of the American decision to stop the bombing, "we expect" there would be "prompt, productive, serious and intensive negotiations in an atmosphere that is conducive to progress." Later that night Nixon told nineteen thousand faithful at Madison Square Garden that he hoped the bombing halt would "bring some progress" to the peace talks. Then, pointing to Agnew who was sitting behind him on the stage, Nixon said, "Neither he nor I will destroy the chance of peace [by injecting the latest developments into the campaign]. We want peace."

The next morning, November 1, Agnew embarked on his last tour of the campaign—with his head down. He visited six critical states—Missouri, California, Texas, Michigan, Ohio and Virginia—and said little in each beyond the steady drumbeat of his law-and-order theme. In Los Angeles, asked about the impact of the bombing halt on the campaign, he said it had come as no surprise and would have "no significant" effect. It was the party line, and he hewed closely to it as he moved across the country and back, always keeping the matter of the bombing halt—and spontaneity—at a respectful distance. "Periodically," Warren Unna wrote in the Washington *Post*, "Agnew refers to the things he learns as he 'talks' to people around the country. Maybe he does it by lip reading from afar."

In Muskegon, Michigan, on the Sunday before the balloting, Agnew committed one final blooper, but it was all but lost in the rush of other campaign events. Walking alongside the airport fence, he came upon a sixteen-year-old boy named James McDiarmid, holding a sign that said: MUSKIE 4 VICE PRESIDENT. As Agnew approached, the boy and some friends shouted at him, "Stop the bomb!"—a reference, they said later, to the nuclear nonproliferation treaty. Agnew stopped, pointed to the Muskie sign, and told McDiarmid, "Why don't you go show that sign to Ho Chi Minh?" Shortly afterward George White walked into the press room to try to tout the traveling reporters off the story. "He didn't say, 'Show that sign to Ho Chi Minh,'" White insisted; Agnew really was referring to what the youths had called out, and he had said, "Go tell that to Ho Chi Minh." But McDiarmid confirmed that Agnew had indeed referred to the Muskie sign. To the reporters, an angry White said, "You guys can make up anything you want, but that's not what he said. You guys have been all through this campaign and you haven't heard him say a bad word about Ed Muskie. Why don't you find out who paid that kid to be here?" Efforts by the reporters to get a clarification from Agnew about what he had meant were unavailing; aides said only that he hadn't realized the sign referred to Muskie. But the youths said Agnew had looked up at the sign and pointed directly at it when he made his remark.

The incident might have created more of a stir had it not been that the campaign now was awash in a last-minute development that could rescue the Nixon-Agnew ticket. On Saturday morning the word raced eastward across the Pacific that Saigon had thrown a monkey wrench into the peace-talks deal. President Thieu, under pressure from associates who saw the broadened talks as a one-way ticket to surrender, had backed off. "The Government of South Vietnam deeply regrets not to be able to participate in the present exploratory talks," Thieu announced, and suddenly the whole arrangement that had made the Humphrey camp euphoric was unraveling. Nixon reacted warily at first, observing only that in light of Thieu's statement "the prospects for peace are not as bright as we would have hoped." But he soon moved quickly to plant the idea that Johnson for obvious political reasons had claimed a breakthrough before it really had been achieved, to boost Humphrey over the top in the campaign's final days. Nixon dispatched Bob Finch to tell two wire-service reporters on his campaign plane that the Thieu statement had come as a surprise, because from what Johnson had told Nixon on the phone Thursday night, "we had the impression that all the diplomatic ducks were in a row." On *Meet the Press* the next day, Nixon tried to dissociate himself from the ploy, but not very effectively. It didn't matter; Thieu's recalcitrance spoke for itself. Nixon and Humphrey went into the election nose to nose in the Gallup and Harris polls: on the final weekend Gallup had 42 percent for Nixon, 40 percent for Humphrey; Harris had 43 percent for Humphrey, 40 percent for Nixon. In the polling business, both results were rated "too close to call," and after a stormy year for both Gallup and Harris, their final efforts proved to be right.

On the day before the election, Humphrey, using his popular running mate to the fullest, joined Muskie in an uproarious motorcade through downtown Los Angeles. The very fact that Muskie was at Humphrey's side in public demonstrated what a positive factor Muskie now was regarded as in the Democratic campaign. That night, in a marathon telecast, Humphrey and Muskie again appeared together while on the other side of town, in the Burbank studio that housed the Rowan and Martin *Laugh-In* show, Nixon did a solo. Agnew was clear across the country in Virginia, one of the safest Nixon states.

The impression among many was that Nixon did not want to risk another blooper, and hence had chained Agnew to a bedpost in the attic. That may have been true concerning Agnew's physical presence that night, but Nixon "made it perfectly clear" at the outset of his telethon—which went not only to New York, Boston and Chicago, but also to Nashville, Louisville and Raleigh—that Agnew was his boy. For all the appearances of spontaneity, the Nixon telethon was a contrived show, with former football coach and Nixon idolater Bud Wilkinson asking carefully screened questions. The very first one intentionally gave the presidential candidate the chance to get one message across above all others to the early viewers: his selection of Spiro T. Agnew had been no mistake, and what Agnew had been saying represented the Nixon position, even if Nixon himself had not been as blunt about it as Agnew had. If Nixon could make that choice again, after all that had happened, Wilkinson asked in his best batting-practice pitching style, would he pick Agnew? "I most certainly would," Nixon replied on cue. "I'm not unaware of the fact that Agnew has been the subject of some pretty vicious attacks by the opposition, but he's a man of great courage. He doesn't wilt under fire. . . . If he had to hold the highest position in the country, he'd be cool under pressure. . . . If anything should happen to me Agnew will be a strong, compassionate, good, firm man."

This answer was obviously a counter to the Democratic tactic of ridiculing Agnew as a buffoon whose ascendancy to the Presidency would be a gigantic and disastrous joke on the country. The Democrats had been running one television commercial mentioning Agnew, followed by canned laughter, and another that showed his face, with the sound of a beating heart in the background. Agnew's own bloopers, contrasted with Muskie's much ballyhooed "Lincolnesque" performance, had prompted Humphrey to elevate the choice of running mates to the status of a major issue. But in Middle America, Republican polls had found, Spiro was a hero, not a joke, and Nixon acted accordingly. His telethon actually was split into two one-hour segments, one for prime-time viewing in each half of the country. At the start of the second segment, as in the first, Wilkinson served up his soft, underhand pitch about Agnew as the first question, to make sure it was heard by the maximum audience.

"In regard to what Agnew's function was in 1968, he'd done it well," a Nixon strategist noted later. "His stock by that time had been growing by leaps and bounds in the Border States, and in '68 that's what we were concerned about more than anything. We went there with a strong feeling we could take Ohio, Illinois and California, and New Jersey was a possibility. But the real trick would be to hold against Wallace all the states Nixon had carried in 1960 and add North Carolina and South Carolina. Well, we did all of that, and a lot of that was Agnew's responsibility. Nixon campaigned down there a good deal, but by the time the campaign was nearing a finish, it was Agnew who was cutting into Wallace. So when Wilkinson threw that question up, Nixon wanted to be darned sure that all those people who might be viewing from all those places would understand that right off the bat, before they got to any other questions, he thought Agnew was one hell of a good guy."

On Election Day Agnew voted in Annapolis, going early in the morning to the fire station across from the city hall to cast his ballot. Then, as was his custom on election days, he went out and played golf. That night he and his family dined at the mansion while the campaign staff and some of his old Baltimore County and Annapolis friends enjoyed a relaxed buffet downstairs. After dinner he watched the television returns in a private sitting room upstairs, accompanied by George White and Mrs. Alice Fringer, his long-time secretary, and from time to time other close aides came to visit. Occasionally he would wander downstairs to talk to his guests, who were watching on several television sets in various rooms. Twice he went over to the Annapolis Hilton to greet his campaign workers and volunteers, then returned to the mansion.

Some of the first election returns were ominous. Connecticut went for Humphrey, and it soon became clear that three of the seven most populous states, New York, Pennsylvania and Michigan, also would be his. According to some of those present, Agnew became very downhearted, and felt that he and Nixon had lost. The Republican ticket failed to carry Agnew's home state, and later a report circulated high in Maryland Democratic circles that Nixon had phoned his running mate that night and chewed him out for it. Nixon aides who were in the Nixon headquarters in New York deny the story emphatically. "Late in the evening," one of them says, "Nixon called him and told him not to worry about it; we still thought we had it in the bag, but it probably wouldn't be sure until the morning, and don't sweat it. We never figured to carry Maryland. We never did much campaigning there; Agnew campaigned over in Towson, his home town, which he had to do, and Nixon sure didn't beat a path into the state. It never was in our plans to carry Maryland; we just didn't think we could do it. It would have been a nice bonus if we had, and actually we came pretty close. Maybe we should have done more there." (The Nixon-Agnew ticket lost Maryland by 21,600 votes; 43.6 percent for Humphrey-Muskie, 41.9 percent for Nixon-Agnew, 14.5 percent for Wallace-LeMay.)

Agnew followed the returns until about five o'clock in the morning, then retired, confident the Republican ticket had won. It was not until several hours later, when the pivotal states of Illinois and California were safely in the Republican column, that Humphrey conceded defeat to Nixon. The final margin of victory out of 73 million votes cast was only 500,000; 302 electoral votes for Nixon-Agnew to 191 for Humphrey-Muskie and 45 for Wallace-LeMay. Agnew was only the running mate, but Nixon strategists readily admitted that he had made a contribution where it counted, in Kentucky, Tennessee and North and South Carolina, whose total of 41 electoral votes put the Republican ticket over the 270 needed to win. In the last three states Wallace ran second, and loss of those three would have cut Nixon's electoral vote to exactly 270. So close was the possibility that the election would be forced into the Democratic-controlled House of Representatives that the Agnew camp could argue with much justification that the presence of the Governor of Maryland on the Nixon ticket, far from being a disaster, actually was a salvation.

Only eleven years earlier, Ted Agnew had been appointed a member of the Baltimore County board of zoning appeals, and here he was, amazingly, Vice-President-elect of the United States. He had taken due note of his phenomenal rise when he told the Republican National Convention that nominated him of the "deep sense of the improbability of the moment" he felt in standing before it. Now, three months later, he was about to become, in that so very trite but so unshakably true phrase, just a heartbeat from the Presidency. It was a prospect overwhelming for any man to contemplate who had come to national prominence—indeed to political awareness—in such a short time.

For Spiro Agnew, whose emergence had been marked not simply by public surprise but by public ridicule, the circumstance to which he now ascended was a particular challenge—to his sense of responsibility to his country, to his party, to Richard Nixon and to himself. He knew, of course, the Alexander Throttlebottom tradition of the Vice-Presidency, but he was, in still another very trite but unshakably true phrase about himself, a very proud man. He had indeed, as he had promised, made Spiro Agnew a household name. Now, in the trappings of high national office, he had the opportunity, and the personal obligation, to make it more, much more, than a comedian's punch line.

15

◆·◇·◆·◇·◆·◇·◆

PITCHER OF WARM SPIT

AT midday on January 20, 1969, Spiro Theodore Agnew of
Maryland, at the age of fifty, took office as the thirty-ninth
Vice-President of the United States. The oath was administered to
him by Republican Senator Everett McKinley Dirksen of Illinois
on the steps of the United States Capitol. Agnew raised his right
hand and placed his left on a Bible borrowed from his daughter
Pamela, and when he completed repetition of the oath, he said
nothing more and sat down. This was, certainly, the biggest day
of his life, but it was not *his* day. The inauguration belongs first of
all to the man sworn in as President, and so Ted Agnew remained
silent and listened as Richard Milhous Nixon repeated the oath
and then made his simple and conciliatory address to the people
who had narrowly elected him to lead them for the next four
years.

"Greatness comes in simple trappings," the new President said.
"The simple things are the ones most needed today if we are to
surmount what divides us, and cement what unites us. To lower
our voices would be a simple thing. In these difficult years,
America has suffered from a fever of words; from inflated
rhetoric that promises more than it can possibly deliver; from
angry rhetoric that fans discontent into hatreds; from bombastic
rhetoric that postures instead of persuading. We cannot learn
from one another until we stop shouting at one another—until we

speak quietly enough so that our words can be heard as well as our voices."

As Nixon said these words, the man he had selected to be his Vice-President sat stolid and unsmiling to one side, intent on his leader's message. For the better part of a year Spiro Agnew would heed it, as he addressed himself to his new role with diligence and determination. He was, of course, aware of all the derogatory characterizations of the office he now filled; that, in the words of Peter Finley Dunne's Mr. Dooley, the chief function of the Vice-President was "to inquire each morning afther th' hilth of th' President"; or, in the less elegant homily of John Nance Garner, that the office was "not worth a pitcher of warm spit." In the same vein, Mr. Dooley had observed that "th' Prisidincy is th' highest office in the gift iv th' people. Th' Vice-Prisidincy is th' next highest an' th' lowest. It isn't a crime exactly. Ye can't be sint to jail f'r it, but it's a kind iv disgrace. It's like writin' anonymous letters." There was Alben Barkley's favorite: "Once upon a time there was a farmer who had two sons. One of them ran off to sea. The other was elected Vice-President of the United States. Nothing more was ever heard of either of them." And, in more lofty prose, Woodrow Wilson in his doctoral thesis on congressional government said of the Vice-President: "His position is one of anomalous insignificance and curious uncertainty . . . The chief embarrassment in discussing his office is that in explaining how little there is to be said about it, one has evidently said all there is to say."

Constitutionally, it was true that Agnew's only assigned role, as he waited in the wings as the President's understudy, was to be President of the Senate with "no vote, unless they [the senators] be equally divided." But Richard Nixon before him had been Vice-President, and Nixon determined at the outset of his Presidency to rescue Agnew from the idleness, boredom and most of all the feeling of unproductiveness that he knew often descended on the occupant of the Vice-Presidency.

Two days after the election, the President-elect had invited the Vice-President-elect to join him at his Key Biscayne retreat to discuss the role Agnew would play in the Nixon Administration. Nixon reported to the press afterward that he intended to make full use of Agnew's experience as governor and county executive in his Administration's work in urban affairs and federal-state relations. As an outward manifestation of the new importance the

Vice-President was to assume, Nixon assigned him offices within the White House itself, just six doors down from the President's, an unprecedented move. (This gesture was interpreted by some as a determination by Nixon to keep the outspoken Agnew on a tight leash. The White House denied any such intent.)

There were, however, everyday reminders that the Vice-President was almost everything and practically nothing. For example, there being no official residence for him, he was obliged to rent an apartment in a Washington hotel, the Sheraton Park; it was the same eight-room suite leased by Lyndon B. Johnson for a time before fate elevated him to national leadership. (The Agnews actually did not mind the lack of an official residence. For one thing, it gave them an excuse to limit official entertaining, which they did not relish, and it gave them more privacy, which they did relish. They made their apartment dwelling as much like home as they could, even to the point where the Vice-President had a pool table installed in the hotel basement where he could shoot a game or two with his Secret Service bodyguards—much as he had done with state troopers at the governor's mansion in Annapolis.)

Still, the knowledge that the man now at the top had been in his position eight years earlier gave Agnew reason to believe that he would be, as Nixon himself had said, the most active and utilized Vice-President in the nation's history. Agnew wanted greatly to be a working and respected Vice-President. As a result of his campaign bloopers, the public was more than willing to accept him as a Throttlebottom, and unless he used his new office to elevate his public image, he would be sentenced to a four-year term as the national laughingstock. There always were those who were ready to capitalize on that image. In time, a California entrepreneur introduced a Spiro Agnew watch and it became an overnight success. Soon the gag circulated widely that Mickey Mouse was wearing a Spiro Agnew watch. Spiro Agnew sweat shirts, dolls and toys were next. Clearly, Agnew had his work cut out for him.

As a first order of business, he determined to handle his one constitutional role with intelligence and taste. Traditionally, the job of presiding over the Senate is assumed by the Vice-President mainly when his constitutional function of breaking a tie vote seems required; the routine day-to-day chore of recognizing speakers and occasionally making a ruling—always on the advice of a veteran parliamentarian—is left to a senator, usually the most junior one present. For all this, Agnew surprised the Senate by opening every session during his first two months in office; in his first year he logged in more time in the chair than any predecessor since Alben Barkley. Meanwhile, he undertook a crash course on the workings of the Senate under the tutelage of Walter Mote, for more than a decade a ranking Republican staff member of the Senate Rules Committee. Mote took charge of the Vice-President's small office on the Senate side of the Capitol. As the first Vice-President in twenty-four years who had not been a United States senator (the last previous non-senator had been Henry A. Wallace in 1945), Agnew received extensive briefings from Mote and from Dr. Floyd M. Riddick, the Senate parliamentarian, and made efforts, in his fashion, to get to know the Senate membership.

Through the first half of 1969, the Vice-President held a series of lunches at the Capitol with small groups of senators. He maintained cordial if not chummy relationships with others in the cloakrooms and corridors of the Senate. At first he trod softly on the fringes of senatorial prerogatives, conferring with senators on embryo Nixon Administration legislative ideas but doing no arm-twisting. He was so successful at the outset that one day in mid-March a group of senators, led by Senate Democratic Leader Mike Mansfield of Montana, rose to commend him for, in Mansfield's words, "a job well and assiduously done."

At the same time Agnew was busy educating himself about the intricacies of the federal bureaucracy, White House politics and power relationships. True to his word, the President heaped a heavy load of administrative responsibilities on the Vice-President —some real, some showcase. As a member and, in the President's absence, substitute chairman of the Cabinet, the National Security Council, the Urban Affairs Council and the Cabinet Committee on Economic Policy, Agnew was interjected into the heart of the new Administration's formative discussions. In the first weeks the President established a new Office of Intergovernmental Relations under the Vice-President's direction as the official Administration contact point for state and local governments. Also, by statute or presidential direction, Agnew then or later became chairman of such diverse executive units as the National Aeronautics and Space Council, the Marine Resources and Engineering Development Council, the Council on Recreation and Natural Beauty, the Rural Affairs Council, the Cabinet Committee on Desegregation, the Indian Opportunity Council, the Council on Youth Opportunity, and the Council on Physical Fitness and Sports. It was, in a favorite Nixon expression, "a full plate" that ought to have satisfied Agnew's appetite for work and involvement.

In those early months he did seem to most observers to be earnestly and contentedly involved. "I feel right now as volatile as gas does," he said on creation of the intergovernmental office. "I am constantly expanding. The only problem I have is time." After breakfast with his wife at the Sheraton Park apartment, and perhaps a hundred pulls on a rowing machine he had installed, or a congressional leadership breakfast at the White House, Agnew most often would begin his workday by reading foreign news summaries and intelligence reports prepared for only the highest Administration officials. Next he would scan the domestic news summary compiled by the President's own staff, then enter a round of committee and staff meetings. He might go up to the Senate for a few hours, return downtown for more work, and finally hit the obligatory social circuit for an hour or two. Although Nixon had given him a White House office, Agnew preferred another suite across the way in the Executive Office Building, occupied by Lyndon Johnson in his vice-presidential days.

In White House staff meetings, the new Vice-President did not hesitate to speak out, particularly concerning domestic affairs, the area in which he felt most comfortable. As a former county executive he was a constant, vocal reminder to other urban specialists that there was such a subdivision, that it was growing in influence. "Most standard social scientists thought in terms of mayors, governors, President," one former White House urban expert says. "In the course of a normal meeting of the Urban Affairs Council, you'd talk cities, cities, cities, and the Vice-President would say, 'Well, what about the counties?' But the focus is very resistant to this. We would say, 'Hey, that's right, isn't it?' and then go right back to talking mayors, governors, President."

At the first meeting of the Urban Affairs Council, Agnew proposed that a "National Urban Policy" be established to guide all departments and agencies of the Administration. It was done and was circulated among members of the council. Hess, then Deputy

Assistant to the President for Urban Affairs and a man who had watched both Nixon and Agnew as Vice-Presidents in White House meetings, said later: "Agnew did not play the same role that Nixon did as Vice-President in the Eisenhower Administration, which was to listen and then synthesize at the end. Agnew was an aggressive talker; he pitched in, he spoke from the governors' viewpoint, and was most often an advocate of the states. Nixon treated him respectfully and Agnew deferred to Nixon. Once, early in the Administration, an extraordinary meeting of the domestic council was called and the President was not there. It fell to Agnew to preside, but he walked in and occupied his usual seat across from the President's chair. Others at the meeting suggested he take it, but he declined."

In this gesture, of course, Agnew was following the prudent lead of Richard Nixon as Vice-President, who even in the critical weeks of Eisenhower's heart attacks had avoided appearances of political ghoulery. When Nixon went off to Europe, after only a month in office, Agnew hewed closely to his normal routine and underlined that he was still no more than the No. 2 man. "The Presidency travels with the President," he reminded reporters. Being No. 2 would probably not be as difficult for Agnew, after all, as it was for Lyndon Johnson, who had been a Washington power as Senate majority leader, or even for Hubert Humphrey, for that matter, who had been on the national scene for nearly twenty years. The altitude still was pretty heady for a man who a decade earlier was spending his time reviewing county zoning decisions.

In the early months of the Nixon Administration, Ted Agnew's determined efforts to eschew Throttlebottomism bore considerable fruit in the public prints. Stories about his diligence, his prudence and his constructive attitude abounded. (The slips of the past, however, were destined always to haunt him. On Nixon's return from Europe, Agnew greeted him personally, and Chicago's *American* ran a cartoon that had the Vice-President inquiring: "How are things with the Limeys, Krauts, Dagoes and Frogs?") Yet those who saw and heard him beyond the public glare were aware that his bitterness toward the social unrest still loose in the land, which had been so apparent in the 1968 campaign, was undergoing no softening. The nation's governors were beleaguered in the winter and spring of 1969 by campus disorder, and Agnew, appointed the President's liaison man on this particular matter, used them as a sounding board for his own fears.

At first the Vice-President expressed his concern in mild and balanced terms. At a governors conference in Washington in late February he observed that "we have the obligation to protect the freedom of others, including students who go to college and want to learn. No government should try to dictate academic policy. We don't want to tell them what to teach or how to teach. But we want to make sure that college administrators and faculty are able to teach" once they have made decisions concerning the curriculum. "Let us not allow the dissenters," he warned, "to confuse our purpose by raising the issue of academic freedom."

In April, when the Republican governors met in Lexington, Kentucky, in the wake of an episode at Cornell University where protesting blacks were photographed with guns, Agnew said some schools had exceeded the "reasonable limit of permissiveness." Congress, he said, should set a limit beyond which besieged colleges would have their federal aid cut off. And concerning the then lively issue of local police on campuses, he said any student as a citizen had a right to call them in against personal attack. "If an individual seeks to prosecute, it should not be the concern of the college president or the faculty," he added.

Two days later, in Honolulu, Agnew warned that vigilantes would take the law into their own hands unless college officials faced up to illegal protest on the nation's campuses. "If the people who can do something don't start acting," said the man who had shut down Bowie State and castigated Baltimore's black leaders for what he saw as a leadership lapse in the 1968 riots, "I tremble at the thought of what forces could fill this vacuum. . . . Unless sage debate replaces the belligerent strutting now used so extensively, reason will be consumed and the death of logic will surely follow. What we have witnessed in the past weeks is not mere disruption. [Such] words dismiss too lightly the grave implications of campus disorders and the reaction to them that is reverberating across the country. We have college administrators confused and capitulating. We have sophisticated faculties distraught and divided over issues as basic as the criminality of breaking and entering, theft, vandalism, assault and battery."

These remarks came on the heels of a speech by Nixon to the

U. S. Chamber of Commerce in which he said there could be "no compromise with lawlessness" on American campuses. School officials, he said, should show some "backbone" in coping with campus violence. Thus, though Agnew's rhetoric was strong and righteous, it was widely seen as the normal affirmation of a President's views by his loyal second. It would not be until about six months later that Agnew would step out conspicuously and alone on the firing line of national debate in the role that would be the hallmark of his Vice-Presidency.

Yet there was occasional evidence that as presidential stand-by he was seething at the growing domestic protest, particularly among youth, against what he unabashedly called "the establishment." The Nixon Administration was negotiating with Hanoi in Paris and was preparing a wide range of domestic reforms, including basic revision of the welfare and tax systems; thus at home and abroad, in Agnew's view, the President was working diligently within the system to cure America's ills. If only, Agnew was saying more and more often now, the other partners in "the establishment"—leaders of industry, education and the religious life—would assert themselves, the destructive elements in the body politic would be weeded out. In June, as a stand-in for Nixon, Agnew told Ohio State's graduating class:

"We are in trouble because my generation has apparently failed to define and defend either its achievements or its inheritance from past generations of Americans. A society which comes to fear its children is effete. A sniveling, hand-wringing power structure deserves the violent rebellion it encourages. If my generation doesn't stop cringing, yours will inherit a lawless society where emotion and muscle displace reason. . . . Ask yourselves which kind of society you want for tomorrow—tomorrow when you are the establishment . . . Democracy's greatest flaw rests in its intransigent commitment to individual freedom. When social change depends on persuasion, rather than coercion, it comes slowly."

Amid Agnew's pleas to the country to work within the establishment, however, there were signs that he was finding it harder and harder to work effectively within the Nixon Administration. In the first months, before the structure-minded Administration really had sorted itself out, many loose tasks had fallen Agnew's way, particularly in the area of domestic affairs. But by the summer of 1969, as the Administration shook down and the men in key positions of influence on the President's White House staff emerged and solidified their positions, more and more functions were pulled into the staff structure. At the same time, Cabinet members were settling into their own bureaucracies. "In the first months," said one key White House staff man with experience in other administrations, "everybody lives in the White House. All the Cabinet members also did, because they didn't know anything about their departments. Little by little, as Cabinet officers were getting hold of their departments, they were spending more time there and worrying about their departments' problems. They worry about firing this or that bureau chief and they almost forget to come over to the White House. But the Vice-President doesn't have a department." Perhaps without quite realizing it at first, Agnew, according to one insider, was methodically being "structured out" of the decision-influencing mechanism. Just as the heads of Cabinet departments were finding that the White House staff system—contrary to Nixon's early assurances that each Cabinet member would run his own show—was centralizing most basic policy decisions, the Vice-President was learning what it meant to be a fifth wheel. "As one who knows something about county and state government and domestic affairs," one insider says, "he felt he might have a large slice of running domestic policy. He got the vice-presidential blues. I think he felt he could honcho the domestic side of it and have a larger hand in it. But we had Arthur Burns, Pat Moynihan and George Shultz, and HEW over there. I think he was looking for a role for himself."

While still loyal to the President, Agnew on occasion would "go public" with his viewpoints, possibly as a way to rally some support for them. As a man of candor, he seemed not to be reluctant to do so. In June, when the Administration proposed limits on the federal tax deductions allowable on municipal bond interest, Agnew as a former county official who knew the problems of raising local revenue urged the Advisory Commission on Intergovernmental Relations to lobby against the idea. As governor Agnew had been a member of the group, composed of federal, state, county and local officials; he told them the limitation would impair the ability of states and cities to sell their bonds.

Also, just before the launching of the Apollo 11 spacecraft that put the first men on the moon, Agnew held a Cape Kennedy press conference and proclaimed publicly that as a minority voice within the Administration, he had privately been urging that the United States set a new goal of landing men on Mars by the end of the twentieth century. After the successful lift-off, he walked into the firing room and proclaimed to the jubilant launching team: "I want to tell you I bit the bullet for you today as far as Mars is concerned. But on the other hand, I want to let you know that I may be a voice in the wilderness." While boosting spirits at Cape Kennedy, the outspoken declaration made sober discussion of space goals within the Administration more difficult and stirred up critics in the country against continued high priorities for space. Congressional supporters of greater space appropriations complained to the Administration that Agnew's candor had undermined their already sensitive task by alerting the opposition. At the annual National Governors Conference in Colorado Springs over Labor Day, Agnew endorsed "as a final objective" a resolution urging full federal takeover of the welfare program—at a time the Administration had just hammered out a new $4 billion welfare reform plan that fell far short of that goal, retaining instead the state-based structure with federal aid funneled in under new criteria.

Agnew's failures to get his way in some policy areas, however, did not lessen his efforts across the board in behalf of the Administration. In general, with the governors and with members of the Senate, he became an aggressive lobbyist for the Administration's proposals, once adopted within the White House. When the Administration revised plans for an antiballistic missile defense system, gave it the more defensive-sounding name of Safeguard and tried to get it through Congress, Agnew became a prime huckster, both in and out of the Senate. Yet he continued to push his own views in other areas. Once, in anticipation of a possible tie vote in the Senate on the ABM, Agnew had to leave a key meeting at Camp David on the welfare package he opposed. As the Vice-President broke off his arguments to fly back to Washington, President Nixon said to him in jest: "You know how to vote on that, don't you?" Agnew replied: "If it's a tie on the ABM, Mr. President, I'll be on the phone about the welfare program."

In the Senate, after months of learning the parliamentary and diplomatic niceties of his position, Agnew nevertheless let his zeal as a lobbyist for the Administration get out of hand. The President had decided to seek an extension of the 10 percent federal income surtax and Agnew became an aggressive nose-counter, rather than leaving that detail to a subordinate. His eleventh-hour inquiries were taken by some senators as only the most thinly veiled pressure, and they deeply resented it. One of them was conservative Republican Len B. Jordan of Utah, who, when asked by Agnew whether the Administration had his vote, replied curtly, "You did have, until now." Shortly afterward, at a lunch of Republican senators, the mild-mannered Jordan announced that he believed firmly in the separation of the legislative and executive branches and would be guided from then on by "the Jordan Rule" —that if the Vice-President tried to lobby him on anything, he would automatically vote the opposite way. Agnew later apologized to Jordan and henceforth was more circumspect in his efforts in behalf of the Administration on Capitol Hill.

Such irritations in the Senate, and the innovations of policy making and implementation within the White House that were freezing him out of policy decisions, weighed heavily on Agnew. Also, after high visibility in the press in 1968 and in the first months of the new Administration, he now appeared to be slipping steadily into the bump-on-a-log image that was traditional for Vice-Presidents. White House staff aides who screened news coverage and digested it for the President's eyes noted a definite drop in Agnew's media fortunes. "He wasn't just being ignored, he was being pounded," one aide said later. "On everything. He was in bad shape in the media." The President, of course, read the anti-Agnew stories and columns about "the Jordan Rule" along with everything else and was aware of his Vice-President's low state.

At about this time Agnew was involved in early Administration discussions concerning an area in which he was well versed and in which he was destined soon to play a dominant role—the politics of 1970. As early as June 1969, Agnew began meeting with then Republican National Chairman Rogers C. B. Morton; Harry Dent, the chief White House political adviser and operative; and the G.O.P. congressional campaign committee chairmen, John Tower of Texas in the Senate and Bob Wilson of California in the House. Although the off-year elections were more than a year away, the Administration perceived early that they would offer the Republican party a rare opportunity to make substantial gains. For one thing, in spite of the most expensive presidential campaign in American political history in 1968, the party was solvent. (Nixon's finance chairman, later Secretary of Commerce, Maurice Stans, put the cost of electing Nixon at more than $33 million.) Not only did the party enter 1969 in the black; it also had one of its own in the White House, armed with patronage, skilled technicians in the craft of fund raising, and the willingness to use both to the maximum.

Coupled with those facts was what the professional politicians call "the arithmetic"—the cold statistical evidence of political opportunity. The Senate would be a major target in 1970; in the national impatience toward the Vietnam war, the most vocal and influential voices of dissent against Nixon policy were coming from that body. In 1970, of thirty-three Senate seats at stake, twenty-five were held by Democrats and one by a Republican increasingly hostile to the President on the war—Charles Goodell of New York. The list of 1970 Senate vulnerables would include such other Vietnam doves as Albert Gore of Tennessee, Joseph Tydings of Maryland, Philip Hart of Michigan, Vance Hartke of Indiana, Harrison Williams of New Jersey, and Ralph Yarborough of Texas. Also, several of the twenty-five Democrats were members of what was known as the class of '58—candidates who had been swept into office in the recession of 1958, re-elected in 1964 on the tide of the national rejection of Barry Goldwater, and hence considered particularly vulnerable. For the Republicans, the 1970 elections offered a quarry well worth talking about, even a year before the battle would be joined.

In their hearts as well as in their minds, the political types in the Administration, Agnew included, already were warming to the prospect of taking on the opposition at the polls again. The customary honeymoon enjoyed by a new President had been prolonged somewhat through the spring of 1969 as Nixon held his foreign policy cards close, particularly regarding Vietnam. He had been elected in 1968 without having spelled out what his Vietnam policy would be, and he extended that exemption from public and congressional accountability by citing the sensitivity of peace talks in Paris and intimating progress without claiming it. But as it became clear that the negotiations were getting nowhere, Democrats in the Senate demanded to know the new President's policy. The honeymoon was over, and partisan criticism increased.

On the domestic front too, heavy-handed lobbying techniques and failure to consult sufficiently with the congressional leadership hardened attitudes toward the Administration, even among some veteran Republicans on Capitol Hill. Like congressional veteran Lyndon Johnson before him, former Congressman and Senator Nixon at times demonstrated remarkable political and diplomatic myopia about the care and feeding of his erstwhile colleagues. The nomination of Judge Clement F. Haynsworth, Jr., of South Carolina in August to fill a Supreme Court vacancy, and the subsequent Custer-like fight for his confirmation in the face of strong conflict-of-interest charges, capped a spring and summer in which the President had managed to poison the well in record time. By the time Ted Agnew sat down with the political heavies of the Republican party to think and talk about 1970, the ill feeling that is the natural condition between Republicans and Democrats already was approaching election-year intensity.

In the country too, and particularly among those chronic gripers of American democracy, the young and the press, the Nixon plea for lowered voices was being ignored. At the onset of fall and the return to the nation's campuses, student protest geared for its most ambitious drive. Protest leaders seized on a new idea—to persuade the country to halt business-as-usual, not only to demonstrate against the war but also to discuss its impact in hundreds of communities from Maine to California. A target date of October 15 was selected and called Vietnam Moratorium Day. Campus groups formed a national radio network to air the speeches and discussions of war critics; political leaders of the antiwar community fanned out to virtually every major campus and many smaller ones. Politicians who had not been identified particularly with the war protest joined in what was planned as a broad-based but low-key confrontation with the ramifications of the war. This broadening in turn led to wider press coverage, even by those conservative news organizations that up to now had looked upon the antiwar protest as an unsavory and ineffective aberration.

The Administration's response, predictably, was to poor-mouth the whole enterprise and try to ignore it. In a nationally televised press conference less than three weeks before Moratorium Day, President Nixon said flatly, when asked about the demonstration: "Under no circumstance will I be affected whatever by it." The remark was taken by the organizers and avid supporters of the Moratorium as a studied insult, and it only spurred them in their undertaking.

All this while Spiro Agnew, Vice-President of the United States, his hoped-for role as a domestic policy shaper in the Administration eroded by the expansion of the White House bureaucracy and circumscribed by the powerlessness of his elected office, watched and listened—and seethed. His loyalty to the President and to his Administration remained high, and as both objects of his fealty came under heavier and heavier fire—particularly from the Senate liberals, the antiwar students and the press—his irritation increased. In meetings at the White House and in other private sessions, there was considerable discussion about how all the attacks could be countered. In an Administration that had already demonstrated a tendency to view all opposition as conspiratorial, the unspoken premise was that "they"—the Senate doves, the student protesters, the press—were ganging up. The Administration had to find some way to defend itself, to throw the carping of critics back in their teeth, to get the Administration off the defensive and onto the attack.

The President agreed. "Nixon himself was not the world's greatest champion of the press," one insider noted later. "He felt he was not getting a fair shake. Somebody ought to take on the press especially. Some felt, why not let Agnew do it? He was good at it, and he was close to the top. A few thought, too, he really was a dumb guy and this might be a way to get rid of him. There were some who didn't want him to do it, but they weren't in the important discussions. Agnew himself took to the idea with relish."

There is no hard evidence that Agnew was ever specifically assigned by the President to the role he now was about to undertake with such dramatic result. Rather, most White House aides and men around Agnew insist the Vice-President decided on his own how, when and where he would start to counter the Administration's critics across the board. Nevertheless, such a decision inevitably evolved not only from Agnew's personal vexation but also from the climate of irritation and defensiveness that permeated the White House at this critical juncture.

Richard Nixon, of course, always had been a firm believer in the maxim that the best defense is a good offense. Not only did he believe it; he had acted on it at almost every stage of his mercurial political career. So, too, had Spiro Agnew; he was, in one of sports fan Nixon's highest accolades, "a fighter." The President of the United States, having already said he would "under no circumstance" be affected by Moratorium Day, had taken himself out of the ring this time. That, no doubt, was the way Dwight Eisenhower would have handled it—aloof, unruffled by a little insubordination in his command. From 1953 through 1960 there had been political uprisings that needed attention, and Eisenhower had preserved his presidential aura by leaving the skirmishing to his lieutenant, Dick Nixon. That was the way it was supposed to be. In a 1966 interview Nixon recalled that although the Republicans lost the 1954 and 1958 off-year elections, in which he had carried the brunt of the Administration political burden, "Eisenhower didn't lose, because he was always apart. He maintained the dignity of the President." Nixon was not one ever to forget that lesson. So in October 1969, he played Eisenhower. Somebody else would have to play Nixon.

16

❖◦❖◦❖◦❖◦❖◦❖

THE BIRTH OF AGNEWISM

IN the fall of 1969, Spiro Agnew came to the role of the Nixon Administration's dragon slayer with formidable oratorical weaponry. Overshadowed by his bloopers in the 1968 campaign, by his careless use of words, there was in Agnew a strangely paradoxical personal infatuation for the well-turned, even ostentatious phrase. This reverence for language made the earlier faux pas even more incomprehensible to those close to Agnew than to the general public; his associates thus regarded them as mere aberrations, an unfortunate occasional fallout attributable to the man's exceptional candor. When Ted Agnew exerted the same painstaking care in dressing up his public utterances that he demonstrated in his personal appearance, the result was much the same; oratorically and sartorially, the man in person exuded a precision and self-discipline that belied any reputation as a political alley cat.

In the era of mass-media communications, when the visual perception and the decibel level accompanying what a man says can have more impact than the substance of his words, Spiro Agnew was himself a paradox. He uttered some of the most inflammatory phrases ever recorded in the lexicon of American politics, but he uttered them under such a veneer of benignity, of personal placidity, that they did not *sound* or *seem* all that inflammatory to those who heard or saw him. It was mainly when the words were stripped of that oral and visual veneer and reduced to cold print —in newspaper headlines and stories—that their divisiveness, their hostility and often downright meanness emerged in fullest force.

One White House speech writer who has worked with the Vice-President says of his stump style, "He can read a text better than anyone I've ever seen. It's almost like a priest up there saying mass. He's got the hands going quietly—he's calm, he comes across benign, he comes across as friendly, with a sense of humor, thoughtful. I think this is attributed to the fact that he didn't come into American politics at the time of the Truman era, as President Nixon did. The political stump speech was the forte then; Humphrey has the style, the President has the style. The Vice-President came into national politics in a time when that was no longer the forte; I guess it was even post-Kennedy. I think that's good. This newer style, Gene McCarthy has it very much; without gestures or the modified gesture. It's the Vice-President's personality. Sit and talk with him. He's a very relaxed guy."

How Agnew's words appear in print, this aide says, when Agnew himself knows he has delivered them with a minimum of visual or oral bombast, may account in part for his disenchantment with his press coverage. "That's the fault of our writers, the way the speech is drafted, and the imperatives of the wire copy and the news writers," this aide says. "They go through a speech and take that phrase and this phrase—and this is legitimate, it's what he said—and you put that in the lead; you take this sharp paragraph and you put it number two; that stuff comes smoking across that wire, and that's hot copy."

What does not come "smoking across the wire," of course, is the physical Spiro Agnew. In person, or on television, the look of the man has a kind of mesmerizing effect. There is first of all a self-contained, assured quality, a manicured coolness that is accentuated by small, spiritless eyes, his erect carriage and impeccably understated dress. He clearly is fussy about his personal appearance, but never ostentatious; his head appears to be the same width as his neck, giving him a ferretlike look that is accentuated by the way he slicks back his slightly graying hair. The word for him as one sees him in person for the first time is likely to be "sleek"—a greyhound in repose. He does not always photograph well; the small eyes, the shape of his head and nose taken full-face, often give him a vacant, sleepy look, not unlike Kilroy of World War II peering over the fence. Among friends, Agnew can break into an open and attractively warm grin that crinkles the small eyes and softens them; among those he perceives to be unfriendly or predatory, the cool gaze dominates and underlines a pervading wariness.

Agnew's immaculate appearance already has generated a small anthology of wisecracks and anecdotes, many of them bitingly on the mark. Reporters and other associates from Annapolis days recall him explaining that he never crosses his legs, thus keeping a crisp crease in his trousers at all times; one tells of Agnew's explanation for avoiding wrinkles in his suit jacket—"Never let your back touch the back of the chair"; Frank DeFilippo's description is that Agnew looks "as though Judy pushes him out the front door on a skate board every morning." All of these suggest an antiseptic quality about the man, and a privateness, that are anathema to the stereotype of the rumpled, shirt-sleeved, back-slapping politician on the make. It is as if Spiro Agnew were playing Henry Higgins to his own Eliza Doolittle and triumphing over all the Zoltan Kaparthys who try to strip his mask away. The only chink is the harshly inflammatory language, and that, as noted, often must be converted to type before it starts to smoke.

Marshall McLuhan would probably say that Spiro Agnew ideally combines the hot and the cool in terms of impact on the television generation—cool in appearance and audio volume; hot as a pistol in the substantive. It is for this reason that those who see Agnew as just another ranting, raving Joe McCarthy engage in rampant oversimplification—one that is particularly objectionable, his intimates say, to the Vice-President.

In appearance and style, and above all in the use of language, Agnew is light-years ahead of McCarthy, who looked like, talked like and was a streetfighter with a limitless repertoire of rank misstatement, twisted logic and gross brutality. McCarthy assaulted everything in sight—the truth, personal reputation, personal appearance and the English language, wielding an oratorical meat cleaver with abandon. Agnew administers a surgical scalpel, using fancy words never uttered on a streetcorner, taking care to dispatch his victims without mussing a strand of hair on his own head or getting a drop of blood on his custom-tailored, perpetually creased trousers. McCarthy did not hesitate to employ oral and visual histrionics: the growling, rasping voice of accusation, the waving of meaningless sheets of paper purported to contain lists of Communists in the State Department. Nor did he shy away from cheap-shot use of the language by ridiculing men's names— "Senator Halfbright" for Senator J. William Fulbright, or "Sanctimonious Stu" for Senator Stuart Symington. By contrast, Agnew appears to loathe the physical and has too much respect—even reverence—for the language, too much confidence in his own use of it, to stoop to those tricks very often. It is an element in his strength that he seems to stand above it all, throwing his spears from out of range. There was in McCarthy a physically intimidating force, an ever-present suggestion that if sufficiently aroused, the man would not hesitate to wrestle an opponent to the ground. George Wallace gives off the same sparks of imminent violence. With Agnew, one gets the distinct feeling that he would rather not touch anybody, or be touched, with a ten-foot pole.

The "priest" imagery that Agnew's associates mention is particularly apropos in this respect. "His image is not of the guy who's going to fall on the button as they had him painted in the 1968 campaign," says Baltimore ad man Bob Goodman, "and it's not of the great antagonizer. He's a very sensible, reasonable, logical guy. On the other hand, he's always run upstream. What amazes me is why the radical left doesn't dig this guy, and why youth doesn't think he's marvelous, because he's doing the same kind of thing they're doing, on his side of the fence. He's antiestablishment in that he doesn't believe a politician has to be a compromiser, a liar, a mealy-mouther, a pacifier, a bullshitter. And in a way he's a priest in terms of his politics; he's kind of apolitical. If the press believed in him I think he would be striking, in terms of his life style and his ways, to youth. Because he's on the right what they are on the left, in terms of 'Do your own thing,' 'Let it all hang out,' even 'Right on!' Take all these expressions. My God, there's Agnew."

Such a reading, however, does not take into consideration the possibility that in doing his own thing—smiting the opposition with what he perceives to be elevated language—Agnew may only be serving up simplistics behind a façade of erudition. It is noteworthy to observe that it was not until the fall of 1969, when Agnew carried the public debate to the opposition with a type of oratory more heavily peppered with multisyllabic words than he had used before, that he really began to nail down a national constituency. The complaints he set out to air in the fall of 1969 were familiar ones, but he dressed them not in the language of the gutter or simply of Main Street, but in the dialogue of intellectualism. At last middle-class America—Middle America, in the new shorthand—had one of its own, a card-carrying suburbanite, who had the stuff to take on "the intellectuals" on their own highfalutin ground; he was a kind of word-power white hope. George Wallace, for all his efforts to be a dandy, was anchored to his back-country constituency and to his own grammatical shortcomings. He scored points by imitating the "pseudo-intellectuals" in an exaggerated style designed to amuse the uneducated; Ted Agnew sought not so much to amuse as to impress and even dazzle. George Wallace repeatedly would tell redneck and hard-hat audiences that he was just as good "as them Yankee governors," but his words and manner betrayed a transparent inferiority complex; Ted Agnew in the fall of 1969 began to show Middle America, by his articulate and righteously confident style, that he was indeed as good as, or better than, those other well-educated, high-sounding public men who took Main Street for granted.

The Vice-President's campaign to arouse "the silent majority" opened without advance fanfare and was hardly noticed at first. According to some insiders, there was no notice or warning to the White House staff or the President about what his Vice-President planned to say, or how. The effort was launched, appropriately and safely, in the South, where Agnew already had won wide acceptance in the 1968 campaign. At a Republican fund-raising dinner in Dallas, on October 9, after the usual politic remarks defending the oil-depletion allowance, he launched the oratory of societal purification that soon would be called Agnewism.

"Should the establishments of this country, industrial, business, educational and governmental, cringe and wring their hands before a small group of misfits seeking to discredit a free system because they can't effectively compete and find success anywhere?" he asked. "I find it hard to believe that the way to run the world has been revealed to a minority of pushy youngsters and middle-aged malcontents." He called the impending Vietnam Moratorium Day "ironic and absurd," staged against the one man who was working above all others to end the war. "Only the President has the power to negotiate peace," he said. "Congress cannot dictate it, the Vietnam Moratorium Committee cannot coerce it, and all the students in America cannot create it. By attacking the President, the protesters attack our hope for peace. They weaken the hand that can save."

Two days later Agnew flew to Montpelier, Vermont, for another party fund-raising event and said: "The man who believes in God and country, hard work and honest opportunity is denounced for his archaic views. The nation which has provided more justice, equality, freedom and opportunity than any nation in world history is told to feel guilty for its failures. The time has come to call a halt to this spiritual Theater of the Absurd, to examine the motivation of the authors of the absurdity and challenge the star players in the cast."

Neither the Dallas nor the Montpelier speech received much attention nationally, and three days later, on the eve of Moratorium Day, Agnew met Nixon at the White House. Afterward the Vice-President condemned the organizers of the Moratorium for failing to repudiate a telegram they had received from the North Vietnamese wishing them success. The President, true to his word, stayed aloof, with his Vice-President on the firing line.

Finally the Moratorium Day dawned that Agnew had cast in apocalyptic terms and that Nixon had said would have no impact on him. Hundreds of thousands of Americans, mostly students, marched and held discussions in a subdued and orderly manner in Washington, and on campuses and town squares around the country. Everywhere the mood was in marked contrast to past demonstrations; the emphasis was on dialogue, on turning the protest inward on local communities, using the lower voice for which President Nixon had called in his inaugural speech. Leading critics of the war participated in different ways; many went to college campuses to lead or join discussions. Typical was Allard K. Lowenstein, the man credited with organizing the 1967–68 effort to dump Lyndon Johnson, who flew in a small plane from the University of Connecticut to Yale, Princeton, Villanova and Georgetown, rallying his campus forces. In early afternoon his plane passed over Shea Stadium in New York, where the American flag flew at half-staff over a World Series game between the Mets and Baltimore Orioles. For most Americans as for Richard Nixon and Spiro Agnew, life went on as usual in spite of Moratorium Day, but even this small gesture at Shea Stadium was a tell-

ing indication of how far the country had moved toward tolera-
tion of the war protest. A year or two earlier such a display of the
flag over one of the grand rites of sports-minded America would
doubtless not have occurred.

The Moratorium Day demonstration was a restrained and responsible protest. Nixon, for all his pledges of aloofness, relented
and went unannounced to the Lincoln Memorial in the early-
morning hours to talk to the camping students—about football!
To the distinctly non-jock generation of protest, Nixon's gesture
was the ultimate in obtuseness and bad taste.

Agnew was not of a similar mind to make conciliatory gestures.
He was scheduled the next Sunday night to deliver yet another
speech at a $100-a-plate Republican dinner in New Orleans. His
speech writer, Cynthia Rosenwald, had prepared a text that defended in a most restrained way the Nixon Administration's policies on issues of concern to those who had staged Moratorium
Day: Vietnam, the Paris peace talks, the draft, strategic arms limitations, federal spending, welfare and tax reform, and a new national attack on hunger and malnutrition. It was a straightforward, dull speech which, if read as written, would have been
standard fare at a Loch Raven Kiwanis meeting. With Moratorium Day as his inspiration and prod, Agnew took the nine-page
text in hand and wrote a one-page introduction that more than
any other single act rescued him from Throttlebottomism and
opened the most controversial chapter to date of his stormy political life. That personally authored revision, as he read it to the
audience of spellbound party faithful in New Orleans, set the tone
and style for all that was to follow in the weeks and months of
bitterness ahead.

"Sometimes it appears that we are reaching a period when our
sense and our minds will no longer respond to moderate stimula-
tion," Agnew said with his deceptive calm. "We seem to be approaching an age of the gross. Persuasion through speeches and
books is too often discarded for disruptive demonstrations aimed
at bludgeoning the unconvinced into action. The young, and by
this I don't mean by any stretch of the imagination all the young,
but I'm talking about those who claim to speak for the young, at
the zenith of physical power and sensitivity, overwhelm themselves with drugs and artificial stimulants. Subtlety is lost, and
fine distinctions based on acute reasoning are carelessly ignored

in a headlong jump to a predetermined conclusion. Life is visceral rather than intellectual, and the most visceral practitioners of life are those who characterize themselves as intellectuals. Truth to them is 'revealed' rather than logically proved, and the principal infatuations of today revolve around the social sciences, those subjects which can accommodate any opinion and about which the most reckless conjecture cannot be discredited.

"Education is being redefined at the demand of the uneducated to suit the ideas of the uneducated. The student now goes to college to proclaim rather than to learn. The lessons of the past are ignored and obliterated in a contemporary antagonism known as the generation gap. A spirit of national masochism prevails, encouraged by an effete corps of impudent snobs who characterize themselves as intellectuals. It is in this setting of dangerous oversimplification that the war in Vietnam achieves its greatest distortion.

"The recent Vietnam Moratorium is a reflection of the confusion that exists in America today. Thousands of well-motivated young people, conditioned since childhood to respond to great emotional appeals, saw fit to demonstrate for peace. Most did not stop to consider that the leaders of the Moratorium had billed it as a massive public outpouring of sentiment against the foreign policy of the President of the United States. Most did not care to be reminded that the leaders of the Moratorium refused to disassociate themselves from the objectives enunciated by the enemy in Hanoi. If the Moratorium had any use whatever, it served as an emotional purgative for those who felt the need to cleanse themselves of their lack of ability to offer a constructive solution to the problem. Unfortunately, we have not seen the end. The hard-core dissidents and the professional anarchists within the so-called 'peace movement' will continue to exacerbate the situation. November 15 is already planned—wilder, more violent, and equally barren of constructive result."

The Agnew-authored portions constituted perhaps only 10 percent of the total speech, but they were the raw meat of it, and when they were extracted by the press and sent "smoking over that wire," they were indeed hot copy. The phrase "effete corps of impudent snobs" was seized by writers and editors and rushed onto page one in newspapers large and small across the country on Monday morning. Spiro Agnew was back in business. For the next year, seldom did more than a few days pass without Americans picking up their newspapers, or turning on their radios and television sets, to read or hear "Spiro's latest." Not excluded from this exercise, importantly, was Richard Nixon, who through the daily news summary painstakingly prepared for him had a better idea than most of the impact his Vice-President was making.

Now Agnew was off and running. The very next night, in Jackson, Mississippi, he focused his incendiary rhetoric on critics who were charging the Nixon Administration with a "Southern strategy" of appeasement on racial matters. "For too long," he said at another Republican fund-raising dinner attended by many Democrats as well, "the South has been the punching bag for those who characterize themselves as liberal intellectuals. Actually, they are consistently demonstrating the antithesis of intelligence. Their reactions are visceral, not intellectual; and they seem to believe that truth is revealed rather than systematically proved. These arrogant ones and their admirers in the Congress, who reach almost for equal arrogance at times, are bringing this nation to the most important decision it will ever have to make. They are asking us to repudiate principles that have made this country great. Their course is one of applause for our enemies and condemnation for our leaders. Their course is a course that will ultimately weaken and erode the very fiber of America. They have a masochistic compulsion to destroy their country's strength whether or not that strength is exercised constructively. And they rouse themselves into a continual emotional crescendo—substituting disruptive demonstration for reason, and precipitate action for persuasion. This group may consider itself liberal, but it is undeniable that it is more comfortable with radicals."

The crowd loved it. But there were Republicans in high places who didn't. The very next morning, at a meeting of Administration political and congressional leaders, the ramifications of the Agnew speeches headed the agenda. Even before the New Orleans speech, according to one White House insider, Agnew's language, and his independence, had concerned some presidential aides who thought he ought to clear his speeches with somebody close to the President. But the concern then was internal. Now, as soon as word of the New Orleans speech had spread, party leaders from urban centers around the country began calling the Republican National Committee in protest. Many themselves had participated in some phase of the restrained Moratorium Day or had party subordinates or even members of their own families involved; they liked neither the tone nor the sweeping scope of the Vice-President's indictment. (Agnew acknowledged later that his daughter Kim, then fourteen, had wanted to participate but that he "wouldn't let her" and she survived her disappointment. "Parental-type power must be exercised," he said. "Some parents have forgotten how.")

Rogers Morton, then the party national chairman, was said to be particularly upset, and the House and Senate party leaders, Gerry Ford and Hugh Scott, were hearing the criticism on the Hill. The President's two chief political advisers, Attorney General John Mitchell and Harry Dent, were at the White House meeting, but not the President himself or Agnew. Dent defended the idea of going after the protesters, but the consensus was that Agnew was exacerbating an already unfavorable public attitude toward the Administration.

In and out of the Administration, one central question was being asked: Was Agnew speaking for himself, or was he merely playing Charlie McCarthy to the President's Edgar Bergen, with some White House wordsmith writing the script? Few seemed to know for sure, although in Towson and in Annapolis, those with longer memories had no doubt it was Agnew himself who wrote the most biting phrases. Ronald Ziegler, the President's press secretary, was asked repeatedly at his twice-daily briefings whether Agnew had cleared his speeches with Nixon and whether he was speaking at the instruction of the President. The answer always was the same—that the Vice-President never had to clear what he wanted to say because he was speaking for himself. Concerning the precise language, there is little doubt now that this was true; concerning the thrust of the Agnew message, the President himself soon would make his feelings clear.

Two days after the Jackson speech, Agnew was in the headlines again with a charge that Democratic Senator Muskie was playing "Russian roulette with United States security" by proposing a unilateral moratorium on testing of multiple nuclear warheads (MIRVs) on missiles. Democrats screamed in protest, but the White House said nothing. For a week the guessing game continued: Was Agnew intentionally bucking Nixon's lowered-voice edict or had he received the presidential blessing? Then, on the morning of October 30, the President walked into a White House reception for the Ethnic Groups Division of the Republican National Committee. With Agnew standing just behind him, Nixon said, "The Vice-President from time to time feels he's very much in touch because of his Greek background. . . . Now, I'm not Greek but I'm very proud to have the Vice-President with his Greek background in our Administration, and he has done a great job for this Administration."

That same night Agnew boarded a plane for Harrisburg with Pennsylvania's two Republican senators, Hugh Scott and Richard Schweiker. According to one insider, the moderate senators had been forewarned by aides not to go because they wouldn't like the speech they would hear. They went along, anyway, and sat stony-faced as the Vice-President, the President's blessing fresh in memory, outdid himself.

"A little over a week ago," he began, "I took a rather unusual step for a Vice-President. I said something. Particularly, I said something that was predictably unpopular with the people who would like to run the country without the inconvenience of seeking public office. I said I did not like some of the things I saw happening in this country. I criticized those who encouraged government by street carnival and suggested it was time to stop the carousel. It appears that by slaughtering a sacred cow I triggered a holy war. I have no regrets. I do not intend to repudiate my beliefs, recant my words, or run and hide."

The Harrisburg speech made the New Orleans and Jackson tirades seem namby-pamby and was a classic of the Agnew style. Again attacking the Moratorium's leaders, he said participants had been "used by the political hustlers who ran the event." He warned: "Ironically, it is neither the greedy nor the malicious but the self-righteous who are guilty of history's worst atrocities. Society understands greed and malice and erects barriers of law to defend itself from these vices. But evil cloaked in emotional causes is well disguised and often undiscovered until it is too late. We have just such a group of self-proclaimed saviors of the American soul at work today. . . .

"Small cadres of professional protestors are allowed to jeopardize the peace efforts of the President of the United States. It is time to question the credentials of their leaders. And if, in questioning, we disturb a few people, I say it is time for them to be disturbed. If, in challenging, we polarize the American people, I say it is time for a positive polarization. It is time for a healthy in-depth examination of policies and a constructive realignment in this country. It is time to rip away the rhetoric and divide on authentic lines. . . .

". . . We have among us a glib, activist element who would tell us our values are lies, and I call them impudent. Because any-one who impugns a legacy of liberty and dignity that reaches back to Moses is impudent. I call them snobs, for most of them disdain to mingle with the masses who work for a living. They mock the common man's pride in his work, his family and his country. It has also been said that I called them intellectuals. I did not. I said that they characterized themselves as intellectuals. No true intel-lectual, no truly knowledgeable person, would so despise demo-cratic institutions. America cannot afford to write off a whole generation for the decadent thinking of a few. America cannot afford to divide over their demagoguery, or to be deceived by their duplicity, or to let their license destroy liberty. We can, however, afford to separate them from our society—with no more regret than we should feel over discarding rotten apples from a bar-rel. . . .

"America must recognize the dangers of constant carnival. Americans must reckon with irresponsible leadership and reck-less words. The mature and sensitive people of this country must realize that their freedom of protest is being exploited by avowed anarchists and communists who detest everything about this country and want to destroy it. This is a fact. They are the few; these are not necessarily leaders. But they prey upon the good in-tentions of gullible men everywhere. They pervert honest concern to something sick and rancid. They are vultures who sit in trees and watch lions battle, knowing that win, lose or draw, they will be fed.

"Abetting the merchants of hate are the parasites of passion. These are the men who value a cause purely for its political mile-age. These are the politicians who temporize with the truth by playing both sides to their own advantage. They ooze sympathy for 'the cause' but balance each sentence with equally reasoned reservations. Their interest is personal, not moral. They are ideo-logical eunuchs whose most comfortable position is straddling the philosophical fence, soliciting votes from both sides. . . .

"People cannot live in a state of perpetual electric shock. Tired of a convulsive society, they settle for an authoritarian society . . . Right now we must decide whether we will take the trouble to stave off a totalitarian state. Will we stop the wildness now before it is too late, before the witch-hunting and repression that are all too inevitable begin?"

Considering Agnew's own sweeping accusations and scapegoating, this last question was suggestive of the American commander in Vietnam who burned down and destroyed a village "to save it." For sheer bitterness and divisiveness, there probably had not been such a speech by a responsible national figure in years, certainly not since Barry Goldwater's "extremism in the defense of liberty is no vice" remark at the 1964 national convention. Goldwater, for one, loved it. "If Ted Agnew keeps on expressing the sentiment of the vast, overwhelming majority of the American people," he said, "he may find himself being boomed for President before it's even his turn."

The call to "divide on authentic lines" and to discard "rotten apples" was in content as well as tone directly at odds with Nixon's inaugural call to lower voices and bring the country together. Here, finally, in an Administration that often seemed to practice intentional ambiguity, with one official saying one thing and another something else on the same subject, was a bell ringing loud and clear. Or was it, after all, just the most audacious application of the same tactic of intentional ambiguity—the old low-road, high-road track of the Eisenhower-Nixon years, with Nixon now moving up to the remote, isolated Eisenhower track and Agnew taking over on the old Nixon track?

In another three weeks there would be no doubt of it. Agnew may have started it all on his own, but he rapidly was embraced as an Administration weapon. In Philadelphia on November 11, he condemned what he called "a carnival in the streets" by a "student minority" raising "intolerant clamor and cacophony." Alluding to Nixon's inaugural plea for tempered discourse, Agnew said, "I, for one, will not lower my voice until the restoration of sanity and civil order will allow a quiet voice to be heard once again."

Two days later, in Des Moines, he proved as much in a major escalation of his drive for the allegiance of the silent majority—a broadside against television news analysis. On November 3,

Nixon had gone on nationwide television to discuss his Vietnam policy. The objective was clear: to try, by projecting a posture of reason and firmness, to diffuse the next and potentially much more volatile antiwar demonstrations, scheduled for November 15 by more radical elements than the organizers of the Moratorium. The President gave a particularly artful performance, and when he finished, network staff and guest analysts presented the customary commentary. They noted that there was little new in the substance of Nixon's remarks and pointed out how he had placed his position in the best light. The guest analyst on one network, ABC, was W. Averell Harriman, who had been President Johnson's chief negotiator in the Paris peace talks. Now, with all this as a backdrop, Agnew turned his sights on the television networks.

Several hours before delivery of the Des Moines speech, texts—which his aides insisted had not been seen or cleared by the White House staff—were released in Washington and the networks were alerted. They reacted as if the Vice-President were about to announce his resignation. They scurried frantically to put the speech on the air live, managing finally to arrange pool coverage for all the networks in what obviously was a determination to demonstrate their fairmindedness. Agnew himself seemed to be surprised that the speech, to a meeting of Midwestern Republicans, was being carried live.

With unprecedented free time afforded to a Vice-President, Agnew made the most of it. He went immediately on the attack against "instant analysis and querulous criticism" of Nixon's November 3 speech. "The audience of seventy million Americans—gathered to hear the President of the United States—was inherited by a small band of network commentators and self-appointed analysts," he complained, "the majority of whom expressed in one way or another their hostility to what he had to say." Agnew said it was "obvious that their minds were made up in advance," and although "every American has a right to disagree with the President of the United States and to express publicly that disagreement," the President also had the right to communicate to the people, and they in turn had the right to make up their minds "without having the President's words and thought characterized through the prejudices of hostile critics before they can even be digested."

Agnew singled out Harriman's comments (which had been rather restrained), and noting Harriman's tenure as chief negotiator in Paris, observed, "Like Coleridge's Ancient Mariner, Mr. Harriman seems to be under some heavy compulsion to justify his failures to anyone who will listen." He charged that ABC had "trotted out Averell Harriman for the occasion" and he in turn "had recited perfectly" in criticism of the President. Not content with that implication of puppetry, Agnew charged that Harriman had "swapped some of the greatest military concessions in the history of warfare for an enemy agreement on the shape of the bargaining table." He doubtless was alluding to the halt in bombing against North Vietnam that had brought about a broadening of the peace talks in November 1968—which Nixon had approved at the time and had continued when he became President.

The argument between the negotiators about the shape of the table was a totally unrelated issue, and the whole attack on Harriman was gratuitous at best. A transcript of Harriman's remarks showed that he had begun by saying, "I'm sure you know that I wouldn't be presumptuous to give a complete analysis of a very carefully thought out speech by the President of the United States. I'm sure he wants to end this war and no one wishes him well any more than I do. He approaches the subject quite differently from the manner in which I approach it. Let me say, though, that I'm utterly opposed to these people that are talking about cutting and running. I'm against the Republican senator from New York's proposal, Senator Goodell, to get our troops out in a year, willy-nilly. I think we should have a responsible withdrawal. I think he [the President] has got the full support of the people. He certainly has got my support in hoping he will develop a program for peace." After having expressed differences of approach, Harriman then observed, "There are so many things we've got to know about this, but I want to end this by saying I wish the President well. I hope he can lead us to peace. But this is not the whole story that we've heard tonight."

As for the regular news commentators, Agnew called them "this little group of men who not only enjoy a right of instant rebuttal to every presidential address, but more importantly, wield a free hand in selecting, presenting and interpreting the great issues of our nation. . . . For millions of Americans, the network reporter who covers a continuing issue, like ABM or civil rights, becomes in effect the presiding judge in a national trial by jury." The networks had focused national attention on many important problems, Agnew conceded, "but it was also the networks that elevated Stokely Carmichael and George Lincoln Rockwell from obscurity to national prominence. . . . Nor is their power confined to the substantive. A raised eyebrow, an inflection of the voice, a caustic remark dropped in the middle of a broadcast can raise doubts in a million minds about the veracity of a public official or the wisdom of a government policy. . . .

"What do Americans know of the men who wield this power? Of the men who produce and direct the network news, the nation knows practically nothing. Of the commentators, most Americans know little, other than that they reflect an urbane and assured presence, seemingly well-informed on every important matter. We do know that, to a man, these commentators and producers live and work in the geographical and intellectual confines of Washington, D.C., or New York City—the latter of which James Reston terms the 'most unrepresentative community in the entire United States.' Both communities bask in their own provincialism, their own parochialism. We can deduce that these men thus read the same newspapers, and draw their political and social views from the same sources. Worse, they talk constantly to one another, thereby providing artificial reinforcement to their shared viewpoints. . . . [The fact that television newsmen are among the most widely traveled in the world, and that many of the most prominent do not come from the East, was not mentioned by Agnew.]

"The American people would rightly not tolerate this kind of concentration of power in government. Is it not fair and relevant to question its concentration in the hands of a tiny and closed fraternity of privileged men, elected by no one, and enjoying a monopoly sanctioned and licensed by government? The views of this fraternity do *not* represent the views of America. That is why such a great gulf existed between how the nation received the President's address—and how the networks reviewed it. As with other American institutions, perhaps it is time that the networks were made more responsive to the views of the nation and more responsible to the people they serve. I am not asking for government or any other kind of censorship. I am asking whether a form of censorship already exists when the news that forty million

Americans receive each night is determined by a handful of men responsible only to their corporate employers and filtered through a handful of commentators who admit their own set of biases."

The Vice-President concluded by noting that the public could register its complaints on television bias by writing or calling local stations. The response was immediate and overwhelmingly in support of Agnew's charges; phone calls flooded local stations throughout the country. At once, network executives responded with indignation. Dr. Frank Stanton, president of CBS, called the speech "an unprecedented attempt by the Vice-President of the United States to intimidate a news medium which depends for its existence upon government license." Julian Goodman, president of NBC, accused Agnew of making "an appeal to prejudice. More importantly, Mr. Agnew uses the influence of his high office to criticize the way a government-licensed news medium covers the activities of the government itself. It is regrettable that the Vice-President of the United States should deny to TV freedom of the press." Leonard H. Goldenson, president of ABC, said he was "fully confident in the ultimate judgment of the American people."

The fearful words of Stanton and Goodman were predictable, but they took on more substance the next day when it was revealed that shortly after Nixon's November 3 speech Dean Burch, the Nixon-appointed chairman of the Federal Communications Commission that licenses commercial television, had called the chairmen of the major networks requesting transcripts of what their commentators had said following the Nixon speech. Burch, who had been a ranking lieutenant in Barry Goldwater's drive for the Republican presidential nomination in 1964, and Goldwater's party national chairman during that campaign, dismissed the telephoned requests as routine. In the prevailing climate, however, the revelation sent shudders through the television news industry, especially when Burch praised Agnew's speech as "thoughtful, provocative and [deserving of] careful consideration by the industry and the public." A New York TV executive told the Los Angeles *Times*'s Robert Donovan concerning the Agnew speech, "It conked us on the head. This has raised utter hell with the networks. Everybody is scared about licenses. You can't have a television station without a government license and you can't have a network without stations. Dean Burch is a friend of Agnew's. Agnew's speech may now enlarge the area of challenge to present licensees. Challenges are increasing anyway and now 'slanting the news' may be a cause of challenge. But 'slanting the news' will be saying things that aren't in line with the President's policy. You can look for a lot more challenges from the right wing."

Adding substance to this viewpoint, ominously, was a request submitted a few weeks later by a group involving Charles G. "Bebe" Rebozo, President Nixon's closest personal friend, that the license of a Florida station, owned by the Washington *Post,* not be renewed and instead be given to the Rebozo group. This application was eventually denied, however, and the FCC shortly afterward declared as a matter of policy, to assure stability in the field, that it would grant renewals except in cases of clearly demonstrable failure to meet license obligations.

Still, there were plenty of indications—Agnew's denials of intent to censor or intimidate to the contrary—that the networks did feel the hot breath of government regulation on their necks, and did react. The next time the President appeared on nationwide television, the networks put their analysts on immediately afterward as usual to demonstrate that things hadn't changed—then limited them to the most perfunctory rehash of what Nixon had said. ABC's commentary was on and off the screen so fast as to be almost subliminal. Agnew and other Administration officials insisted that there had been no intimidation; it was true that no licenses were lifted for "slanting the news." But it is not necessary to hit somebody over the head with a club to intimidate him. Holding the club in striking position often is enough, and that was what Agnew's speech did. For months afterward the networks "behaved" after presidential television talks and press conferences. (Nearly a year later, when the sales director of a major station in New York was asked about the purchase of television time by candidates in the New York gubernatorial and senatorial campaigns, he declined to discuss it because "we're still up-tight over the Agnew speech.")

Once again after Des Moines, the question was raised about the authorship of Agnew's remarks and whether they had the President's blessing. Again came the official answer: the Vice-President spoke his own mind and the White House hadn't cleared the speech. It was an exercise in semantics; only the most naïve observers could doubt now that while the words might be Agnew's, the music was Nixon's. According to one Agnew aide, the original idea for the attack on the television networks came from Herb Thompson, then working for Agnew as part of Herb Klein's press agentry office. Clark Mollenhoff, a former Washington correspondent who had joined the Administration as a special counsel to the President, told reporters that while the precise origin of the speech might be in doubt, there was no question but that what Agnew had said reflected the predominant view at the White House about television news. White House Press Secretary Ziegler conceded that Pat Buchanan "may have, and I think did have, some thoughts" on the preparation of the Des Moines speech; another White House source spoke more plainly to the Los Angeles *Times*'s Don Irwin. It was, he said, "Buchanan's speech." For the record, Ziegler said Nixon "didn't discuss this subject with the Vice-President" but had "great confidence in his Vice-President and he supports his Vice-President in the office."

Actually the conservative Buchanan, who had helped nurture Nixon's interest in Agnew in 1968 by funneling in news accounts of the Marylander's hard-line pronouncements on law and order, and had taken a turn as a campaign speech writer for him, had found a soul mate in Agnew. As chief compiler of the daily news summary for the President, he had observed Agnew's low state in media treatment during the first six months of the Nixon Administration; as one who saw what leading newspapers and television networks were saying, he could quickly gauge the impact of Agnew's speeches. According to one of Agnew's chief staff aides, Agnew and Buchanan often talked issues and media coverage, and out of those talks came many of the ideas on television and the press that Agnew later expressed. "It was out of the Buchanan-Agnew style that issues developed" as speech themes, this aide said. Of the earliest controversial speeches, "I think the Vice-President was testing what the press was doing about covering him." The Des Moines speech, he said, grew out of Agnew's feeling that his Southern speeches had not really been adequately covered. In taking on television, there was a feeling on Agnew's staff "that the press is a big establishment, that it's a no-win issue." But when the Des Moines speech received wide coverage, this aide said, Agnew's reaction was that "they want more of the same."

Thus confirmed in his course, Agnew went after the next

"enemy" of the Administration—the hated "Eastern establishment press." One week after the Des Moines attack on the television networks he flew to Montgomery, Alabama, and unloaded on his old nemeses, the *New York Times* and the Washington *Post*. He accused the *Times*—incorrectly, it turned out—of ignoring a letter in which 359 members of Congress had backed the Nixon Vietnam policy. By clear inference, he said the paper had grown "fat and irresponsible" as a result of dying competition. (Arthur Ochs Sulzberger, publisher of the *Times,* explained later that the paper had run a story about the congressional letter, but not in the early edition that reached Washington.) The *Post*, Agnew noted, also owned one of Washington's four major television stations, an all-news radio station and *Newsweek* magazine, "all grinding out the same editorial line"—a sweepingly inaccurate charge, as both the editorial structure and comment of the four news-gathering organizations repeatedly proved.

As usual in Agnew broadsides, there were the necessary disclaimers of intent to shoot dirty pool. "I am opposed to censorship of television or the press in any form. . . . for the purpose of clarity, before my thoughts are obliterated in the smoking typewriters of my friends in Washington and New York, let me emphasize I am not recommending the dismemberment of The Washington Post Company. I am merely pointing out that the public should be aware that these four powerful voices harken to the same master."

What Agnew did not bother to point out was that the *Times* and the *Post* were probably the two major newspapers most consistently and aggressively critical of the Nixon Administration; or that the two daily newspapers in Montgomery, where he was speaking, were owned by Multimedia, Inc., a conglomerate communications corporation; or that some of the strongest supporters of the Administration outside the East also had multiple-media interests. Instead, he concluded by warning that "the day when the network commentators and even the gentlemen of the *New York Times* enjoyed a form of diplomatic immunity from comment and criticism of what they said—that day is over. Just as a politician's words—wise and foolish—are dutifully recorded by the press and television to be thrown up to him at the appropriate time, so their words should likewise be recorded and likewise recalled. When they go beyond fair comment and criticism they will be called upon to defend their statements and their positions just as we must defend ours. And when their criticism becomes excessive or unjust, we shall invite them down from their ivory towers to enjoy the rough and tumble of the public debate. I do not seek to intimidate the press, the networks or anyone else from speaking out. But the time for blind acceptance of their opinions is past. And the time for naive belief in their neutrality is gone."

It always has been a special tactic of Agnew's to sound as if he were the first fool ever to rush in where angels have feared to tread. It came as startling news to anyone who had been in television or the press for any time at all to hear that they had been enjoying "a form of diplomatic immunity from comment and criticism of what they said." Politicians and the public have criticized the press, often validly, since Colonial days; similarly, Agnew's plea for self-examination by the press ignored a tremendous amount of hand-wringing and soul-searching that has gone on in newsrooms for as long as ink has touched paper, and today nowhere more than within the major newspapers about which he was complaining.

Agnew's criticism of the *Times* and the *Post* might have been more credible had it not come from a member of an Administration that had elevated attempted manipulation of the press to an art form, and had sought to take advantage of American journalism's greatest weaknesses as had no previous Administration. For all of Agnew's accusations, the *New York Times* and the Washington *Post* today consistently stand head-and-shoulders above most other American newspapers in breadth of coverage. In terms of thought, money and effort to produce daily newspapers that above all else inform the reader, the eastern seaboard, and isolated pockets of enterprise and initiative elsewhere—in Chicago, St. Louis, Los Angeles and a few other cities—provide overwhelmingly the strength of American print journalism today. What is wrong with American journalism is not the excessive exercise of power by the big-city giants, but the under-exercise of resources, initiative and energy by the vast majority of American newspapers of the Middle America to which the Nixon-Agnew Administration pays constant court. This is the soft underbelly of American journalism; the Administration, through Agnew's attacks on the "liberal establishment press," and its more direct and insidious wooing of the go-along, no-enterprise press of Middle America, constantly seeks to probe that weakness.

Under the direction of the Administration's chief institutional propagandist and apologist, former newspaper editor Herb Klein, not only has the Nixon Administration courted the small-town and small-city press as never before; for the first time a major effort has been made to exploit the shortcomings of the hundreds of radio and television stations around the country that have neither the wherewithal nor the will to cover the federal government themselves. It is, in part, an unabashed effort to circumvent the handling of Administration news by the Washington press corps, which by and large is better educated about the ways of the federal bureaucracy than are local newsmen and editors, and has numerous Washington sources through which to evaluate government programs and proposals.

When a policy is announced in Washington, the procedure for correspondents is not only to interrogate government officials supporting the policy but also to seek out informed critics. It has been Klein's job, as Director of Communications, to try to avoid, minimize or at least neutralize the impact of this responsible journalistic practice by getting Administration programs before the press of Middle America in undiluted form. He end-runs the Washington press corps by putting the Administration on the road—by sending out teams of bureaucratic experts, including Cabinet members—to sell their programs directly. The euphemism is "bringing the government to the people," and from the Administration's point of view the exercise is infinitely preferable to having policies analyzed by newsmen who are more familiar with the subject and who have ready access to other experts.

Editors in small towns and smaller cities, who unquestionably are experts about their own local governments, do not take kindly to the suggestion that they may not know as much about how the federal government operates as do newsmen who work in Washington. But for years the larger newspapers have been training some of their best reporters and sending them to Washington precisely because they want expert analysis and reporting of national affairs. Also, local editors have their hands full keeping themselves and their readers informed about local affairs. When the Administration road show comes into town, often headed by a Cabinet member, many local editors and television news directors are sitting ducks for it. Klein sends briefing teams to the larger, better metropolitan newspapers too, but their more specialized staffs usually have better resources to assess what they are told and to sift substance from propaganda, than do the smaller-town journalists. It would have been more in the interest of an informed American public had Agnew criticized those elements of the nation's press that treat national news as a necessary evil—to be crammed into a few columns each day, hitting only the high spots—rather than those relatively few that strive nobly to give their readers a fuller, more sophisticated and more balanced fare.

As far as President Nixon was concerned, however, Agnew was doing just fine. At a press conference in early December, he told reporters he thought Agnew had "rendered a public service in talking in a very dignified and courageous way" about press coverage. He himself had no complaints, Nixon said, "just so long as the news media allows, as it does tonight, an opportunity for me to be heard directly by the people and then the television commentators will follow." And follow they did—ABC for barely a minute, CBS for four, NBC for eight—all straight recapitulation. Doubtless Ted Agnew was pleased.

Although the President said he was satisfied with Agnew, and he was the Vice-President's only constituent, others around the White House were not. Among some of the few staff liberals, who never had wanted Agnew on the 1968 ticket in the first place, there were grumblings that the President had "created a Frankenstein monster." One aide said later, "There's always been division among the President's staff people with regard to the effectiveness of the Vice-President, the wisdom of having chosen him, his ability and the benefits of what he does. There's been that division going all the way back to the convention and postconvention at Mission Bay. As we moved into this period, the doubts on the one hand and the feeling that the Vice-President was a valuable ally on the other endured. There's an ideological fault right down the middle of the White House, just as there is in the G.O.P." Once the political effectiveness of Agnew's speeches could be seen, however, some critics changed their minds, this aide said.

Among Nixon's own speech writers there were frequent meetings and discussions about the Vice-President's rhetoric. After the New Orleans speech one of them said, "The reaction here was pretty cool to it, even at what somebody described as the highest level of the White House. I took that to mean maybe the President. I don't think at any point they felt strongly enough about it to say to the Vice-President, 'We don't like that direction. Cool it.' Some comment was made [among the Nixon speech writers] that, 'Gee, if anybody happened to be talking to anybody on the Vice-President's staff you might raise the question.' But if any body felt that way [critical of Agnew's speeches], nobody ever got to the point of trying to act on the basis of that feeling. And then that negative feeling changed. The reaction to those speeches among people who are considered the Nixon constituency was favorable enough so that after a period of time, if there were doubts, those doubts were alleviated, and the President found ways to indicate he stood right squarely behind the Vice-President. Since then, when the Vice-President tries out a line of argument or attack, there are some misgivings among some of the more cautious people here. But if it seems to work, the misgivings are dissolved. With each burst of speeches, this procedure has been repeated. There was a point when somebody suggested that if we provided him more 'constructive' materials, we might be able to get that tone into the speeches more strongly. In that connection I did do a rough draft on some very technical policy issue, but as far as I know it was never used. Others may have done things like that at the time, but that operation never took."

As 1969 drew to a close, some people were still laughing at Spiro Agnew, as they had been doing at the year's start. But not many. Instead, out of his personal restlessness and boldness, and an opportunity born of his President's need for a hatchet man, Agnew now was a figure to be admired or feared. His strength was as the strength of millions because—he never doubted—he was right. Within the official Nixon family, not all the reservations about him were resolved, and some louder voices were yet to be raised against him. But one thing was certain now. In the nation at large, if not always in the inner circles of the Administration for which he spoke, the voice of Spiro Agnew had become a most effective political instrument.

17

◇•◇•◇•◇•◇•◇

STRONG RIGHT ARM

THE conversion of Spiro Agnew from fifth wheel to the High Priest of the Great Silent Majority was so sudden and dramatic that for a time he became bigger news than the President himself. When, at the end of 1969, Nixon decided to send Agnew on his first mission abroad, to Asia, there was inevitable speculation that the trip was designed to shunt him out of the domestic spotlight and cool him off for a while. The prospect of the nation's new phrase-making discovery addressing himself to international problems triggered a rush of applications from newsmen to accompany him. Only ten of thirty-two applicants were given seats on the plane, and the selection was clearly arbitrary; the *New York Times,* so recently a target of Agnew's tongue, was chosen, but the Washington *Post,* also a target, was not; an obscure, decidedly pro-Agnew correspondent for Southern newspapers was given a seat; Agnew's hometown paper was not because, the Baltimore *Sun* quoted press secretary Herb Thompson as saying, "to be quite honest, he doesn't like the *Sun.*" Thompson later denied it. Agnew had become so controversial now that there was little he said or did that did not kick off a row with someone.

For all the advance trepidation about turning him loose on foreign soil, however, Agnew's twenty-three-day, eleven-nation Asian tour proved to be a quiet success, with hardly a misstep, though he never had been to that part of the world before. His official mission was to represent President Nixon at the second inaugural of President Ferdinand Marcos in the Philippines, and then to provide explanations and assurances about Nixon's newly enunciated Nixon Doctrine toward American commitments overseas. The policy, in brief, was to reduce the American presence wherever possible while continuing American financial and moral support of overseas allies who helped themselves. Agnew's job was to reassure these allies in Asia that they were not being abandoned, but that American policy expected them to shape up. It was a delicate task for a man with no diplomatic background and with a penchant for most undiplomatic candor.

A flock of staff aides accompanied Agnew and his wife, whose only previous trip outside the United States had been to Canada. Two foreign policy experts, one from Henry Kissinger's National Security staff at the White House, and one from the State Department, were aboard to advise Agnew and keep him out of trouble. All three men appeared to accompanying reporters to be apprehensive as *Air Force Two* headed for Manila by way of Honolulu and Guam. While the newsmen relaxed in the back of the plane and let visions of international bloopers dance in their heads, the experts supplied Agnew with thick briefing books on each country to be visited, providing him with details of history, current political, economic and social problems, plus all the niceties of diplomatic protocol. Agnew was a serious and obedient student, cramming for his new and sensitive mission. As the trip progressed, the experts told newsmen that the Vice-President was following his instructions to the letter.

In Manila, known for brands of political protest and freewheeling journalism that make the United States seem tame, Agnew got a taste of each and did not flinch. Leftist students, denied a police permit to demonstrate, did so anyway, one of them throwing what accompanying reporters thought was a large firecracker at Agnew's limousine. It went off with a bang and a puff of smoke as it hit the car's roof outside the American embassy. Agnew said nothing. Neither did he comment when a Manila columnist expressed puzzlement about "the big fuss over the coming here of America's biggest nobody." Instead he played the diplomat, congratulating the Filipino people at the inaugural dinner for having elected Marcos "to an unprecedented second term by the will of the people and, I believe, possibly by more than that—by divine will."

On a previously unannounced side trip to South Vietnam, Agnew visited the 24th Air Evacuation Hospital in Long Binh and unpolitically refused to let cameramen go with him as he toured wards of American wounded. En route to Taiwan he told reporters it was time for a "meaningful dialogue" with mainland China, then on arrival reassured Chiang Kai-shek of U.S. fealty. In Bangkok he reassured King Bhumibol that the United States would honor its defense commitments to Thailand despite congressional snipers. "Some of the people back home are so anxious to make friends of our enemies," he said in one of his few lapses into domestic political comment, "that sometimes they even seem ready to make enemies of our friends." In Nepal he spoke of progress being made there in "India," causing U. S. Ambassador Carol Laise to whisper urgently, "Nepal!" In Kabul, Afghanistan, some students tossed garbage; in Malaysia, Singapore and Indonesia he played the tourist, distributing tiny "moon rocks" to the heads of state as gifts from President Nixon. In Australia and New Zealand he again turned the other cheek to demonstrators, one of whom in Canberra shouted, "Say something stupid, Spyro!" It was, in all, an impressive exercise in self-restraint for one so given to being outspoken. "I expected the whole thing to be a million laughs," James Naughton of the *New York Times* confessed later. "I wondered how I as a domestic reporter was going to write the story I came to write—you know, 'Agnew screws up.' He just didn't."

The Asian trip gave Agnew's domestic targets a respite, but it also gave Republicans around the country time to assess his impact. It was, they soon realized, tremendous; now, with the start of a congressional election year, wherever party leaders turned their thoughts to fund raising, the name of Spiro T. Agnew headed the list of drawing cards. Invitations, as many as fifty a day, came pouring in. A year earlier, according to Herb Thompson, Agnew had been speaking mainly as a fill-in for the President; now he was the one everybody wanted.

From now on, public speaking would be the Vice-President's main forte. Yet he continued to play a role within the Administration as time and the confining internal structure would allow. In this period, the winter of 1969–70, he made what one ranking White House insider later termed Agnew's major contribution to the early Nixon years, as chairman of the Cabinet committee on school desegregation. "I took the committee very seriously and felt the thing had to work," this insider said. "The Administration had set a very bad name for itself in the first go-around on school desegregation in the fall of '69. When the Administration took office, it was fourteen years after *Brown v. Board of Education,* and the dual school system in the South was still virtually intact. It disappeared in the aftermath of mounting court decisions, but a very sustained effort over the winter of 1969–70 by the Administration made it possible for this to happen.

"There was no question about the law. The question was, How do you get the law obeyed? We worked up very elegant strategies to reward school districts that abolished their dual system rather than to punish those that did not. The strategy was to make the absolute minimum presence of the federal government; we created committees in each state and brought them to the White House, where they met for hours in the old Fish Room with Agnew or Shultz, the vice-chairman, and other members of the committee. I'll bless [then Postmaster General Winton M.] Red Blount to this day. He'd stand there at the entrance; black educators and white businessmen from Georgia, Alabama, Arkansas, Mississippi would come in, and Red Blount would be a receiving line by himself, with that thick Southern accent of his: 'How do you do, sir; how very nice to see you, sir,' to each one of them. We had a little routine; we'd take about two hours, then we'd open the doors and march into the President. The President would pass out golf balls and he'd say, 'It's wonderful that you're going to do this, because you've decided to do it yourselves. You're not being forced by Washington.'

"We didn't know they were going to do it. At that point the court orders were awfully hard, and you could have had misery. You could have had people shooting at each other. But we got rid of that dual school system and nobody ever pointed a gun at anyone."

The ironic part about this effort, in which Agnew played a key role, was that by its very nature the Administration could not boast about it. "The only condition on which you could achieve this was to deny that you were doing it," said the same White

House insider, who also had worked in the Kennedy Administration. "If I may say so, it was great fun in the early Kennedy days to get on an airplane and zip down to some Southern city and stuff an affidavit into the hand of some Southern redneck politician and get back to Georgetown in time for cocktails. And what you got out of that was the Wallace movement."

Another reason the techniques and results of the do-it-yourself desegregation effort were not trumpeted by Agnew and the publicity-conscious Nixon Administration, this staff adviser acknowledged, was that "taking credit for elimination of the dual school system might not have been politically advantageous for them in some parts of the country." What voters, particularly in the South, wanted to hear was the smoking Agnew rhetoric, going on the attack.

For an aspiring politician, the clamor for his oratory offered a rare opportunity to build and cement a personal constituency; Richard Nixon, with much less public acclaim and demand, had taken precisely that route in the mid-1960's to repair his party standing and put the party leaders in his debt. With Agnew, however, there was little evidence that he was thus motivated. He seemed to be joining the battle more for the sheer zest of it and to acclaim the President, to whom his loyalty was boundless. Although Agnew continued work with various committees, public speaking became his predominant function, yet he did not conduct himself at all the way Nixon had in the mid-1960's, prowling the country looking for Republican leaders' shoes to be shined.

Whereas Nixon had spent every waking hour backslapping and handshaking local politicians, listening respectfully to their problems and bestowing his tactical wisdom on them in his favorite business of electing Republicans, with Agnew the speech was the thing. Usually, he would fly into a city and retire to his room to chat with his aides and the Secret Service men or watch a sports event on television. He would skip the local reception, sometimes eat dinner in his room, and appear at the money-raising function shortly before he was to speak. Afterward, whereas Nixon would have invited some of the local pols to his room for more chit-chat, Agnew would often leave town or just go back to his room. It was no way to build up a loyal army of political troops, and in fact his conduct offended many of his hosts who worked hard for his appearances, wanted to get to know him better, and saw in his political climb a possible future windfall for themselves. But that was the way he was, and they could take it or leave it.

If this attitude suggested, however, that Ted Agnew was all business and no fun, it was deceiving. In his own circle he was much given to needling his associates. Arriving in his suite on a speaking trip arranged by a new advance man, he would call the young man in and blithely inquire of him, "What am I doing in this town?" When he was told by the nonplused advance man that he was due to make a speech in a few minutes, Agnew would freeze and say, "Oh, no. I'm not going to make any speech." Then, with the advance man on the edge of apoplexy, Agnew would break into a grin and inform his victim that he had just been through "the advance man's initiation."

When Agnew returned from Asia, he plunged into a heavy round of Lincoln Day fund raising. He was destined in the next months to establish himself as the G.O.P.'s champion money raiser, supplanting Governor Ronald Reagan of California. Bids from the South in particular were plentiful, the faithful wanting him for himself alone as well as for the coin he could gather; but the Northern industrial pockets of party liberalism wanted him too, once it was clear how the Agnew message played on the cash register. Soon new Agnewisms were being heard and reported "smoking across the wires" from every corner in the land. In Lincoln, Nebraska, he said Democrats complaining about how long it took the Republican Administration to clean up the Democrats' eight-year mess had the public "ready to run for the Rolaids"; in Chicago he blasted "supercilious sophisticates" who advocated open-admissions policies in the nation's universities; in Atlanta, where antiwar pickets paraded all afternoon around the Marriott Hotel, he claimed the silent majority as his own constituency and challenged his critics in language that reached new heights, even for him, of ridicule and bitterness:

"The liberal media have been calling on me to lower my voice and to seek accord and unity among all Americans. Nothing would please me more than to see all voices lowered; to see us return to dialogue and discuss and debate within our institutions and within our governmental system; to see dissatisfied citizens turn to the elective process to change the course of government; to see an end to the vilification, the obscenities, the vandalism and the violence that have become the standard tactics of the dissidents who claim to act in the interests of peace and freedom. But I want you to know that I will not make a unilateral withdrawal and thereby abridge the confidence of the silent majority, the everyday law-abiding American who believes his country needs a strong voice to articulate his dissatisfaction with those who seek to destroy our heritage of liberty and our system of justice. To penetrate the cacophony of seditious drivel emanating from the best-publicized clowns in our society and their fans in the fourth estate, yes, my friends, to penetrate that drivel, we need a cry of alarm, not a whisper. . . . Let the few, the very few, who would desecrate their own house be made fully aware of our utter contempt."

By party estimate, Agnew raised nearly $2 million dollars for the G.O.P. by making this and other Lincoln Day speeches in Phoenix, St. Louis and Minneapolis. Now most of the internal debate about his role was muted by the overwhelming response. Besides, the Administration was again entering a spring of discontent on the nation's campuses and in the troublesome Democratic-dominated Senate, and Agnew's attention-grabbing voice was a most valuable commodity. Rebuffed in 1969 in his attempt to put Haynsworth, a Southern conservative, on the Supreme Court, Nixon had come back with a Floridian named G. Harrold Carswell who turned out to be an even more disastrous choice. An early political speech had been uncovered in which Judge Carswell vowed his undying commitment to racial segregation, and the disclosure spurred a deeper examination of his record, leading to his rejection. Nixon immediately sought to extract what political capital he could from the defeat by charging that the Senate "as presently constituted" would never confirm a Southerner for the Court—a totally unwarranted conclusion. There were scores of qualified and acceptable Southerners but rather than nominate one of them, Nixon chose to exploit the issue. The phrase "as presently constituted" was pregnant with the implication that the Senate would be reconstituted in the 1970 off-year elections and then Nixon would be able to get his Southerner on the Court.

With that objective in mind, Agnew went south in late April. In Columbia, South Carolina, he characterized the opposition to Haynsworth and Carswell as "learned idiocy" and told a cheering crowd of two thousand at the largest fund-raising dinner in the state's history that Nixon "intends to redeem his campaign pledge to balance the Supreme Court." The speech was an unvarnished invocation of the Southern strategy: "I bring you greetings tonight from *your* President, and I underscore that pronoun, 'your.' He thanks you and the other people of South Carolina for standing by him at the national convention, for delivering South Carolina to the Republican column in the 1968 election, and for staffing the Administration in Washington with more Southern voices than it has heard since *Gone With the Wind* enjoyed a record run at Loew's Palace. . . . I'll admit that we haven't yet succeeded in getting a second strict constructionist appointed to the Supreme Court to join Chief Justice Burger, but I'm sure you'll acknowledge that the President has been giving it an all-out try. If we had a little more help from some senators in our own party, and if a few fair-weather Southern Democrats had been willing to brave the storm, the matter would have been settled long ago. Judge Clement Haynsworth would have made it in a breeze and South Carolina would have contributed an outstanding Justice to the Supreme Court. Instead he went down to defeat on the most nebulous set of trumped-up charges ever contrived by the labor and civil rights lobbies and their allies in the news profession. To prove it was no accident, these same forces combined to defeat G. Harrold Carswell by using the flimsy subjective excuses of 'insensitivity' and 'mediocrity.' "

Agnew spoke to the South Carolinians in a huge hall on the state fairgrounds after a glowing introduction by Senator Strom Thurmond, who said, "Now you understand why I favored Spiro Agnew for Vice-President in 1968, and with South Carolina will favor Spiro Agnew for President in 1976." As usual, Agnew delivered his speech with a minimum of audible bombast, introducing his serious remarks with some well-chosen gags designed to amuse the Dixie audience. But these introductory "jokes" betrayed a venom that belied the monotone delivery. The only argument he ever had with Nixon, he said, "was when the President decided to convert the White House swimming pool into a sumptuous new press room. It wasn't that I objected to using the swimming pool for this purpose. It was just that I resented his insistence that the water be drained out." The crowd roared its approval. Then he told how Nixon had suggested he play golf with Democratic Senators William Fulbright, George McGovern and Edmund Muskie as "a great bipartisan gesture." But, Agnew said, "I really didn't want to play golf with them. I just might accidentally tag one with a golf ball. And then he might respond the way they usually do to aggressive and brutal treatment. And I hate to be kissed on a public golf course." Another roar of laughter and wild applause. And then: "Speaking of Ed Muskie reminds me that a politician who tries to please everybody often looks like a small dog trying to follow four boys home at the same time."

In each of these three gags, there was a certain intentional heavy-handedness: the drowning of the critical press; a man kissing another man; likening Muskie to a dog. Agnew was benign in delivery, but he was crude in substance and innuendo. The faint suggestion of perversity in the golf-course gag particularly delighted rednecks in the audience; they rebel-yelled their pleasure. It was akin to his use of words like "effete" and "eunuch." There was the occasion, too, when Agnew rose to offer a toast at a White House stag dinner for England's Prince Philip and, seeking to assure nervous diplomatic types that he would not commit a blooper, said: "All of you with tightened sinews and constricted sphincters can relax." And once, playing with professional golfer Doug Sanders, whom he earlier had hit in the head with a golf ball, Agnew started off the round by inquiring of his golfing companions whether they were keeping their sphincters constricted. Homer Bigart had told Agnew in the 1968 campaign: "Governor Agnew, one thing you must remember. Locker-room humor should never be equated with running for Vice-President of the United States." Or, he might have added, with being Vice-President. But it all made for great stumping among the screaming, raucous silent majority.

Agnew went to Edgefield, South Carolina, the next day for the state's tricentennial celebration and in the presence of Haynsworth said that the Nixon Administration was the first in more than a century "to welcome the South back into the Union." He said Haynsworth and Carswell knew what he meant, as did millions of others who saw the attempt to place them on the Supreme Court. He called himself a "Southern vice-presidential candidate" in 1968 and said the "Southern strategy" was nothing more than a determination to give Dixie a fair shake in Washington.

From Haynsworth's home state Agnew went on to Carswell country for a major Republican fund-raising affair in Hollywood,

Florida. His task was complicated by the fact that since Carswell's rejection the judge had succumbed to the lure of political opportunity and had entered the Republican senatorial primary against a man who already had been given the White House blessing, Congressman William Cramer. In an airport interview Agnew resolved the dilemma, much to Cramer's consternation, by calling Cramer and Carswell "both fine men."

In his speech Agnew somehow forgot to mention that the Senate had rejected Haynsworth and Carswell. Instead, he reopened an attack on a front he had been assaulting intermittently since his election—campus leadership. For sheer brutality, it rivaled even the Harrisburg "rotten apples" speech. He not only assailed a university president, Kingman Brewster, Jr., of Yale, but also called on alumni to oust him for, among other things, criticizing the manner in which Nixon had been elected President. Before Agnew was through, campus demonstrators, black radicals, President Robben W. Fleming of the University of Michigan, Dr. Benjamin Spock, the Washington *Post* and Cornell University all had felt his lash.

Agnew's primary target, Brewster, had expressed sympathy with a strike by his students against the Bobby Seale Black Panther murder trial in New Haven, and had labeled Nixon's election "a hucksterized process." Though Agnew's audience of tuxedoed and bejeweled Floridians was distinctly non-Ivy League, and the Cramer-Carswell split was more on their minds than Yale, Agnew went after Brewster as if the Yale president were running against both of them. First he scored radical students: ". . . the heady wine of intellectual elitism courses through their veins . . . they resemble probationers of some esoteric organization—eager to the point of sycophancy to do all the right things and make all the right noises so that they will be accepted into the group . . . each year a new group of impressionable consumers falls victim to the totalitarian ptomaine dispensed by those who disparage our system. . . .

"The true responsibility for these aberrations and the nurturing of arrogance and contempt for constitutional authority rests not with the young people on campuses, but with those who so miserably fail to guide them. I can well understand the attitude of the majority of the student body at Yale University when most of the Yale faculty votes to endorse a strike in support of members of an organization dedicated to criminal violence, anarchy and the destruction of the United States of America. And when the president of that respected university describes the election of a President of the United States by the people of the United States as a 'hucksterized process' under which they could not expect much better 'whichever package was bought or sold,' it is clearly time for the alumni of that fine old college to demand that it be headed by a more mature and responsible person."

In any academic community, the improbable phenomenon of a high governmental official instructing the university's alumni to fire its president doubtless would have created an uproar. Here, approving Floridians listened with amusement as the G.O.P.'s new star administered the gratuitous suggestion as if he were providing a recipe for chicken soup—the flat, measured monotone and unsmiling countenance cloaking the effrontery of the performance.

Again the imagery of personal brutality and violence was surfacing increasingly in Agnew's rhetoric. Recalling a similar attack he had made on Michigan's President Fleming for agreeing with black radicals on an admissions quota, Agnew explained "the vigor" of that assault on "an old Cub Scout theory that the best way to put a tough crust on a marshmallow is to roast it." He blamed not only university administrators for campus unrest but also "affluent, permissive, upper-middle-class parents who learned their Dr. Spock and threw discipline out the window— when they should have done the opposite." That remark generated a roar of approval. So did this one: "To most academicians the traditional enemy has always been on the right. The sixties showed how pitifully unprepared the academic community was for an assault from its ideological rear. They had best learn how to deal with it, for their survival is at stake. One modest suggestion for my friends in the academic community: the next time a mob of students, waving their nonnegotiable demands, start pitching bricks and rocks at the Student Union, just imagine they are wearing brown shirts or white sheets—and act accordingly."

Precisely what Agnew meant by "act accordingly" he did not say, but the suggestion was fraught with vigilantism. The remark was typical of the call to man's baser instincts that lurked behind the veneered Agnew harangue; again, it was delivered in the most placid tones, as if volume rather than content determined whether the remark was incendiary. There was, in the Vice-President's style, a particular irresponsibility. Quick to accuse and hold responsible, he was revealingly insensitive to the damage he might inflict on others' reputations, or to his personal responsibility for doing such damage. In an earlier speech he had attacked educational practices at, of all places, the University of Rome, and had earned a sharp protest from Italian officials. Of that protest, he now said, "Criticism of my speech also came from Italy, where it was contended my charges about the University of Rome were unsubstantiated. If that be the case, my apologies—but the source of my facts was an analysis in the Washington *Post*. That is where the diplomatic protests should be lodged. And if any of the information that the *Post* printed was in error, I am sure they will come forward with their usual prompt retraction."

Also in the Hollywood speech, Agnew mentioned "students at Cornell who, wielding pipes and tire chains, beat a dormitory president into unconsciousness," and he added: "This is the criminal left that belongs not in a dormitory, but in a penitentiary." The next day Dr. Dale R. Corson, president of Cornell, sent a telegram to Agnew: "No such incident has ever occurred at Cornell University. . . . It is incredible that the Vice-President of the United States should make such a public statement for which there is no basis in fact. The damage you do through such irresponsible and widely publicized statements is irreparable. May I ask how you propose to make such amends as it is possible to make?"

The question brought an acknowledgment from Herb Thompson that the beating to which Agnew referred had taken place at the University of Connecticut, not Cornell. But violence was no stranger to Cornell, Thompson said. "University authorities had to obtain restraining orders to prohibit violence . . . these orders were tested by SDS and the Black Liberation Front with no action taken against them." Again, Dr. Corson took issue. Thompson's statement, he said, "displays both inaccuracies and disrespect for the judicial process." Cornell had obtained a temporary restraining order, but "it was not tested by violent action" by anyone. "I look forward," he went on, "to the personal effort of the Vice-President of the United States both to establish the facts on which he bases his public remarks and to set the record straight." He is still waiting. All he got was another letter from Agnew's office saying, "The Vice-President regrets this inaccurate attribution ["through an error in reporting received in this office"] and has issued a public statement correctly identifying recent actions of students on your campus." Attached was a copy of the first letter from Thompson, for which Dr. Corson had asked the Vice-President's public correction in the first place!

There was, of course, method in Agnew's assault on academia. The White House could stand aloof and say the attacks were no more than one independent member of the Administration speaking his mind, but by design or happenstance Agnew's broadsides were giving voice to all the scapegoating going on in a country racked by the divisions of an unpopular war abroad and social and economic conflict at home. The protest against the war and the fight for racial progress were centering increasingly on the American campus; it was easy to cite as the cause of the nation's ills not the war or racial injustice but the "revolutionaries" who opposed both, and to point to the campus as a breeding ground for them. There always had been a strong streak of anti-intellectualism in Middle America; George Wallace had tapped it boldly and often, but never behind the façade of erudition Agnew used to give his brutal thrusts the trappings of responsible dialogue.

Even before the Florida speech, American campuses were seething over Agnew's remarks. A study by a special committee on campus tensions of the American Council on Education reported that "political exploitation of campus problems by some public figures," notably Agnew and Ronald Reagan, had become one of the most divisive elements in campus life. Agnew was drawing most of the lightning for the Nixon Administration; Nixon himself was not beloved on American campuses, but students found in Agnew a more stimulating object for their critical energies.

Now, however, in late April of 1970, a decision by the President regarding Indochina suddenly ignited the campuses to such pervasive opposition to Nixon that not even the dislike of protesting students toward his deputy could siphon off the anger. In an attempt to buy more time for his Vietnamization policy, Nixon approved and implemented an invasion—or "incursion," as the Administration called it—of neighboring Cambodia by American and South Vietnamese forces, to decimate enemy sanctuaries from which military operations against South Vietnam were being mounted. Nixon sought to justify the move as a way to protect American lives in South Vietnam; critics immediately attacked the invasion as a needless and dangerous expansion of the war, and nowhere did that chorus erupt with greater volume and intensity than on American campuses.

Agnew and other Administration spokesmen were thrown into the breach; on CBS's *Face the Nation*, the Vice-President argued that efforts by the enemy to extend the sanctuaries and establish new supply lines to the sea required the action. "Our emphasis and thrust," he said, "is to protect that flank so that the Vietnamization program can go forward and that Americans can disengage from Vietnam and come home." And of criticism of the move at home by "the dissident and destructive elements in our society," Agnew said, "I don't think many of them are really honestly sincere about the cause. I think they are simply utilizing this as a vehicle to continue their antisocial, outrageous conduct. And I think if the war were over, for example, they would find something else to use an excuse for throwing firebombs into the Bank of America." This last was a reference to an act of violence in California, and the Vice-President preceded it with an observation that he was not talking about all critics of the Cambodia invasion. But as so often when Agnew assaulted the "disruptive elements" in the society, any distinction was blurred. Thousands of college students who deeply and honestly opposed the war and this latest action saw Agnew's words as a red flag. Still, this was not the segment of American society for whom and to whom he was speaking. He made that quite clear at the close of the TV program. Reminded of Nixon's plea for lowered voices, he was asked whether he thought he had "increased divisiveness in this country and, if so, to what end?" Agnew replied that he had not. ". . . It is necessary," he said, "for the frustrations of the American people, as they sit back and observe the steady erosion of the fabric of our society taking place, with hardly a word raised in its defense, to have a strong spokesman. When a fire takes place, a man doesn't run into the room and whisper, 'Would somebody please get the water?'; he yells, 'Fire!' and I am yelling 'Fire!' because I think 'Fire!' needs to be called here."

The very next day a fire did take place, at a little-known university called Kent State in Ohio, the flames of which touched every corner of the land. The spark was the decision to go into

Cambodia, fanned—college students across the nation later told itinerant White House missionaries—by the rhetoric of Administration spokesmen like Spiro Agnew against those who opposed the war. Students had marched through the town of Kent three nights earlier protesting the Cambodia action, committing some vandalism against local businessmen along the way. The disturbances were deemed too much for local police to handle and Governor James Rhodes called in the National Guard, who took up positions on the campus. In a moment of tension, emotion and panic, the guardsmen fired on the students, killing four of them.

Agnew was in Washington at the time, preparing to speak to the American Retail Federation. He had a tough speech ready to go and nothing was going to stop him. Some in his audience, he told the federation members, might think his remarks "show a certain insensitivity" expressed at that particular moment, but they were addressed to "a general malaise that argues for violent confrontation instead of debate." What happened at Kent State, he said, was "a tragedy that was predictable," for which assessment of blame would have to await investigation.

Then he launched into his prepared text without a phrase altered. He assailed "tomentose exhibitionists who provoke more derision than fear" (*tomentose* is defined by *Webster's* as "covered with densely matted hairs") and "elitists" like Mayor John Lindsay of New York who "in their feverish search for group acceptance are ready to endorse tumultuous confrontation as a substitute for debate, and the most illogical and unfitting extensions of the Bill of Rights as protections for psychotic and criminal elements in our society." (The month before, Lindsay had criticized officials who "are ready to support repression as long as it is done in a quiet voice and a business suit"; Agnew shot back at officials "ready to support revolution as long as it is with a cultured voice and a handsome profile." He called them exponents of "philosophical violence . . . born on the social ladder . . . formally educated. . . ." who scoff at "honesty and thrift and hard work." No wonder, he observed, "we have traitors and thieves and perverts and irrational and illogical people in our midst.") The "tomentose exhibitionists," the Vice-President said, were obvious in their threat to systems of higher education, and hence less dangerous than "the moral relativists, the creators of the 'era of moroseness'" among the "elitists" in American society.

In the anguish that gripped American campuses over the Kent State slayings, Agnew's words were predictably incendiary. But even within the Nixon Administration, which had shown an unusually united front to the outside world, the words were having a divisive impact. One of the most loyal Nixon supporters of 1968, Secretary of the Interior Walter J. Hickel, was moved to write a letter to the President imploring him to rebuild lines of communication to the nation's young shattered by such factors as Agnew's rhetoric. "I believe the Vice-President initially has answered a deep-seated mood of America in his public statements," Hickel wrote. "However, a continued attack on the young—not in their attitudes so much as their motives—can serve little purpose other than to further cement those attitudes to a solidity impossible to penetrate with reason." (Six nights later, still having heard nothing in reply from the President, Hickel appeared on the CBS News *60 Minutes* television show with Mike Wallace. He repeated his general observations, without mentioning Agnew. It was an appearance the White House did not soon forget, and it was an element in Nixon's decision seven months later to fire Hickel.)

But Nixon was not in any mood to make peace with the young. Like Agnew, he had his back up over these unsightly, unseemly, unmanageable campus troublemakers who refused to get into line. In a visit to the Pentagon to discuss Cambodia a few days after the Kent State shootings, he referred to campus demonstrators as "these bums . . . blowing up campuses"—a characterization, Agnew later explained, Nixon used after he learned that the life project of a California professor had been destroyed in an antiwar demonstration.

Agnew's and Nixon's remarks also stirred the concern of college presidents. They urged Nixon and members of his Administration to refrain from making hostile observations about college students in this volatile time. The President assured them their advice would be followed, but only hours later Agnew taped a television interview with TV personality David Frost and said he thought Nixon's use of "bums" was "a little mild." Nevertheless, the Vice-President did acknowledge that if it was established that the national guardsmen had fired first at Kent State, they might be held responsible for murder. "As a lawyer I am conversant, and I suppose most people who follow the courts are conversant, with the fact that where there is no premeditation but simply an over-response in the heat of anger that results in a killing, it's murder," he said. "It's not premeditated, but it's a murder, and certainly can't be condoned." If the demonstrators hadn't thrown rocks and attacked the guardsmen, Agnew said, there would have been no shooting. Frost suggested that had there been no Cambodian operation, the students may not have demonstrated. That was possible, Agnew conceded, but there were certain elements who were ready to riot over anything, including the length of their hair. As for Hickel, Agnew said, he didn't believe his "old friend" had read his speeches completely. Young people were being heard, he said, "but the fact that they are heard does not necessarily mean they must be heeded." That remark, presumably, was intended to be conciliatory.

Despite later denials, there are indications that around this time Nixon called Agnew in and told him that while he wouldn't think of suggesting what his deputy should and shouldn't say, it might be time to lower his voice for a while. Scripps-Howard reporter Dan Thomasson first wrote of the meeting in mid-May and said the President had assured Agnew he would be his running mate again in 1972. In the presence of Attorney General John Mitchell—a great Agnew booster—Nixon told Agnew not to worry about criticism from Hickel and other Cabinet members and reminded him, according to Thomasson, "You're my Vice-President, not theirs." He personally agreed with Agnew's assessments about campus and street demonstrators, Nixon said, but in light of the inflammatory situation on American campuses—an equally brutal assault on black students by police at Jackson State College had killed two others—Agnew "should not go out of his way to irritate matters further."

When Thomasson's story broke, the Administration moved quickly to discredit it, particularly the part about an assurance to Agnew that he would be on the ticket in 1972. En route to Key Biscayne for a long weekend, Press Secretary Ronald Ziegler told reporters traveling with the President that the story was "totally without fact," that no such meeting had taken place, and that the President had neither asked the Vice-President to cool his rhetoric nor assured him he would be his running mate again. Another White House official, however, told Don Irwin of the Los Angeles *Times* that such a meeting had occurred the previous week, and that after Thomasson's story appeared there had been another high-level meeting among White House staff members to discuss how word of the Nixon-Agnew session had leaked. That night, at Dan Thomasson's home in the Washington area, the phone rang. It was Ziegler. He was, according to Thomasson, in a most apologetic and mollifying mood. "I'm sorry I had to shoot you down on that one," Ziegler told him.

Events subsequent to the reported Nixon-Agnew meeting gave more credence to Thomasson's story. On May 8, Agnew went to Boise, Idaho, to speak at a Republican dinner. On arrival he told newsmen at the airport that a Nixon staff member had called him concerning the President's earlier promise to tone down Administration criticism of students. "The President wanted me to understand thoroughly he was not attempting to put any kind of muzzle on me and that he was not opposed to the kind of things I have been saying," Agnew told them. He would continue to criticize "criminal conduct" in the antiwar protest but "we never meant to imply that a great majority of the students were involved in this kind of conduct," he said. That same night President Nixon stated at one of his infrequent press conferences that he would not attempt to tell his Vice-President what to say but did ask all members of his Administration to remember that "when the action is hot, keep the rhetoric cool."

Meanwhile Agnew's prepared text had been released in Washington before delivery in Boise. It began: "At every period of great challenge in this nation's history, debate has always included a cadre of Jeremiahs; normally a gloomy coalition of choleric young intellectuals and tired, embittered elders." These Jeremiahs were speaking out now "in what could only appear as a conscious attempt to rekindle the debilitating fires of riot and unrest that had been banked by the continuing commitment of President Nixon to end the war." Specifically, Agnew charged that Senator Fulbright had made "the baldest and most reactionary plea for isolationism heard in that chamber [the Senate] since the heyday of the 'America Firsters.'" When the Vice-President rose to speak in Boise, however, he announced he was abandoning these portions of his text because in light of Nixon's press conference remarks, he wanted "in some small way" to help cool the volatile mood of the country. He did not "author" the paragraphs he was cutting, he said, but he wouldn't apologize for them, either, because while "the rhetoric was not mine" it did reflect his thinking.

(Up to this time, notably, the Vice-President had taken pains to stress that the words he spoke were his own. Thus, he could still say nobody was "muzzling" *him*.)

Agnew also cooled it in Atlanta the next day, where he substituted for the President at the dedication of a Confederate memorial of Robert E. Lee, Jefferson Davis and Stonewall Jackson carved on the side of Stone Mountain. The substitution had brought sharp protests from Georgia. An Emory history professor, Dr. Bell Wiley, called the decision an affront to Lee, who believed in dissent and "risked his life and forfeited his career in order to defend it." Lee, he said, "did not believe students and professors are bums." When Agnew arrived in Atlanta he was greeted by an Atlanta *Constitution* editorial labeling his selection to make the dedication "a shame and a disgrace. . . . Honorable men rode that rocky ledge, General Robert E. Lee among them. . . . As general-in-chief of the Confederate Armies, Lee had traits sorely needed in this hour of the nation's history. His temper and patience seldom failed him. Self-control was his nature. On those rare times when his wrath did get away from him, he followed it with a particularly gracious act to the one who had felt his displeasure. Spiro Agnew has none of these redeeming qualities. He has the grace of a drill sergeant and the understanding of a 19th-Century prison camp warden. He has come very close to doing with ill-tempered language what Lee and Jackson and Jefferson Davis failed to do by force of arms: divide the nation. . . ."

Such a diatribe from the press under other circumstances almost surely would have generated a rousing return volley from Agnew. Instead, he remained unavailable to the press and followed a noncontroversial text at Stone Mountain. That same weekend, though strident antiwar demonstrations were going on in Washington and elsewhere to protest the Cambodian operation and the killings at Kent State and Jackson State, the Vice-President kept his mouth shut. Only after the demonstrations were over did he comment in a radio interview that their speakers were "the same old tired radicals that everybody in the country's sick of listening to. . . . I certainly don't agree that the demonstrations are really indicative of deep-seated student hostility to the Cambodian decision." Rhetoric should be cooled, he agreed. "I think the best place and the first place it should begin is on the editorial pages of some of the Eastern newspapers."

Dan Thomasson's story of Nixon's request to Agnew to cool it had also stated that "to dispel any thought that he is being muzzled by Nixon, Agnew is preparing a speech for delivery in Texas later this month in which he will make subtly many of the same points he has made before. But White House insiders said the Vice-President's Texas appearance will leave no doubt that Agnew is not going to be beaten down by campus, cabinet or congressional critics."

The only thing wrong with that prediction was the use of the word "subtly." Sure enough, in Houston a week after that was written, Agnew said at a $500-a-plate fund-raising dinner:

"Lately, you have been exposed to a great deal of public comment about vice-presidential rhetoric and how I should 'cool it.' The President is getting this advice daily from many quarters . . . some of them inside the government. But mostly it has come from persons who have been in the target area of some of my speeches. Nowhere is the complaint louder than in the columns and editorials of the liberal news media of this country, those really illiberal, self-appointed guardians of our destiny who would like to run the country without ever submitting to the elective process as we in public office must do.

"The President has refused to curb my statements on behalf of this Administration's policies, or to tell me what words to use or what tone to take in my speeches. And on my part, I have refused to 'cool it' . . . until those self-righteous lower their voices a few decibels. This I am sure they are unwilling to do, and there is too much at stake in the nation for us to leave the entire field of public commentary to them."

Then followed one of the most scathing assaults on the press and individuals in it ever to come from the pen of Spiro Agnew or any other critic. Hardly anyone of note escaped his attack—neither the editorial writers and columnists of the *New York Times,* the Washington *Post,* nor his most recent tormentor, the Atlanta *Constitution.* Agnew called the *Post*'s prize-winning cartoonist, Herblock, "that master of sick invective" for a cartoon showing a national guardsman with a box of bullets, each labeled with an Agnew phrase, plus one marked with Nixon's "bums" comment. "And they ask *us* to cool the rhetoric and lower our voices," he said to wild cheering and applause. Other columnists' and publications' words criticizing Agnew were quoted as examples of excessive rhetoric, with such descriptive phrases from Agnew as "hysterical," "overwrought," "apoplexy," "pure unbridled invective" and "irrational ravings."

Then Agnew calmly went on: "Ladies and gentlemen, you have heard a lot of wild, hot rhetoric tonight—none of it mine. This goes on daily in the editorial pages of some very large, very reputable newspapers in this country—not all of them in the East by a long shot. And it pours out of the television set and the radio in a daily torrent, assailing our ears so incessantly we no longer register shock at the irresponsibility and thoughtlessness behind the statements. 'But *you* are the Vice-President,' they say to me. 'You should choose your language more carefully.' Nonsense. I have sworn I will uphold the Constitution against all enemies, foreign and domestic. Those who would tear our country apart or try to bring down its government are enemies, whether here or abroad, whether destroying libraries and classrooms on a college campus, or firing at American troops from a rice paddy in Southeast Asia. I have an obligation to all of the people in the United States to call things as I see them, and I have an obligation to the President to support his actions in the best manner that I can. I choose my own words and I set the tone of my speeches. As he [Nixon] said at his recent press conference, I am responsible for what I say. And I intend to be heard above the din even if it means raising my voice."

As usual in his speeches, Agnew entered the disclaimer that he didn't mean to criticize everybody in the press, but he said it did bother him "that the press as a group regards the First Amendment as its own private preserve. . . . That happens to be *my* amendment too. It guarantees my free speech as much as it does their freedom of the press. So I hope that will be remembered the next time a 'muzzle Agnew' campaign is launched."

From then through the summer of 1970, there was little more of the earlier speculation that cooler rhetoric from Spiro Agnew might be just around the corner. In early June, in the wake of the Houston harangue and a commencement speech at West Point at which Agnew deplored the glamorizing of "the criminal misfits of society" and the eulogizing of foreign dictators by "charlatans of peace and freedom," eleven University of Minnesota professors called on him. They warned him that he was "driving moderates into the arms of extremists" with his talk. Their spokesman, Professor of Economics Walter W. Heller, late of the Kennedy and Johnson administrations, came away observing, "I have my fingers crossed." It proved to be a wasted gesture.

One of the Minnesota professors had proposed to Agnew that he devote a full speech to defining what he considered to be responsible dissent, to underline to American youth that he was not trying to curb all opposition to Administration policy. Agnew took up the idea and later that month delivered such a speech in Detroit. He called for "rational dissenters" to balance out "the emotionaries, a relatively small group of anti-intellectuals that has snatched the standard of dissent from their hands." But he observed, in regard to appeals that he de-escalate his own rhetoric, that "no argument is fair that appeals exclusively to emotion [and] no argument is realistic that rules out all emotion." Rather than de-escalating, he said, "we have to elevate the rhetoric," and this he intended to do "forcefully, factually and fearlessly."

Within the White House, too, Agnew heard complaints that his speechmaking was alienating campus youth. After the anti-Cambodia demonstrations, a group of eight young White House aides led by Jeb Magruder was dispatched to college campuses all over the country to mingle with students and get their sentiment about how the Nixon Administration was handling the war. "The most frequently repeated comment on the campuses," says Lee Huebner, one of the eight, "was that the Vice-President's rhetoric was a thorn in their flesh, and we had to go back and tell him to cool down. So we did. We were quite direct, and we were surprised in some ways. He is such a terribly candid person—that's his strength and his weakness, I suppose—that he responded in a way that made us be even more candid. We felt terribly comfortable and terribly ready to report things just as we had heard them. At the beginning he listened a lot, and then he talked a lot, and forty-five minutes were gone. We made motions to leave and he said no. Another forty-five minutes went by. There was a sense that he really wanted to get at the bottom of it, to talk it out. I'm not sure that he wanted to find out where he had gone wrong. It may be that he wanted us to fully understand where he stood. I got the impression he was committed to the notion somehow that if you really thought about something clearly enough, everybody would agree. And if people disagreed, either they weren't thinking clearly or they were badly motivated. And in order to accept that point of view, he had evolved that notion as possible for himself.

"When he finished, he did say he didn't think it was time to go after the college students any more and he was going to cool it on that front; he was going to lay off the students. And he did. But he kept insisting on what the point really was—he accepted the fact that it was politically wise or in the interests of national morale at this point not to exacerbate this problem, but what concerned him far more was whether the things he was saying were accurate or inaccurate. And by God, if they were accurate, we ought to be saying them. He kept saying things like this: 'Well, I must be going wrong somewhere. So many intelligent people are criticizing me. Jump on me. Tell me where I'm wrong.' He's very proud and he doesn't like to be disliked. . . . Our main conclusion [from the campus visits] was that there was a newly emergent group of moderate students, moderate in tactics at least, who had become very hostile to the Administration but shouldn't be confused with the radicals; that they wanted help from us in drawing that distinction, but they thought we were blurring the distinction. That was the point on which we focused with the Vice-President."

In at least one prominent case, however, that lesson did not take. Shortly afterward, the President appointed a twenty-two-year-old Harvard junior fellow named Joseph Rhodes, Jr., to a new presidential commission on campus unrest. Rhodes, an acquaintance of White House aide John Ehrlichman's, had been acting as an unofficial adviser and informant to the Administration in this area. In an interview with the *New York Times* after his appointment, Rhodes said that one of the things he wanted to find out as a member of the commission was whether public statements by Nixon and Agnew "are killing people"—an obvious reference to the Kent State and Jackson State shootings and charges of Administration responsibility for creating the climate in which they occurred. Agnew immediately jumped in, charged that Rhodes lacked "the maturity, the objectivity and the judgment" to serve on the commission and called for his resignation. Rhodes had "misused" his relationship with Ehrlichman, Agnew said, had engaged in "verbal posturing" and had displayed "a transparent bias that will make him counterproductive to the work of the commission." He was "no longer entitled to the cloak of dignity that a presidential appointment would throw around him."

On the face of the situation, Agnew's attack was a most injudicious thing to do. Young Rhodes not only was a friend of the President's No. 2 aide but also had been appointed by the President. An internal complaint against him would have been one thing; this was out in the open, with the risk of a presidential rebuff. It did in fact come quite quickly, in a report from Ziegler that there were no plans to change the commission membership. "We want a wide range of views—a diversity of views—represented on the commission," he said. According to Rhodes, his friend Ehrlichman called him at Harvard the same day and told him: "That son of a bitch! Don't worry about it. The President wants you to know he's not happy about it."

The Vice-President's decision to "go public" with his gripe against Rhodes either was evidence of his apolitical thinking or was required because his line to the President was being clogged. Both possibilities fed Administration scuttlebutt that Agnew was being frozen out, especially since the Vice-President's continuing unhappiness about being downgraded on domestic policy making touched inevitably on the man who was emerging in that realm, Ehrlichman.

But Spiro Agnew was not a man to stay down for long. Four days after the Rhodes rebuff he was back on the attack, this time choosing critics of the President who he could be certain would not be defended by the White House—seven leading Democrats and then-Republican John Lindsay. At a Cleveland fund-raising dinner, Agnew called them "Hanoi's most effective, even if unintentional, apologists" and he singled out Lindsay as one of his own party's "summertime soldiers and sunshine patriots" who had abandoned Nixon to save his own political skin. In some of his bitterest language, Agnew said Fulbright had supported the build-up of American forces in Vietnam in 1964 "but when the seas became choppy, the storm clouds arose and the enemy stubbornly resisted, one could soon glance down from the bridge and see Senator Fulbright on the deck demanding that the ship be abandoned and staking out a claim to the nearest lifeboat." He listed Johnson aides Clark Clifford, Cyrus Vance and his favorite target, Averell Harriman, as men "whom history has branded as failures." Harriman had "succeeded in booting away our greatest military trump—the bombing of North Vietnam—for a mess of porridge." He added: "As one looks back over the diplomatic disasters that have befallen the West and the friends of the West over three decades at Tehran, Yalta, Cairo—in every great diplomatic conference that turned out to be a loss for the West and freedom—one can find the unmistakable footprints of W. Averell Harriman." He charged Harriman with U.S. acceptance of the 1962 Geneva Agreement on Laos that, he said, ignored the future likelihood of North Vietnamese use of the Ho Chi Minh Trail to send supplies into South Vietnam. ". . . Down Harriman's Highway," he said, "have come half a million North Vietnamese troops to bring death to thousands of Americans and hundreds of thousands of South Vietnamese."

That Cleveland tirade marked the end of the very brief cooling-off period, if indeed it had ever existed. Pussyfooting never was in the Agnew style, as he noted in one of the best examples of his utter candor. "In a desire to be heard," he told a British television audience in a taped interview, "I have to throw them [the press] what people in America call a little red meat once in a while and hope that in spite of the damaging context in which these remarks are repeated, that other things which I think are very important will also appear."

In the next weeks Agnew provided ample red meat by hitting every target in sight: the national drug scene; supporters of the Cooper-Church amendment against future use of U.S. troops in Cambodia ("Cassandras of the Senate . . . trying to forge new chains upon the President's freedom of action"); the "Fulbright claque in the Senate" that was providing "great comfort" to the enemy; the McGovern-Hatfield end-the-war amendment ("a blueprint for the first defeat in the history of the United States"; he wondered whether its sponsors "really give a damn"). This last broadside, delivered to a very receptive Veterans of Foreign Wars convention in Miami Beach, drew protests from Fulbright, McGovern and Hatfield that Agnew was trying to intimidate them, and that in so doing, as President of the Senate he was making, in Fulbright's words, "a direct attack on our constitutional process." But Agnew had more limited objectives. He simply wanted to use the amendment, already ticketed for sure defeat, as a vehicle in the most important political assignment given to him to date by the President—leading the Republican party's off-year attempt to purge the Senate of Vietnam doves and, if possible, grasp Senate control.

The Vice-President's emergence as a speechmaker may primarily have been his own idea, and his success his own doing. But others in the party—notably the President—had not watched and listened without grasping the fact that in the personal phenomenon of Spiro Agnew, a very valuable party implement was developing. Throughout the spring Agnew had tucked into his speeches at G.O.P. fund-raising affairs—which by now had brought more than $3 million into the party till—reminders that it would take a Republican Congress or at least a Republican Senate to make a real difference in the fortunes of Nixon Administration programs. Now his mission was to obtain that shift. In an interview with Associated Press reporters Walter Mears and Carl Leubsdorf in mid-July, Agnew spelled it out. "I have the political assignment for the Administration," he said when asked about the forthcoming campaign. "I wouldn't say this is a hard-line role in its entirety but it certainly is to some extent a partisan one." From such an oratorical bomb thrower, that description ranked as one of the classic political understatements. In the campaign of 1970 ahead, Agnew was to teach even the masters like Richard Nixon a thing or two about partisan invective.

As a last assignment before plunging into that campaign, Nixon sent Agnew on his second Asian trip, this one a nine-day dash through five countries, again to reassure American allies that the withdrawal of American troops from South Vietnam did not mean the end of U.S. aid to them, provided they were ready to assume their share of the defense burden. The first and diplomatically most difficult stop was South Korea, where Agnew had the task of smoothing over concerns by the Seoul government about American plans to withdraw twenty thousand Americans from Korea and substitute more military hardware. Korean President Chung Hee Park kept Agnew in conversation for six hours in an unscheduled marathon session, but the Vice-President held firm in what his diplomatic escorts later indicated was a commendable demonstration of coolness and resolution. The Koreans weren't any happier about the decision, but they hadn't changed it.

In stops in Taiwan, South Vietnam and Thailand, and a surprise visit to Cambodia, Agnew continued the smooth transition from unshackled partisan warrior at home to diplomat on a tight rein abroad. The only remark he made that came close to being a blooper occurred at the outset, en route to Korea, when he told accompanying reporters that the United States was going to "do everything we can to help" the newly installed regime of General Lon Nol in Cambodia, because "the whole matter of Cambodia is related to the security of our troops in Vietnam." He warned that "if Cambodia falls" it would be impossible for the Vietnamization program and the disengagement of American troops from South Vietnam to succeed. The remarks sounded strongly like an advance justification for sending American troops into Cambodia again, but Agnew refused to speculate on the possibility, which would have been a violation of the Cooper-Church amendment. The White House backed the Vice-President but insisted that he was making no new pledge to the Lon Nol government, and when Agnew arrived in Phnom Penh he "clarified" the situation. After having conferred with Cambodian leaders, he told reporters that "beyond assistance of an economic and material nature I made no commitments whatsoever. . . . I explained that we would not become militarily involved." Agnew's second diplomatic assignment was hailed by the White House as effective salesmanship of the Nixon Doctrine. It was all the more impressive, Administration aides said, because the Vice-President had been treading on unfamiliar ground.

Now, on return, Agnew was to set out on very familiar ground. The off-year elections were at hand; his job was to sell the domestic Nixon Doctrine—that a band of willful men in the Democratic-controlled Senate was obstructing progress and unity at home and should be thrown out. About this doctrine, he would need nobody to tutor him along the way. The theme had been the inspiration for most of what he had said since that night in New Orleans when he had identified the "effete corps of impudent snobs" and had harangued his way into the hearts of Middle America. That was ten months earlier; in the intervening time he had come from next-to-nowhere to third, just behind the President and Billy Graham, on the Gallup poll's list of America's most admired men. Five of every eight Americans surveyed expressed a favorable opinion of him. The task now was to convert that sentiment into votes for the Republican party and the Nixon Administration.

There was little doubt that Ted Agnew would throw himself into the effort with determination and relish. Senator Eugene Mc-Carthy, who was leaving the Senate voluntarily, had watched the last months with his customary detachment and had dubbed Agnew "Nixon's Nixon." The description was apt, and it would be all the more so in the two months ahead, as the great silent majority was summoned to be heard and counted. Now at last the political potency of Agnewism would be measured.

18

❖·❖·❖·❖·❖·❖

WAR ON RADICLIBS

IN early August of 1970, President Nixon called his Vice-President to the Oval Office to discuss the approaching campaign. During the previous ten months the President had been content to let Ted Agnew roam at will through the countryside and the English language with only the broadest direction or none at all, confident that Agnew would stay within the framework of Administration policy. Agnew had not breached that confidence, but the importance of the exercise ahead, and Nixon's own deep interest and self-declared expertise in it, dictated presidential masterminding.

During the spring Agnew had been laying the groundwork for an assault against those in Congress, and especially in the Senate, who had been the chief obstructionists of Administration policy, particularly on the Vietnam war. In this preparation he had emulated the role Nixon himself had played as Vice-President in off-years in the 1950's, and more recently and with more effect in 1966. At that time, private citizen Nixon had worked vulnerable congressional districts tirelessly, eventually playing a pivotal role, or being so credited, in a resounding party gain of forty-seven seats in the House of Representatives. The scope of the victory, which Nixon practically alone had predicted, had propelled him once again into the forefront of G.O.P. leadership, with a great if unwitting assist from then President Johnson. Johnson made the tactical mistake of singling out Nixon as a "chronic campaigner" shortly before the off-year election, thus rallying Republican sentiment around him and positioning Nixon to emerge from the campaign as the party's savior. Nixon wisely had seen 1966 as an election of great opportunity because the party's lot in the House was so low that it was bound to spring back, and he now pictured 1970 as a similar opportunity in the Senate.

"That suggested itself," a Nixon associate of 1966 says. "How many senators they had up, how many we had up. We didn't have a snowball's chance of getting the House, and they had guys up in the Senate from that damn class of '64 that came in with Goldwater's defeat. A lot of them just eased in, or came first in '58 in the recession, so they were vulnerable. I think anybody who looked at it would have realized the strategy would be to get the Senate, although you don't say you're going to ignore the House. It was just like 1966. All the guys [Democrats] who won in the House in '64, the freebies, they were all vulnerable in '66. So too, their Senate guys who won in '64 would be vulnerable in 1970."

Agnew of course knew the arithmetic of 1970 as well as Nixon did: with fifty-seven Democratic seats in the Senate, a Republican pickup of only seven would mean control, with the Republican Vice-President breaking the tie. But the President, always so much a captive of his own political past, had other lessons to convey to his deputy. One article of Nixon faith was that winning meant attacking: in 1946 he had campaigned for a House seat as an "out" and won; in 1950 he had campaigned for a Senate seat as an "out" and won; in 1952 he had campaigned for the Vice-Presidency as an "out" and won; in 1968 he had campaigned for the Presidency as an "out" and won. In 1954, 1958 and 1960 he had campaigned as an "in"—carrying the record of the Eisenhower Administration on his back—and lost. The trick was obviously, even though one was in office, somehow to take the "out" posture. Harry Truman had done it effectively in 1948, escaping a defensive attitude about his own conduct in office by going on the offensive against the Republican-controlled Congress—the "do-nothing Congress" that blocked every important aspect of his program. The parallel with the 1970 situation was clear; the Nixon Administration would make war on its own version of the do-nothing Congress, this time with a twist happily provided by Senate Democratic opposition to the war.

And, with Nixon's own perception of history again as a guide, the attack would have to be carried by the Administration's lightning rod, the Vice-President, so that Nixon could remain—Eisenhower-like—the aloof statesman above the battle. Johnson's error in 1966, Nixon said in an interview after that election, had been to come down from the pedestal where the American people want their President to stand; Eisenhower had stayed up there in the off-year elections of 1954 and 1958 and came through the setbacks without much diminution of his own stature. Nixon took the heat then, like a good soldier; now he was on the presidential pedestal and it would be up to Agnew to draw the fire, go on the attack, play Nixon to Nixon's Ike.

There would be at least one important difference, though. Nixon had been there; he knew the personal pitfalls of such an assignment and he was going to back his surrogate to the hilt, with money, staff and moral support. In the inevitable comparisons made between Nixon and Eisenhower, the younger man nearly always came off second best: in public appeal and adoration, certainly; in command presence; in, yes, projection of strength and manliness. But when it came to politics, that was Nixon's department, and when it came to treating a Vice-President the way he deserved to be treated, Richard Nixon knew something about that, too. He might not be able to best Ike in many ways, but this certainly was one of them. This Nixon desire to be more generous and understanding toward his understudy was a strong psychological factor Spiro Agnew had going for him in his Vice-Presidency, and it would continue to be so.

One very tangible way to assist the Vice-President in his difficult assignment, backed to the hilt by the President, was to make sure Agnew and the party's candidates had plenty of money with which to conduct a winning campaign. The man selected to oversee this totally unpublicized effort was Jack A. Gleason, a New Yorker who first became associated with the Nixon entourage in 1967 when the candidate's staff was looking for a professional fund raiser. He was assigned to Maurice Stans, the Nixon finance chairman, and later came to Washington when Stans was appointed Secretary of Commerce. In early summer of 1970, Gleason had, with little fanfare, been transferred from Stan's staff to the White House, as assistant to Harry Dent, and after a while quietly detached in advance of the 1970 campaign.

Gleason established a minuscule office in the basement back room of an obscure row house off Dupont Plaza, about eight blocks from the White House, where he organized and implemented what probably was the most lucrative and complex fundraising effort ever launched in an off-year campaign. While Spiro Agnew provided the visible fuel for the attack on the opposition, Gleason, with the knowledge, consent and assistance of the White House, pumped in the invisible fuel.

In 1968 the Nixon camp had learned a thing or two about raising money, when Stans masterminded the record intake of $33 million for the primary and general election campaigns, more than doubling the previous high by Goldwater in 1964. Now, with the name of the President to pry open wallets, purses and checkbooks on Wall Street and all over Middle America, the sky seemed to be the limit. Gleason reached for it. To properly assess whether Nixon and Agnew won or lost in 1970, it is necessary to understand how much they laid on the line, and the Gleason operation as much as the Agnew travels was a measure of the commitment.

The system worked this way: in order to field the strongest possible opponents to the Senate Democrats, Nixon himself asked prominent Republicans to run against them. Congressmen holding safe seats were enticed into Senate races by a combination of presidential flattery and exhortation, pledges of postelection jobs for any losers, and the promise of ample campaign funds. Once the candidates were selected, Gleason traveled to Republican target states surveying the local situation and setting up the machinery through which campaign money would be funneled.

For example, one of the anointed G.O.P. congressmen, Tom Kleppe of North Dakota, was prevailed upon to run for the Senate seat held by Democrat Quentin N. Burdick. At the outset of the campaign Gleason telephoned Kleppe's campaign treasurer, Harold Anderson, and told him what had to be done to hook up the money machine at his end. "He wanted the names of committees to send the money to," Anderson said later, "and I told him of ten or twelve independent committees we set up—'Friends of Tom Kleppe' and the like." After that, Anderson said, he heard no more from Gleason, but checks began arriving to the various committees he had named. "All I was, was the treasurer—the conduit the money was funneled through," he explained. "I was informed by the congressman that he had arranged for there to be certain monies coming in for the campaign."

For all its surreptitious character the operation, repeated in numerous states, apparently was entirely legal, since it was based in the District of Columbia, where laws on reporting of campaign spending did not apply. It provided distinct advantages over normal fund raising. Centralization within a White House-connected structure gave the President and his political strategists closer control over each campaign being helped. According to one source close to the Administration, one particular Republican candidate who tried to set himself off from Agnew and his campaign methods had to curb his criticism, for fear that the White House money pipeline might suddenly be shut down.

Being able to invoke the President's name was a tremendous help to Gleason, who already knew the fund-raising ropes. "If you can call up somebody and say, 'The President is very interested in such-and-such campaign and they need such-and-such amount of money right away,'" one Republican politician observed, "you have a much better chance of getting it." Also, the special operation avoided the pressure that often descended on the national committee and the G.O.P. congressional and senatorial campaign committees to share funds equally among all party candidates. In this underground procedure, in which few knew how much money was being raised or where it was going, the White House could assess which candidates had the best chance to win and which needed money the most, and then inject financial transfusions at will. In the last weeks, phone calls were placed to big contributors telling them the President wanted a certain amount of money funneled immediately into a specific campaign. The contributors were given the name of the appropriate committee; checks went out in a matter of hours.

According to one Republican politician importantly involved in an Eastern campaign favored by the special White House operation, Gleason boasted after the election that more than $12 million had been raised for Republican candidates through it. The only trace of the whole underground effort that could be found later was an occasional listing in campaign contribution reports filed on Capitol Hill, such as $2,500 to Republican candidate J. Glenn Beall, Jr., in Maryland by the Nixon-appointed U.S. ambassador to Great Britain, Walter H. Annenberg, "care of Jack A. Gleason" at the Dupont Plaza basement address.

Money, of course, was not everything. The Nixon-Agnew meeting in August was the first of several during the summer at which the tactical considerations behind the political arithmetic of 1970 and the fund raising were mapped out. The President indicated the priority he placed on the campaign by assigning as its chief operations officer one of his most trusted and capable all-round counselors, Bryce Harlow, who also was a veteran of the Eisenhower Administration political wars. Harlow invited two Nixon speech writers, the conservative Pat Buchanan and the ideologically ambidextrous Bill Safire, and a top issues man, young Dr. Martin Anderson, to join the Agnew entourage, and all four met with the President and Vice-President to outline the campaign. From the start, the operative word was "attack"—attack on opposition to the Vietnam war and on softness toward the enemy; attack on softness toward crime, toward campus protest and violence; attack on permissiveness toward the younger generation, on the breakdown of law and order. Intimately involved in the attack strategy was the man who had taught it to Nixon—Murray Chotiner. After a year in political limbo, the architect of Nixon's early victories in California had been brought right into the White House in late 1969 specifically to oversee preparations and strategy for the 1970 congressional elections. By August 1970, Chotiner knew who was vulnerable and to what, and in Agnew he had a worthy successor to his prize pupil in the craft of victory through political vilification.

In all this, it was obvious, the Spiro Agnew who had emerged as a stump fire-breather over the previous ten months was made to order for the assignment. He would say what was required of him, and make money while saying it. In every state where Republicans were running, plans were made for huge fund-raising affairs, at which one man above all was asked to speak—Spiro Agnew. It was decided early that with a few exceptions, Agnew would focus on the Senate, going directly after those vulnerable doves whose defeat in itself would reduce the intensity of anti-Administration clamor on Capitol Hill, as well as contribute to a possible party takeover in the Senate. One of the most prominent doves, Ralph Yarborough of Texas, had already been defeated in the primary, and if one of 1970's eight Republican Senate candidates—Charles Goodell of New York, now one of the most outspoken critics of the war in either party—went under too, nobody at the White House would be heartbroken.

There was, of course, more to the campaign than raising money and putting Agnew in a chartered jet plane and sending him off around the country attacking the opposition. In mapping out the campaign, the White House team took inspiration from two political books, one intended to help the G.O.P., one not. A young 1968 campaign aide to John Mitchell named Kevin Phillips had written a tome called *The Emerging Republican Majority,* in which he professed to see in the demographics of the country the makings of a new era of conservative Republicanism. He based his optimism on the growth of an essentially white middle-class society settling in a great arc from the South through the Southwest to California—a sweeping "Sun Belt" of self-centered affluence whose determination to hold on to what it had could be nurtured into an era of conservative political power. This "emerging Republican majority" bore a striking resemblance to Spiro Agnew's "great silent majority" and to Richard Nixon's "forgotten Americans" of the 1968 campaign, whose concerns were a roll call of the contact points of the Nixon-Chotiner-Agnew attack strategy, summed up in the catch phrase "law and order." The book became required reading in the Nixon Administration.

The unintended inspiration came from a book that by design or not constituted a Democratic reply to Phillips. Written by Richard M. Scammon, former chief of the U.S. Bureau of Census, and Ben J. Wattenberg, a speech writer for Lyndon Johnson, it was called *The Real Majority* as an obvious counter to Phillips' title. Its central message was that the deciding vote in American politics was not in any newly emerging bloc on the right, but smack in the center. In contrast to Phillips' ponderous style, Scammon and Wattenberg took the reader through their unsurprising theory in a breezy and simplified fashion that entertained as it sought to instruct. The operative phrase in their book was "the Social Issue"— what everyone else since the Goldwater campaign had been calling "law and order." "The Social Issue" meant how voters reacted to elements in their social community—questions of race, crime, attitudes toward youth, and so on. The voters, said Scammon and Wattenberg, were not being bigots or racists or rednecks when they expressed concern about the real problems that emerged from these areas. The winning candidate had to address himself to this widespread, central concern in a responsible way, and in the prevailing climate had to take the Social Issue away from the Republicans or go under. They called on Democrats to undertake a drive "to the center" by accepting the public concern about the Social Issue as valid and responding to it. They also noted that another governing factor in elections, "the Economic Issue"—pocketbook politics—could overshadow the Social Issue, and they urged the Democrats to make use of it in 1970.

Naturally, the Scammon-Wattenberg book fell into Republican hands early. In the minds of the White House campaign strategists, it confirmed the course outlined for the fall—to jam the Social Issue down the Democrats' throats from Maine to California. Nixon himself always had preferred occupying the center of the political spectrum to risking the isolation of one of the wings; he often referred to himself as a "centrist." His 1968 Republican nomination had been fashioned by occupying and broadening the central ground between Reagan and Rockefeller, his 1968 election by holding the middle against Humphrey on the left and Wallace on the right. He wanted an emerging Republican majority, all right, but he intended to carve it out of the center, easing the center over to the right, no doubt, but expanding it against the extremes on either side. In Scammon-Wattenberg politics, which was essentially common-sense, if followship, politics, this was the way a "real majority" was built. If there was going to be a battle for the center in 1970, Nixon knew how it would have to be undertaken by the Republicans; not by moving much themselves, but by painting the Democrats as extremists on the left, thereby making the right-of-center Nixon Administration seem more moderate by contrast. If a Democrat was a moderate, call him a liberal; if he was a liberal, call him a radical; if he was an "intellectual," call him both.

In his precampaign sessions with his wordsmiths, Buchanan and Safire, the Vice-President played around with the proper phraseology for nailing the Democrats, and maybe a few Republicans too, with the extremist label. Because the Republican party by every yardstick remained the minority party, Kevin Phillips notwithstanding, it was important to play down the party label and talk in terms of conservative and liberal, or preferably, radical. "Radical" was such a good all-purpose denigrator; it conjured up images of bearded hippies making and throwing bombs, of "effete" academics blissfully giving secrets to the Communists, of obscenity-shouting students waving the Viet Cong flag and calling policemen "pigs."

But "radical" was also an old word, without particular identification with Agnew or the impending effort to purge the Senate liberals. How about some distinguishing combination? Agnew, Buchanan and Safire toyed with several, including "radillectuals," but that somehow didn't come off. Why not just "radical-liberals"? As with any good political slogan, this one said everything and nothing. Agnew liked it, started using it, and according to one of the speech writers, "later shortened it to 'radiclibs' himself." But did Agnew, who always boasted that "my words are my own," actually think up this most famous of labels he slapped on the opposition? "Well," says another of the speech writers, "I think we have to say he was the author. There were a number of ideas and thoughts, but that was the one he opted for, and the genesis of it doesn't make that much difference."

White House thinking for the 1970 campaign was so well advanced that on August 6, before Agnew's Asian trip and a full month before he was to hit the trail, he was able to announce some details of what he called "the traditional role of a Vice-President of the United States during the off-year-election season" —meaning, of course, the Nixon tradition. "Most especially," he said, in what was a tip-of-the-iceberg comment, "I will be urging the election of a more responsible Congress that will help—rather than frustrate—President Nixon's efforts to do what he promised the American people in 1968 he would do." The President, he said, "has promised to give me his maximum personal assistance in this undertaking." And because of the scope of the job, he had "asked the President to increase the normal availability to me of members of the White House staff"—Harlow, Buchanan, Safire, Anderson and Lamar Alexander, a Nixon staff assistant. Agnew had a way with words, but no matter how he put this arrangement, he could not obscure the clear evidence that this operation was being run out of the West Wing—the power center in the White House.

Agnew came out of the chute fast. On September 10 he met with Nixon at the White House, then headed out on his Boeing

727 jet, chartered by the Republican National Committee, for Springfield, Illinois, the first of six states he would visit in seven days. Making the trip were twenty-two staff members and an equal number of Secret Service men, plus a press entourage of about thirty, all of whom had their baggage carefully X-rayed before boarding the plane. At noon on the steps of the state capitol, Agnew spoke to four thousand persons in behalf of Republican Senator Ralph Smith, rated an underdog against Democrat Adlai Stevenson III, son of the two-time Democratic presidential candidate. He declared his remarks the start of a "national campaign to determine the leadership of the seventies . . . a second critical phase in the historic contest begun in the fall of 1968—a contest between the remnants of the discredited elite that dominated national policy for forty years and a new national majority, forged and led by the President of the United States—a contest to shape the destiny of America. . . .

"As the stream of contemptuous commentary has poured forth from America's old elite, small wonder it has been embraced by the disgruntled who seek the reason for personal failure everywhere but in themselves. The objective, then, of this campaign as in 1968 is not simply to win or hold offices; it is also to give America a new leadership of faith, courage and optimism. It is to replace those who moan endlessly about what is wrong with their country with men and women of the wit and will to stand up and speak out for what is right about America."

If the encouragement of faith, courage and optimism were to be the objectives of Agnew's 1970 campaign, it was doomed to failure from the start, because from the moment he uttered those words he was off on an odyssey of divisiveness and personal vilification seldom matched in recent times. Ralph Smith had to be returned to the Senate, the Vice-President said, "because your country just cannot afford any more ultraliberals in the United States Senate. There was a time when the liberalism of the old elite was a venturesome and fighting philosophy—the vanguard political dogma of a Franklin Roosevelt, a Harry Truman, a John Kennedy. But the old firehorses are long gone. Today's breed of radical-liberal posturing about the Senate is about as closely related to a Harry Truman as a Chihuahua is to a timber wolf."

There it all was, in the first mouthful. For loyal downstate readers of the Chicago *Tribune*, it must have been a shock indeed to hear Franklin Roosevelt, Harry Truman and John Kennedy thus elevated. But before you could castigate someone as a radical-liberal, you had to say what a plain old liberal was, who in retrospect, Agnew was saying now, was not such a bad guy. But, he elaborated, "ultraliberalism today translates into a whimpering isolationism in foreign policy, a mulish obstructionism in domestic policy and a pusillanimous pussyfooting on the critical issue of law and order." Throw in a word to connote cowardice, like "whimpering," a big word or two, season it all with outrageous alliteration—just for fun, of course—and *voilà!* Grilled radical-liberal.

Agnew heaped it on: "The troglodytic leftists who dominate Congress . . . the tired irrelevant liberalism that made the Ninety-first Congress a citadel of reaction; . . . Rejected and written off by the old elite, the workingman has become the cornerstone of the New Majority." On pornography and crime: "How do you fathom the thinking of these 'radical-liberals' [now in quotation marks] who work themselves into a lather over an alleged shortage of nutriments in a child's box of Wheaties—but who cannot get exercised at all over that same child's constant exposure to a flood of hard-core pornography that could warp his moral outlook for a lifetime. It's high time these ultraliberals put *their* priorities in order." On the economy: "It is about the economy that the weeping and wailing of the congressional left wing has been loudest—and least convincing." On the press: "If any of you are regular readers of the liberal Eastern press—the organ-grinders of the old elite—you will probably read on your editorial pages tomorrow, 'That terrible Mr. Agnew has done it again.' Don't let this bother you as, assuredly, it does not bother me. When you have been head-to-head with our Korean ally for six hours of tough negotiation, you are not likely to be stampeded off the range by an editorial writer for the Washington *Post*. Let them run right up the wall. We are going to be out with the other 'happy warriors' on the campaign trail this fall, roasting marshmallows along the way."

Shortening the label now to "radiclib," Agnew noted that young Adlai Stevenson had blamed the riots of the 1968 Democratic convention on denial of public parks "for peaceful assembly and peaceful protest" and had called the Chicago police "storm troopers in blue." Said Agnew: "Any public official, especially from the state of Illinois, who still believes the riots at the Chicago convention were the result of 'denying parks for peaceful protest' has no business in the United States Senate. Any individual who, in these times, will slander the men of the Chicago police force by calling them 'storm troopers in blue' ought to be retired from public life."

With his assault on Stevenson's "storm troopers in blue" comment, the Vice-President was on the mark. The Democrats reacted defensively. Former Vice-President Hubert Humphrey, seeking election to the Senate in Minnesota with Ben Wattenberg on his writing staff, peddled hard the Scammon-Wattenberg pitch for Democrats to get right on the Social Issue. Also, Democratic National Chairman Lawrence O'Brien attacked extremists in his own party ranks. Word of the latter remarks was flashed to the Agnew plane. At the next stop, in Casper, Wyoming, the Vice-President inserted in his speech a warning against radical-liberals "trying to pull the fastest switcheroo in American politics" by taking a new, get-tough line on law and order.

Not all Democrats running for the Senate, of course, were radiclibs. In Wyoming, one of Nixon's most strenuous supporters on Vietnam, Democratic Senator Gale McGee, was up for re-election against Republican Representative John Wold, who had been persuaded by the President to oppose him as part of the critical Senate challenge. Agnew solved the problem by not mentioning McGee by name, but pointing out that his re-election "would help to guarantee that those who oppose the President up and down the line in Congress stay in their positions of majority power. . . . A vote for John Wold is therefore a vote for new leadership of the Senate Foreign Relations Committee." The argument was a weak and punchless one compared to Agnew's harangue against Stevenson. The voters apparently thought so, too; they returned McGee in November. In most places, though, the Vice-President found clear-cut ideological targets.

From Casper the Agnew entourage went to Southern California for one speech and a leisurely weekend. Like the Nixon and Agnew campaigns of 1968, this one was carefully mapped out to avoid overtaxing the star, to take maximum advantage of television and to give the press only one mouthful of news at a time to chew on. It had been a cardinal principle of the Nixon strategists in 1968 to avoid giving the press multiple choice about what they would write. Instead of the traditional morning-to-night stumping, with perhaps six or eight speeches—and an exhausted candidate, he spoke once or maybe twice before a crowd all day. The main appearance usually was in morning or midday, to provide time for film or tape to be processed and sent east for the network evening news shows. In 1970 the same procedure was observed, with one exception. Agnew also had an important fund-raising function to perform, so evening speeches at party dinners were scheduled. But as in Springfield, he tried to get the "red meat" out early so it could be packaged by the TV newsmen and served to Middle America's viewers at dinnertime.

The Springfield speech, which introduced the Nixon-Agnew strategy and its catch phrase to public and press, gave the reporters a big mouthful to chew on over the weekend. Who, exactly, were these radiclibs Agnew was talking about? Stevenson obviously was one, but who were the others? Were they to go through the campaign as phantoms, castigated collectively, or would Agnew provide a shopping list? The newsmen inquired of Agnew's aides and received coy assurances that when the time came, they would have no doubts. In the theater of political attack, suspense also had its role.

In San Diego the next night, at a $125-a-plate party dinner, Agnew hit out at four "professional pessimists" among the Democrats—Senators Fulbright, Edward M. Kennedy, Joseph M. Montoya, seeking re-election in New Mexico, and Democratic National Chairman O'Brien. Also, Agnew aides had heard that the Democratic Senate candidate, Representative John Tunney, of late had taken to riding around—and being seen—in police cars. The Vice-President threw him in as a "Tunney-come-lately" to the law-and-order issue. He observed: "In the United States today, we have more than our share of the nattering nabobs of negativism. . . . [They] have formed their own Four-H Club—the hopeless, hysterical hypochondriacs of history." Nor did he talk about Democrats only. "Any candidate of any party who voices radical sentiments or who enjoys the support of radical elements ought to be voted out of office by the American people," he said. Now, who might that mean? Reporters asked the White House aides and were told that the Vice-President meant, of course, Goodell, the only liberal among the Senate Republicans seeking re-election. Agnew believed, one White House aide said, that it was necessary to include Republicans in his attack on radiclibs to establish the credibility of his charges against the Democrats. The reference proved to be the opening shot in what would be the most controversial skirmish in the Nixon-Agnew battle plan of 1970.

In that battle plan, Nixon left the words to the masters, but he gave them the music. At one pre-campaign meeting with them he had made it clear that he wanted a free-swinging, Harry Truman-type campaign. "What I came away with," one of the speech writers said later, "was the idea that the Vice-President would go on the campaign trail in a manner reminiscent of Al Smith and Harry Truman, smiting the opposition hip and thigh, frankly and openly partisan, and enjoying the campaign. That's why you'll find in many of Agnew's speeches references to the Happy Warrior—Al Smith."

Early in the campaign, this aide recalled, a local paper in a town in the Midwest noted that twenty-two years earlier Truman had come through on his whistlestop campaign. The speech writer tore out the item and handed it to Agnew, who then told his audience, "Harry Truman always used to say, whenever anybody said 'Give 'em hell': 'I never give 'em hell, I just tell the truth and they think it's hell.' That was a big applause line and it characterized his visit there—that of the lusty, happy warrior out on the campaign carrying his cause to the people."

Happy warrior? Spiro Agnew? The speech writer saw no irony in the comparison. Of the Vice-President's performance, he said, "There was no element of viciousness or meanness in it, or intended to be. Quite the contrary, the use of alliteration, for example, was slightly tongue-in-cheek. You can't use 'nattering nabobs of negativism' with enormous seriousness. You can use it mock seriously. It was our counterpart to 'prophets of gloom and doom'—Stevenson's line. I gave him that one, and 'hopeless hysterical hypochondriacs of history'—the new Four-H Club. James Reston called it the worst alliteration in American political history. But that's what we were after. I gave the Vice-President both of those and asked him which one he wanted to use, and he said, 'Oh, hell, let's use 'em both.' When you use that kind of exaggerated hyperbole or alliteration in a speech, obviously you intend it to be humorous, and it was received humorously by the audience —and taken seriously by some people who felt it was intended seriously and was rough stuff."

To underline that it was all meant to be a joke, the speech writers had a large *Webster's Dictionary* placed on the plane for the reporters' use. "This was all fairly conscious. It's amusing, titillating, interesting, exciting; to give writers color and bite in speeches. That's how you get a lead, that's how you get attention. And above all, in a good-natured fashion. That was the idea. We weren't being quasi-intellectual when we used a big word. We didn't say, 'Here comes a big word.' He made fun of himself, but what he was doing there was calling attention to his message, and the alliteration and the big words captured exactly what we intended. Then the press went overboard on them. After they did that, you just leave it and do something else."

If Agnew and his writers meant the Vice-President's rhetoric to be one big joke, that intention was never transmitted to the reporters who traveled with them, nor—more importantly—to the thousands of citizens who gathered to hear him or to the millions who heard him on radio and television. What came across was that Agnew was being very serious indeed, and the individual targets of his sweeping harangues and personal attacks didn't see much jest in them either. The rationale for Agnew's rhetoric reflected the same insensitivity that the man himself had demonstrated repeatedly in the 1968 campaign and throughout his year of vituperative attack on the nonestablishment in 1969. The idea that you figuratively could knock a man down, kick him, suggest that he was a traitor to his country, then smile and say you were only kidding, indicated at best naïveté about public discourse, at worst brutality.

On Saturday morning, September 12, the Vice-President went off to Palm Springs by helicopter to play golf, leaving the press in San Diego to play "Who's the Radiclib?" In the course of eighteen holes in 100-degree heat, he decided he'd have a press conference to pique their curiosity further, so the press was piled into buses and driven across the desert—a six-hour round trip—for the twenty-minute session. Under intense badgering, Agnew refused to identify any of the radiclibs specifically by name. "I want to keep your interest alive," he said, but the list was about seven or eight names long, including "a Republican or two."

Radical-liberals, Agnew explained, were members of Congress

who "applaud our enemies and castigate our friends and run down the capacity of the American government . . . who seek to overthrow tradition, whether or not it is effective, and whether their solutions are workable or not, and seek to write all solutions on the most unusual periphery of American opinion. They never look to our historic system for their solutions, but to some dramatic, theatrical, attention-getting device which will not work, but provides good copy." For all that, Agnew cautioned the press, he did not "impugn their patriotism," nor was he "calling for a congression investigation. . . . What I impugn is their judgment, which I think is perfectly horrible . . . and so I call on the majority of the people to turn them out of office." While many of them were engaged in a "rush toward the center, they aren't really fooling anybody . . . and I'm going to blow the whistle on them."

Agnew did promise to name the radiclibs shortly. As for including Goodell, he said, the senator "has requested that neither President Nixon nor I appear in New York for him or anyone else," and he would "probably discuss that particular matter" later in the campaign. He would, he said, "have to make a future judgment" on whether he might endorse James Buckley, the Conservative party opposition to Goodell in New York's three-man race.

It was all, of course, a fun game. One of the more comical diversions came as Agnew headed back east, stopping first at Las Vegas. Landing at the airport, he told a thousand schoolchildren bussed out to greet him that they needed "a Congress that will see to it that the wave of permissiveness, the wave of pornography and the wave of moral pollution never become the wave of the future in our country." Then he drove into town, past garish hotel marquees that proclaimed: WELCOME VICE PRESIDENT AGNEW —KENO—POKER; THE NOW YEAR—FOLIES BERGERE—WELCOME VICE PRESIDENT AGNEW and ALL YOU CAN DRINK, $2.25.

At a $100-a-couple rally at the Frontier Hotel, he told a thousand good Republican citizens of Las Vegas that the country was going to hell because of—drugs. Rock songs, movies, books and underground newspapers all were brainwashing American youth into a "drug culture . . . a depressing life style of conformity that has neither life nor style." Part of the blame, Agnew proclaimed—in one of the great fun, games, booze, skin and vice capitals of the land—rested with "pill-popping" parents and "growing adult alcoholism," which led some youngsters "to do some experimenting on their own." But the real villains, he said, were the rock songwriters and the media outlets that were pushing their lyrical wares. He quoted the Beatles song that goes, "I get by with a little help from my friends, I get high with a little help from my friends." It was "a catchy tune," he said, "but until it was pointed out to me, I never realized that the 'friends' were assorted drugs." And who would have guessed, he said, that the title "Lucy in the Sky with Diamonds" really stood for LSD? Also, there was the movie (*Easy Rider*, apparently) that promoted as heroes "two men who are able to live a carefree life off the proceeds of illegal sales of drugs." Some members of the news media were warning against drug abuse, Agnew said, but "far too many producers and editors are still succumbing to the temptation of the sensational and playing right into the hands of the drug culture." Maybe he would be accused of "advocating song censorship," the Vice-President acknowledged, but had his audience—including those listening on a statewide TV hookup—"really heard the words of some of these songs?"

The first radiclib after Stevenson to be called one fairly straight out was Senator Philip Hart of Michigan. At an airport rally in Saginaw, Agnew was blessed with an assemblage of bearded, raucous protesters standing under a banner that said: IMPUDENT SNOBS UNITE HERE. When Hart's Republican opponent, Mrs. Lenore Romney, tried to introduce the Vice-President her voice was drowned out by their obscenities. Agnew stepped up, tense, and said into amplifiers turned up full volume, "That's exactly what we're running against in this country today. With enemies like that, how can we lose? . . . You people out there preach a lot about dissent. But you're afraid to tolerate dissent. You're afraid of other points of view because you don't have the strength of your convictions. And you're not intellectual; you're intellectually stagnant."

"Agnew is a social disease," the protesters replied in a steady chant. Agnew stopped, listened, then waved his hand as if conducting them. "You're pathetic," he said finally, turning his attention to Hart. His defeat, he said, would "help rescue the Democratic party from radical-liberals so that America can stand safe and secure in this dangerous world."

. . .

The Agnew entourage returned buoyant from this first cross-country campaign trip. In about a week's time, the Vice-President had nailed the opposition with a label that everybody already understood—as much as it meant anything and was intended to lend understanding. He had thrown the Democrats on the defensive about crime, violence, protest—"the Social Issue"—and thus had successfully established the "attack" posture for himself and Republican candidates everywhere. As the Democrats now scrambled to get off the extreme-left wing on which Agnew had pushed them, he was right there pushing them back out again. When Ted Kennedy addressed students at Boston University and urged them to reject violence, Agnew called him a "Kennedy-come-lately" (later familiarized to "Teddy-come-lately"); he told a G.O.P. rally for Stanley Blair, his old lieutenant running an impossible race for governor in Maryland, "Look around the country and you'll see what I mean. Kennedy-come-latelies speaking for law and order. They all take their polls and then decide what they think that week. They're all rushing toward the center now, where the President of the United States has been since you elected him."

The Nixon staff was surprised at how rapidly the Vice-President was able to establish the issue and seize the offensive posture. Even after 1968, some had underestimated their own ability to generate the kind of press they wanted. "We didn't apprehend well enough," one Nixon lieutenant said later of the 1970 effort, "what we did know in 1968. Being in power, the Vice-President can command a kind of media attention that is just incredible when you consider what the President [Nixon] was trying to get out in 1966." The aide recalled those days, four years earlier, when private citizen Nixon campaigned for congressional candidates. "Sometimes there was only one correspondent along. We'd get two sticks of type; no television. But this was the Vice-President. Every night he's on nationwide television; *Life* magazine's got a cover on him; you've got a planeload of correspondents there, and you don't realize the whomp-whomp, the intensity of that thing. So what happened was, we made the issue in about six or seven days. Adlai Stevenson got an American flag lapel pin on; Teddy Kennedy's talking about 'campus commandoes'; Jack Tunney's getting in and out of police cars on the Coast.

They all shifted themselves and talked about war records. That was successful; we made our issue. We're the party in power, yet we went on the offensive; we had to, because we were trying to oust guys from the Senate, and we threw them on the defensive. But the thing was, then they rearranged their advertising campaign, their issues campaign personally, they defensed it all the way down the line, and fairly effectively. They blunted the issue we wanted to draw."

In doing so, however, the Democrats invited the charge of opportunism, and before they were able to bolster their defense, Agnew was on the road again, this time taking dead aim on the major targets among Senate Democrats. Perhaps the prime opponent of all was veteran Senator Gore in Tennessee, a genuine and powerful liberal critic of the Vietnam war and opponent of the Supreme Court nominations of Southern judges Haynsworth and Carswell. A full year earlier, the White House had set its sights on Gore's seat and had encouraged a hard-hitting young conservative, Republican Representative Bill Brock, to take him on. Ken Reitz, the youngest partner of Harry Treleaven, Nixon's own media mastermind of 1968, was dispatched to Tennessee, where for a year he built the organization for Brock's bid. Agnew anointed the sharp and expensive operation in the third week in September at a mass rally in Memphis.

One of the prominent Tennesseeans to greet the Vice-President was Gore himself, trailing and desperate for all the free television time he could get. "I was happy to see Senator Gore here," Agnew told reporters. "It's in the tradition of civility in politics." Then, presumably in the same tradition, he went downtown and accused Gore of consorting with—not being one of—the Senate's radical-liberals. Agnew called Tennessee's senior senator "for all intents and purposes Southern regional chairman of the Eastern liberal establishment. . . . You do not see him bringing down to Memphis the radical-liberal friends he hobnobs with up in Manhattan and Georgetown, because those friends would not sit very well with the people of Tennessee." Of Gore's votes against Haynsworth and Carswell, he said, "Be aware, citizens of Tennessee, that the assault on these judges was aided and abetted by your own senator. He found the temptation to be loved by his Washington and Manhattan friends irresistible, and he found his obligations to the citizens of Tennessee secondary to his liberal community credentials." Agnew disclaimed that he was challenging the "patriotism or sincerity" of Gore. "Indeed, he is most sincere in his mistaken belief that Tennessee is located somewhere between the *New York Times* and the Greenwich *Village Voice.*"

Earlier, in a Memphis studio, the Vice-President was asked by an interviewer whether jokes about Spiro Agnew watches and the like "get to you a little bit." He answered, "No, they really don't. And I have to admit that I've gotten very callous and hardened to those things, because I'm not an uncertain man. I think that what I'm doing is right. I'm totally committed to the course that I'm following." (Agnew was also asked about the possibility he might be dropped from the ticket in 1972. "It wouldn't disturb me in the slightest," he said. ". . . All I'm 'trying to do is do the best job of being Vice-President that I can do, and that means supporting the President. We intend to re-elect President Nixon. Now, whether I'm part of that or not is virtually unimportant because the President is the important office.")

Anyone traveling with Agnew into the dens of the radical-liberals could not have had the slightest doubt of the man's certainty and commitment. He attacked with the same air of righteousness that had marked his public conduct since his zoning-board days in Towson. From Memphis he went to Indianapolis, where he administered the same treatment to another prime Administration target, Senator Vance Hartke. Identifying him only as "the senior senator from Indiana," and not saying he *was* a radical-liberal, Agnew charged that Hartke "has proudly voted with the radical-liberals of the Senate in their unsuccessful attempts to cut off funds for the war in Vietnam and pull out American troops in a way that would surely sow the seeds of future wars." He called Hartke's associates "this little band of obstructionists and isolationists" and said Hartke "has taken a stand with the radical-liberals on the side of permissiveness. . . . He represents some people in Berkeley, California, some people in Madison, Wisconsin, and some people at Columbia University in New York [all scenes of recent campus revolt]—and he does *not* represent the view of the people of Indiana."

In Indianapolis, Agnew took his guessing game one step further into the realm of the ridiculous by noting that a "far-out foreign policy adviser" of Hartke's, a "New York adviser and fund raiser," had come into the city, met privately with Democrats and had said in a subsequent statement that an end to America's involvement in Vietnam would strengthen its "voice for peace in the Middle East." Said Agnew, "That sort of topsy-turvy reasoning is absolute poppycock. But your present senior senator has not repudiated it in any way, and we must assume he agrees with it." Who, a reporter asked Safire, was the mystery visitor from New York? It was, Safire said, Harriman, quoted in a local newspaper. Well, why not say it was Harriman? "Because it is in the tradition of political discourse not to name your opponent," Safire replied. But Harriman was not running for any office. Safire insisted that the nonidentification was traditional, and that nothing was implied by calling him a "New York adviser" in ultraconservative, notoriously anti-Eastern establishment Hoosierland.

Agnew's Indianapolis speech, televised throughout the state without cost to the G.O.P., grossed $460,700 for the state party, according to Dr. Earl L. Butz, the state finance chairman (later Nixon's second Secretary of Agriculture). It brought the total Agnew had raised since Labor Day to more than $1 million.

The final stop of Agnew's second swing was Milwaukee, where the local radiclib, Democratic Senator William Proxmire, was considered unbeatable. Instead of a rerun of the bare-knuckle, patronizing anti-Gore, anti-Hartke pitches to Middle America, the Vice-President this time spelled out his campaign objective in loftier, less personal terms. "My mission," he said, "is to awaken Americans to the need for sensible authority, to jolt good minds out of the lethargy of habitual acquiescence, to mobilize a silent majority that cherishes the right values but has been bulldozed for years into thinking those values are embarrassingly out of style." He conceded that sometimes he used "colorful language" because "you cannot awaken people with a whisper. . . . A call to intellectual combat cannot be issued by a flute. It needs a trumpet." The trouble with America, he said, was that "during the past generation, a philosophy of permissiveness has permeated American life. . . . We have gone through a debilitating, enervating age of indulgence." And with youth, he said, part of the problem was "the hero-villain lineup. . . . To many of us, and especially to many young people, the world appears divided into good guys and bad guys. If somebody is not with you all the way, he is against you."

The speaker was, of course, the same man who in the previous two weeks had crisscrossed the country separating bad guys from good; the same man who played transparently on local prejudices and stereotyped Mid-American impressions of the evils of "Manhattan and Georgetown," in a manner worthy of George Wallace and his sly backwoods references to "Harvard pointy-headed intellectuals and Washington bureaucrats." But the best was yet to come. The trumpet that was summoning the silent majority to intellectual combat was about to call on the faithful to separate out the No. 1 Bad Guy of the 1970 campaign—the terrible and awesome Senator Charles E. Goodell, Republican of New York.

19

GOOD-BYE CHARLIE

A politician can always generate a laugh at a colleague's rally by offering to speak for or against him, whichever will help most. The line is among the most tired of political gags but it lives on, perhaps because it touches on the eternal willingness of the public to believe that politics really is a dirty, or at least only modestly principled, game. In his similarly eternal quest to be accepted as a regular guy, even Richard Nixon has invoked the old turkey for the laughs that come so hard to him. Yet extremely rare is the occasion when a politician is so Machiavellian that he actually will speak out against a friend with the intention of creating a backlash reaction that will help that friend.

In the Administration's 1970 drive to gain control of the Senate, however, Nixon and Agnew produced a new wrinkle. Agnew would speak out against an undesirable (the party's nominee in New York, Senator Charles E. Goodell), but just enough to create sympathy and a switch of sufficient liberal votes to him from the Democratic candidate (Representative Richard L. Ottinger) to ensure the victory of the Administration's own choice—the third contender (Conservative candidate James L. Buckley). The initial "beneficiary"—and ultimate victim—of the three-way ploy, Senator Goodell, was appointed by Governor Rockefeller in 1968 to complete the unexpired term of the late Senator Robert F. Kennedy. Goodell, one of the bright young Republican stars in the House, a solid conservative on most issues who was rising rapidly within the party leadership ranks, had undergone a remarkable transformation in the Senate. Exposed to a statewide constituency for the first time—and dependent on it for re-election—he had shifted almost overnight, both politically and stylistically. Although his record of support for the Nixon Administration on domestic affairs was as good as most, his apostasy showed glaringly in his position on the Vietnam war. He became one of its most bitter and sweeping critics, proposing early withdrawal of American troops and joining forces with a few other Republicans as well as a growing number of Democrats in the Senate.

A quiet, pipe-smoking, conservatively dressed middle-roader in the House, Charlie Goodell soon became a member of the Now Generation—long hair, lively striped shirts, fat ties, and suits with wide lapels. The cynics on Capitol Hill—and they constituted a small army—concluded at once that Charlie had taken a hard look at his broadened constituency, in which Manhattan now loomed much larger than his native Jamestown, and had acted accordingly. Concerning his dress, it was perhaps a valid conclusion; his strong views on the war, however, had evolved at a time many Americans, disheartened and skeptical of U.S. policy, were joining the peace movement with conviction. As a critic of Vietnam, Goodell spoke with an intensity that grew out of a personal soul-searching, and those who wrote him off as no more than an opportunist on this issue did not properly gauge his commitment.

One who did, however, was Richard Nixon. The President had a professional politician's respect for Charlie Goodell's performance in the House and for his mind, and that was all the more reason to regret his switch on the war, and his endless sniping on the issue in the Senate. But Goodell was, after all, a Republican, and as such preferable to the Democrat running against him, an equally vociferous Vietnam critic, Representative Richard Ottinger. At least Goodell would vote with the G.O.P. on organizing the next Senate.

In August, when the White House political strategists began discussing the fall campaign in detail with the President, it became increasingly likely that Goodell was going to lose. There had been some hope at the White House that a Nixon supporter on the war could be found to run against him in the Republican primary, but Goodell pressed hard and early for a commitment from Rockefeller, and once he got that, primary opposition faded. Nevertheless, there was enough conservative sentiment within the state party and within the state itself to make Goodell's prospects for re-election exceedingly dim. The Republican party, in spite of Rockefeller's three straight terms and prospects for a fourth, continued to be on the short end of voter registration in New York State. Of growing influence in the picture was the Conservative party, which in the 1960's had given Republicans at war with Rockefeller and blue-collar Democrats disenchanted with liberal trends a place to go. The party had been a vehicle for a hopeless but happy romp by columnist William F. Buckley, Jr., in the 1965 mayoralty race, but since then it had grown beyond the status of a joke or a haven for political cranks. Now Bill Buckley's brother Jim, who had lost one Senate bid as the Conservative candidate in 1968, decided to make it a three-way race for the Senate, encouraged by the outspoken displeasure of many Republicans with the new Charlie Goodell.

Running under the Conservative banner, Buckley could forthrightly declare himself the Nixon candidate in the race, though the President was obliged by G.O.P. orthodoxy and his own track record of party loyalty to support, at least nominally, the Republican nominee. A basic element in Richard Nixon's political success was his party regularity. In the dark days of the party's eclipse after the Goldwater debacle, he had preached and implemented a policy of party unity at all costs. Ideology had to be shelved and the party revived with the election of Republicans and more Republicans, of all shapes, sizes and convictions. But now, of course, the party was not simply breathing again but was robust, with an opportunity, or so the White House strategists convinced themselves, to make a historic breakthrough in party alignment by 1972. A strong Conservative party in New York could at a minimum exert pressures on the liberal Republican organization and should be encouraged, within realistic limits.

Goodell and Rockefeller, who also was up for re-election, made clear early in the campaign that they did not want either Nixon or Agnew going into New York. In the early White House discussions, the thinking therefore was that Agnew would indeed stay out of the state. There was little he could do; Goodell was going down the drain anyway at the hands of Ottinger, with Buckley running third.

As the campaign progressed, however, an odd phenomenon developed. Ottinger, who with a massive television campaign in the Democratic primary had sent his recognition factor skyrocketing, suddenly began to taper off. He had overdone a good thing; his spending itself became an issue, forcing him to adopt a low profile. At the same time Buckley, running an unabashed law-and-order campaign, began to climb, as Goodell made little impact. It began to look as if Buckley might finish second to Ottinger. The phenomenon was observed with interest at the White House and on the Agnew plane; the ghost of Niccolò Machiavelli began to rear its conniving head.

By the time the Vice-President had returned from his second campaign swing, reports from New York were impressive enough to warrant a bold move. The President, departing on a politically timely European tour, gave his blessing, under ground rules that were supposed to observe, for the record, the niceties of presidential party fealty. Republican National Chairman Rogers Morton, in a sop to Rockefeller, would go to New York, appear with Goodell and say a few kind words for him. Then, having thus thrown up the façade of Administration support, Morton would duck and run for cover. Next, the Vice-President would come wading in— strictly on his own, of course—and start belting Goodell, who he already had hinted was on his list of radical-liberals. Meanwhile the President, safely in Europe, could cry, "Who, me?" The purpose of the Agnew attack, however, would not be simply to rally anti-Goodell support to Buckley; the Conservative candidate already was doing quite well enough on his own. The hooker in the ploy was the expectation—well founded, it turned out—that the Agnew sledgehammer, applied in one of the very epicenters of radical-liberalism, would generate a wave of sympathy for poor old Charlie. It was an operation, for all its brutishness, that required a certain precision; just enough clout to cause a sufficient shift of liberals from Ottinger to Goodell to undercut Ottinger and permit Buckley to go ahead; not enough to make a galloping hero of Goodell, and thus elect him. The White House strategists were gleeful at the prospect of it all, and the chief executioner, Spiro T. Agnew, headed west for the third time primed to fire a long-range missile in the direction of New York—at the proper time.

His first stop was the small town of Minot, North Dakota, hardly the place to launch such a cunning gambit. Nor was

Agnew supposed to do so there. As the Vice-President headed westward, Morton was on his way to Rochester, New York, to provide the smoke screen that would enable President Nixon to maintain his reputation as the supporter of all Republicans, all the time. After that, there would be time enough to go after the victim.

Goodell, meanwhile, was trying to get his own Agnew-based sympathy wave started. Without knowledge that the boom was about to be lowered on him, he attacked the Vice-President for criticizing the recently released Scranton report on campus unrest, which Agnew had called "pablum for permissiveness." "Mr. Agnew has long been saying that it is the duty of men in public office to speak out against violence in our universities," Goodell said. "That is precisely what this report does—only the report, unlike the Vice-President, speaks in balanced and moderate language." At this point Goodell wanted to separate himself only from Agnew, not from Nixon. "In no conceivable sense is it [the Scranton report] scapegoating the President for a problem which, as we all know, has long antedated his accession to office," Goodell said. The President was "far ahead of Vice-President Agnew in exercising constructive leadership on the issue."

Back in Minot, Agnew was asked in a local television interview to identify any Republicans on his list of radiclibs. "Well," the Vice-President said, suddenly abandoning the pre-arranged timetable, "I'm not going to weasel on that question; I'm going to forthrightly say that I would have to put one Republican senator who seeks re-election this year in that group. That is Senator Goodell. . . . He has certainly proposed and stimulated the kind of leadership that encourages the dissident elements of our society. . . . Senator Goodell has left his party." There. He had said it. When you tell it like it is, you have to tell it like it is all the time. So what if Rog Morton was in Rochester placing the official mantle of party endorsement around Radiclib Charlie?

Morton, not surprisingly, was flabbergasted. The ax was not yet supposed to fall. In a joint press conference with Goodell, the national chairman said Agnew "spoke on his own." As for himself, Morton said of Goodell, "If he's a Republican in New York, he's a Republican with me. . . . I'm trying to develop a team. I'm trying to build a party. I'm looking at it from an entirely different point of view." Goodell, for his part, saw the development as the break he desperately needed. He was sure, he said, that "the people of New York will not allow Spiro Agnew to pull the lever for them in November."

From Minot, Agnew went on to Salt Lake City and let Goodell have it again: "When a man consistently opposes a President of his own party on the greatest issues of the day; when a man makes public opposition to all his party stands for a major article of his political faith; when a man also goes out of his way publicly to reject support of his President that has not yet been offered; when a man attempts to curry favor with his party's leading adversaries by gratuitous attack on many of his fellow party members—then I think that man has strayed beyond the point of no return." (Agnew did not leave' Salt Lake City without delivering two more of his more noteworthy phrases. He called demonstrators who chanted against him members of the "Spock-marked generation," and after interrupting his prepared speech several times to admonish them, he pleaded: "Please don't contribute to the kind of climate in this country that raises emotions beyond reason. . . . Listen, argue, debate, condemn where you must, but do it with your mind, not with your—butt.")

The attack on Goodell threw the party into temporary turmoil. Agnew confirmed the next day that he would go to New York in a few days to speak at a private fund-raising luncheon for New York candidates for national office supporting the Nixon Administration—meaning Buckley. In a press conference in Salt Lake City, Agnew said that in endorsing Goodell, Morton "has a little different job than I do—he's strictly a party functionary. Rogers Morton is there to elect Republican candidates, and as such, he has to be a party loyalist. . . . But I think there's a time when the Vice-President has to leave his party if he feels in good conscience he can't support its candidates. And that's what I'm doing." Some liberal, antiwar Republicans, like Senator Edward Brooke of Massachusetts, disagreed. Goodell, he noted, "is the nominee of the Republican party; he has the backing of the Republican governor of New York and the chairman of the Republican National Committee. It's obvious he has not left the party."

But Brooke was wasting his time. The purge effort was well under way. Some in the White House could not contain themselves; Murray Chotiner told a reporter that Agnew in his attack was also representing the President's views. Such a candid admission was not part of the game plan, but neither was the timing of Agnew's first outburst, while Morton still was at Goodell's bedside, assuring the patient of survival. As for Goodell, he refused at first to consider that the President was part of the plot to do him in. Nixon, he said, "was for me, [and] I still think he supports me." An even more naïve voice came from Capitol Hill, where the ever-trustful Republican Senate leader, Hugh Scott of Pennsylvania, offered: "I'll be glad when the President gets back. When the President is away, those who are not President are disposed to play."

At the heralded private luncheon in New York, Agnew did not endorse Buckley by name; he just said the other candidates were unacceptable. The supposed cuteness was in keeping with Agnew's curious idea of political civility—as if the victim's blood would not spurt out this way. Then he left the meeting without talking to reporters and hit the trail again in pursuit of Democratic radiclibs.

In Pittsburgh, the Vice-President made clear that Nixon himself was "the prime mover of our concerted effort to root out of positions of power those radical liberals who frustrate progress at home and undercut our efforts for an honorable peace abroad." And when Rockefeller disclosed he had called the White House and asked that the President keep Agnew out of New York, the Vice-President replied defiantly: "I want to emphasize here that I have no intention of—simply because of cries to quiet me—of being quieted. And I don't think the President has any intention of indicating any displeasure with what I've said so far." Speaking with the confidence of a man who had touched the necessary bases with his boss, which of course he had, he added: "I think the President is aware of the thrust of my remarks. He certainly hasn't condemned me for them or tried to modify them in any way. He leaves it up to me what I want to say." And to another question about presidential support: "That's something the President will have to answer. Let me put it this way—you notice I'm still talking."

He was indeed. In New Orleans, the scene of the "impudent snobs" crack, he met privately with newspaper editors and delivered his most brutal remark of all. "If you look at the statements Mr. Goodell made during his time in the House and compare them with some of the statements I have been referring to,"

he told the editors in what he believed was an off-the-record comment, "you will find he is truly the Christine Jorgensen of the Republican party."

Surprisingly, this equating of the senator from New York with
the first person known to have undergone surgery for a change of
sex in Denmark created little reaction at first. Some reporters accompanying Agnew did not even mention it in their stories.
Rockefeller's chief political adviser, George Hinman, did hear
about it, however, and sent a telegram to Agnew in care of the
White House. "It is a matter of the deepest regret to one who is
bound to our party and to our national Administration by deep ties
of friendship and loyalty," Hinman wired him, "to have our proud
banner so lightly dipped in filth against another Republican
whose only offense is an independent view of the issues of life and
death in our time. Reasonable men can and do differ on Senator
Goodell, but no fair-minded person can do anything but deplore
your references to him today in New Orleans."

Christine Jorgensen didn't like it either. She too sent Agnew a
telegram complaining that "the blatant use of my name in connection with your political feud with Senator Charles Goodell is
not only unfair but totally unjustified. I am proud that I was born
a U.S. citizen and I resent the implication that I am in any way
lending aid to radicals or any subversive groups. It is contrary to
my personal conviction. I request that some effort be made to correct these wrongful impressions." And in an interview in Hollywood, she expressed her views of the Vice-President. "Mr. Agnew
in the past couple of months has been rather too much a bull in a
china shop, striking out at anyone and using a form of comedy
which I don't think is appropriate to his office. I've felt at various
times after reading his remarks, 'My goodness, we have a clown
in the White House, and this man is one breath from the Presidency.' The first trait of comedy is to be able to laugh at oneself,
but I don't like being used as a political pawn. Playing with the
masculine-feminine thing is old comedy material but I think it's
completely tasteless when it comes from so high an office. I don't
think dirty politics is necessary." Asked if she planned legal action, Miss Jorgensen said, "No, there's a certain immunity to the
Vice-Presidency, and you have to prove malicious intent. I don't
think it was malicious. It think it was said to be kind of smart
aleck. You know, I think he has a problem that many writers

have, me included. He falls in love with his own words. I think Mr. Agnew has a case of the 'cutes,' and I think there are many Americans who don't care for it."

Calling for "a politics of reconciliation, not vituperation," Goodell challenged Agnew to a debate. "I'm challenged to debates every day," the Vice-President replied. "I guess I'd be debating all the time if I listened to those requests." Miss Jorgensen's demand for an apology likewise got short shrift. "This is one of the most widely publicized lives in our history," Agnew said of her. "And publicized in a calculated way. Publicized not by accident. Therefore, I think that that publicity, even publicity to the extent of promoting a motion picture on this life, puts the life in a public domain. I don't feel that, because it is in the public domain, it is any more than a calculated additional attempt at publicity that the subject has come up. . . . When a person seeks that kind of publicity, that person has to be expected to be speculated about, conjectured about and commented about." Somehow, it sounded as if Christine Jorgensen had started it all by comparing herself to Charlie Goodell.

While the Goodell controversy simmered, Agnew went blissfully about his business of assailing radiclibs. In Texas, where the resident radiclib, Senator Ralph Yarborough, already had been disposed of in the Democratic primary, he stumped for Republican Representative George Bush, running for Yarborough's seat, and for Paul Eggers, the G.O.P. gubernatorial candidate. In the face of the solidly Democratic state legislature, Agnew made an elaborate case for divided party responsibility in the executive and legislative branches—the precise condition nationally that he was saying was ruining the country! The split, he said, created "a constructive adversary climate" because "if you have a government that's dominated by one party, you have tranquillity politically, but tranquillity doesn't mean that people are totally aware of what's going on in government. It generally means just the opposite. It means that too many things are happening behind the scenes in closed decision without the knowledge of the media or the people of the state. When you have an adversary political climate even though it may slow . . . the implementation of reform and programs, it does assure that they receive the fullest debate and consideration, and it does assure that the poor parts of those programs will be opened to the public scrutiny before they are enacted into law." And having delivered that little civics lesson, the Vice-President was off to try to purge more Democrats so that the existing adversary climate in Congress might be reduced.

Consistency was not one of the great pillars of the Agnew campaign. In Wilmington, Delaware, he castigated "elitism" and extolled blue-collar workers while campaigning for the election of one Pierre S. du Pont IV for Congress. In Birmingham he told a Republican rally that "I will never go forked tongue in this business, saying one thing in one section of the country and another thing elsewhere." Then, on a local television interview, he was asked about his seeming inconsistency in praising split party responsibility in Texas. "I was in a position where my politics and my mission required me to emphasize that side of it," he answered blithely. "If I were talking in a Republican state, I would emphasize the other side of it. . . . Certainly my declaration there was politically pragmatic. I'm not going to stand here and say that I would tell you that I was not seeking a way to appeal to the voters of Texas who were being appealed to by the other party that the way to really get everything done was to have one party. There are some advantages one way. There are some the other way." And that, of course, explained it all. Only the opposition, apparently, spoke with "forked tongue" in Agnew's view; when *he* worked both sides of the street it was merely a matter of "emphasis." Later in the campaign in Chicago, he was asked whether he too hadn't executed a Christine Jorgensen-type political transformation by changing from a liberal in 1966 to a conservative in 1970. "I challenge anyone," he responded, "to find an issue on which I have changed my stance since I was governor of Maryland. I challenge you or anyone in the country to show me where I have flip-flopped on any issue."

And so it went. In Orlando, campaigning hard on his favorite law-and-order theme, Agnew gave fulsome praise to one of 1970's most prominent law-defiers, Republican Governor Claude Kirk of Florida. Earlier in the year, in defiance of a federal order, Kirk had seized control of a county school system, to stop a court-ordered plan for busing to implement desegregation. And in Jacksonville, after a year of railing against reporters who quoted him out of context, Agnew quoted former Vice-President Humphrey out of context in accusing him of committing "the political turn-coat act of the year" when he said that President Johnson was "absolutely paranoid about the war in Vietnam." Humphrey had said that, all right, but not in the context of blaming his 1968 defeat on Johnson, as Agnew indicated. Actually, Humphrey had used the remark in defense of Johnson's unbending attitude, and to explain why he hadn't taken a position on Vietnam at the 1968 convention that would have embarrassed Johnson.

On another occasion Agnew accused the press of "casually dismissing" the allegations of others against himself while "no matter what I say it's immediately dissected." He criticized reporters for not checking the transcript of the David Frost show to prove he was right when he accused a student leader of having told the Scranton Commission unqualifiedly that "the only way to get the attention of the society is to bomb buildings." Reporters on the Agnew plane duly checked the transcript supplied by his staff, and found that the student had made quite clear she was reporting on prevalent campus views, not stating her own. At times Agnew seemed to be running as hard against the press as against the radiclibs, even proposing at one point that TV commentators submit themselves and their views to television-panel interrogation by government officials. He himself would be willing to be one of the questioners—after the election. Veteran Eric Sevareid responded, "What really hurts is the thought that maybe nobody's been listening all this time."

Consistency was no more of a byword at the White House than it was in the Agnew entourage. While some presidential aides let it be known that before leaving for Europe, the President had given his consent to the attack on Goodell, others continued to deny it. Presidential Counsellor Robert Finch, who was supposed to play a key role in the 1970 campaign but didn't, insisted as late as mid-October that the White House was adopting a hands-off policy in the New York election, despite what Agnew was saying. To that, the Vice-President said of Finch: "I suppose he was expressing a personal hope, or a conviction, or possibly even a straddle. Let me just make one thing clear. As the Vice-President in the Nixon Administration, I'm not on a frolic. I'm out here doing a job for the Administration. And while everything I say has not received the express clearance of the President, I have a sense of purpose and definition in what I'm attempting to accomplish. We'll just leave it at that."

A few days later, Finch conceded in a Washington backgrounder (in which he could not be named by those present as a source) that the get-Goodell campaign was not an Agnew initiative, but a strategy planned by the White House. Nixon had entered into "a gentleman's agreement" with Rockefeller to stay out of New York, he said. "But then a poll showed Goodell running third, and we figured if it was going to be a throwaway vote, we might as well go for Buckley because he would be a vote to organize the Senate for the Republicans."

By now the President was back from Europe and taking soundings on the campaign. What he heard from aides and party polls was depressing; for all of Agnew's rantings, prospects were dim that the party could pick up the seven seats it needed to win Senate control. The Democrats had pretty well defensed the law-and-order issue with their "rush to the center," and now they were going onto the offensive with attacks on the Administration's stagnant economic policy—the pocketbook issue, pinning the old "party of the Depression" label on the Republicans with good effect. Although Nixon had mouthed all those axioms about a President maintaining a statesmanlike posture above the partisan battle, the old warhorse in him was snorting now. He hadn't stayed out of a national election in eighteen years; he wasn't going to now. In all those years as an "out," he had stood in awe and sometimes in fear of the power of a President to impose the prestige of his office onto a campaign. Johnson had given him a first-hand lesson at the close of the 1968 race, but had not gone about it right. Nixon was confident he knew how to use the Presidency to beat the opposition, and in the remaining weeks of the campaign he was going to apply its political weight to the side of the Republican party as never before.

All the pomp and circumstance of a traveling chief of state accompanied Nixon on the campaign trail—*Air Force One*, the ruffles and flourishes announcing the approaching Chief Executive at each stop, the presidential seal on every podium. It was, indeed, awesome to see, especially when the huge light-blue and silver jet with the words "United States of America" emblazoned on its side, or even the smaller Jetstar, came into some modest-sized airport. *Air Force One* had to be used frequently, it was explained, because the President needed its complex communications equipment to keep the reins of government and national defense firmly in hand at all times. The cost of using the plane for campaigning—nearly $2,000 an hour of flying time—was borne, it was reported, by the Republican National Committee. It seemed a good investment. In terms of voter impact, money could not buy that kind of clout.

The President joined the campaign on October 17 in a sweeping jet-stop tour to the Vermont hills, the New Jersey seashore, Pennsylvania Dutch country and the Mecca of professional football, Green Bay, Wisconsin. Partly by circumstance, partly by design, the day's outing provided both the style and the substance for his political efforts over the next three weeks. At the airport in Burlington, Vermont, two rocks about the size of golf balls were tossed in Nixon's direction but fell far short of him. Still, he and his aides seized the incident and milked it for all it was worth. The aides quickly spread the word to reporters who hadn't seen the rocks or who had thrown them. The President labeled the rock throwers part of a small group who constantly sought to "tear America down," echoing a theme of his own 1968 presidential campaign, and of Agnew's 1970 efforts. "You hear them night after night on television," Nixon said, "people shouting obscenities about America and what we stand for. You hear those who shout against the speakers and shout them down, who will not listen. And then you hear those who engage in violence. You hear those, and see them, who, without reason, kill policemen and injure them, and the rest. And you wonder: Is that the voice of America? I say to you it is not. It is a loud voice but, my friends, there is a way to answer. Don't answer with violence. Don't answer by shouting the same senseless words that they use. Answer in the powerful way that Americans have always answered. Let the majority of Americans speak up, speak up on November third, speak up with your votes. That is the way to answer."

Nixon and his aides climbed back aboard *Air Force One* little short of elated at the heckling and the tossing of rocks, which were quickly gathered up by presidential aides like two nuggets of gold. Said Charles Colson, one of Nixon's political lieutenants, "Those rocks will mean ten thousand votes for [Senator Winston L.] Prouty"—the Vermont Republican seeking re-election. Actually, Colson was understating the White House's expectations. Repeatedly after that, Nixon mentioned the rock-tossing incident, embellishing as he went, in an effort to convert it into votes not simply for Winston Prouty in Vermont, but also for every Republican candidate everywhere.

At a huge airport hangar in Teterboro, New Jersey, admission to the President's speech was to be strictly by ticket from the local Republican organization. Those admitted then had to walk a gauntlet of more than fifty Air and Army national guardsmen. Any with long hair or hippie garb were searched by state and local police. Because of this procedure, the structure was less than half filled when the President arrived. When all the Nixon partisans were in position up front, the local police—on cue from a White House advance man—let everyone else in: hecklers, long-hairs and all. The protesters, chanting their slogans and obscenities from the rear, were drowned out by shouts of "We Want Nixon!" from the faithful up front. Nixon, grinning, raised his arms over his head in V-formation and then launched his speech, playing the obscenity-shouters like a violin. "One vote," he said later at Green Bay, "is worth a hundred obscene slogans." In the Nixon strategy, quite obviously, it was just the other way around: one obscene slogan was worth a hundred votes—and one rock, ten thousand.

Once on a later visit to a local campus in eastern Tennessee, Nixon professed to hear shouts of obscenities from the rear amid loud and constant cheering from the Republican multitude. Nobody else seemed to hear the blasphemies, but that fact did not deter him; he launched into his antiobscenity theme with customary relish. At stop after stop in the next weeks, no sticks or stones broke Nixon's bones, but names—those everyone heard and those only he did—sent him into paroxysms of law-and-orderism.

The President's trading on real or supposed acts of violence and shouts of obscenity became so transparent that reporters were inspired to write a special campaign song for him. They sang it over the public address system on the White House press plane, to the tune of "Three Little Words." It went:

> *Four-letter words;*
> *Oh, what I'd give for*
> *Some four-letter words.*
> *To hear those four-letter words;*
> *That's what I live for*
> *On campaigning days.*

> *And when obscenities come, I hope they're smutty*
> *Those are the words that make the voters putty.*
> *Four-letter words,*
> *Four little letters,*
> *That simply mean*
> *Bleep-bleep-bleep.*

To the rock-throwing bonanza, Agnew added his particular specialty: he criticized the press for inadequate coverage when the President was "the target of a shower of rocks by young radical thugs" in Burlington. And he continued to fire his volley of verbal missiles against assorted radiclibs. In Chicago, called "a peddler of hate" by Stevenson, Agnew replied: ". . . By putting vote-mongering ahead of long-held leftist convictions, by placing a yen for publicity ahead of the nation's striving for an honorable peace, by smearing others in public life—I say that Adlai the Third has demeaned his great name. . . ." In Baltimore he alluded to conflict-of-interest charges faced by Democratic Senator Tydings and dubbed him a radiclib "who takes all the advice he can get from Hyannisport." In Hartford he tried to head off the election of Democrat Joseph D. Duffey by attacking the Americans for Democratic Action, of which Duffey was national chairman. In Raleigh, where no radiclibs were running, he hit at "smug elitists back in Georgetown", and promised that if enough radiclibs were retired by the voters "we'll have a strict constructionist from the South on that Supreme Court whether Birch Bayh and Ted Kennedy like it or not." In Greenville, South Carolina, under the admiring eye of Strom Thurmond, who called him "the greatest man this country has produced since John C. Calhoun and Robert E. Lee," Agnew accused the radiclibs of "aping other apologists—those who indulged the Nazi excesses in the late twenties and early thirties." After that mouthful, he told the rebel-yelling crowd that "those red-hots who complain about vigorous rhetoric are the world's worst in scurrility and libel and intemperance of expression. I wouldn't stoop to such invective." All this with the customary straight face, well-modulated voice and absence of arm-waving theatrics.

In Agnew's heavy-handed pursuit of radiclibs, he was not without his own brand of humor. His press secretary, Vic Gold, extremely conscientious but also quite excitable, was a perfect foil. Once, when the good-natured but intense Gold first worked for him, Agnew called him into his office and handed him what Agnew said was a copy of an AP story attributing some particularly outrageous remarks to the Vice-President. "What are you going to do about it?" Agnew asked. "Did you say it?" asked Gold, formerly a press aide to Barry Goldwater. "Yes, I didn't know he was a reporter," Agnew replied, stony-faced. "Then we'll have to live with it," Gold said. "One thing I learned from Goldwater. Never clarify. If you do, it'll get you in worse trouble." Agnew broke up laughing. The story was a fake.

Sometime later, Agnew called Gold in and handed him what appeared to be a UPI story reporting that a senator had called Agnew all sorts of names, capping off his diatribe by saying, "not only that, he has a Goldwater retread working for him." Gold was about to spring into action when Agnew burst out laughing again. "Okay," Gold said, "you've got me 2–0." The press secretary went to his office, got some wire-copy paper, and typed a story that said the head of a federal agency had challenged Agnew to a debate. He wrote in the story that he, Gold, said when he learned of the challenge: "If the Vice-President debated every braying jackass, he wouldn't have time to do anything else." Gold sent in the fake story to Agnew in a stack of other papers, and waited. Two days later, his phone rang. It was Agnew. "Vic? You really told that so-and-so!" Gold answered: "Mr. Vice-President, remember two days ago I said you had me 2–0? Now it's 2–1." Agnew roared.

About a week before election day, with the President now on the campaign trail reminding the voters about that avalanche of rocks and dirty words that had descended upon him, the White House strategists decided it was time to administer the *coup de grâce* to Charlie Goodell. To their glee, the reverse-twist Machiavellianism being employed in New York—to stimulate a sympathy vote for Goodell by Agnew's blatant intercession, for Buckley's ultimate benefit—was working marvelously. The foundering Goodell had taken the bait and was trying desperately to make maximum capital of Agnew's intrusion, but the severe defections in his own party ranks could not be overcome. A measure of his plight came at an annual dinner-dance of Queens County Republican clubs, at which both Rockefeller and Goodell appeared. The crowd, well boozed by now, cheered the governor lustily, except when he tried to put a word in for Goodell. Then Buckley signs and chants went up everywhere. And when the hapless Goodell rose to speak, he was drowned out in a chorus of boos; indeed, he appeared for a time to be physically in danger. A blowsy blonde picked up her drink and threw it, including the glass, at another lady of similar description at a table below Goodell. The tumult was so great that the young senator finally shouted a few words and escaped.

Into this politically ripe climate came Spiro T. Agnew. With the AGNEW STAY OUT signs still posted by Rockefeller, the Vice-President made his incursion into New York under cover of a supposedly nonpolitical speech at the annual dinner of the Navy League of the United States. Reporters traveling with the Vice-President were told that the speech would indeed be nonpolitical, but of great importance because it would touch on national security. And that it did. It called for defeat of the radiclibs, including Goodell, "before they irretrievably damage the security of the United States."

In that peculiar Agnew habit of exempting himself from the rules that bind other men, Agnew started out by telling the Navy officers that he had been out politicking, "but tonight, constrained by your nonpartisan, or should I say bipartisan, environment, I checked my political hat at the door." Then he said, "So I will not dwell this evening on the Senate contest in this state. After all, it seems to be going rather well [laughter] but, so that no one can possibly be offended, I will chastely observe that there are three candidates in New York. I oppose two, and don't oppose one—but to keep things nonpolitical I will not give the names. I trust you will construe that in the spirit intended."

Next came a strong defense of the Nixon Administration's national security policies. The audience settled back to hear the nonpolitical speech traditional for that forum. But suddenly, they heard this: "Which leads me to discourse now on why I have been on the campaign trail for these past six weeks. It bears directly on this meeting tonight. Out on the hustings I have sought to present, admittedly with a pinch of candor, the concerns of the Nixon Administration with a group of highly influential members of Congress, principally in the Senate, whom I have come to characterize as radical-liberals. Certain of my objections to this group fall into areas not directly relevant to this organization, so I will, most reluctantly, put those aside this evening. But one aspect of what I call radical-liberalism is, I believe, actively of concern also to the Navy League. I refer to the national security criteria by which I identify these people. Let me reassure you on one point before proceeding with this phase of the discussion. I am not— very definitely *not*—attempting directly or indirectly or slyly to intrude this 1970 campaign into your deliberations. Rather, I want you to understand the concerns I am expressing to the nation, and why I am expressing them—because I regard these concerns as transcending conventional politics and going to the very foundations of our nation's security. As a matter of fact, I submit that the nature of my involvement in the Senate race in New York manifests my determination to reach beyond the ordinary practices of American politics in order that larger national needs may be served." Not only was he not intruding on the nonpolitical tradition of the Navy League; he was doing it in the noblest of causes.

Agnew gave the Navy men a definition of radical-liberal that would ring a special bell with them: ". . . a neoisolationism . . . a conviction that our defense establishment is far too large, far too costly, infested by jingoists, guided by martinets professionally incapable of fashioning realistic defense programs, the whole apparatus entangled in a massive conflict of interest with American industry and political leaders, creating what President Eisenhower called 'the military-industrial complex.' . . . These are people so viscerally antagonistic toward the whole defense complex that they have become . . . almost paranoid on the war, so much so that they have persuaded themselves that the United States can win in Asia only through ignominious defeat."

Agnew entered his customary disclaimer: "It bears restating that every one of these members of Congress is no less patriotic than you are or I am—I haven't the slightest question about that. But I profoundly disagree with their views. I believe that these people, so sincere in their beliefs, must be replaced, regardless of which party they belong to, before they irretrievably damage the security of the United States of America." And then, having pointed out he had checked his political hat at the door, the Vice-President of all the people left New York—still, somehow, wearing it.

(Agnew had also used the nonpolitical Navy League dinner to reply to a report that the President was thinking of dumping him

in 1972. David Broder of the Washington *Post,* in a column preceding a Nixon trip to Texas, reported that the President was particularly interested in the Senate race there of George Bush, who
might replace Agnew on the 1972 ticket. Agnew reminded his
audience that he had said in an earlier TV interview "that I'm not
an uncertain man, and I meant that. Some of my friends in the
liberal media are already plotting my demise . . . to my friends
in the media who would like me replaced, gentlemen, I'm not an
insecure man, either." The next day, he repeated to reporters, "I'm
not an insecure man. I have a sense of purpose in what I'm doing.
I have a close relationship with my President. Just because someone makes a comment that I'm about to be dumped down the
drain, I don't subscribe to it." And from Longview, Texas, where
the President was trying to help Bush, Nixon said he thought Agnew was "doing a wonderful job. I must say that he's one of the
greatest campaigners in all history." After the election, White
House sources said that the story had been floated to help Bush's
sagging chances in Texas, but he lost anyway. Later, Bush was
named U. S. Ambassador to the United Nations by Nixon.)

In that last week the Vice-President did not take off his political
hat at all, even in jest. The combined assault of Nixon and Agnew
on the radiclibs, rock throwers and obscenity shouters hammered
away at the same basic themes Agnew had carried alone since
Labor Day. Because their staffs had neither the foresight nor the
time to make adjustments to the Democrats' responses, all the Republicans could do was pour it on, and give them more of the
same. By now, as already noted, the Democrats had done much to
neutralize the law-and-order issue and had switched to the economic issue. They operated on the premise that blue-collar
America was more concerned about its jobs than its racial and
anti-intellectual prejudices and fears. The Democrats saw in the
oratorical excesses of Nixon and Agnew a possible backlash that
they could convert to their own advantage, not by outshouting the
Republican pair, but, ironically, by following Nixon's 1969 inaugural advice and lowering their own voices.

A critical event in the whole battle of strategies occurred on the
Thursday night before the elections, in San Jose, California.
Nixon had given a speech without incident inside the municipal
auditorium. Meanwhile, outside, a large crowd of extremely raucous young demonstrators gathered in protest. When the Presi-

dent came out, closely protected, he suddenly climbed on the hood of his car and threw his arms over his head, flashing the V peace sign with each hand. The crowd, incensed, began to shout obscenities and throw bottles and rocks at him. Martin Schram of *Newsday*, standing right below Nixon, heard him say through a frozen smile, "That's what they hate to see." Although rocks came close, the President was whisked away without harm. Aides, however, immediately began to circulate reports that the President had narrowly escaped injury, and for the rest of the campaign San Jose replaced Burlington in the G.O.P. harangue.

In Belleville, Illinois, Agnew referred to the incident, arguing that "when the President of the United States . . . is subject to rock and missile throwing it is time to sweep that kind of garbage out of our society. Yes, I say separate them from the society in the same humane way that we separate the other misfits who interfere with social progress and interfere with the conduct of the business of one of the greatest nations in the world." And in Boise he boasted that his attacks on radiclibs had brought "the prodigal sons of permissiveness . . . knocking on the door of their father's house." The radiclibs "one by one on the great question of law and order in this society . . . have recanted and hit the sawdust trail to the mourner's bench. Men who once snickered at and scorned the majority of Americans as 'flag wavers' are now sporting flag pins."

Meanwhile Nixon was speaking to a tumultuous Republican rally in Phoenix, laying on the law-and-order theme with the same harsh language that Agnew was using, but also employing his old, fire-breathing prepresidential stump style, forgetting some of his own maxims about presidential aloofness and the dignity of the office. "For too long," he said, "we have appeased aggression here at home, and as with all appeasement, the result has been more aggression, more violence. The time has come to draw the line. The time has come for the great silent majority of Americans, of all ages and of every political persuasion, to stand up and be counted against appeasement of the rock throwers and the obscenity shouters." Nixon named nobody, but said people who believe "that violence will end as we give more power to those who demand more power . . . [have] led us down a path of appeasement." It was a low point in one of the lowest off-year campaigns, and the White House capped it all with an act of sheer stupidity. Nationwide television time was bought and Nixon's performance in Phoenix was shown—on poor-quality tape no less —on election eve.

Nixon and Agnew met in San Clemente on the final Sunday to compare notes. It was clear by now that the Democrats were counting heavily on their argument that the Nixon Administration was letting the country fall apart economically. Agnew came out of the two-hour meeting charging the Democrats with "scare tactics" and "the big lie" on the economy. "The gross national product has been steadily growing, housing starts are up, prime interest rates are down," he said. But it was too late to start peddling prosperity, after eight weeks of law and order, radiclibs and the Christine Jorgensen of the Republican party.

On election eve, immediately after the nation's television viewers had been treated to fifteen minutes of the President of the United States in Phoenix in full partisan attack, Senator Muskie, representing the Democrats, came on sitting quietly in the kitchen of an old Maine house. When he taped his election-eve presentation, Muskie did not know that the Republicans would show the disastrous Nixon rerun; it was a stroke of great good fortune for Muskie personally and for his party. He delivered an extremely low-key appeal to reason and moderate discourse that directed just enough controlled anger at the Nixon-Agnew tactics of vilification to strike the most advantageous contrast for the Democratic cause.

"There are those who seek to turn our common distress to partisan advantage," Muskie said, "not by offering better solutions but by empty threat and malicious slander. They imply that Democratic candidates for high office . . . men who have courageously pursued their convictions in the service of the Republic in war and in peace, that these men actually favor violence and champion the wrongdoer. That is a lie, and the American people know it is a lie. . . . How dare they tell us that this party is less devoted or less courageous in maintaining American principles and values than are they themselves. This is nonsense, and we all know it is nonsense. And what contempt they must have for the decency and sense of the American people to talk to them that way, and to think they can make them believe." It was a performance that was to have great personal significance for Muskie;

largely on the strength of it, he was catapulted into the front-running position for the Democratic presidential nomination of 1972.

On election night, high-level Administration officials took a suite at the Washington Hilton to watch the returns on television. Many members of the Cabinet dropped by—Attorney General Mitchell, HEW Secretary Elliot Richardson, Postmaster General Winton Blount, Wally Hickel, and others. Agnew, who was giving a party on a lower floor for his staff and all those White House aides who had accompanied him during the fall, joined them. The bad news came in—a net pickup of only two Senate seats; a House loss eventually reaching nine; a calamitous defeat in the gubernatorial races, with Democrats gaining eleven, including the large states of Pennsylvania and Ohio. After all the rhetoric, spread over 32,000 miles of flying in thirty-two states, all Spiro Agnew had to show for his efforts, beyond an estimated $3.5 million raised, was an even bigger reputation for divisiveness.

"He was down," one of those present that night said later. "He didn't think we'd done as well as we should have, especially because he saw these governors he knew; all these governors who had come in with him in 1966 were going down the tube, one after another." Then came word of a few bright spots shining through—the defeat of Gore in Tennessee, Tydings in Maryland, Duffey in Connecticut, and Goodell in New York, and the victory there of Buckley. Hickel later reported in his book, *Who Owns America?*, that "the overwhelming attitude was not one of victory and joy, but rather of revenge." When one of the television networks reported that Goodell had lost, Hickel wrote, "Agnew strode over to the TV set and said: 'We got that son of a bitch!' He was far more elated about having helped defeat Goodell than in winning in some other area of the country."

Hickel said he was so offended by the remark and the mood that he "quietly and quickly" left the room. Others present insist, however, that Agnew made no such remark, and that although it was natural that the Vice-President was pleased at some of the results, there was no exultation. "We were glad we won some," this Nixon aide said. "We worked hard for some; we were delighted Goodell went down the tube, but we were more delighted Buckley won. We knew Goodell wasn't going to win the damn thing as of September; he wasn't going anywhere, he had fifteen percent or something. But Hickel's account, that's ridiculous. Hickel's problems stem from the fact that he went and made a big hero of himself on the Mike Wallace show and you just don't go out and publicly air your grievances with the President of the United States if you're a member of his team."

Whatever the mood in the Washington Hilton suite that night, the incontrovertible fact was that on the whole, the big purge of 1970 had been a dismal failure. And because Ted Agnew had been the chief visible implementer of the effort, he stood to be the chief loser, aside from those Republicans thrown out of office. That, at least, would be the orthodox political reading. Agnew himself had observed late in the campaign in an interview with Walter Mears of the Associated Press that "I'm tremendously vulnerable. These races are very close. There could be circumstances . . . that could make this a typical off-year." If so, the elections analysts, everybody—particularly the columnists and commentators he had attacked—would blame him. "No matter what happens," he said, "you can be pretty well assured that the adverse results will be laid at my doorstep, the good results will be attributed to something else."

But was it all that incontrovertible that the Republican purge had failed? Who said so? Those elections analysts, those commentators who took it easy on the radiclibs and who never gave Ted Agnew or Richard Nixon or the Republican party an even break? It all depended on how you looked at it.

At Republican National Committee headquarters on Capitol Hill shortly before two o'clock that early morning, Agnew met with reporters and called the results "bittersweet—things to be disappointed about and things to be elated about. . . . on balance we have done very well . . . not as well as I, as a campaigner, would have had us do," but better than average for an off-year. In the Senate, while a Republican majority was not achieved, Agnew said the results had brought a "very definite ideological change regardless of party," giving Nixon "a working majority he hasn't had before." Even the victory of conservative Texas Democrat Lloyd Bentsen over Nixon's hand-picked favorite, George Bush, constituted a "philosophical" victory, the Vice-President contended.

Before long, once Agnew and his colleagues had recovered

from the shock of the returns, they would be seeing even brighter silver linings in the cloud that had just passed over. And once again, as so often in the past, immediate reports of the political demise of Spiro Agnew would require re-examination.

20

◇•◇•◇•◇•◇•◇

DON'T BLAME ME

O N the morning after the 1970 elections, finding anybody in the Nixon Administration who owned up to having predicted Republican control of the Senate was as difficult as spotting a radiclib cheering at an Agnew rally. Nobody, it seemed, had ever really believed that the G.O.P. could achieve a numerical majority. What the Administration had been talking about all along, it turned out, was something now called an "ideological majority," and the gloom of the previous night suddenly vanished in the realization that this other goal had been reached. Immediate protestations from the likes of Texas' Lloyd Bentsen that he was and remained a Democrat both organizationally and ideologically, and was not in Richard Nixon's pocket, were brushed aside in the Administration's determination to change black to white, or at least to gray. Before long the propaganda machinery was spewing out a variety of reassurances that the Republicans had really won.

First, the President himself told reporters at San Clemente that he had won a "working majority of four" in the Senate—counting Bentsen. The results, he said, would not go unnoticed abroad, and would "enormously strengthen our hand at home."

Next, the Administration's all-purpose fall guy, Bob Finch, wrote a memo accommodatingly circulated to Washington correspondents and editors around the country by Herb Klein. It was said to be Finch's "expanded notes from a Cabinet and White

House staff meeting" at which the President had explained why what seemed like a crushing defeat to others was actually a dandy victory. "These thoughts seem to be a more reasonable and accurate assessment of what was and will be than one finds in the media," Finch wrote. "At least this should serve as an antidote to the Chicken Little syndrome that seems to have beset many politicians and pundits in the wake of Tuesday's returns." The memo argued that 1) the President's intervention had been "decisive" in cutting losses and making slight gains; 2) ideological gains had given him a "working majority" in the next Senate; 3) his base for 1972 remained strong.

Finally, the President called in a select group of favorably disposed columnists and personally gave them the benefit of his thinking on the election results. It was supposed to be a backgrounder of the sort that has been held in Washington for years, with any information conveyed coming from nameless sources "close to the White House." But one of the invited newsmen, conservative columnist James J. Kilpatrick, apparently didn't understand the ground rules. When it was over, he went out and clearly attributed all that was said to the President.

In a column relating the same presidential optimism without any attribution, Richard Wilson of the Cowles Publications went on from this strange reading of the past to a more interesting look at the political future through Nixon's eyes. On the basis of the backgrounder, Wilson wrote that "it turns out that Vice-President Agnew is expendable. It also turns out that the Democrats successfully defused the law-and-order issue. In discussing the outlook with his associates, Nixon is becoming increasingly circumspect about Agnew. Nixon is the first to recognize Agnew's great effort in 1970 and the last to criticize him for how he performed and what he said. Far be it for Nixon to criticize Agnew for doing the same thing Nixon did as Vice-President in 1954 and 1958. Still, don't take any bets on Agnew being on or off the ticket in 1972. A prospective bettor really won't have enough information until he sees all the horses in the race. . . . So it appears that Vice-President Agnew is a hostage to President Nixon's political prospects. If Agnew is needed in 1972, he will be kept; if not, so long, Spiro."

Thus, within a matter of days after Agnew had put his prestige on the line in the off-year elections, speculation was flying that he was on the skids. It was a condition that, as Agnew had expected, would continue to hang over him throughout the next year leading to the 1972 campaign. Just as his public statements as governor of Maryland constantly were read for indications of a shift from liberal to conservative, and just as all he said in 1969 and 1970 had raised questions about whether it was Ted Agnew or Dick Nixon speaking, so everything he was to say through 1971 would be assessed in terms of one question: Would he be on the ticket again in 1972?

Several times in the previous year Agnew had said that the answer was a matter of indifference to him, that he was not an uncertain or insecure man. But as events evolved through 1971, there was increasing belief among his associates that while he would step aside for the good of Richard Nixon, he would not be cast aside as a failure. What he had said in 1969 and 1970 had been political, of that there could be no doubt, but the man had also spoken from his convictions and fierce personal pride. Also, he had talked often of giving voice to the aspirations and feelings of the silent majority and of refusing to abandon that voiceless group. If the past year had proved nothing else, it had shown that the silent majority, whatever its size, constituted a considerable and staunch constituency that would not take kindly to any dump-Agnew move. Thus, while it may have been true as Wilson said that Agnew was a hostage to Nixon, it could be argued just as strenuously that Nixon was a hostage to the creature he had helped create, the Agnew-loving silent majority.

In addition, Nixon was a hostage to his own past. Meeting with reporters as part of the postelection whitewash job, Klein claimed that the 1970 strategy had paid off, and then gave his personal opinion that "presuming that President Nixon runs [in 1972], Agnew will be on the ticket." Concerning the criticism of Agnew's campaign attacks, Klein said, "President Nixon remembers he had a lot of criticism in 1954 and 1958" in a similar vice-presidential role.

Not only as a loyal member of the team but also as a prideful man with a reputation to defend, Agnew joined zestfully in the effort to paint the 1970 election results as rosy as possible. A week after the balloting, Republicans in the Capital paid $150 apiece to honor him for his campaign efforts. Invitations called the affair "an intermingling of interested individuals aimed at animated acclamation and appreciation for guess whom? Household word Spiro." With her husband, the Attorney General, benignly observing, Martha Mitchell contributed a silly mock telephone routine, and Al Capp as master of ceremonies said of Jim Buckley's victory over Goodell, "The big question is, will Bill Buckley and Gore Vidal kiss and make up? I think Vidal would love that." It was all good clean silent-majority fun.

On this occasion the Vice-President conveyed the Administration line in vintage Agnew: "Lately I see that various pursed-lip pundits with twenty-twenty hindsight have heartburn over this campaign—not simply over my part in it, but the President's part as well. Well, here's my view: first, these were our initial off-year elections, a season for every new administration that is historically a time of mourning; second, Richard Nixon is our first President in one hundred and twenty years who has had to contend with a hostile Congress from the first day he took office—and I don't have to tell this sophisticated audience how difficult that is; and third, economic stress, the bane of incumbent administrations, has been unavoidable because this President has had the character and courage to wind down both a runaway inflation and a runaway war. Considering it all, my friends, I'll say simply this: on November third we Republicans made political water run straight uphill."

In claiming that the G.O.P. had bucked the traditional trend against the party in power, Agnew did not mention the special vulnerabilities of Senate Democrats of the classes of '58 and '64. Instead he ticked off the relatively few victories he could name, called them a "parliamentary revolution" and claimed a "climactic victory for reason and order" by forcing the Democrats to counter his law-and-order assault. "In the heat of the campaign," he said, "a whole bevy of Democrats who spent the last three years cozying up to radical dissenters turned tail and ran, unclenching their fists in their frantic rush to middle ground. As they fled, they stripped off their leather jackets, pinned on sheriff's badges, then turned to their constituents, transformed—now all Wyatt Earpy and swearing evermore to stand foursquare for law and order."

The issue, Agnew said, had been an obstructionist Congress, and he had offered "as positive a message as ever a political campaign offered the country; where it fell short of our hopes, I concede only that we undersold our message. . . ." And in an extemporaneous observation, he warned any future Goodells. "The party is big enough to accommodate many points of view," he said. "But there is such a thing as gratuitously engaging your party in warfare for personal aggrandizement." Nixon, returning from Paris where he had attended the funeral of Charles de Gaulle, wired his appreciation of Agnew as "one of the most able and devoted Republican leaders I have known," and said that his Vice-President, "the great campaigner of 1970," had been unfairly criticized. So much for the dump-Agnew talk—for a while.

Predictably, Agnew's campaign antics did nothing for his relations with the Senate. When he presided over his first postelection session, Senate Majority Leader Mansfield expressed regret in a Democratic caucus that unnamed persons had gone "back and forth across the nation unwarrantedly criticizing the Senate." He hoped senators of both parties would reject "the blanket condemnations, the snide innuendos, the inferential alliterations" of that campaign, but "without reproducing the pattern of arrogant half-, quarter- and no-truths which were so much the hallmark." Agnew sat in the chair blissfully unconcerned, with six of his campaign targets before him. "It's always serene in the Senate," he told a reporter.

Amid the growing speculation about his future, the Vice-President went to Honolulu for a short vacation, taking his staff, Secret Service men and their wives along with him. There he granted a long and revealing interview to James Naughton of the *New York Times* that reinforced the impression that not being Vice-President of the United States for a second term would not signal the end of the world for him. "I suppose," he said, "it's basically because there're a lot of things that I'd like to do someday that I won't be able to do until I'm out of politics. I've always looked at life in this fashion, that there's a great amount to enjoy in life no matter what you're doing, so long as it's something that you want to do. The political side of it's been very enjoyable to me. I've always treated my political life as a sort of furlough from the practice of law. So I suppose your public life has to come to an end sometime or another, and it's just reality to believe that's true, that you're not always going to be a public man. . . . I've always looked at it as public service, not as a job, and one that someday will terminate and I'll revert to private life. And it doesn't distress me to think that that may happen—any time."

The Vice-President said he wasn't interested in becoming rich, but "would like to, in my latter years, at least be comfortable." He'd like to write a column or do "something in the electronic medium—commentary or some sort of interview program," and "do some traveling, in a manner similar to [what] President Nixon did in the years he was away from government, to learn more about that side of government. Possibly special assignments, if whomever was in the White House felt I was qualified to do that sort of thing."

During his Honolulu stay, Agnew spoke to the Associated Press Managing Editors Convention. He gave a calm and balanced speech that tempered the few criticisms he had to make with fulsome praise for the American press. "I have not the least doubt that the United States has the most self-demanding, least self-satisfied, most ingenious, least inhibited, best informed, least controlled, most professional, least subjective, most competitive, least party-line, fairest and finest journalistic complex in the entire world," he told the doubtless astonished editors. "I have found newscasters and reporters, in large majority, as fair and as objective as they are emotionally and psychologically able to be, and I have found the great preponderance of them very conscientious in their calling. I have found most news accounts of my deeds and words adequate and factual; indeed, time and time again I have found surprisingly complimentary coverage of my viewpoints by journalists who I happen to know do not suffer from ardor for Agnew. I have seen Niagaras of words and interpretations erupt almost overnight from your fraternity over political events, inundating the American people with astonishingly detailed information about important people and issues—and I have marveled how well you have made this the best-informed nation on earth. The entire process, as well as most of its people, I admire immensely. I regard America's press as the best and strongest in the world . . ."

Was this the same Spiro Agnew who in late 1969 and throughout 1970 had laid much of his party's woes at the feet of American journalism? Had the editors been able to ask him that, he doubtless would have pointed to the disclaimers he had tucked into most of his speeches, to prove he was being consistent. But it did sound suspiciously like the occasion in Dallas when he campaigned for Republican Paul Eggers for governor on grounds that split executive-legislative responsibility would be good for Texas —while he was saying it was bad for America.

In early December, Agnew returned to a Washington that seemed to be recovering from the postelection gamesmanship over who had won and lost. President Nixon held his first press conference in five months and struck a most conciliatory tone. He was going to wear his presidential hat through 1971, he said, and he gave a categorical pledge that in 1972 he would not be going after any Republicans who, like Goodell, disagreed with him. The White House political operation of 1970 was largely disassembled, and a new, slugging national chairman, Senator Bob Dole of Kansas, was selected—to be, some said, "the New Agnew," freeing the Vice-President for a less divisive role in 1971. The move was viewed in many quarters as part of an image-rebuilding program for Agnew, to make him more acceptable as a candidate in 1972, but he denied any such intent.

Nevertheless, Agnew did appear finally to be lowering his voice. In a few speeches and informal remarks after the mild Honolulu talk, he was decidedly benign, naturally giving rise to speculation that he had been muzzled or advised—in a favorite Nixon Administration expression—to keep a low profile. Actually, there was a practical need at this juncture for a cool Agnew. A grand new Administration policy was being hatched, involving reorganization of the federal departments and shifting of responsibilities back to the states and localities through an ambitious revenue-sharing plan. Agnew, of course, would be one of its chief salesmen. As a former governor he long had been an advocate of revenue sharing, and he was the Administration's liaison with the governors. But as he branched out into other endeavors, particularly partisan speechmaking and fund raising, he had neglected his old colleagues. Fortuitously, the G.O.P. governors were meeting in Sun Valley, Idaho, in mid-December; the conference would give him an opportunity to renew old friendships, mend political fences and maybe talk to some of the lame ducks about federal jobs.

The governors, however, were not in a conciliatory mood. While Ted Agnew and the President had been racing around the country castigating Senate radiclibs, Republicans in gubernatorial races were, in their view, being given short shrift. Some, in fact, felt they had suffered a backlash from Agnew's intemperate remarks. After Republican Governor Winthrop Rockefeller's loss, the Arkansas G.O.P. wired the President blaming Agnew because of the way he had derided Dale Bumpers, the Democratic candidate. Other losers, gathering in Sun Valley for a last fling and—some hoped—a crack at a federal appointment, grumbled among themselves about how Agnewism had contributed to their own downfall.

As is customary at such gatherings, the nation's political reporters arrived early to extract any remaining election postmortems from the governors and to gauge the intensity of obvious intraparty unhappiness over the results. It was not hard to do, with so many losers around. Usually tight-lipped, circumspect men, like Governor Dewey Bartlett of Oklahoma, who had been defeated in an upset, acknowledged to newsmen that the campaign run by Nixon and Agnew had not been of any help to them, and indeed had been most discordant. Others agreed that the President and Vice-President should have sounded a more positive theme in their campaigning. It was no revolt, but it was a noteworthy disaffection, and reporters wrote about it. Before the end of the conference, one of them, Raymond W. Apple of the *New York Times*, was to be elevated to the status of prime villain, along with Sander Vanocur, then of NBC.

As Agnew flew west to Sun Valley, he read Apple's account of the gubernatorial grumbling and became so disturbed that he scribbled out a speech to the governors, half of them lame ducks, that would strike exactly the wrong note. While the Vice-President thus prepared for the meeting, the governors were visited by Republican National Chairman Morton, who brought commiserations to the losers, and some news—dispatched to him by phone from the White House just as he was about to speak. In what surely was a classic example of bad political timing, Morton announced to this disgruntled collection of federal-job seekers that President Nixon was indeed going to appoint a former governor to his Cabinet—Democrat John Connally of Texas. The news that Connally was to be Nixon's new Secretary of the Treasury hit the assembled Republican governors like a wet mackerel across the face. They all knew Connally and most of them admired him as a tough, no-nonsense authoritarian—a kind of developing Lyndon Johnson, for whom he bore a great friendship and a striking personal resemblance, both physical and stylistic. But he was, after all, a Democrat, and this came at a time when Republican governors out of work were tripping over each other. "Can he add?" asked Governor Frank Sargent of Massachusetts.

It was a considerable irony that news of Connally's appointment reached the Sun Valley conference, and in a sense muddied the waters, before Agnew's arrival. Through the next year, as speculation continued that Agnew might be dumped from the 1972 ticket, the name that rose increasingly as a substitute was John Connally of Texas. His predictably rapid rise as the strong man of the Nixon Cabinet, and the bounty of Texas electoral votes that his presence on a 1972 Nixon ticket might bring, fed the talk in Washington and around the country. If Agnew was found expendable, here was a man who could hold on to the conservative constituency, especially in the South. Richard Nixon liked strong men; in fact, he seemed at times to be mesmerized by them, and there was none who came on stronger than Lyndon Johnson's look-alike, act-alike protégé.

But Ted Agnew was not a lame duck, not yet. Into this decidedly unhappy environment strode the resident strong man, primed to respond to all the griping. "This can hardly be described as a halcyon year for Republican governors," he told them. ". . . But out of adversity comes a familial closeness that never exists in times of plenty. So in 1971, Republican governors must close ranks solidly behind our leaders who remain in state houses around the country and behind our President in the White House. Some of our most talented associates have fallen in political combat. But I would remind you that they are not dead, they are only temporarily disabled. They need our rehabilitative political care so that those who wish to can return again to active duty. And we hope it's soon." So far, so good.

But then, so suddenly and harshly that those in the packed hall seemed not to grasp at first what he was saying, Agnew let go. "What they do not need, those who have fallen in the political wars, are excuses and rationalizations for their defeats," he said. "What is not needed is the assessment of blame—they don't need it, and neither do those whose shoulders occasionally become repositories of the fault. They don't even need it when it masquerades as constructive criticism." Judging from what he was to say later, Agnew's intent here was to complain about the press. Some of the governors, however, took his words as straight-out criticism of themselves for having dared to express displeasure at the Nixon-Agnew campaign.

"Who," he asked, "is in a position after an election to decide the factors that contributed to a victory or to a defeat? I contend that the causes of victory or defeat in a political election are as opaque and indefinable after as before the vote. Therefore, the assignment of blame—even though it may be labeled as constructive criticism—is an opinion exercise which may very well, if taken seriously, mandate changes in strategy which could be conducive to further weakening. You know, it is possible to make a wrong judgment on what lost or won an election. I, for one, am not ready to accept the analyses of columnists and commentators who are ideological antagonists.

"Such changes in direction that we, the Republican establishment, decide to make as a party should result from our own analyses—not that of the opinion makers of academe and the media. I mean, after all, where were they when we needed them?" Could this be the same media about which Agnew was so lavish in his praise in Honolulu?

The Vice-President told the stunned governors that he had come "in this time of trial and tribulation to consult with my brothers, and if necessary to debate with them, and if convinced by logic to make changes and to be their advocate for change." They would be meeting the next morning, he reminded them, and out of that meeting would come "the strength of consolidation and unity, regardless of certain outside attempts to generate chaos and division, mostly for the excited consumption of the sensation-minded among the so-called expert observers."

Others, however, were not so hopeful. Oregon's Governor Mc-Call, one of the most outspoken critics of Agnew, stormed out of the hall. He called Agnew's remarks a "rotten, bigoted little speech" that sadly misread the mood of the country. McCall had met with Agnew before the speech and had reported there "wasn't the slightest contrition, not the slightest yielding" to the governors' criticism. Yet McCall had expressed hope that the evening speech would indicate some conciliation. Instead, afterward, he called the remarks "the most divisive speech ever given by such a high official," and he said of Agnew, "He's not going to learn, and I'm sorry about it." Governor Robert Ray of Iowa said he was "amazed" at Agnew's accusatory remarks, and others agreed. Only Governor Reagan said he thought the speech was "fine, right and proper."

The governors went into the next morning's private meeting with Agnew as if they were going into battle. It lasted three hours, and proved to be a no-holds-barred confrontation. Unusual security provisions were invoked to keep the press out, but they did not prevent some of the governors from reporting what had gone on. Apparently still operating on his campaign theory that the best defense is a good offense, the Vice-President came in with all guns blazing. Circulating newspaper clippings reporting the governors' gripes at the conference to prove his point, he accused the press of trying to drive a wedge between him and his old colleagues. Most of the governors' difficulties, Agnew said, stemmed from this hostile press and the zest with which some Republicans wooed influential newsmen. "The thrust," one governor reported later, "was that all of the press was here to crucify the Republican party and the Vice-President, and none of the press was here to do anything constructive." Agnew singled out Vanocur and Apple as particular culprits, this governor said; he quoted Agnew as saying, "Some of the problem with a lot of Republicans is they go out of their way to pat Sandy Vanocur on the ass and get on his boob tube." The most prominent clipping circulated was Apple's story reporting dissension in the governors' ranks. Agnew told the governors, "I don't know him but I think he's out to get me."

Most of the governors were appalled at the Vice-President's attack. Bartlett, one of the mildest of the lame ducks, complained, "I told you not to attack Fred Harris"—the Oklahoma Democratic senator who hadn't even been up for re-election. Bartlett also called on Agnew to "stop this war with the press," and others seconded the recommendation. From all accounts, some of the liveliest exchanges were between Agnew and McCall, a former radio newscaster who matches Agnew in candor and colorful language. Agnew confronted McCall with the "rotten, bigoted speech" comment. "I'm not sure I said 'rotten,'" McCall replied. The original remark had not appeared in any newspapers reaching Sun Valley that morning, but an Agnew aide, C. D. Ward, had learned of it from a reporter and had told the Vice-President. And McCall de-

nied that he had ever called for the President to dump Agnew
from the 1972 ticket. He simply had raised the question, he said,
whether the President would want to run with someone who had
campaigned "with a knife in his shawl."

Aside from his castigation of the press's performance in Sun
Valley, Agnew also blamed newsmen again for what he said was
an erroneous impression among the governors concerning the
kind of campaign he had waged in the fall. When a number of
them said they wished he had taken a more positive approach, he
insisted he had done just that. Governor Linwood Holton of Virginia told Agnew that the Vice-President's speech the night before
had been particularly disappointing because it had been negative
and had produced a letdown in a conference that up to then had
been constructive.

In the speech, Agnew had defended his campaign style in these
words: "When you have to fight the establishment of an in-group
there is only one way—attack. We attacked—we think constructively. Everything we said certainly was not negative." And he had
asked, "What is an election if it is not an attempt to divide the
voters of the country between two or three candidates who are
seeking an office? Heavens, if they didn't divide, we might never
have a result." In the morning meeting, Agnew returned to this
defense. As for his campaign style, one governor later reported
Agnew as saying, "You've got to chop their nuts off before they
chop off yours." And he ridiculed the idea that he had been some
kind of wild horse, galloping off on his own. "Any schoolchild," he
said pointedly, glaring at his critics, "would *know* the Vice-
President is just an extension of the President."

It was hot-and-heavy going, with Agnew taking some heat too
about the lame-duck governors' troubles in the Administration job
market. One of the losers, Frank Farrar of South Dakota, wanted
to know why it was that several defeated Republican congressional and senatorial candidates already had received jobs but
none of the lame-duck governors had. Not all of them griped,
though. Ronald Reagan recalled California's "Eleventh Command-
ment"—"Thou shalt not speak ill of another Republican"—and
said he observed it "except where John Lindsay is concerned."
Agnew said he observed it too, "except where Charlie Goodell is
concerned." Governor Raymond P. Shafer of Pennsylvania, said
to be seeking an Administration post, contributed little to the dis-

cussion, a colleague reported. "When you've got the application in one hand, you don't grab the microphone with the other," he said.

There was talk, too, about the Administration's neglect of the governors, and about a remark Nixon had made trying to minimize the national importance of the eleven G.O.P. gubernatorial losses. Agnew told the governors that Nixon's remark had been misconstrued by the reporters to whom it was made. All in all, it was a black day for the press fraternity, which the Vice-President only recently had called "the best and strongest in the world." The meeting, however, did seem to clear the air for the governors. McCall called it "the most genuine eyeball-to-eyeball meeting I've ever attended anywhere," and he and others vowed that all was well again in their relations with Agnew.

The whole episode provided an instructive example of Agnew's thinking, and problem, concerning rhetoric. For a man who obviously takes such pride and care in his use of the language, the number of times he complains that he is misunderstood and misquoted by the press is remarkable. In this instance, he came winging into Sun Valley to tell the governors how the press had performed there, when he had not been present at the time and the governors had. When he arrived, he told the governors the press was at fault for reports that he had run a negative campaign; actually, he said, they focused on his attacks on individuals and gave short shrift to all the positive things he had said. But then, when several of the listening governors grumbled about the negative tone of *that* speech—which of course they heard with their own ears, unfiltered by the press—Agnew went before them again in private to tell them *they* had misunderstood him.

"I went into the meeting this morning," he told a press conference afterward, "aware that several governors had been rather upset with some of the things that I said last night, or some of the connotations that they read into my intention in making those remarks. So I began by stating what I had intended to convey in those remarks, and I circulated a copy that was taken off the tape of those remarks, and there was some discussion. And some governors, I'm frank to say, felt that the remarks could have been said in a way that would have not left open the possibility of the construction they put upon them. But I'm confident that each of them, after we had had this full discussion this morning, was aware that the thrust of the remarks was positive and aimed at getting us working together in the right direction and not negative in any sense."

Asked about his antipress remarks to the governors, Agnew said "there was some discussion as to whether my comments about the press were misunderstood, in the context that many members of the press whom I did not mean to criticize, considered themselves included in the criticism." Agnew said he had pointed out to the governors that in his Hawaii speech "I was very laudatory and very commendatory to the press. . . . I believe we do have the finest press in the world. This doesn't mean that everyone is above criticism, and those who exhibited what I consider to be an advocate's position for the opposite party, they're entitled to be questioned by me from time to time about the efficacy of their viewpoints." Thus, whether it was the press or Republican governors listening, Agnew seemed to be suggesting, the confusion was not in what he said, but in how it was interpreted by others.

His conviction that this was so was no better illustrated than in his response when asked at the press conference whether he regretted having said that Goodell was "the Christine Jorgensen of the Republican party." He answered, "I don't regret saying it in light of what I said today, but I certainly regret saying it in light of the way it was reported. All I intended to mean by that remark was that this was a very dramatic change in a person's life who was a public person. Senator Goodell's change was an equally dramatic change in a person's life who was a public person. The metaphor was not intended in any way to be nasty or vicious to Senator Goodell."

"Well," Agnew was asked, "what was the matter with the reporting?"

"Because the implication was that I had indicated there was something wrong with Senator Goodell," he replied. "That sounded bad. Don't you think that was bad?"

"Well," he was asked again, "didn't you think there was something wrong with Senator Goodell?"

"I'm talking about in the context of Christine Jorgensen, that he had some problem of a physical nature," Agnew answered.

The way the original remark had been reported by the major wire services and major newspapers was precisely the way the Vice-President had said it, without characterization. Yet he obviously thought it was the press's fault, not his own, that it had been widely received as a physical slur against Goodell. It is most interesting and revealing in this regard to note that Agnew, unlike most other major politicians on the national scene today, much prefers speaking to reporters on the record than on a background basis, and in fact prefers that discussions and interviews be recorded. Whereas other public figures are intimidated by the presence of a tape recorder, Agnew appears to gain assurance from it. Others fear that they may be quoted exactly as they have spoken; if Agnew has any fear, it is that he will not be quoted precisely and accurately. In this he is notably different from Richard Nixon, who often has banned tape recorders in backgrounders or interviews; indeed, he is said to feel that insisting on their use is an insult to the professionalism of note-taking reporters and writers. Agnew, on the other hand, not only demonstrates in his preference for the recorded interview a supreme confidence in his ability to express himself lucidly; he also conveys a basic mistrust in the press's ability or willingness to transmit to the public exactly what he says. The press is a middleman between him as the manufacturer of ideas and the voter as the buyer, and Agnew obviously feels that when his product goes through that middleman, there is a corrosive markdown. His attacks in late 1969 on television analysts and newspaper columnists, particularly, sharply revealed this attitude, but so does his wary, day-to-day relationships with reporters—bred of a history of candid remarks accurately, if at times unfairly, transmitted to the public. Agnew's conviction that the fault lay not with himself but with how others interpreted him, one governor said after Agnew's press-conference rationale of the Christine Jorgensen remark, was the key to the communications problem existing between him and his critics. "He is very defensive," this governor said after the meeting, "and when people are defensive and think they're right, they don't change very easily."

Agnew left the Sun Valley conference confirming that view. "I don't feel that I have conducted the kind of campaign that needs any particular change," he said. "There has been much said about my divisive rhetoric but I can promise you that things that were said about me were much more divisive and intolerant than anything that I ever said when I went out on the hustings." Would he do anything differently? "Sure, you'd do something different," he said. "You'd look at some of the misconstructions of your actions and you'd say, 'Well, probably I'm vulnerable. If I had been more careful in how I'd documented that particular statement I would not have been vulnerable to that misconstruction,' and I wouldn't do it again."

One might have concluded from this remark that a more prudent, if no less aggressive, Vice-President Agnew departed from Sun Valley. But the history of his public life had been marked by complaints of "misunderstandings" and "misinterpretations" and "misconstructions" of his public utterances. The odds were that he would continue to say what he pleased, and to complain later about how it was reported and interpreted.

The odds were right. Through the winter and early spring of 1971, Agnew addressed himself mainly to shoring up the wounds opened among the governors, and to selling the Nixon Administration's legislative proposal on revenue-sharing and government reorganization, now wrapped up in a hard-sell, hucksterized package called "the New American Revolution." There was a new American revolution going on, all right. But it was happening in the streets, on the campuses and even in the armed forces, as the generation called on to fight in Vietnam continued in various ways to say, "Hell, no." While Agnew in this period did say his piece when the spirit moved him, by and large he showed unusual restraint. By White House design or personal decision, he did keep his rhetoric cool, adopting a low profile as he moved around the country expounding the virtues of revenue-sharing. Some in the White House thought they had in the 1971 legislative package the ingredients to inspire the voters to a new sense of participation in local government—some even used the New Left slogan of "participatory democracy," so carried away were they. But revenue-sharing proved to be a sexless issue, not well understood by the public and further complicated by the determination of Democrats on Capitol Hill to remake it to their own liking and with their own label on it.

Periodically, there were outbursts of the old Agnew fire. In late January he took off after Democratic Representative William Anderson of Tennessee, the first commander of the atomic submarine *Nautilus*, for coming to the defense of Daniel and Philip Berrigan in the alleged conspiracy to kidnap national security adviser Henry Kissinger. In mid-March, at a Boston fund-raising affair before the conservative Middlesex Club, Agnew sharply criticized the CBS documentary *The Selling of the Pentagon*, as "a subtle but vicious broadside against the nation's defense establishment." When the network decided to rerun the show with critical comment from Agnew and two other officials, he challenged CBS to let him edit his own remarks. CBS refused.

Just down the hall in the Sheraton-Boston Hotel as Agnew spoke to the Middlesex Club, 130 members of the Ripon Society, the liberal G.O.P. group that was calling for Agnew's replacement on the 1972 ticket, listened to various antiwar speakers. One of them was Republican Representative Paul N. "Pete" McCloskey, Jr., of California, who was positioning himself to challenge Nixon in the 1972 primaries. Yet Agnew said nothing about him, nor about five thousand antiwar demonstrators who stood outside the hotel chanting obscenities about the Vice-President. His bland conduct in this respect seemed a far cry from the Spiro Agnew of 1969 or 1970, and speculation continued that he had been muzzled on McCloskey or was keeping his head down to fortify his chances to be on the 1972 ticket. This talk, however, failed to take into account Agnew's strong-willed determination to speak his mind whenever events or circumstances moved him, particularly when he felt President Nixon was being unjustly criticized.

Such a time was now at hand. Earlier in the month, South Vietnamese forces had moved into Laos in a drive to disrupt supply lines on the Ho Chi Minh Trail, in much the same way they and American forces had gone into Cambodia nearly a year earlier. This time, restrained by congressional action against committing U.S. ground troops outside South Vietnam, Nixon had limited American assistance to airlift and support of the South Vietnamese. After first reports of success, the enemy had stiffened and the South Vietnamese were pulling out sooner than it had been announced they would. Accounts of a rout immediately emanated from the front and were fanned by antiwar senators on Capitol Hill. The Administration denied the reports, saying the South Vietnamese were engaged in "mobile maneuvering." Asked about the situation at a press conference in Boston the day after his speech, Agnew replied, "This was not a rout. This was an orderly retreat. It was an orderly withdrawal in accordance with plan. They were not forced out." Nevertheless, Agnew's remarks constituted the first time an Administration spokesman had suggested a "retreat." It was another example of Ted Agnew compelled to go to the defense of his leader in his high-risk fashion.

(Accompanying Agnew to the Boston press conference was Senator Edward Brooke, himself a frequent critic of Administration policy on Vietnam. Agnew made clear he would not back a brewing Conservative party challenge to Brooke in Massachusetts in 1972 as he had supported the Conservative party fight against Goodell in New York. "I certainly don't consider him a radical-liberal," the Vice-President said. Brooke listened patiently, but the next week, at an unpublicized White House meeting of G.O.P. senators due to seek re-election in 1972, he complained to Attorney General Mitchell and others that Agnew had to be harnessed. His attack on CBS was "negative" politics, Brooke said.)

But when it came to his pet peeves, nobody was going to silence Ted Agnew, short of the President, who said nothing. In early April, in the wake of the conviction of Lieutenant William L. Calley, Jr., in the Mylai murders, Agnew hit out at "home-front snipers" for fostering a negative attitude toward American combat veterans. In a Los Angeles speech he charged his critics, including the press, with "accentuating the negative" about everything, specifically the abortive invasion of Laos. "Masochism replaces pride," he said. "Guilt becomes the new intellectual standard, the badge of neosophistication." Even the Gallup poll came in for criticism for reporting that 12 percent of Americans said they wanted to move to another country, twice the percentage found in 1959. Agnew cited higher figures for seven other countries, including 41 percent for Great Britain. "The headline in the *New York Times* said, 'Gallup Finds Twelve Percent Want to Quit U.S.'" he noted. "It was not 'Eighty-eight Percent Prefer U.S.,' or 'U.S. Lowest in Dissatisfied Citizens.'"

Compared to 1969 and 1970, however, Agnew was behaving himself, and when he did speak out, it always was in staunch defense of the President and the Administration. More often, he was heavily engaged in the dreary task of selling the New American Revolution, which made a lot of sense to local and state politicians and administrators, but was just one big yawn to the public. Meanwhile, important policy decisions, domestic and foreign, were being considered in Washington, and Agnew was only on the periphery of them. By this time George Shultz, head of the newly reorganized Office of Management and Budget, and John Ehrlichman as overseer of all domestic affairs, had solidified their positions, effectively depriving Agnew of a decisive role in the making of the New American Revolution, rather than simply the selling of it. As a former county executive and governor, Agnew felt he had the credentials to make a major contribution, but the avenues were closed. He seldom had a chance to discuss deep policy with the President in privacy, and increasingly he received messages from various White House aides telling him the President wanted him to do this or that. " 'The President says'—that's a favorite expression around here," said one White House aide sympathetic to Agnew's plight. "Well, he's learned about it. He doesn't go for it. He wants to be told by the President, not some underling. He doesn't forget he's the Vice-President of the United States."

On the occasions when Agnew did have an opportunity to get his viewpoint across, he did not hesitate to do so. One important time came in early spring when the National Security Council, of which the Vice-President is a statutory member, discussed relations with China. The President, determined to break the impasse, had encouraged a thaw by such small gestures as referring to Peking as "the People's Republic of China" instead of "mainland China" or "Communist China." He spoke hopefully of the time Peking would be brought into the family of nations and of the need for better U.S.-Chinese relations to achieve stability in Southeast Asia. However, one reason the Vice-President had stopped twice in Taiwan on his Asian trips was to underline the continued American commitment to Chiang Kai-shek, and in White House discussions Agnew was among those who cautioned a wary approach in any dealings with Peking.

In April, there occurred what seemed to be a momentous breakthrough when Peking suddenly invited an American table-tennis team on tour in the Pacific to visit China for exhibition matches with the crack Chinese players. The offer was seized upon, and the young American players were among the first Americans to penetrate the Bamboo Curtain since Mao's takeover. World-wide publicity attended the visit and the matches, in which the Chinese used second-rank players to avoid humiliation of their less experienced guests from America.

Stories of "ping-pong diplomacy" filled American newspapers and television screens as the Republican governors gathered for yet another conference, this time at Colonial Williamsburg. In his role as chief gubernatorial fence-mender, Agnew arrived the Sunday before the formal sessions were to begin. At around midnight, in a most unusual gesture for him, the Vice-President suggested to Vic Gold, his press secretary, that a few of the reporters covering the conference be called in for a drink. Gold, who always is on red alert, dashed down to the lobby of the Williamsburg Lodge in search of likely prospects. Because it was late, not many reporters were to be found. He phoned some in their rooms, rousting them out of bed; others he caught going through the lobby. Because it was to be an off-the-record affair, and because not all reporters were to be invited, Gold darted about with a furtiveness and frenzy that exceeded even his usual style. One observer of Gold's quest likened him to the cartoon character, "The Roadrunner," zooming up and down stairways and through corridors like a mini-cyclone, generating great gusts of wind in his wake as he raced by, screeching to a stop to whisper a message clandestinely, then dashing off again in a blur—always with a look of impending holocaust.

In short order Gold rounded up nine newsmen—several more than originally sought—and they dutifully trooped up to the Vice-President's suite. They found Agnew relaxed and cordial, accompanied by two other aides, Roy Goodearle, his advance man, and Pete Malatesta. The reporters were invited to sit down, and Gold spelled out emphatically—more emphatically than usual for such affairs, the newsmen present noted—that the gathering was to be completely off the record. The Vice-President seemed to have nothing special in mind; the group fell into easy discourse on a wide range of subjects. According to some who were in the room, the discussion was at all times friendly and proper, if occasionally animated. Agnew made his usual points about the need for more self-criticism in the press, and a tougher skin toward outside criticism. He was complimentary toward individual reporters, critical of their editors and management.

In the course of the dialogue, the subject turned to the ping-pong diplomacy story. There was some light banter about it at first, one of the reporters asking Agnew whether he played ping-pong, and whether he was any good. The Vice-President allowed that he was a pretty fair player and in fact probably could beat Mao Tse-tung and Chou En-lai. But soon the talk took a more serious turn, and Agnew had some definite ideas about the handling of the ping-pong diplomacy by the press. He was particularly disturbed about a story from China by John Roderick of the Associated Press Tokyo Bureau, in which Peking was credited by the writer with a diplomatic coup for using second-stringers against the less experienced Americans. Roderick had written that the gesture "could be described as an exquisite display of Chinese tact and politeness to guests," when a team of the host's most powerful players "could have humiliated their American guests." Agnew, according to some of those present, expressed specific distaste for the use of the word "exquisite" and he worried that the glowing accounts of China by the inexperienced young observers on the U.S. team would give Americans a severely distorted impression of the hard and repressive life inside China. He was particularly worried, he said, that an unwarranted mood of euphoria might be gripping the American people, leading them to expect too much in terms of solid progress toward peace with China as a result of the modest diplomatic relaxations.

All in all, the Vice-President told his guests, the United States had taken a propaganda beating in the visit of the ping-pong players. At a National Security Council meeting before the visit, he told the reporters, he had unsuccessfully argued against facets of the Administration's course toward easing relations with China. He felt the United States had been trapped by the Chinese invitation; the visit had been a mistake because it might tend to undermine American support for Taiwan. He did endorse the recent lifting of some trade and travel restrictions against Peking, but was concerned about a pace in U.S. policy that might appear to suggest this country was overly eager for an accommodation. Such an impression could adversely affect American public opinion toward the Taiwan regime.

The discourse and the drinking went on for about three hours. At one point Agnew candidly said he wasn't sure whether he would be an asset or a liability on the G.O.P. ticket in 1972, but that he hadn't decided whether he would want to run again. The reporters finally made their way out after three o'clock, bound to secrecy.

In spite of the strict secrecy imposed, three reporters not present at the gathering found out about what was said in considerable detail. Not bound by any agreement, two of them went to

Gold, told him what they knew, and asked for an opportunity to interview the Vice-President about his remarks. Gold respectfully declined, thanking the reporters for coming to him. The Vice-President, he said, had spoken off the record and as far as he was concerned that arrangement still stood.

The circumstances created a bizarre situation. As word of the developing story spread, other newsmen began to go after it. The first to get an account of the midnight meeting into print was Tom Ottenad of the St. Louis *Post-Dispatch,* who made an afternoon edition. Others soon swarmed all over the story, except the unfortunate nine who had been in the room with the Vice-President. They still felt bound to write nothing, though some went to Gold to ask that they be relieved of the stricture imposed the night before. Agnew declined. As a result, the nine select reporters were captives of their own story. On the bulletin board in the press room, somebody chalked the words FREE THE WILLIAMSBURG NINE, but they never were released from their promise.

The story hit Washington and the Administration hard. Here, for the first time on a major issue, the Vice-President had expressed reservations about important Administration foreign policy—second-guessing the President, or so it seemed. Even while reporters in Williamsburg were sniffing out the story, Agnew was telling the Republican governors in a private luncheon meeting pretty much what he had told the Williamsburg Nine the night before: that he had some reservations about easing relations with Peking, but that the policy had been set and he supported it. At the White House, steps were taken quickly to smother the suggestions of a disagreement. Press Secretary Ziegler told reporters that contrary to the stories from Williamsburg, Agnew "fully supports" the Administration's initiative toward China. He said he had talked to Agnew by phone that morning and had been authorized to say "there is absolutely no disagreement over policy." Later in the day Ziegler tried to throw more cold water on the matter. "You should not pursue the story that there is a difference of opinion within the Administration, particularly a difference of opinion between the Vice-President and the President regarding the recent initiatives that the United States Government took toward the Republic of China. There is no difference of opinion."

Ziegler did not, nor did anyone else at the White House, deny that Agnew had said what was reported. Nor was any explanation given why he had said it in a postmidnight meeting with strict prohibitions about publication. In an Administration often accused of speaking out of both sides of its mouth, and practicing "studied ambiguity" to keep all its friends happy and its foes uncertain, there was wild speculation as to motive. Was Agnew floating a trial balloon for the Administration, to test the public impact of a détente? Was he letting the ultraconservatives know they still had a friend in court? Was he making a daring, independent bid for the hard-line anti-Communist constituency? Was he "going public" with a fight he had lost within the Administration? Or was he just saying what he thought, in the relaxed atmosphere of a late-night bull session? When all the opinions were in there was no clear consensus, though in light of later developments the latter seemed as close to the truth as any hypothesis.

Through all this there was nothing but silence from the President. In the past he had often offered praise for Agnew, but this time he said nothing. There were widespread reports within the White House that on this occasion Agnew had gone too far, either by intent or just plain carelessness, and that the President didn't like it. Later developments clarified why he would not have been pleased by his Vice-President's garrulousness; in mid-July, after a secret trip to Peking by Kissinger, the President announced to an astonished world that he himself had been invited to visit China for talks with its top leaders, and had accepted. The move was a brilliant diplomatic and political stroke, said to have been months in the making. In light of that revelation, for Nixon to have been anything other than chagrined at the Williamsburg incident would have been amazing.

Inevitably, though the Peking breakthrough had not yet developed, Agnew's performance in Williamsburg intensified the speculation that he might be dropped from the ticket. But the President's silence worked both ways. Had Nixon been looking for a reason to unload his Vice-President, that incident surely would have been the ideal rationale, yet he did not seize it—at least not then. So the game called "the Future of Spiro Agnew" continued to be played through the spring, summer and fall, with no better clues about the answer than earlier.

Agnew did not go underground after the Williamsburg flap. Instead he resumed his revenue-sharing salesmanship job, never hesitating to rise up and smite a foe he felt needed smiting. Later in April, when war protesters marched in Washington in an orderly fashion, he called them "well-motivated but confused"; in New Orleans at about the same time, he staunchly defended FBI Director J. Edgar Hoover against "opportunists" seeking the Democratic presidential nomination in 1972; in May, he called the Mayday protesters "the same scruffy individuals that caused the disruptions in Chicago in 1968."

When Senator Fulbright said Agnew had impugned the patriotism of Senate doves, the Vice-President was particularly blunt. "This is a very serious accusation, and one that demands a response," Agnew replied. "My response is this: he lies in his teeth. I challenge him to prove that I have ever made such a statement. . . . The truth of the matter is that on many occasions I have said just the opposite—that the Senate doves are patriotic and well-motivated. Unfortunately, these good intentions do not keep them from being absolutely wrong." There, at last, the insertion of those disclaimers had paid off. Fulbright professed astonishment. "I didn't know there was any doubt about his attitude toward me and many others in the Senate who have criticized the war policy," he said. "It is clearly the thrust and implication of many of his remarks that we were aiding and abetting the enemy . . . to imply that I have betrayed the country. There is no doubt about the thrust of what he said."

In Jackson, Mississippi, two nights later, Agnew repeated the charge, accusing Fulbright and Republican Senator Jacob Javits of "using the tactics of verbal smear in order to discredit and intimidate those who disagree with their viewpoint. I have no intention of being intimidated or silenced by such tactics." And then he observed, "To be a public man is not always easy. But to be a public man who is loyal to one's principles and benign in all of one's pronouncements is wholly impossible. Politics is the arena. Ours is an adversary system. The options are simple—fight for your principles or abandon them. Weasel or take the flack. Give in or fight. I try to make my positions clear. I know they are consistent. They represent what I honestly believe. I shall continue to state them in such a way that I will not be misunderstood." This from the man who constantly complained that he was being misunderstood.

True to his word, Agnew kept on swinging. In June, in Nassau, he criticized what he called "a wave of paranoia" in the news business based on unwarranted fears of government repression and censorship; when the *New York Times* obtained and published parts of the "Pentagon Papers," the secret study of U.S. involvement in Vietnam, he deplored conducting diplomacy "on the pages of a newspaper" and later characterized the publication as "a cheap, common fencing operation." To the National Young Republicans Federation in Phoenix, he said: "The same people who are putting this most distorted viewpoint of American participation in the South Vietnamese war before the American people, the same people who rush to expose those portions of secret documents that support their point of view—even though they may just be contingency plans that were drawn up to take care of events that never happen—these are the same people who are firmly controlling American opinion through a biased and slanted and an oversighted viewpoint of what is taking place around the world."

It was a parting shot before Agnew left in late June on a month-long trip around the world, starting with the inauguration of President Chung Hee Park in South Korea. But this time he did not stop off at Taiwan to assure Chiang Kai-shek that all was well; he was far westward, through Singapore, Kuwait, Saudi Arabia, Ethiopia, Kenya and the Congo by the time Kissinger completed his secret mission to Peking and Nixon made his surprise announcement that buoyed the world, Taiwan excepted. Agnew also visited Spain, Morocco and Portugal on that largely uneventful trip, which seemed by its itinerary designed to keep the Vice-President off the beaten path and out of any highly controversial diplomatic situations.

The immediate surmise, in fact, was that Agnew had been elegantly put on ice in all these faraway places with strange-sounding names, so that he would not somehow gum up the secret overtures to China. The Associated Press's White House correspondent, Frank Cormier, wrote that the Vice-President had not been informed in advance of Kissinger's mission. Agnew remained tight-lipped on China throughout the trip, but privately he seethed at the suggestion that he couldn't be trusted to keep a secret of such global import, or that he would speak out, if he knew, against such a major Nixon initiative. Actually, Agnew aides insisted, as a member of the National Security Council, the Vice-

President certainly knew of the Nixon Administration's plans to seek a détente with China, and supported them.

Feeding the speculation that Agnew had been farmed out was the fact that he made very few personal appearances during the month-long trip, saw the reporters accompanying him infrequently and played golf thirteen times. Although he paid diplomatic calls at each stop, the general impression was that he was on a lark—an impression fanned particularly by one event in Kenya, at the famous Treetops lodge on a huge game preserve, overlooking a watering hole. With a party of about thirty-five guests, including his doctor and his secretary, the Vice-President had dinner and watched the wild animals. He played the tourist —fed sugar to a baboon named Gladys, dubbed one of the performers "the Gina Lollobrigida of the buffalo set," dined on gazelle meat, and when two rhinoceroses proceeded to make love in full view, called the scene "an X movie." To Agnew's understandable outrage, the night was described thus in *Newsweek:* "Aside from hacking up the local golf course, his main outing was to a nearby hunting lodge, where in company with his private physician and his pretty, red-haired secretary, he watched two rhinos copulating." Relations with the traveling press had been cool up to then; thereafter they became frigid, though the *Newsweek* correspondent in Kenya was not part of the traveling press entourage.

The most serious flap of the trip, however, was of Agnew's own making. En route from Kinsasha in the Congo to Madrid, he held a press conference on *Air Force Two* and volunteered his impressions of the black leaders he had met in Africa. America's black leaders "could learn much" from them, he said. Kenya's Jomo Kenyatta (Agnew called him "Yomo"), Ethiopia's Haile Selassie and the Congo's Joseph Mobutu—all political strong men—"have impressed me with their understanding of the internal problems and their moderateness," he said, ". . . in distinct contrast with many of those in the United States who have arrogated unto themselves the position of black leaders; those who spend their time in querulous complaint and constant recrimination against the rest of society."

Nothing he had said on the trip about foreign policy—and that was very little—could match this pointed, long-distance attack on black American leadership for impact in the United States. The comment—volunteered, not pried from him—sounded like a playback of his Baltimore lecture of 1968. Congressman William Clay of St. Louis, a leader of the Black Caucus, said of Agnew on the House floor: "Our Vice-President is seriously ill. He has all the symptoms of an intellectual misfit. His recent tirade against black leadership is just part of a game played by him, called mental masturbation. Apparently, Mr. Agnew is an intellectual sadist who experiences intellectual orgasms by attacking, humiliating and kicking the oppressed."

But Agnew was unmoved, even by this intemperate outburst. Asked later whether his comment had been "wise," he replied, "Well, I don't know whether it was wise in the sense that I should not have known where the emphasis would be placed, but the comment was one that wasn't entirely a spontaneous one. I thought of the implications of it, but I thought it was important that the black population of this country realize that there was a type of leadership which was positive and direct and helpful to the establishment in those countries in carrying out the necessary steps to raise the standard of living and to increase the benefits to all people." The African black leaders, of course, *were* the establishment, and an iron-handed one too, in most places; nor were any of the African states visited particularly known as an economic, political or social Utopia for the average black man.

Agnew's airborne attack on black American leaders, and the speculation that he had been sent into temporary exile while Kissinger went to Peking, made his return to Washington in late July an event of more than usual interest. If the President wanted to end the speculation that his understudy was in the doghouse, he could go to Andrews Air Force Base to greet him. But Nixon did not; instead he sent Secretary of State William P. Rogers. Agnew shook hands with Rogers, said nothing, climbed into a limousine and sped off—to the White House, where the President came out, told him he had done "a fine job," and escorted him into his office for a fuller report. The future of Spiro Agnew was no clearer than it had been.

In succeeding days Agnew told friends he was most unhappy that his round-the-world trip had been cast by the press as jet-age exile to Siberia or, worse, as an extravagant golfing tour. Select newsmen were informed that the Vice-President indeed had been on serious diplomatic business; that his itinerary had been determined not to put him on the shelf but to fulfill long-standing diplomatic obligations and invitations. He told the *Christian Science Monitor* that he supported the President's planned trip to Peking and always had fully supported the policy of improving relations with the Chinese. His remarks in Williamsburg, he said, had been "misunderstood and obfuscated to an extent . . . I was one hundred percent in favor of the initiative then and, of course, still am. But I am distressed with the euphoria with which the initiative was received. There was an immediate assumption that this meant an end to all tensions between the United States and mainland China and a resolution of all our ideological difficulties. This, of course, is not realistic. . . . We've got a long way to go. But at least we've made a step toward discussing these matters. I don't think we should become so optimistic that people would feel that in case these discussions don't bring about an immediate resolution of all difficulties, they should be discouraged."

The circumstances and timing of Agnew's trip abroad, and the China initiative, were not the only elements now contributing to the guessing game about his political stock. In mid-August, President Nixon suddenly summoned his chief economic advisers to Camp David in Maryland for a weekend of important talks. From those sessions emerged another startling reversal in the Nixon Administration—the ordering of a ninety-day wage-price freeze, the floating of the American dollar and other turnabout economic moves that had been anathema to Republican dogma. The President announced the new policy in a nationwide television talk, and the next day out on the firing line as Nixon's chief economic spokesman was none other than John B. Connally—the man most frequently mentioned as Agnew's successor on the 1972 Republican ticket. The combination of Agnew's troubles and Connally's ascendancy in the Nixon inner circle kept the dump-Agnew talk buzzing in Washington's gossip mill. *Newsweek* put Connally on its cover, under the label NIXON's No. 2 MAN? Republicans and Democrats alike on Capitol Hill and around the country professed to see the end of Spiro Agnew in the rapid emergence of the tall, driving, ambitious Texan.

But if Ted Agnew was concerned, he didn't show it. For one thing, a week before, at a private meeting with officials of the Republican National Committee, the President had told them, "Support the Vice-President. Do what you can to help the Vice-President. He's got a tough job and he's doing it well. He's been attacked and maligned unfairly." And on the day after Nixon announced his new economic policy, Agnew was present as the President briefed State Department sub-Cabinet officials on its diplomatic implications. Suddenly he grasped Agnew's arm and raised it with his own over his head. In his own talk to the group, in Nixon's amused presence, Agnew reportedly spoke of "inflation and unemployment—specifically the inflation of the egos of certain economic prophets and the much-discussed possible unemployment of the Vice-President." Several days later, asked on *Issues and Answers* whether he was worried that Connally would replace him on the 1972 ticket, Agnew said, "Not a bit. . . . There is no competition between Secretary Connally and me in the sense that we are trying to elbow each other for the vice-presidential nomination in 1972. Realistically, I think many things would have to happen before I would become concerned about the possibility of a person of the other party receiving the nomination for Vice-President in my party. . . . I don't believe that if Secretary Connally became a candidate for Vice-President he would remain a Democrat. . . ." As for running again himself, Agnew said the President "must select the most potent and powerful Vice-President that he can find." He did not think Nixon would decide before 1972, he said, and "until he decides, it would be fruitless for me to make any decision."

What Agnew was saying was only basic civics. As always in the American system, selection of the Vice-President came down to a one-man constituency—the President of the United States.

Through all the Connally speculation Agnew remained cool, and outwardly at least, good-humored. In mid-September he went to San Juan, Puerto Rico, for the 63rd National Governors Conference and said: "This has been a good year for governors. There are four governors in Washington: the Vice-President, at Transportation [Volpe], at HUD [Romney] and another one in a holding pattern." And he told of picking up the phone in his office a few days earlier and hearing a recorded message that said, "Your four years are up. Please signal when through." In mid-November, at a Republican Governors Conference in French Lick, Indiana, he reported he had just come from Chicago, where he had stayed in the hotel's vice-presidential suite. "Secretary Connally was out of town," he said. "I asked about check-out time, and they said, 'Election Day.'"

Through it all, too, his own desires remained difficult to fathom. At San Juan, he agreed to be a more active White House lobbyist for the governors so readily that some Democrats told reporters he had solicited the job at a private meeting, to obtain an open door to the President's office. Republican Governor Linwood Holton of Virginia, also at the meeting, called the report preposterous. Yet there were signs that Agnew was determined to make himself less controversial, and hence more acceptable as a 1972 running mate. In a distinctly conciliatory mood, he urged Republican and Democratic governors, in discussing the Nixon economic policy, to "raise the exchange rate of our ideas . . . to set aside the kind of petty bickering that interferes with healthy debate and put away the partisan jockeying for position that so clouds the issues and saps the cooperative spirit so urgently needed today." The tone of Agnew's remarks dampened any dump-Agnew thoughts that might have been in liberal Republican minds. Oregon's Tom McCall, who the previous December at Sun Valley had called Agnew's talk there a "rotten, bigoted little speech," told reporters: "The Agnew you saw here today would go over very well in Oregon." Not a Republican governor could be found who openly advocated dumping him, and most said they expected him to be on the ticket again.

No sooner had the governors discovered the conciliatory Agnew, however, than he was off dragon-slaying again. A week later, in Washington, he attacked four Democratic presidential prospects—Muskie, McGovern, Humphrey and Kennedy—for "reckless and appalling" talk in contending that defense spending could be cut deeply without impairing national security. "All of those gentlemen are well-motivated, sincere citizens," he said in the standard disclaimer before lowering the boom, "but in my judgment they are terribly wrong, dangerously wrong, and they should be held accountable if they disastrously tamper with the national security." He compared their call for a "reordering of priorities" with a similar plea from Gus Hall, general secretary of the Communist party of the United States. "I'm sure I'll catch a few editorial slings and arrows for using his name in the same speech with theirs," he observed, as if to take the curse off the technique, "but what he says is germane to our discussion." Again, as so often in the past, speculation that Spiro Agnew had been muzzled or had muzzled himself proved to be inaccurate. At the G.O.P.

governors meeting in French Lick, he unloaded on Representative "Pete" McCloskey, the California Republican and Korean War combat hero who had decided to challenge President Nixon in the 1972 New Hampshire primary. "Pete McCloskey is in such a money bind," the Vice-President reported, "he's been forced to auction off his personal art collection. Yesterday he sold his favorite painting—'Benedict Arnold Crossing the Delaware.' " That one caused some of the liberal governors present to cringe, but they mostly held their tongues.

In early October, at El Paso, Texas, Agnew came full circle by defending his technique of broad-brush attack as "the politics of positive division." He said he enjoyed "the hydrophobic hostility" of "a pompous, unelected, liberal elite" and he resurrected the "radical-liberal" label of the 1970 campaign, serving notice that "come 1972, be assured, we intend to strengthen the hand of the President during the second Nixon Administration by removing most, if not all, of these afflicted souls from the source of their infection," which he described as Potomac Fever. Thus, a year after Agnew's 1970 attempted purge of "radical-liberals" had yielded such meager results and had generated so much criticism, even within his own party, he was announcing that as far as he was concerned, it would be more of the same in 1972. Asked whether Agnew had been speaking for the White House, Press Secretary Ziegler said only that the Vice-President had expressed his view of "a goal the Republican party will seek." From all this, it was clear that Agnew would not sit back and brood over his future. With his President embattled on the right as a result of his heretical overtures to Communist China and his abandonment of conservative economic orthodoxy, Agnew was out on the firing line again protecting that sagging flank—reminding the right what the alternative to Nixon would be.

There always remained in Agnew's words and deeds one consistency—fealty to Richard Nixon. On learning that the ultraconservative Young Americans for Freedom had disavowed Nixon at their mock convention, and had nominated him instead, he wrote: "I feel it reasonable to point out that if my efforts as Vice-President are indeed deserving of such support, it is only because I, as a member of the Nixon Administration, have been working since January, 1969, to help carry out the President's program for our Nation." Even in this thank-you note he was serving his President, telling the young right wing: Love me, love my boss. It was a message Nixon needed telling, and it was a measure of how far Agnew had come since that day of anointment in Miami Beach. The question now was whether this phenomenon—a Vice-President pulling his President on his coattails among the disenchanted right—would determine how far Agnew might yet go.

For all the criticism of Agnew on the left, there was no apparent disposition to put him under wraps; the clamor from the right demanding Agnew's retention, and excoriating the Nixon Administration's foreign policy initiatives, was an effective counter. In mid-October, despite a raging controversy in this country and in Agnew's ancestral home, Greece, over continued American support of the military dictatorship that put democracy on the shelf in Athens in 1968, the President agreed to let his deputy stop there on the way back from Iran's 2500th anniversary celebration, where Agnew had met with exiled King Constantine of Greece for seventy minutes. In Athens, Agnew gloried in an extravagant reception by his fellow Greeks in general and by President George Papadopoulos in particular. The Greek military government took maximum advantage of the visit, using it as a badge of respectability before a critical Western Europe and the world. Agnew played his part, conspicuously avoiding use of the word "democracy" as he spoke in its very cradle, and ignoring the cries of protest from 174 elected deputies of the old Greek parliament that he was playing into the hands of "those who have usurped power and hold it by force." According to reporters accompanying Agnew, a visit to his father's birthplace, the village of Gargalianoi, was a genuinely moving experience for him. But it did not move his critics at home from insisting that he could have picked a more diplomatic time to indulge his yearnings to return to his ancestral home. (Actually, Agnew's attitude toward totalitarianism and political repression in Greece had been on the record since September 1968, when, as the Republican vice-presidential candidate, he told the National Press Club: "The Greek military government that took over in 1967 has not proven itself to be as horrendous a specter to contemplate as most people thought it would.")

Agnew returned to Washington with speculation about his future on the 1972 ticket continuing unabated. A decision by Nixon to send Connally to Saigon for the inauguration of President

Thieu—a mission that many thought would have fallen automatically to the Vice-President—was seized upon as a sign that Nixon was moving to bolster Connally's foreign policy credentials with an eye to making him Agnew's 1972 replacement. For his part, Agnew continued to insist that what he wanted was whatever was most likely to help the re-election of Richard Nixon, even if that meant Spiro Agnew's stepping aside. In an interview with the Associated Press's Walter Mears, he said Nixon should make the decision "without any feeling about sympathy for whatever my situation might be. It's got to be done in a cold, hard, practical political way because the big thing is to get him re-elected."

Throughout the fall of 1971 and into 1972, however, the fate of Spiro Agnew remained prime grist for the political mill. The liberal Ripon Society of the Republican party called for his removal from the 1972 ticket; the President was reported by columnist Jack Anderson to have commissioned a poll on whether Agnew would help or hurt him in 1972; in another poll of delegates to the 1968 Republican convention, 76.5 percent of 861 delegates responding said he should be renominated, and 71 percent said a dump-Agnew movement would damage the ticket's chances of winning in 1972. Beyond the mock presidential nomination of Agnew by the Young Americans for Freedom, other party conservatives formed "Americans for Agnew" and pledged that the group would "do everything in its power . . . to ensure that Agnew will be on the ticket in 1972." Lee Edwards, a young Washington publicist with ties to the G.O.P.'s old Goldwater wing, issued the rallying cry: "In an era of ideological eunuchs, he stands almost alone as a man of principle; yet Washington, D.C., is ablaze with rumors that Vice-President Agnew will be dumped from the G.O.P. ticket in 1972."

It was true; the rumors were flying. White House political adviser Harry Dent wrote the Queens County, New York, Conservative Republican Association that "despite what you read in the press, there is no plan to drop Mr. Agnew from the ticket in 1972," but Dent was an acknowledged Agnew aficionado. Only Richard Nixon, the man who had "discovered" Spiro Agnew in 1968, could confirm the rumors or set them to rest.

21

◇•◇•◇•◇•◇•◇

WHAT PRICE AGNEW?

A S Spiro Agnew embarked on the fourth year of his term as
Vice-President of the United States, he had the satisfaction
of having been the office's busiest and most talked-about occupant. Richard Nixon, who knew personally the feelings of isolation and impotence the office could bring, had made sure his
Vice-President was thoroughly briefed on most major issues, was
included on high-level councils, was given a panoply of advisory
and ceremonial responsibilities and, most important, was given
his head. Concerning the last license, Agnew himself had par-
layed his freedom into a bonanza of publicity and controversy,
making a shambles of the clichés about the obscurity of the Vice-
Presidency. Yet, for all that, as the time approached for a decision
on whether he would seek or be asked to seek a second term, all
those closest to him knew that he shared with all those truly obscure predecessors in the Vice-Presidency one overriding legacy of
that office—frustration.

Although Nixon outdid his President, Dwight Eisenhower, in
the generosity with which he treated his Vice-President, Agnew
confessed to intimates that the job was a disappointment. He had
come into it after four years of administrative responsibility in
one of the largest counties in the nation and after two years as
governor. He had served those six years at a time a whole new
inventory of urban and suburban problems was surfacing. He had

been introduced at the administrative level to federal programs dealing with those problems, and had dealt with them on the receiving end in both local and state contexts. Hence, he believed deeply that he was uniquely qualified among the ranking members of the Nixon Administration to give direction and leadership to the spectrum of domestic programs that went out of the executive branch to Congress, the states and localities. His time in Annapolis, Agnew said later, "was a very, very fine training for me. It was a very active time. We revised the entire tax structure of the state, which revised the education structure and the public safety structure. I had a lot to do with local governments, and my four years as county executive were equally productive because that's again a different ball game. You get to see how each level of government must depend on its own resources and each one has its own problems. I think those years were of tremendous benefit; anyone in the federal system would benefit by training in state and local government."

Nixon had taken note of Agnew's qualifications in assigning him as the Administration's liaison with the governors and mayors, but in that post he was little more than a glorified errand boy. The important roles were in policy making and administration, and Shultz and Ehrlichman had settled in as the key staff men on the domestic front.

To men around Agnew, it was considered short-sighted that Ehrlichman, a man with no notable experience in the field of domestic problems, would be put in charge when a man like the Vice-President, with his experience in administering domestic programs, was available. Agnew had demonstrated in Annapolis, one of his associates said later, that "what was more important than the policy was actually finding out how you could make it work. There are plenty of policy men around, but when you get down to trying to fit and impose a new policy on an ongoing structure, you run into some terrific practical problems. If you don't face up to them when you're talking about changing policy, the policy itself will get killed in the process." Agnew increasingly felt that this aspect had not been thought through adequately at high levels in the Administration. In the building of grand domestic concepts, the practical approach of how things would work was systematically structured out, the Vice-President believed, resulting in lofty programs stumbling over the simplest but unanticipated realities.

He felt, obviously, that he was the man who could make that contribution if only he were given the chance. ". . . More important than words in this campaign and in the next Administration," he had said in accepting the vice-presidential nomination at the 1968 convention, "will be action, the kind of action that flows from involvement in the problems, and from the closest kind of relationship with the people who are involved in the problems." Since then, however, there had been more words than action, and he didn't really participate in enough of what little action there was.

Part of the reason for Agnew's reaction was his limitless self-confidence that he had the answers. But another motive was also his genuine and undiminished loyalty and admiration for Nixon, who, he felt, was being hurt because good advice was not getting through to him, from his Vice-President and others. Agnew retained his belief that Nixon would make the right decisions if confronted with the practicalities of high-sounding domestic policies laid before him, and he was chagrined that the failure of programs not adequately thought out in terms of the practicalities reflected negatively, and in his view unfairly, on the President. He said in private, in fact, that the Administration's much-ballyhooed domestic programs were largely a sham, all theory and promotion, with appallingly little horse sense and substance. He questioned seriously whether the American people would give the Nixon Administration a second term based on how little had been accomplished domestically, and in moments of deepest frustration, whether indeed it deserved a second term. Such pessimistic thinking naturally colored his own views on whether he wanted to be part of four more years of the same—if indeed there were going to be four more years of the same, or of anything, for the Nixon Administration—let alone whether there would be a political future beyond that for him. What persuaded Agnew to persevere and keep his options open into 1972 was, as much as personal motivation, his profound loyalty to the President and his desire to defend Nixon within the Administration as he long and outspokenly had defended him outside it.

This matter of loyalty to Nixon was a key yet little-understood element in the President's power within his Administration. Basically a suspicious man politically, Nixon needed loyalty around him. Over the years he favored those men most unswervingly loyal. Inevitably, a sort of palace-guard atmosphere was created, with ranking aides vying for favor through the coin of the Nixon realm—not always brains or performance, but loyalty. It was a weakness in terms of selection and use of men, but it enabled Nixon to retain, in the eyes of the men around him, a kind of protective armor against error. " 'It's not the President's fault'—it always gets back to that," a Nixon insider acknowledged on one occasion. "Nixon in some way or another always manages to have it come out that way. I suppose it's because, with the higher degree of loyalty he commands from people, he accumulates loyal people, and the others, with whom loyalty might not be so obvious, just don't get in. But he manages to keep those around him, even though it's a very unsettled existence, with such a high degree of loyalty to him that they can never say anything bad about him. And that promotes internal conflict, because you can't blame it on Nixon; you have it in your head that, 'Well, he's a good guy, I know that; every time I see him, he's the finest fellow. He's got everything figured right; he knows what you're saying to him; he's swift, he's smart, so none of this can be his fault; ergo, it's all these other guys around him.' And he thrives on it. Even his unwillingness, or even inability, to deliver bad news, is preserving that image. He's always trying to be a good guy."

Agnew did not escape that same special hold Nixon had on the people around him. It had been importantly involved in Agnew's determination to speak out against the President's critics in the first place; that sense of deep loyalty to Nixon, plus the frustration, even then, that the Vice-Presidency gave him no meaningful way to serve a President ill served by others. Now, in 1971 and 1972, both feelings were stronger than ever and were reflected in Agnew's increasing inclination after the 1970 elections to tell intimates and even interviewers that he was not sure he wanted a second term.

According to Agnew intimates, there was no reason to doubt he meant what he said in suggesting that stepping aside for another man in 1972 would not break his heart. If he were to be convinced in his own mind that his name on the ticket might mean Nixon's defeat, it would be in character for him to withdraw voluntarily, or to bow out gracefully if asked by Nixon to do so. The Vice-President said as much in an interview with Alan Otten, Washington bureau chief of the *Wall Street Journal*, in February

1971. "I am very relaxed about it," he said. "If, when Mr. Nixon decides that he is going to run himself again, he also decides there is some other person who would be more helpful to him as a running mate, I would certainly never contest that judgment. I would not only step aside willingly but I would support and campaign for the ticket." The only exception, he said, would be if his replacement's views were "totally hostile to my own," and even then he would "withdraw and shut my mouth." He was not, he said, "locked into a compelling psychological need to keep this job. . . . It's entirely possible that someone not hungry for the political side of life might not want to continue in government, might want to return to private life. Many people at my stage of life want to consider the welfare of their family. Despite the very substantial pay increases recently [$62,500 salary and $10,000 expenses], the pay here still is not what you could get in outside life for equal responsibility. Nor is the tax structure very helpful; a good part of that pay is on a rubber band, and it snaps right back into the Treasury."

There were, however, other factors to be considered in weighing whether Agnew would be offered and would accept a second nomination. It was a fact, by the end of 1971, that even moderate Republicans, on Capitol Hill and elsewhere, were privately howling for his scalp. In the face of such sentiment, Agnew's disavowal of great interest in a second term was dismissed by some as the defense mechanism of an exceedingly proud man against rejection. Also, there was Richard Nixon's own personality and his special attitude toward the Vice-Presidency—how he felt occupying it, functioning in it, and nearly being dumped from it. "You must remember that Richard Nixon spent eight years being ignored by a President," one White House aide said. "He knows Vice-Presidents are ignored and he knows that's not very nice for Vice-Presidents." Nixon too had shared the usual frustrations, had drawn the same heat and, specifically, had squirmed under the knowledge that there were some in his party who didn't want him on the ticket a second time. To men close to Nixon through the years, and particularly in 1956 when Harold Stassen tried to enlist Eisenhower in a dump-Nixon effort, the idea that the President would be a party to a similar ploy, with Agnew as the target this time, was hard to contemplate.

Even on the personal level, they asked, if Agnew was to be

dumped, who would inform him? "Certainly not Nixon," one old hand insisted with conviction in late 1971. "The mechanics of this would be pretty interesting. You see, the President is not going to call Spiro Agnew in and say, 'I don't want you on the ticket.' He'll never do that. If he doesn't want him on the ticket, somebody will be sent to try to convey gracefully that word. The trouble with that procedure, à la the Hickel episode, is that often the fellow who is to be told doesn't know he's been told. [When Hickel was fired from the Nixon Cabinet in 1970, the blow came only after repeated "hints" to quit. Finally he was called to the White House on the subterfuge that his departmental budget was to be discussed. He was ushered into Nixon's office, where the President, in the presence of Ehrlichman, and after much beating around the bush, told him he was through. "Occasionally he would put in: 'Wally, you know how much I've always thought of you,'" Hickel later told friends.] And you look over the cast of messengers who could be sent to Agnew to accomplish such a task— there could be Haldeman, Mitchell and possibly Ehrlichman, but I really don't think the latter. You're down to about those two; the reason is that if the President sent somebody else to have a delicate discussion with him, Agnew would sense that that didn't mean a whole lot. Mitchell and Haldeman are the only two guys he knows that carry messages—real messages. And for practical reasons, that would narrow it down to Mitchell. If Haldeman went over there, Agnew wouldn't be quite sure of that either, because that might just mean, 'Nixon doesn't really feel that way; Haldeman probably has run me down and has gotten Nixon in a weak moment to do this.'

"Even with Mitchell, it would be a very difficult case to make. With Hickel, that was something that had come to real loggerheads. It just had to be resolved, and had been let go for a long time. In this case, this guy [Agnew] hasn't done anything. The case you can make is that he helped; and Mitchell would make it. So just on the mechanics of it, it's hard to see that coming off— unless, of course, Spiro himself walks over to the White House, braces the guards and slips a note under the door saying, 'Incidentally, in case you're wondering, I've made other plans.' But I don't think he's going to be run off that way. More likely, he'll sit right there, especially if he begins to hear more and more gossip. He feels strongly that if anybody over there is trying to undermine him, he's not going to let them get away with it."

Any conspiracy against Agnew within the palace guard ran great risk of being suspected by Nixon himself, having personally encountered and successfully combatted the dump-Nixon exercise in 1956. Nixon was a man who lived constantly with his past and who measured his progress by his success in making amends for past indignities and injustices inflicted upon him; Stassen's dump-Nixon effort was considered by many old Nixon hands in 1972 to be one of Agnew's best insurance policies for a second nomination if he wanted it.

An equally persuasive argument against a genuine dump-Agnew move was the 1969–71 phenomenon of the man himself as a political commodity. In the process of speaking out in defense of the President and against the protesting and disruptive elements in the society, Agnew had developed a large and volatile constituency in the country, in Middle America, and particularly in the South. The arithmetic of 1972 suggested that an inevitable fall-off in large Northern industrial states Nixon had carried in 1968—like Ohio, Illinois and New Jersey—required a compensatory pickup of 1968 Wallace states in Dixie, plus retention of the critical Border States where Agnew had been so helpful in 1968. Not only could he help keep that critical constituency in 1972; any attempt to oust him from the ticket could trigger noisy and divisive rebellion against the Republican ticket within that constituency. In four years the forgotten Americans about whom Richard Nixon had talked principally in the 1968 campaign had become Spiro Agnew's forgotten Americans, and dropping him would be asking for trouble. Scott Moore, Agnew's old lieutenant and sidekick in Towson who accompanied him to the raucous 1964 Republican convention that nominated Barry Goldwater, put it this way: "Looking back to the San Francisco convention, you knock Agnew off that ticket, you've got hell to pay. Next time, if Nixon goes to get the liberal vote, Republicans won't like it. And what will happen if he dumps Agnew?" Moore's point was underlined in late July 1971 when twelve leading conservatives, led by columnist William Buckley, met in New York and announced they had "suspended" their support of Nixon out of disappointment in his national security policies, including his overtures to mainland

China. They did not mention Agnew, but the move suggested an unsubtle application of pressure from the right, of which Agnew would be a natural beneficiary.

In the last days of 1971, the disenchanted Republican conservatives took the ultimate step by persuading Representative John M. Ashbrook of Ohio to declare his candidacy against Nixon in the New Hampshire primary. In an effort to head off the challenge, Agnew himself met Buckley in New York, but his efforts were unavailing. Ashbrook, in his announcement, said he intended to pressure Nixon to stop his "leftward drift," and he emphasized that his argument was against the President, not against Agnew. In fact, Ashbrook said, he hoped Agnew would be renominated.

For all the general expectations that political expert Nixon would make a pragmatic choice on his 1972 running mate, intimates also were aware that emotional strains on him could counter pragmatism. The strong pull Nixon had on the loyal men around him worked both ways, and again there was the Eisenhower syndrome to be considered—how Ike had treated Nixon. Nixon had done all that was asked of him as Vice-President and had to scheme to stay on the ticket in 1956; Agnew had done all that was asked of him as Vice-President—indeed, had done just what Nixon had done, only more so. How could he be faulted—or punished—for that?

It was said that Agnew had become Nixon's Nixon. In fact, Agnew had in many ways actually out-Nixoned Nixon, even at his most astute. In 1967 and 1968, one of Nixon's most effective stratagems was his conversion of the press's past performance toward him—particularly in 1960 and 1962—into a weapon to neutralize it. By constantly telling reporters that they twice had done him in—but that he had no hard feelings, mind you, and they were perfectly within their rights—he had encouraged a mass guilt complex among them and had softened their professional diligence toward him. From 1969 to 1971 the Vice-President had gone Nixon one better; he had dragged the press and television kicking and screaming before Middle America and had administered a good old-fashioned whipping, to the great glee of a nation of onlookers. He had not, of course, sought to intimidate the press and TV. Hadn't he said so? In 1968 Nixon had shamed the press into taking it easy on him; in the next immediate years Agnew browbeat the press and TV to ease off. He called his assault a plea for self-examination; it was, especially for the federally licensed television business, the plea of the Damocles sword, and to a fair degree it worked.

Not only did Agnew do in spades what he had been asked to do; he also became the personification of the Nixon Administration, perhaps even more than the President in this sense: in an Administration that used words without comprehending their impact, then cried "foul" when called to account for what the words had wrought, Spiro Agnew was the chief practitioner. Like Agnew, the Nixon Administration talked more, with an unprecedented publicity and propaganda machinery to process and exploit its words, than any before it. Like Agnew, the Nixon Administration systematically set up façades and smoke screens of words to obscure lack of program in some areas and foot dragging in others. John Mitchell had told black parents complaining about seeming contradictions in desegregation policy, "You would be better informed if instead of listening to what we say, you watch what we do." It was a remarkable comment for an Administration that was so much words and, at least on the broad domestic front of prime interest to the Vice-President, so little action. Finally, for all its words the Nixon Administration, like Agnew, did not seem to understand that words could be as inflammatory and divisive in the society as the bombs it constantly saw in the hands of its real and imagined foes. Rejection of Spiro Agnew by the Nixon Administration would be, clearly, a rejection of self. The only way out, if there was to be a way out, had to be a voluntary withdrawal by Agnew himself, confronted by evidence that he might hurt Nixon more in 1972 than he could help him.

As 1972 opened, the expectation was that the country would have to wait until the Republican National Convention in August to learn Agnew's fate. On the second night of the new year, however, in an one-hour television interview with CBS White House correspondent Dan Rather, Nixon gave his Vice-President a delayed Christmas present. Right off, Rather asked the President whether he could give assurances, "categorically and unequivocally," that he wanted Agnew as his running mate again and that the Vice-President would be on the 1972 ticket. That decision would be made at the convention, Nixon said, but "if I am a candidate I obviously will have something to say about it. My view is that one should not break up a winning combination. I

believe that the Vice-President has handled his difficult assignments with dignity, with courage; he's at times been a man of
controversy, but when a man has done a good job in a position,
when he has been part of a winning team, I believe that he should
stay on the team. That is my thinking at this time." Suddenly, all
the months of rampant speculation, all the talk of John Connally,
was swept aside. The Nixon Administration was not going to engage in a denial of self; barring the unforeseen, it was going to be
Agnew again—if he wanted a second nomination.

In all of this, as the 1972 presidential election approached, and
with it Agnew's political fate, one reasonably might have asked:
What if Spiro Agnew had become President in his first term as Vice-
President? What if he were re-elected as Vice-President and became President in 1973 or beyond? It was, for all the "heartbeat
away" clichés, a most serious and demanding question. Of the
thirty-six men who had occupied the Presidency when Agnew became Vice-President, twelve of them—one of every three—had
been Vice-President. What, it was legitimate now to ask, if Spiro
Agnew were to become President tomorrow? The nature of his
conduct as Vice-President, and the acquiescence in that conduct
by his President, most likely would plunge the nation into a period
of bickering and disruption that would make the recent past seem
by contrast an era of good feeling.

The most recent succession of a Vice-President held some lessons pertinent to the prospect of an elevated Agnew. Lyndon
Johnson, for all his egoism, entered the Presidency with hat in
hand, having conducted himself in the Vice-Presidency in a way
that gave little offense to anyone, subordinating his pride—at
least the equal of Agnew's—to the limitations of his office and the
requirements of his chief. At the time of his assassination, President John F. Kennedy was growing in public popularity, esteem
and even adoration; his departure left a deep emotional, as well as
political, void. Aware of that fact and acting on it, Johnson moved
into the Presidency on tiptoe, conducting himself in his first
months in office more as regent for the departed leader than as
President in his own right. His deferential yet confident manner
made the most of the public good will built by Kennedy and magnified by the shock of his death; Johnson thus masterfully
brought the country through one of its most perilous and emotion-
laden transitions in history.

Could Spiro Agnew, as the legatee of the Nixon Administration, do the same? First of all, Richard Nixon as candidate and President never had generated great, deep and widespread warmth. A successor under circumstances of national crisis, especially Spiro Agnew, probably could not count on the same depth of public confidence and trust that greeted Johnson in November 1963. Also, Johnson, after thirty-two years in Washington, brought to the White House a reputation as one of the most knowledgeable men about making the national government work. By contrast, Agnew was best known—and widely known—for his bombastic and divisive speeches. His name was now, as he wanted, a household word, and the word meant polarization. If he suddenly became President, Agnew might well subordinate his own personality to the image projected by his predecessor, as Johnson did to the style and programs of Kennedy in those first months of 1964, but would the public climate provide the same opportunity for a new Spiro Agnew to take hold?

Or would the apprehension of his critics deepen and even explode into more demonstrative opposition? The years since 1963 had taken a heavy toll on the American people's confidence in its leaders. The Vietnam war had worked a particular alienation among the young. In the Johnson and Nixon administrations, actions and deceptions had fanned disaffection, and words had spread and intensified the disaffections. In this context Agnew's rhetoric had been especially incendiary and destructive. And what would happen if after a presidential death, Agnew, like Johnson before him, said to the American people, "Let us continue" what went before? Would such a rallying cry in the early seventies summon up unity, or deepen division?

When a presidential candidate selects a man to be his running mate, he always pays lip service to the one criterion that should be used in the selection—that the vice-presidential candidate is the best-qualified man available to assume the Presidency if that step should be necessary. And then, in nearly every case, the presidential candidate proceeds to reject that criterion out of hand. The roll call of obscure Vice-Presidents speaks dismally in support of that fact: George M. Dallas, William R. King, Schuyler Colfax, Henry Wilson (real name Jeremiah J. Colbaith), Thomas A. Hendricks, Levi P. Morton, Garret A. Hobart, and so on. Richard Nixon said in Miami Beach in 1968 that he had picked Spiro

Agnew because he had no doubt that Agnew could take over as President. The real reason was that Agnew was deemed at the time to be the least offensive to party conservatives, that he might even help a bit in the Border States and would not outshine the presidential nominee.

The framers of the Constitution gave very little thought to the Vice-Presidency. It was clear, however, that they intended that he be the second most qualified man for the Presidency. The require- ment that the states through the electoral college—not, at the time, by popular ballot—vote for two men from different states was an attempt to reach out for men who had appeal beyond their own state boundaries. "It was believed," wrote Dr. Louis C. Hatch in *History of the Vice-Presidency of the United States,* "the clever device would ensure, if not the election, at least the nomination, of men honored throughout the Union. . . . Presuming the non- existence of concerted action through political parties and the continued solidarity of the states' electoral votes, it must follow that the Vice-President would always be the person most desired for President after the one actually elected." By most judgments the Vice-Presidents were so qualified in the earliest years of the Re- public, when the runner-up in the election became Vice-President —John Adams (twice), Thomas Jefferson and the brilliant but erratic Aaron Burr. Ratification of the Twelfth Amendment to the Constitution in 1804, after a tie in 1800 between Jefferson and Burr in the presidential balloting had demonstrated a practical flaw in the system, instituted the present separate selection of Vice-Presidents.

On that occasion Representative Roger Griswold of Connecti- cut, a staunch Jefferson critic, warned that "the man voted for as Vice-President will be selected without any decisive view to his qualifications to administer the government. The office will gen- erally be carried into the market to be exchanged for the votes of some large state for President, and the only criterion which will be regarded as a qualification for the office of Vice-President will be the temporary influence of the candidate over the electors of his state. . . . The momentary views of a party may perhaps be promoted by such arrangements, but the permanent interests of the country are sacrificed."

So concerned were some Federalists that the Twelfth Amend- ment would radically change the original conception of the Vice-

Presidency that they sought a constitutional amendment abolishing the office altogether. They failed, and nearly 170 years later, regional ticket balancing remains a major product of the system, often summarily ruling out selection of the most qualified men available.

Even conceding the remote possibility that Richard Nixon selected Spiro Agnew in 1968 because he believed he was the next best qualified man to run the country, the manner in which Nixon had used his Vice-President had to be considered. The Agnew Vice-Presidency had been extremely destructive in terms of preparing the man to be President—to govern effectively. For all the briefings on national security affairs, and the assignments of committee and council chairmanships, for all the travel abroad, Spiro Agnew would come to any future Presidency severely handicapped to lead, precisely because he had been so misused politically—not in terms of party needs, but in terms of national demands. Despite Nixon's references to the "traditional" role of Vice-Presidents to campaign hammer-and-tongs for the party, there had been no such notable tradition, save that established by Nixon's own divisively partisan campaigning as Vice-President. No amount of experience in the National Security Council, or on the overseas protocol circuit, would help Spiro Agnew if he had to govern a nation in which his name was anathema in most inner cities and on most campuses, and a rallying cry to the baser instincts of middle-class and blue-collar America.

Who was at fault? Richard Nixon, certainly, for—after having chosen Spiro Agnew and voicing such lofty intentions about his role in the Nixon Administration—so callously employing the man as a political battering ram. Spiro Agnew, certainly, for his reckless performance in office. Both of them, for their short-sightedness about how that performance might jeopardize the political stability of the country in time of a crisis of succession. Finally, the system itself, which permits the nomination and election of less than the most qualified men, and subsequently their employment in office in ways that not only demean the office but undermine their ability to govern, if it should come to that.

What needed to be done? For a start, the public interest demanded that both Nixon and Agnew consider whether Agnew's performance in one term as Vice-President had rendered him unable to rebuild public confidence against the time when he might have to assume the Presidency; or whether his pursuit of and service in a second term could be conducted in such a way as to overcome the destructiveness of the first term. Spiro Agnew had demonstrated that he was not the unintelligent dolt his most severe detractors pictured him to be. According to a former Nixon White House intellectual, although Agnew's own staff was "a bunch of creeps," in seeking help from the academic community the Vice-President "had pretty good taste in intellectual horseflesh. Man for man, it was the best collection of such people that I've ever seen in Washington." Also, he was one of the most imaginative users of words ever to occupy the Vice-Presidency; his drawback was not the words he used, but how he used them—to incite and divide rather than to inspire and conciliate. Perhaps, had Richard Nixon employed him as he might have, and as Agnew had hoped—as a pragmatic tester and challenger of domestic concepts as they came off the drawing board—the public image of Spiro Agnew, and his acceptability as a President in a crisis of succession, could have been much different. But whether Agnew jumped off the edge or was pushed into the public role of polarizer, that was how he was perceived by friend and foe alike; it was not the image of a President in a time of crisis.

In an article on "the Nixon style" in October 1971, Nixon-Agnew speech writer Bill Safire noted that "the critical three words in the Nixon lexicon" often were "in a way"—indicating the President's concern that whatever goals are sought, they must be pursued in a manner that will not diminish the goal itself; "the rights of the accused must be protected—in a way that does not overlook the rights of the victims of crime; . . . segregation should be ended—in a way that does not harm the process of education." By the same token, should not a President employ his Vice-President to advance the goals of his Administration—in a way that will not severely handicap that Vice-President's chances to rally the country to his side if fate in a split second so requires?

And what of the system? Is there no way that a President can be encouraged, if not obliged, to make use of his Vice-President in a more constructive manner? Apparently there is no way to prohibit a President himself from engaging excessively in partisan politics if that is his inclination, nor should there be, beyond the force of public opinion and the extreme pressures of his office that often crowd out such excesses. He is, after all, also the leader of his party. But what of a Vice-President? Part of the reason Richard Nixon used Spiro Agnew as a political bludgeon, and indeed part of the reason Agnew embraced the role with such zest, was the fact that the Vice-President, for all the make-work assigned to him by the President, did not have the same pressures on him that keep a President gainfully occupied. Surely, however, the prospect that the Vice-President may be President in the flash of a second is sufficient reason to make certain his time is spent grooming him for the staggering responsibilities he may inherit— not sniping at the opposition like an idle boy shooting tin cans with a BB gun.

Perhaps more duties of great influence now handled by appointed officials within the White House ought to be assigned by statute to the Vice-President. His lack of a constituency within the Administration—a major responsibility and a department or bureau through which to implement it—handicaps him. Why not amend the Constitution to strip the Vice-President of his role as President of the Senate, and make more active use of him within the Administration in which he is supposed to be the No. 2 man? His Senate role is, after all, an anachronism that violates the separation of the executive and legislative branches and is only a nuisance to Vice-President and Senate alike.

The idea actually is not very new. In 1956 a Senate government operations subcommittee, chaired by then Senator John F. Kennedy, held hearings on a proposal by former President Herbert Hoover for creation of an Administrative Vice-President, to be appointed by the President and approved by the Senate. His task would have been to relieve the overburdened President of administrative detail in such areas as the appointment of postmasters, supervision of reorganizations within the executive branch, resolution of conflicts among various executive agencies, coordination of interdepartmental committees and overseeing of independent agencies.

The idea met with mixed reactions. Then President Eisenhower, speaking through the man in his Administration who came closest to being an Assistant President, Sherman Adams, said he would have no objection provided the appointee "have the prestige, through title or otherwise, to enable him to assure that those tasks are effectively carried out." But former President Truman flatly opposed the suggestion. He said it was "not possible [for a President] to delegate any of the functions of his office as set out in the Constitution," and that the "powers and functions of the President [should] in no way be limited beyond the restrictions set out in the Constitution." Clark Clifford, former special assistant to Truman and later Secretary of Defense under President Johnson, pointed out that the President "could bestow all of the powers suggested in this plan upon the Assistant to the President as that exists today, if he chose to do it." Eminent historians also warned of a dilution of presidential powers through appointment of an Administrative Vice-President.

Faced with such opposition, one Republican member of the subcommittee, Senator Margaret Chase Smith of Maine, raised the obvious question: Why create a new office of Administrative Vice-President, when the constitutional Vice-President was there, waiting for something worthwhile to do? Why not give him greater executive responsibilities, thus providing administrative relief to the President and giving the Vice-President valuable on-the-job training at the same time? "It does seem to me," said Democratic Senator John L. McClellan of Arkansas, chairman of the full committee, "that the office of Vice-President of the United States should be related to the executive branch of government where the Vice-President, in performance of functions that might be assigned to him in that branch of government, would become equipped from experience, from direct contacts with the problems involved, to assume the duties of the President in the event a vacancy should occur."

Clifford agreed. "I believe that the Vice-President could well be moved from the legislative branch where he is now to the executive branch," he said. "It would take a constitutional amendment, but the enormity of the problem is such that it will take far-reaching measures to satisfy anything like the need that exists at this time . . . I think the Vice-President should be the second officer in the executive branch of the government. He could take over from the President a vast amount of administrative detail." The move would enhance the Vice-President's prestige greatly, Clifford said, and would provide "the process of preparing a man for succession to the Presidency. No matter how many committees you put the present Vice-President on, no matter what functions you give him in attending Cabinet meetings and National

Security Council meetings, I do not believe he is prepared to the degree that he would be if he were the day-to-day working assistant to the President of the United States."

Senator Kennedy, questioning Clifford, observed that "the reason that under the Constitution the Vice-President was given a limited function is because it was assumed in the beginning that he would be in opposition to the President, and therefore his functions were rather wisely limited." By upgrading a Vice-President who could not be dismissed by the President, Kennedy suggested, "there would be a number of problems created for the President. Perhaps it would weaken his prestige, particularly under the constitutional amendment which limits the President from running for a third term, if during the second term of his office he would possibly be introducing a number of problems that would complicate the problems of the next President." In this comment, ironically, Kennedy brushed aside the possibility of the Vice-President himself becoming that next president by succession. "I am not saying it would complicate the problems of the Vice-President in case the President died," Kennedy said. "That has happened only in a few cases."

Clifford disagreed with Kennedy that the upgrading of the constitutional Vice-President would create more problems than it solved. "From a practical standpoint," he said, "when a convention met they would know that they were selecting a President and the operating or Executive Vice-President. And I think it would change the whole concept of the selection of Vice-President . . . from that of a geographical or philosophical consideration to one of practical common-sense selection of a headman and his assistant to do the job. And I would not feel any concern that it would cause a diminution in the authority or prestige of the President . . . I think that the presidential powers are so tremendous that if by chance a Vice-President would get off the reservation, I have no doubt but that a President could trim him down to size in no time at all."

"You think," Kennedy asked, "that as far as picking a Vice-President who might be President—which is a fairly responsible job for any convention—you think they would act differently, they would pick a different man, possibly, if they felt he was going to be an Administrative Assistant to the President?"

"I do," Clifford replied. "I think that a great deal more thought would be given to the selection of a Vice-President under such circumstances than has been given in the past."

Hoover balked, however, on grounds that the Vice-President, contrary to the popular impression that he always is and must be under the President's thumb, is constitutionally his own man and should not be subjected constitutionally to the President. "I have never thought it necessary to change the functions of the Vice-President," he said. "In the proposals I have made, I do not in any way or in any fashion impose upon his province . . . He is separately elected to an office of the government. We are not always sure that his policies are going to run parallel with those of the President. In any event, in order to give the President full executive authority, he [the Vice-President] would have to be placed subject to the President, [and that] would be a pretty vital change in the whole constitutional concept of the Vice-President."

Hoover said he did not see how the administrative duties under consideration could be imposed on a Vice-President by law, "even if you removed his legislative duties. . . . If the President did not like what the Vice-President was doing, if he had administrative or executive duties, he could not remove him." If Congress wanted to make the constitutional Vice-President "a sort of Executive Vice-President," Hoover suggested, it would have to amend the Constitution to make him an appointive, not an elective, officer—which brought it back to his original idea, plus abolition of the constitutional Vice-Presidency. "I do not think you could maintain him as an elective officer and maintain any cohesion in administration," the former President, an expert in government reorganization, said.

Scholars also raised a red flag. Dr. James Hart of the University of Virginia warned the subcommittee that such action "would weaken the Presidency by tending to split it in two." The upgraded Vice-President would not be chosen by the President, he said, but "would be saddled upon the President by the political considerations [of the time] at the national convention . . . Once chosen, he would be tied around the President's neck for the whole term . . . Stuck with a Vice-President he could not fire, I should expect and hope that no President would assign to him very important tasks . . . I regard this proposition as a very dangerous threat to the integrity of the President."

Confronted with such views, the subcommittee backed off. "Before a constitutional change of this radical nature is undertaken," its report on the hearings said, "there should be extensive and thorough consideration of all aspects of this matter." The President already had sufficient authority to delegate the performance of many administrative functions to subordinates, the report said, and besides, "Congress should not take the lead in diluting the President's responsibilities or functions in order to lessen his burden, unless such legislation is actively sought from Congress by the President."

There the matter has rested, for sixteen years, as the President's burdens have grown infinitely heavier and the frustrations of the Vice-President, through succeeding administrations, have been little diminished. By administrative action, it is true, Presidents Eisenhower, Kennedy, Johnson and Nixon did attempt to make greater use of their Vice-Presidents. Statutory authority was sought and granted to place them on the National Security Council and other executive bodies, and other duties were parceled out. Still, Vice-Presidents have continued to complain to intimates that without major responsibilities and large numbers of bureaucratic troops with which to meet them, they find themselves far down in the pecking order of Washington power politics.

It has been a complaint, in fact, that Vice-Presidents do not have nearly the political clout of the appointed department heads in any Administration. The lament suggests a radical but provocative thought: Why not require by law that the Vice-President serve as head of one of the great Cabinet departments? A presidential nominee, and a convention, would think harder about a man if he might turn out to be the next Secretary of State or Defense. And what better training for a man who might be President tomorrow, in a world and a time when the Chief Executive's foreign policy role so often dominates his Administration?

It would be argued that such grooming for the Presidency— either through a major, constitutional expansion of his duties or such assignment to one of the two prime Cabinet posts—might give the Vice-President an unfair advantage over other ambitious politicians aspiring to the Presidency. But what is wrong with making the Vice-Presidency truly a stepping stone to the Presidency? It has become that already: Agnew's three predecessors— Humphrey, Johnson and Nixon—all have been their party's presidential nominee, and the Democratic front runner going into 1972, Senator Muskie, was his party's vice-presidential nominee in 1968. The Vice-Presidency no longer is a Throttlebottom office in terms of its political potential; it should be one no longer in terms of its functions.

In the last decade, events have generated an increased awareness among public and politicians alike that the Vice-Presidency does have a future. Many politically ambitious men now covet the nomination, instead of running to hide from it. It would seem to be a propitious time to elevate the office in purpose as well as political potential, so that Americans in time will demand of their Vice-Presidents the same qualities of leadership and responsibility they expect of their Presidents.

Agnew himself does not favor any significant change in the role of the Vice-Presidency. Asked whether he would like to see the office function differently, he says, "I wouldn't, because I think right now it functions entirely at the whim of the President, which is the only way it should. To stultify it with a list of statutory restrictions or constitutional prohibitions would not make the Vice-President valuable to the President. So I think it's good that what the Vice-President does, ninety percent of what he does, is what the President wants him to do."

Agnew says he has found "particularly rewarding" the fact that the President "has tried to keep me in the policy-making counsels of the government and has been very meticulous about making certain that I attend all the leadership meetings, the joint leadership meetings, the Cabinet committee on economic policy, the National Security Council, and the domestic council, and that I'm not left out of the flow of the interchanges that lead to his ultimate decisions in these matters." But he acknowledges at the same time that "the most debilitating thing about the Vice-Presidency is that it's not in the circuit of government; it's an appendage." As a result of thoughtlessness or carelessness on the part of a Cabinet member, he says, the Vice-President can go uninformed about a development or decision on a matter in which he is actively involved. "It happens," he says. "Not in important ways. But suppose HEW reaches the decision-making stage [on a particular issue]; they may forget to notify me." He claims he has gotten used to it. When such a case occurs, he has to say, "Wait a minute, I'm in that." In an economic matter, the Secretary of Treasury will be notified as a matter of course, "but I could be up to my neck in something and don't know," because he is not in the direct, administrative line of command.

Agnew says he would not favor removing the constitutional role of the Vice-President as President of the Senate because "the tie-breaker has its uses." He interested and informed himself about the Senate when he first took office, he says, because he felt if he was going to have to preside over it, he had to know what he was doing. But now, like most Vice-Presidents before him, he recognizes that the function of routinely occupying the chair is not constructive and can be left to junior members of the Senate.

As for this Vice-President's most controversial role as the political spokesman for his President and his party, Agnew is most enthusiastic. "Clearly President Nixon wants me to do this," he says, "just as he did it for President Eisenhower. It's the most virile role I have. It makes a decision maker out of me." For a man who has been in executive government, he says, the adjustments in the Vice-Presidency have been formidable. As a former governor, he says, he has been used to saying when he disagrees with something, " 'We're not going to do it.' But if the President says, 'We're going to do it,' we do it." And he grins with good-humored acquiescence.

Clark Clifford, long one of Washington's most successful lawyers, has not changed his mind about the need to expand the duties and responsibilities of the Vice-President, and to relieve him of his role as presiding officer of the Senate. But he acknowledges that, as Agnew's observation conveys, no matter what changes in the concept of the Vice-Presidency may be made, how the President elects to employ him will always be the governing factor. "After all," Clifford says, "the Vice-President operates under the direction and control of the President. You can't change that; that's our system and it's the right system; you give one man the responsibility and the authority, and you hold him to the accounting of the American people." Agnew has had a partisan speechmaking role, Clifford says, "because President Nixon has chosen that role for the Vice-President."

The former Secretary of Defense says he does not oppose a functional political role for the Vice-President; indeed, he would favor the Vice-President taking over not only the ceremonial duties of the President, but also his normal party role. "The President should not give his time to being head of his political party; he should be able to delegate that to the Vice-President. The party would accept it, except in rare instances, when the President would enter into discussions."

But such a delegation should not be a license for excessive partisanship, to the detriment of a Vice-President's ability to unify the country in a crisis of succession, Clifford says. Under present circumstances, and because of the manner in which Agnew has functioned in the office, he contends, Agnew's sudden ascendancy "would be a calamity—a real tragedy. But that's a risk that they take. They're conscious of it; they've chosen to do it that way."

One of the positive aspects of an augmented, elevated Vice-Presidency, Clifford says, might well be an enhanced view of the office, not only by the public and the man who might seek it but by a President who still will determine how the occupant of that office is used. "You still have to face the fact, though, that if a President chose to use the Vice-President as President Nixon is now," he says, "there's not very much the Vice-President could do about it." Of course, Vice-President Agnew, by his own testimony, would not have it any other way as far as his partisan speechmaking role is concerned.

Senator Humphrey, who served on the Kennedy subcommittee in 1956 and was Agnew's predecessor as Vice-President, agrees with Clifford that the existing Vice-Presidency should be upgraded, especially on the domestic front. Although he, like Agnew, served productively on a great many committees and councils, Humphrey says, "It's my judgment that the Vice-President ought to be the man who the President designates as the super-Cabinet officer in charge of all domestic programs. Presidents now ought to look upon the Vice-Presidency as a strong right arm in the operation of government, and to use that office for administrative purposes, not just for show, for receiving foreign guests and so on; but to be actually a sort of super-administrator."

As a veteran member of the Senate and as its presiding officer for four years, Humphrey says the Vice-President's constitutional role could easily be dropped. "The Vice-President has little influence if any in the Senate," he says. "Even a man who was as close to the Senate as I was, I doubt that my presiding over the Senate did very much for it, or for me. It's at times pleasurable, but the Senate immediately is suspicious of you."

A Vice-President freed of that role ought not, however, to become a political weapon for the President and his administration, Humphrey says. "I think it demeans the office. You become the hatchet man; I don't think a man who's Vice-President ought to do any more of that than other members of the Cabinet or the President himself. I think you ought to conduct yourself as best you can, as if you were President, without having the authority." Agnew's political role as Vice-President, Humphrey says, would have an adverse effect on his ability to unite the country, should circumstances thrust the Presidency on him suddenly. "But I'm sure he'd be a different man when he became President," Humphrey suggests.

Though the manner in which Agnew has used the office of Vice-President is controversial, nearly everyone interested in that office, Agnew included, acknowledges shortcomings in the Vice-Presidency as now constituted. Certainly the time has come for a full and scholarly examination of the constitutional and practical roles of the Vice-President, preferably by a blue-ribbon presidential commission, to help Congress and the President chart a more constructive framework in which future Vice-Presidents will function. In addition to Agnew himself, other men who have served in the office are available to present their views, as well as a great many men like Clifford and Sherman Adams who have served overburdened Presidents and frustrated Vice-Presidents in the era of mushrooming American responsibilities since World War II.

Quite apart from the role of the Vice-President, the present method of selecting nominees for the office is unsatisfactory in a democracy. Of course the President and Vice-President must be politically compatible and, hopefully, personally compatible as well, if there is to be continuity in an elected Administration in time of constitutional succession. Still, there should be some means to bring the public will to bear on the choice of the man who statistics indicate stands a one-in-three chance of becoming President. One way would be to require party conventions to choose the vice-presidential nominee from among those men who have fared best in the state primaries, or have received a minimum number of votes in the balloting for President.

Obviously, the abolition of the electoral college, and institution of the direct popular election of President and Vice-President, could go a long way to raising the caliber of Vice-Presidents. Presumably it would matter less which state a nominee came from, and more how he appealed to the mass of voters. Such an approach would doubtless favor men from the larger population centers, but the field of potential candidates almost certainly would be broadened.

The best and most practical safeguard, really, is the sincere determination of the presidential nominee to meet the requirement to which most merely pay lip service—that the man he selects really will be qualified to take over the Presidency if necessary. One would think that the stormy and unpredictable course of American presidential succession would be enough to persuade men nominated to run for President to decide on that basis, and that basis above all else.

It would be the greatest of ironies if, out of the divisive Vice-Presidency of Spiro T. Agnew, there came a constructive overhaul of the office and of the manner in which its occupant is selected and used. In his speech before the Middlesex Club of Boston in March 1971, Agnew gave his views of the Vice-Presidency and the license offered to him by a permissive Constitution:

"There is no doubt that the framers of our Constitution considered the Vice-Presidency an office suitable for men of energy. Until the ratification of the Twelfth Amendment in 1804, the defeated major presidential candidate was usually elected Vice-President. This created some interesting stresses. Over the years, however, the Vice-Presidency has lost its political punch and become the most placid and uncontroversial of political positions. Indeed, as presently structured, it may be compared to an adjustable easy chair. The occupant has his choice of either reclining sleepily or sitting up alertly. The posture adopted is inconsequential, because it is virtually certain that no one will notice which attitude has been selected.

"Whatever his decision, however—whether he has dozed amiably or listened attentively—it has been traditional for a Vice-President to be indulged by the intellectuals and opinion-makers of his time with nothing harsher than a deprecating comment or a condescending joke. In recent years, the rules have been amended to allow Vice-Presidents to talk—so long as they are careful to say absolutely nothing. This privilege was heavily exercised and refined to a high degree during the last Administration.

"And in regard to vice-presidential strictures, it seems appropriate to note—on the occasion of a Lincoln Day address before the oldest Republican organization in Massachusetts—that, following four years of lassitude as Abraham Lincoln's Vice-President, Hannibal Hamlin suddenly found himself Collector for the Port of Boston. In my own case, I found it an onerous choice between the ennui of easy-chair existence and pointless verbosity. And so, quick constitutional research revealing no authoritative reason why a Vice-President is required to choose between catalepsy and garrulity, I forsook the comfortable code of many of my predecessors, abandoned the unwritten rules—and said something."

Say something, Spiro T. Agnew certainly has. What he has said, and the way he has said it, offer persuasive reasons for giving future Vice-Presidents of the United States something much more and much better to do.

INDEX

Abbott, George, 231
Abrahams, Al, 9, 195–99, 204
Acheson, Dean, 242
Adams, Elaine, 161
Adams, John, 440
Adams, Sherman, 443, 451
Administrative Vice-President, proposal for, 443–47
Advisory Commission on Intergovernmental Relations, 291
Agnew, Elinor ("Judy") Judefind, 38, 39, 150, 229–30
Agnew, Kim, 307
Agnew, Margaret Akers, 30, 35
Agnew, Pamela, 39, 283
Agnew, Spiro T.
  accepts Vice-Presidential nomination, 232
  Army, 39–43, 45
  Asia, 322–24, 347–48, 420
  assessment as Vice-President, 429–53
  attacks "radical liberals," 358–92, 426
  beginnings in politics, 54–73
  boyhood, 30–37
  campaign (1970), 350–95
  campaigns for Vice-Presidency, 239–82
  changes in Vice-Presidency, 448–49
  city slums, 265–66

  compares U.S., foreign black leaders, 421–22
  "conversion" to conservatism, 174–78, 211–12
  county executive, 74–115
  courts Rockefeller, 180–99
  deals with Bowie State, 10–16, 28–29, 157, 163–68, 171–73
  decision to speak out, 294–97
  defends 1970 performance, 398–99, 404–11
  disclaims national ambitions, 207–8, 213
  disenchantment with role, 430–33, 448–49
  drug culture, 365–66
  early employment, 38, 43–49
  early Vice-Presidency, 283–97
  election night (1968), 281–82
  election night (1970), 393
  fights with human relations commission, 75–100
  governor, 150–79
  gubernatorial campaign, 137–49
  Gwynne Oak controversy, 75–83
  humor, 329–30, 386–87
  "impudent snobs" speech (New Orleans), 305, 320, 348, 378
  inaugurated as Vice-President, 283
  lectures Baltimore black leaders, 16–26, 28–29, 157, 169–71
  loyalty to Nixon, 431–32

Agnew, Spiro T. (*continued*)
  newspaper criticism, 317–19,
    341–42, 360, 436
  nominated for Vice-President,
    216–33
  open housing, 92–95, 107–10,
    157–59, 175–77
  personification of Administra-
    tion, 437
  places Nixon's name in nomina-
    tion, 224
  "positive polarization," 308
  public speaker, 298–302
  purge of Goodell, 372–95
  questions Administration China
    policy, 414–18, 423
  relations with press, 60, 71–71,
    113, 143–44, 251–63, 266–67,
    310–20, 401–2, 409–11, 436–37
  renomination in 1972, 369, 389–
    90, 400, 416, 431–33
  runs for county executive, 74–
    115
  "rotten apples" speech (Harris-
    burg), 308–10, 331
  seeks judgeship, 59–60
  seeks gubernatorial nomination,
    121–36
  student, 36–39, 49
  Supreme Court appointments,
    328–30
  switches to Nixon, 200–15
  TV criticism, 310–17, 382, 436–
    37
  travels around world, 420–23
  tries to head off Ashbrook chal-
    lenge, 436
  urban renewal fight, 103–7
  visits Greece, 427
  visits South Vietnam, 324
  watches Rockefeller TV an-
    nouncement, 3–10
  youth and dissenters, 264–65,
    289–90, 302–5, 308–10, 327–
    28, 343–45, 366, 376, 382
  zoning board, 56–63, 111–12
Agnew, Theodore S., 30, 32–37, 272
Ahepa society, 8, 35, 197
Akers, "Teddy," 30, 136
Alexander, Lamar, 358
Alton, Joseph W., 15, 128
American Broadcasting Company,
  209, 255, 262, 267, 311–12,
  314–15, 320
American Council on Education, 334
American Nazi party, 24
American Retail Federation, 336
Americans for Agnew, 428

Americans for Democratic Action,
  107, 141, 386
Anderson, C. M. ("Andy"), 36
Anderson, Dale, 61–62, 114, 129,
  274
Anderson, Harold, 353–54
Anderson, Jack, 428
Anderson, Martin, 202, 355, 358
Anderson, William, 411
Andrews, John, 226*n*
Annapolis *Evening Capital*, 132
Annenberg, Walter H., 355
antiballistic missile system, 292,
  312
Apollo 11, 291
Apple, R. W., 403, 406
Arends, Leslie, 226*n*
Arrowsmith, George H. C., 68
Ashbrook, John M., 436
Associated Press, 347, 394, 401, 420,
  425
Atlanta *Constitution*, 340–41

Babcock, Tim, 188, 225*n*, 226
Baker, Howard, 219, 227
Baltimore *Afro-American*, 141
Baltimore black leaders confronta-
  tion, 16–26, 28, 29, 157, 169–
  71, 175, 206, 212, 289, 422
Baltimore Colts, 52, 262, 266
Baltimore Law School, University
  of, 39, 43
Baltimore Neighborhood, Inc., 89
Baltimore *News-American*, 224
Baltimore *News-Post*, 70, 224
Baltimore Orioles, 303
Baltimore riots, 16–26, 28–29, 157,
  169–71, 174, 206
Baltimore Sunpapers, 19, 27, 57,
  59, 61, 65, 71, 78, 107, 112–
  14, 131, 143, 155, 170, 246,
  252, 275, 322
Baltimore Urban Coalition, 23
Bancroft, Harding F., 275
Barkley, Alben, 284, 286
Barnett, Ross, 25
Barrett, Lester, 43–44, 49, 51–52,
  54
Bartenfelder, John, 129
Bartlett, Dewey, 403
Bascom, Marion C., 18, 20, 22, 26
Battle of the Bulge, 40
Bayh, Birch, 386
Beall, J. Glenn, Jr., 354
Beall, Osborne, 55, 63
Beatles, 366
Bellmon, Henry, 188
Bentsen, Lloyd, 394, 396

Berrigan, Daniel, 411
Berrigan, Philip, 411
Bevilaqua, John, 40
Bhumibol of Thailand, 324
Bigart, Homer, 250, 255, 262, 330
Birmingham, Michael, 55, 64–72, 121, 124
Black Action Federation, 159, 161
Black Caucus, 422
Black Liberation Front, 333
Black Panthers, 262, 331
Blair, Stanley, 229, 367
Bliss, Ray, 227*n*
Blount, Winton M., 325, 393
Boston University, 367
Bowie State College, 10–16, 28–29, 157, 163–68, 171–73, 206, 289
Bowie, William B., 162–63
Bradley, Brooks, 61–62, 69–70
Braun, Ted, 194, 196
Bresler, Charles, 12–13, 19, 148, 157, 164–65, 170–72, 250
Brewster, Daniel J., 63, 102–3, 119
Brewster, Kingman, Jr., 331
British Broadcasting Company, 142
Brock, Bill, 226*n*, 368
Broder, David S., 207, 390
Brooke, Edward W., 231, 247, 377, 413
Brown, H. Rap, 24–25, 159–62, 175, 178, 187
Brown, Kenneth, 14, 15, 166–68
Brown v. Board of Education, 325
Brownell, Herbert, 226*n*
Buchanan, Patrick J., 27, 202, 215, 217, 219, 225*n*, 250, 316, 355, 357–58
Buckley, James L., 121, 365, 372, 374–75, 377–78, 383, 387, 393, 399
Buckley, William F., Jr., 121, 219, 374, 399, 435–36
Bumpers, Dale, 403
Bunche, Ralph, 81
Burch, Dean, 314
Burch, Francis B., 153, 161, 167–69
Burdick, Quentin N., 353
Burger, Warren E., 329
Burns, Arthur, 291
Burr, Aaron, 440
Burroughs, Leo W., Jr., 87
Bush, George, 219, 380, 390, 394
Butz, Earl L., 370

Cabinet Committee on Economic Policy, 286, 448

Cabinet Committee on School Desegregation, 287, 325–26
California, University of, 262
Callaway, Howard ("Bo"), 225*n*
Calley, William L., Jr., 413
Cambridge riots, 159–63, 187
campaign (1966), 121–49
campaign (1968), 239–82
campaign (1970), 350–95
Cambodia, 334–38, 340, 343, 346, 348, 412
Capp, Al, 399
Cargo, David F., 186, 189
Carmichael, Stokely, 17, 23–26, 159, 162, 175, 313
Carroll, Jack, 125
Carroll, Joseph, 24
Carswell, G. Harrold, 328–31, 368
Chamberlain, Neville, 241, 244, 246
"Checkers" speech, 243, 262
Chesapeake and Potomac Telephone Company, 191
Chesapeake bay-bridge land controversey, 131–35, 154, 271–76
Chesapeake National Bank, 131, 271–75
Chiang Kai-shek, 324, 414, 420
Chicago *Tribune,* 359
Chicago's *American,* 288
Childs, John C., 132
China relations, 414–18, 420–21, 423, 426, 435–36
Chotiner, Murray, 355–56, 377
Chou En-lai, 415
Christian Science Monitor, 423
Chung Hee Park, 347, 420
Churchill, Winston, 241, 244
civil rights, 159, 173–75, 214, 230, 235, 312–13, 325–26. *See also:* open housing; human relations commission
Clark, Bob, 255, 262–63
Clark, James, 158
Clark, Ramsey, 169
Clarke, Alan, 51–52
Clay, William, 422
Cleaver, Eldridge, 262, 276
Clifford, Clark, 345, 444–46, 449–50
Cockey, Joshua A., 105–6
Colbaith, Jeremiah J., 439
Colfax, Schuyler, 439
Colson, Charles, 384
Columbia Broadcasting System, 272, 314, 320, 335, 337, 412–13, 437
Columbia University, 369

Communist party, U.S.A., 240, 425
Congress of Racial Equality, 79, 81,
    83–88, 97–99, 108, 162
Connally, John B., 403–4, 423–24,
    427–28
Connecticut, University of, 303,
    333
Constantine of Greece, 427
Constantine, Gus, 122
Constitutional Convention, 154–55
Conte, Silvio, 231
Cooper-Church Amendment, 346,
    348
Cormier, Frank, 420
Cornell University, 289, 331, 333
Corson, Dale R., 333–34
Counabaugh, Anna, 32
Council on Physical Fitness and
    Sports, 287
Council on Recreation and Natural
    Beauty, 287
Council on Youth Opportunity, 287
Cowles Publications, 397
Cramer, William, 331
Crampton, Robert O., 132
Cummins Engine Company, 9
Currier, Fred, 191–92

D'Alesandro, Thomas, III, 18, 21,
    28, 169
Daley machine, 257
Dallas, George M., 439
Daly, Robert, 144
Daniels, Samuel T., 25
Darrell, J. Cavendish, 62
Davenport, Kim, 31–32
Davis, Charles, 14
Deardourff, John, 189–90
Democratic National Convention
    (1968), 240–41, 360–61
DeFilippo, Frank, 70–71, 143–44,
    224, 253, 300
De Gaulle, Charles, 400
DeMuth, Isabel, 32
Dent, Harry, 226n, 231, 293, 307,
    353, 428
Des Moines speech, 310–17
Devereux, James P. S., 54, 245
Devine, Sam, 226n
Dewberry, Frederick L., 113–14, 129
Dewey, Thomas E., 226n
Dignan, Joseph, 61–62
Dirksen, Everett McKinley, 227n,
    242–43, 247, 283
Dobbin, Tilton H., 122, 151
Dole, Bob, 402
Donovan, Robert J., 192, 314
Dorsey, Philip H., 155

Douglas, Robert, 194
Duffey, Joseph D., 386
Dukert, Joseph, 220, 223
Dumbarton Junior High School, 51
Dump-Agnew talk, 243, 398, 400,
    418, 421–24, 426–28, 433–38
Dump-Nixon movement (1956),
    433, 435–36
Dump-Nixon movement (1972),
    412, 426
Dundore, Harry, 122, 131
Dunne, Peter Finley, 284
Du Pont, Pierre S., IV, 381

Edwards, Lee, 428
Edwards, Leslie, 36
Eggers, Paul, 380, 402
Ehrlichman, John, 202, 344–45,
    414, 430, 434
Eisen, Jack, 155–56
Eisendrath, Charles, 254
Eisenhower, Dwight D., 117, 120,
    151, 243, 249, 288, 297, 310,
    352, 429, 433, 436, 443, 447,
    449
Eisenhower syndrome, 436
Ellsworth, Robert, 27, 188, 201,
    225n, 227, 258
Emanuel, Meyer M., 158
Emerging Republican Majority,
    The (Phillips), 356
Engers, Mildred E., 66
Esquire, 9, 10
Evans, Dan, 219
Evans, Rowland, 250

Face the Nation (CBS), 272, 335
Fannin, Paul, 226n
Farrar, Frank, 407
"Fat Jap" controversy, 252–63, 269
Federal Bureau of Investigation,
    161, 164, 419
Federal Communications Commis-
    sion, 314–15
Feinblatt, Eugene, 36
Feingold, Edgar L., 56, 78, 79, 85,
    90, 137–38, 141–42, 144, 162,
    170
Finan, Thomas J., 124, 126–28
Finch, Robert, 226n, 227, 227n,
    228, 279, 382, 396–97
Finney, Jervis, 28–29, 100, 129
Fish, Ody, 227n
Flanigan, Peter, 225n, 231
Fleming, Robben W., 331–32
Fong, Hiram, 226n
Ford, Gerald R., 227n, 242–43, 307
Forest Park High School, 36–37

Franklin, Ben A., 265, 271–72
Fringer, Alice, 7, 10, 60, 281
Frost, David, 337–38, 382
Fulbright, J. William, 301, 329, 345–46, 362, 419
Fulton, Eugene, 44

Gallup poll, 222, 270–71, 279, 348, 413
Gandhi, Mahatma, 248, 264
Gardner, John W., 219
Garment, Leonard, 225*n*
Garner, John Nance, 284
Garrison Junior High School, 35
Gates, Thomas, 204
Gaul, Christopher, 19, 113
Gede, James, 66–67
Gelston, George M., 17, 19–20, 162, 169–70
Genet, Jean, 262
Georgetown University, 303
Gerber, Leonard O., 131–32
Gibbons, Gould, 38–39, 44
Gitling, Mae, 26
Gleason, Jack A., 352–53, 355
Gleitsman, Carl, 45–48
Godwin, Mills, 208
Gold, Victor, 386–87, 415, 417
Goldberg, David, 190
Goldenson, Leonard H., 314
Goldstein, Louis L., 153
Goldwater, Barry M., 6, 117–22, 182, 196, 216, 226*n*, 227, 231, 276, 294, 310, 314, 353, 356, 374, 387, 428, 435
Goodearle, Roy, 415
Goodell, Charles E., 121, 142, 294, 312, 356, 362, 365, 371–83, 387–88, 393, 399–402, 407, 409–10, 412–13
Goodman, Julian, 314
Goodman, Robert, 124–26, 136, 140, 144–45, 147, 170–71, 174, 249, 301
Gore, Albert, 27, 294, 368–69, 393
Gore, Louise, 27, 193
Goucher College, 54
Gould, Kingdon, 208
Graham, Billy, 226*n*, 227, 348
Griswold, Roger, 440
Grogg, Lester L., 65–67
Gwynne Oak Amusement Park, 75–85, 87, 102, 108

Haldeman, H. R. ("Bob"), 225*n*, 227, 246, 434
Hall, Gus, 425
Hall, Leonard, 191

Hamlin, Hannibal, 453
Hammerman, I. H. ("Bud"), 36, 122, 149
Hampshire, Paul, 122
Hardesty, Edward, 69–70, 128
Harlow, Bryce, 355, 358
Harriman, W. Averell, 311–12, 345–46, 370
Harris, Fred, 406
Harris, Sam, 239
Harris poll, 279
Harrisburg speech, 308–10, 331
Harrison, John, 51
Harrison, Lee, 51
Hart, James, 446
Hart, Philip, 294, 366
Hartke, Vance, 294, 369
Harvard University, 249, 344–45, 371
Hatch, Louis C., 440
Hatfield, Mark O., 221, 225, 227, 346
Hay, Everett T., 114
Haynsworth, Clement F., Jr., 295, 328–31, 368
Heller, Walter W., 343
Hendricks, Thomas A., 439
Hennegan, A. Owen ("Gus"), 77, 79, 84, 91, 95
Henry, William E., 11
Herblock, 341
Hess, Stephen, 249–51, 257–58, 272, 287
Hickel, Walter J., 201, 225*n*, 226, 337–38, 393–94, 434
Hinman, George, 9, 190, 193–97, 204–5, 379
History of the Vice-Presidency of the United States (Hatch), 440
Hitt, Pat, 225*n*
Hobart, Garret A., 439
Ho Chi Minh, 278, 346, 412
Hoffheiser, Katie, 65
Holmes, W. Maurice, 87
Holofcener, Michael, 77, 79–86, 88–92, 95–96, 98, 107
Holton, Linwood, 225*n*, 407, 425
Homan, Richard, 153, 156, 235, 253–54, 258–59, 261–62
Hood, Wayne, 225*n*
Hoover, Herbert, 443, 446
Hoover, J. Edgar, 419
Hopkins, Samuel, 168
Howard, Jim, 249
Howard University, 11, 164
Hruska, Roman, 225*n*
Huebner, Lee, 343

Human Relations Commission, 75–100
Humphrey, Hubert H., 204, 217, 222, 240–46, 264–66, 268–73, 276–82, 288, 357, 361, 381–82, 425, 447, 450–51
Hurd, Eliot P., 118–19
Hurley, Tim, 2
Hussey, John H., 39

Iglehart, Francis, 96–99, 108
"impudent snobs" speech (New Orleans), 305, 320, 348, 378
Indian Opportunity Council, 287
Interdenominational Alliance, 159
Irish, Charles, 57
Irwin, Don, 207, 316, 338
Issel, W. Ernest, 132
Issues and Answers (ABC), 209, 424

Jackson, Allen C., 132
Jackson State College, 338, 340, 344
James, Richard A., 48
James, William S., 152
Javits, Jacob K., 419
Jefferson, Thomas, 440
John Birch Society, 24, 103–4
Johns Hopkins University, 37, 39, 49
Johnson, Jim, 127
Johnson, Lyndon B., 72, 102–3, 119, 151, 183, 185, 203–4, 212, 236, 268–70, 272, 276–77, 279, 285, 287–88, 295, 303, 311, 343, 351–52, 356, 381–83, 404, 438–39, 444, 447
Johnson, Mary, 30, 32
Jones, J. Walter, 122–23, 131–35, 152, 174, 191, 205, 220, 229
Jones, Marshall W., 28
Jones, Rudolph T., 83, 86, 88, 162
Jordan, Len B., 293
"Jordan Rule," 293
Jorgensen, Christine, 379–81, 392, 409–10

Kahl, Christian H., 64–65, 68–69, 72, 122, 124
Kaufman, Nathan, 57–58
Kellett, Don, 95
Kelley, Robert A. L., 65
Kelly, Jerome, 131–33, 143
Kempton, Murray, 182
Kennedy, Edward M., 362, 366, 386, 425
Kennedy Institute of Politics, 249

Kennedy, John F., 91, 117, 142, 144, 326, 343, 359–60, 438, 443, 445, 447
Kennedy, Robert F., 26, 196, 203–4, 210–11, 372
Kent State University, 335–37, 340, 344
Kenyatta, Jomo, 421
Kerner, Otto, 177
Kerner report, 177, 214
Kiesinger, Kurt, 177
Kilpatrick, James J., 397
Kimmel, Sam, 42–43, 48–49, 54–56, 61, 63
King, Eugene L., Sr., 75–77, 79, 82, 96, 99
King, Martin Luther, Jr., 15–17, 24, 159, 162, 168–69, 206, 211, 248
King, William R., 439
Kinnamon, Bruce G., 160
Kirk, Claude, 381
Kissinger, Henry, 323, 411, 418, 420, 422
Klein, Herbert G., 225n, 316, 319–20, 396, 398
Kleindienst, Richard, 225n
Kleppe, Tom, 353
Knoll, W. I. E., 2
Kovens, Irvin, 122
Kuchel, Thomas H., 116–18
Ku Klux Klan, 138, 144–47

Laise, Carol, 324
Lally, Robert J., 14–20, 26, 77, 129, 161, 168–70
Langrall, Clarke, 112, 122
Laos, 346, 412–13
LaRue, Fred, 225n
Laugh-In (NBC), 279
Laxalt, Paul, 252
Lazarus, Ralph, 204
LeMay, Curtis, 347
Leubsdorf, Carl, 347
Leuktemeyer, John A., 274
LeVander, Harold, 198–99
Lincoln, Abraham, 453
Lindsay, John V., 121, 141, 217–18, 221, 225, 231, 235–36, 345, 407
Lively, Walter H., 23
Loch Raven Elementary School, 51
Loch Raven Kiwanis, 51, 61, 64, 304
Lodge, Henry Cabot, 119, 190, 218, 219, 225, 269
Long, Clarence D., 131, 133–35, 154
Lon Nol, 348
Los Angeles *Times*, 192, 207, 254, 314, 316, 338

Lowenstein, Allard K., 303
Lumbermens Mutual Casualty Company, 44
Lynch, Connie, 24

McAuliffe, Anthony, 40
McCabe, Thomas, 204
McCall, Tom, 7, 184–85, 190, 195–96, 405–8, 425
McCarthy, Eugene J., 203–4, 299, 349
McCarthy, Joseph R., 240–41, 243, 245–46, 300
McClellan, John L., 444
McCloskey, Paul N., Jr. ("Pete"), 412, 426
McCormick and Co., 132
McDiarmid, James, 278
McGee, Gale, 361
McGovern, George, 177, 329, 346, 425
McGovern-Hatfield Amendment, 346
MacGregor, Clark, 225n
McGrory, Mary, 242
McKeldin, Theodore, 124
McKissick, Floyd, 159
McWhorter, Charles, 225n

Maddox, Lester G., 127
Magruder, Jeb, 343
Maguire, John A., 58
Mahoney, George P., 4, 126–30, 136–49, 174, 177
Makelena, Ted, 261
Malatesta, Pete, 415
Mandel, Marvin, 70, 151–52, 162, 222–23
Mansfield, Mike, 286, 400
Mao Tse-tung, 415
Marcos, Ferdinand, 323–24
Marine Resources and Engineering Development Council, 286–87
Maryland Bar Association, 39
Maryland Casualty Company, 38–39, 42–44
Maryland Institute of Art, 31
"Maryland Mafia," 250
Maryland National Bank, 123, 151
Maryland National Guard, 32, 169, 210
Maryland State College, 172–73
Massenburg, Kitty, 122
Mathias, Charles, Jr. ("Mac"), 208–9
Mathison, Gerald E., 113
Matsunaga, Spark M., 258
Matz, Lester, 132, 134

Matz, Childs and Associates, 132
Mears, Walter Mirch, 347, 394, 428
Medairy, Bernard J., 106
Meet the Press (NBC), 240, 279
Menchine, Albert, 51, 59
Miami *Herald*, 220, 222
Michigan, University of, 331–32
Middlesex Club, 411–12, 452
Miller, Jack, 226n
Miller, J. Irwin, 9, 195, 204
Miller, William E., 227
Minnesota, University of, 342
Mission Bay meetings, 236–39, 243, 320
Mitchell, Clarence, 18, 21, 25, 28, 169–70
Mitchell, John N., 225n, 227–28, 231, 269, 307, 338, 356, 393, 399, 413, 434, 437
Mitchell, Juanita Jackson, 25
Mitchell, Martha, 399
Mitchell, Parren, 22
Mobutu, Joseph, 421
Montoya, Joseph M., 362
Mollenhoff, Clark, 31
Montgomery speech, 317
Monumental Life Insurance Company, 32
Moore, Dick, 225n
Moore, E. Scott, 18–19, 55–57, 63, 68, 70–71, 83, 89, 104, 107, 111, 113, 115–17, 120, 122, 128–29, 435
Moore, Ormsby S. ("Dutch"), 19, 89, 103, 105, 113, 117, 121–24, 129, 133–34
Moore, Robert B., 21
Morrow, Hugh, 194
Morton, Levi P., 439
Morton, Rogers C. B., 201, 219, 223, 227, 227n, 228–29, 231, 293, 307, 375–78, 403
Morton, Thruston B., 204
Moser, Herman, 48
Mote, Walter, 286
Mott, Stewart, III, 195, 206
Mount Vernon Mills Textile Company, 136
Moynihan, Daniel P., 291
Multimedia, Inc., 317
Mundt, Karl, 226n
Murfin, Bill, 226n
Murphy, George, 227n
Murray, Joseph, 52
Muskie, Edmund S., 240, 258, 265, 278–82, 307, 329–30, 392, 425, 448
Muths, Louis, 38, 41–42

Myers, Samuel L., 11, 13, 15–16, 163–68
Mylai, 413

National Advisory Commission on Civil Disorders, 177, 214
National Aeronautics and Space Council, 286
National Association for the Advancement of Colored People, 13–14, 25, 159, 166
National Broadcasting Company, 255, 320, 403
National Governors Conference, 1969 (Colorado Springs), 292
National Governors Conference, 1971 (San Juan), 424–25
National Liberation Front, 277
National Negro Business League, 239
National Press Club, 263, 427
National Security Council, 286, 414, 416, 420, 441, 444–45, 447–48
National States Rights party, 103, 145
National Urban Policy, 287
National Young Republicans Federation, 420
Naughton, James, 34, 42, 324, 400
Navy League, 388, 389
Nebraska primary (1968), 196, 197, 209–10
"New American Revolution," 411, 413–14
Newbold, Robert T., Jr., 80
New Economic Policy, 423
Newell, Frank H., III, 57–59, 87–88, 130
New Hampshire primary (1968), 189–92, 203–4, 436
New Hampshire primary (1972), 426
New Orleans speech, 305, 320, 348
Newsday, 391
Newsweek, 247, 253, 317, 421, 423
New York *Herald Tribune*, 217
New York Mets, 303
New York Times, 3, 8, 34, 141, 195, 198, 201, 250, 255, 265, 271–76, 317–18, 322, 324, 341, 344, 369, 400, 403, 413, 420
Nixon Doctrine, 323, 348
Nixon, Edward, 225n
Nixon, Richard M., 4, 6, 27, 119, 123–34, 127–28, 140, 178–87, 200–15, 258, 263–97, 299, 303–4, 310–16, 320–26, 328–29, 332–35, 337–39, 341–42, 344–47, 350, 352–58, 363, 365, 367, 369–70, 372–78, 383, 385, 390, 392, 394, 396–404, 407–8, 410, 412, 417–18, 422–28, 430, 432–41, 447, 449, 450
  announces New Economic Policy, 423
  announces trip to Peking, 418
  assessment of Agnew, 203, 207, 221, 229–30, 234, 438
  backs Agnew's conduct, 308, 438
  calls for cool rhetoric, 339
  calls students "bums," 337
  campaign (1968), 263–82
  election eve telecast (1970), 391
  enters 1970 campaign, 383
  inaugurated as President, 283–84
  meets Agnew first time, 27, 193
  New Hampshire primary (1968), 189–92
  nominated for President, 216–25
  plans 1970 campaign, 350–58
  rock-tossing incident in Vermont, 384, 386
  San Jose incident, 390–91
  says wants to keep "winning team" with Agnew, 438
  woos Agnew, 201–3
Noel, Sterling, 71
Novak, Robert D., 250
Nunn, Louie B., 226n

O'Brien, Lawrence F., 361–62
O'Connor, Frank, 182–83
O'Donnell, Peter, 227n
Office of Intergovernmental Relations, 286
Ogilvie, Richard, 226n
O'Hara, James, 40
Ohio National Guard, 336
Ohio State speech, 290
Oishi, Gene, 26, 253–63
Olds, Glen, 225n
Olson, Jerry, 199
open housing, 92–95, 107–10, 138–39, 157–59, 175–77
Oregon primary (1968), 190, 195–97, 209–10, 216
Otten, Alan, 432
Ottenad, Tom Cannonball, 417
Ottinger, Richard L., 372–73, 375

Papadopoulos, George, 427
Parker, W. Giles, 68
Patton, George S., 40–42
Pentagon Papers, 420

Percy, Charles H., 217–18, 221, 225, 231, 235
Pericles, Sons of, 35
Pfrommer, Christopher, 133
Phillips, Kevin, 356
ping-pong diplomacy, 414–16
Pittsburgh *Post-Gazette*, 267
"Polack" remark, 247, 249, 254, 257, 259–60, 269
Pollard, W. Roy, 30, 32, 33, 35–36, 41
Pollard, William R., 35
Pomerleau, Donald D., 17, 19, 168–69
Poor People's March, 173, 175, 211
Power, G. Gordon, 68, 73, 77, 79, 91, 95
Prendergast, Bill, 249
Pressman, Hyman A., 131, 133–34, 139–40, 143, 146–47
Price, Arthur, 75–76, 79–81
Price, David, 75–76, 79–82
Price, James, 75–76, 79–82
Price, Ray, 217, 231
Prince Philip, 330
Princeton University, 303
Procaccino, Mario, 182–83
Prouty, Winston L., 384–85
Proxmire, William, 370
Pueblo, the, 193

Quinn, Charles, 255, 267
Queen, Emmett, 36, 256–57

"radical liberals" (radiclibs), 358, 360–62, 364, 366, 368–69, 375–76, 380–86, 388–92, 426
Randolph, A. Philip, 162
Rasmussen, Walter J., 70–71
Rather, Dan, 437
Ray, Robert, 406
Reagan, Ronald, 156, 187, 209, 216–18, 221, 228, 231, 327, 334, 357, 406–7
Real Majority, The (Scammon and Wattenberg), 356–57
Rebozo, Charles G. ("Bebe"), 315
Reed, Paul, 143
Reitz, Ken, 368
Republican Governors Conferences
1967 (Jackson Hole; Palm Beach), 186–89
1968 (Tulsa), 211, 213–14
1969 (Lexington), 289
1970 (Sun Valley), 402, 410–11
1971 (Williamsburg), 414–15
1971 (French Lick), 424, 426

Republican National Committee, 249, 306, 308, 359, 377, 384, 394, 423
Republican National Conventions
1964: 116, 120, 310, 435
1968: 178, 216–33, 282, 426, 428, 439
1972: 437
Reston, James B., 313, 363
Resurrection City, 173, 212
Rhodes, James, 183, 189, 223, 226n, 232, 336
Rhodes, John, 226n
Rhodes, Joseph, Jr., 344–45
Richardson, Gloria, 102
Richardson, Elliot, 393
Riddick, Floyd M., 286
Rinehart, D. Eldred, 122, 223
Ringgold, Jim, 36
Ripon Society, 118, 412, 428
Rockefeller, David, 205
Rockefeller, Margaretta Fitler ("Happy"), 196–97
Rockefeller, Nelson A., 3–11, 27–29, 117–20, 122, 157, 178–202, 204–13, 216, 218, 221–23, 225, 228–29, 231, 236, 357, 373–75, 378–79, 383, 387–88
announces candidacy, 205
fails to tell Agnew he won't run, 3–10, 198–99
meets Agnew first time, 180
meets Agnew (in 1967), 185
promises not to run for Presidency again (1965), 182
says will not run in 1968, 3–10
S.S. *Independence*, 187–88
tries to win Agnew back, 205–6, 208–9
wins third term as governor, 182
Rockefeller, Winthrop, 403
Rockwell, George Lincoln, 313
Roderick, John, 416
Rogers, William P., 422
Rome, University of, 333
Romney, George, 3, 4, 10, 27, 140, 183, 185–94, 209, 219, 223, 231–32, 257, 424
Romney, Lenore, 183–84, 366
Roosevelt, Franklin D., 55, 359–60
Rosenwald, Cynthia, 249, 304
"rotten apples" speech (Harrisburg), 308–10, 331
Rowland, James B., 141
Rubin, Jerry, 31
Rumsfeld, Donald, 226n
Rural Affairs Council, 287

Safeguard, 292
Safire, William, 355, 357–58, 370, 442
St. Louis *Post-Dispatch*, 417
Samuelson, Don, 183
Sanders, Doug, 330
San Jose incident, 390–91
Sarbanes, Paul, 156
Sargent, Frank, 404
"Saturday night group," 51
Scammon, Richard M., 356–57
Schachter, Leon, 49
Schilling Spice Co., 132
Schram, Martin, 391
Schreiber Brothers, 45–48, 73
Schweiker, Richard, 308
Scott, Hugh, 307–8, 378
Scranton report, 376, 382
Scranton, William W., 9, 119–20, 184, 195, 227
Scripps-Howard newspapers, 338
Seale, Bobby, 331
Sears, John P., 188, 201, 225n, 237, 244, 246, 250–51, 258
Secret Service, 285, 326, 359, 400
Selassie, Haile, 421
Selling of the Pentagon, The (CBS), 412
Sevareid, Eric, 382
Shafer, Raymond P., 407
Shakespeare, Frank, 225n
Shane, Edith, 50
Shogan, Robert, 247, 251, 253–54, 257, 259, 262
Shultz, George, 291, 325, 413, 430
Shusterman, Abraham, 81–82, 85, 95
Sickles, Carleton R., 126–28, 141, 149
60 Minutes (CBS), 337
Smalley, Bob, 250, 267
Smith, Alfred E., 363
Smith, L. Mercer, 191
Smith, Margaret Chase, 444
Smith, Michael Paul, 43
Smith, Ralph, 359
Smith, Roland, 10, 11, 13, 14, 16, 164–66, 171–72
"soft on Communism," 241–47, 257, 269
Sohmer, Arthur, 250
Solomon, Harry T., 132
Soul on Ice (Cleaver), 262
South Carolina State College, 164
Southern strategy, 306, 331
Suthern Governors Conference, (1967), 187

Spock, Benjamin, 331–32, 377
S. S. *Independence*, 187–88
Stafford, Emerson, 160
Stans, Maurice, 225n, 294, 352–53
Stanton, Frank, 314
Stassen, Harold, 433, 435
Steinbock, Charles, Jr., 61–63, 111–12, 271
Steinman, Karl F., 48
Stevenson, Adlai E., II, 242, 363
Stevenson, Adlai E., III, 359–62, 366–67, 386
Student Nonviolent Coordinating Committee, 17, 21, 159
Students for a Democratic Society, 333
Sulzberger, Arthur Ochs, 317
Supreme Court, 328–30, 386
Symington, J. Fife, 63, 68, 73, 77, 118
Symington, Stuart, 301

TV criticism (Des Moines speech), 310–15
Tawes, J. Millard, 75, 121, 126, 129, 131, 140, 153–54, 274
Thayer, Walter, 204
Thieu, Nguyen Van, 270, 278–79, 428
Thomasson, Dan, 338–39, 341
Thompson, Herb, 166, 230, 250, 263, 267, 316, 322, 324, 333–34
Thornton, Virginius B., III, 11
Thurmond, Strom, 216, 226n, 228, 231, 276, 329, 386
Time, 187, 254
Tower, John, 206, 216, 219, 227, 227n, 293
Towson State College, 13, 168
Treleaven, Harry, 368
Truman, Harry S, 242, 299, 359–60, 363, 443–44
Tunney, John V., 362, 367
Twelfth Amendment, 440, 452
Tydings, Joseph D., 208, 294, 386, 393

United Steelworkers of America, 71
U-JOIN, 23
Unna, Warren, 278
Urban Affairs Council, 286–87, 448
urban renewal, 103–7
U.S. Chamber of Commerce, 290

Vance, Cyrus, 345
Vanocur, Sander, 403, 406

Vice-Presidents, 284, 286, 438–40
Vidal, Gore, 399
Vietnam, 158, 183–84, 203, 210–11,
    239, 241, 246, 264, 269, 272,
    277–78, 294, 304, 310–12, 317,
    334–35, 345–48, 350, 355, 361,
    369–70, 373, 382, 411–13, 420,
    439
Vietnam Moratorium, 295–97, 302–
    5, 307, 311
Vietnamization, 246
Village Voice, 369
Villanova University, 303
Virginia, University of, 446
Volpe, John A., 219, 221, 227–28,
    424

Wahbe, Vladimir A., 105–6
Wallace, George C., 25, 101–3, 105,
    119, 127, 178, 217, 238, 263–
    66, 271, 276–77, 280–82, 301–
    2, 326, 334, 357, 371, 435
Wallace, Henry A., 286
Wallace, Lurleen, 127
Wallace, Mike, 337, 394
Wall Street Journal, 432
Ward, C. D., 406
Ware, Gilbert, 19, 20, 172, 238
Washington *Post*, 153, 155–56, 160,
    207, 235, 253–54, 278, 315,
    317–18, 322, 331, 333, 341,
    360
Washington *Star*, 141, 242
Wattenberg, Ben J., 356–57, 361
Weiss, Mike, 253
Welcome, Verda, 178
Westinghouse Corporation, 132

White, George W., Jr., 49, 51, 54,
    123, 244, 249–50, 274–75, 278,
    281
Whitney, Jock, 204
Who Owns America? (Hickel), 393
Wilde, Oscar, 262
Wiley, Bell, 340
Wilkins, Roy, 24, 159, 162
Wilkinson, Bud, 279–80
Williams, Harrison, 294
Williams, Wallace A., 108
Williamsburg Nine, 417–18
Williford, Elaine Sturgis, 36
Willkie, Wendell L., 117
Wilner, Ron, 125, 147
Wilson, Bob, 227n, 293
Wilson, Henry, 439
Wilson, Richard, 397
Wilson, Woodrow, 284
Wisconsin primary (1968), 204,
    209
Wiseman, J. A., 13–16
Wold, John, 361
Woods, Rose Mary, 225n
Wroten, Russell, 160

Yale Republican Club, 183–84
Yale University, 303, 331
Yarborough, Ralph, 294, 355, 380
Yates, William, 2nd, 160
Young Americans for Freedom,
    427–28
Young Republicans, 420
Young, Whitney, 24, 162

Zeinog, Richard, 124
Ziegler, Ronald, 307, 316, 338–39,
    345, 417, 426

About the Author

A national political writer in the Washington bureau of the Los Angeles *Times*, JULES WITCOVER has been writing on politics and other subjects of national interest from Washington since 1954 as author, newspaper correspondent and columnist. Winner of the Sigma Delta Chi Award for Washington Correspondence in 1962 and a Reid Fellow in Europe in 1958, he has written for many national magazines, including the *New Republic, Saturday Review, The Nation*, the *Saturday Evening Post, The Progressive, The Reporter* and the *Columbia Journalism Review*. His previous two books (see back jacket) have also examined major political figures at close range.